THE FLOWERING OF NEW ENGLAND

VAN WYCK BROOKS *has written:*

THE FLOWERING OF
NEW ENGLAND

By

VAN WYCK BROOKS

A Dutton **dep** *Paperback*

Everyman

NEW YORK

E. P. DUTTON & CO., INC.

CONTENTS

THE FLOWERING OF NEW ENGLAND

CHAPTER I

THE BOSTON OF GILBERT STUART

AT THE time of the Peace of Ghent, which brought to a close the War of 1812, Gilbert Stuart, the portrait-painter, was an old inhabitant of Boston. He had lived in the town,—for it was still a town, not to become a city for almost a decade,—nine good years. The son of a Rhode Island snuff-grinder, he had made his way up in the world of art until nobody questioned his eminence. He was famous in London and Dublin, where he had been a rival of Lawrence and Beechey. In all American circles, his word was law. No one dared to praise an American poet until the *Edinburgh Review* had done so, but Stuart was the arbiter in painting. In his careless way, he had neglected to answer the letter from the Academy of Florence asking for a portrait of himself. He did not need these testimonials. In the capital of New England, whither he had come to live and die, everyone praised and admired him. Even John Adams, the patriarch of Quincy, who said he would not give sixpence for a Raphael, yielded to the spell of the genial artist. The old man had rejoiced, with a Puritan's fervour, that the age of painting and sculpture had not arrived to corrupt his beloved country. But Gilbert Stuart's witty anecdotes charmed away his prejudices. After his first sitting, he exclaimed that he would be glad to sit to Stuart from one year's end to another.

Times had undoubtedly changed in the Christian Sparta, as John Adams's cousin, Samuel Adams, had called the town of Boston. Gilbert Stuart, who was a no-

table wag, liked to begin his anecdotes by saying, "When
I lived in the Athens of America." Everyone knew what
he meant by the phrase: he was referring to Philadelphia.
And every Bostonian knew that he was mistaken. William Penn's town had taken the lead in all these matters
of enlightenment—thanks to a good Bostonian, Benjamin Franklin; but that was in days past. The real American Athens was the Christian Sparta. At least, it was
advancing towards this position, with large and rapid
strides; and Stuart knew it. He was only indulging a taste
for mischief. In England, when people had asked him
where he was born, he had said, by way of explaining
Narragansett, "six miles from Pottawome and ten miles
from Poppasquash." His sitters were little the wiser when
he added that he had spent his early years at Newport,
where, in some of the old merchants' houses, he had seen
portraits by Van Dyck and Kneller, real or supposititious.
And if he liked to tease the men of Boston, who suffered
from no lack of self-esteem, it was not because he found
them dull. He laughed at blue laws and blue noses, but
so did many of his Boston sitters, those who had not lost
their Tory ways and some of those who belonged to the
younger circles. For the dominant Boston nose was far
from blue: it was a Roman nose, flanked by a full-blown
complexion. Stuart, with his lordly style, his fresh, ruddy
face and downright manners,—not to mention his taste
for the best Madeira, which he poured from a half-gallon
ewer, throwing off tumblers like cider in haying-time,—
was quite at home with the great East India merchants,
whose ships had sometimes carried the Madeira twice
round the Cape, to give it a good rocking. They liked the
hearty freedom of a man who, when one of his sitters fell
asleep, painted him with ass's ears. They liked a man
who, if he used snuff, used half a pound of it a day. They
liked his high spirits and his flowing talk, as well as the
claret he seemed to mix with his paint. And they liked

the uncanny skill with which he dived into their own thoughts,—for they were proud of their thoughts,—and made them live and speak on his eloquent canvas.

This was the golden age of portrait-painting. It was an age of public men. It was an age of family pride, nowhere more marked than in Boston. It was an age of modest wealth, which the recent war had checked but not extinguished. For three generations, since the days of Smibert, Boston had supported its portrait-painters, and Gilbert Stuart was another Copley. It was true that the town had little feeling for art. Stuart was to die as obscure and poor as any tippling poet in the gutter. The Boston people did not cherish him—much as they enjoyed his company—because they were proud that one of the world's artists had chosen to live in Boston. They cherished him because he so greatly added to their own pride in themselves; and when they finally buried him in the Common, near the famous Julien of the "soup," they did not even mark his grave. Boston was torpid in aesthetic matters. Stuart had refused to exhibit his pictures because they had been hung so badly. Boston was congenitally obtuse in all that concerned the senses, except Madeira; and this was still to be true a century later, when, with little more aesthetic feeling, the town possessed so much aesthetic knowledge. It was always to look on the plastic arts, instinctively, as a clever woman said, in the days when New Yorkers liked to tease Bostonians, merely as branches of literature. There was something cold and dry in its perceptions. But the very elements in its social life that nourished the portrait-painters,—the family pride, the wealth, the public spirit,—were obviously creating a situation that fostered all its natural faculties. The merchant-patricians, like those of Holland and Flanders, in times gone by, wished to perpetuate their names and glorify their capital not only in the elegance of their mansions but also in churches, parks and public buildings, in professorial chairs at Harvard College, in schools and asylums and hospitals. Such were the desires and thoughts that Stuart caught in the faces of his sitters.

All the omens favoured these intentions. The recent war had cleared the atmosphere. For twenty years after the Revolution, Boston had been poor and apprehensive. The nation was torn with sectional dissensions, while everyone feared the interference of England and Napoleon was abroad like a wolf in the night. But Waterloo and Commodore Perry had quieted these anxieties. England had ceased to be a menace. The abhorrent career of Napoleon had broken the old connection with France. Europe had become engrossed in problems that had little meaning across the ocean. America, united and free at last, with all its problems solved, as it seemed at the moment, faced a future that was almost dazzling. The "era of good feeling" was beginning, and circumstances had been kind to Boston. The war, which had largely destroyed the commerce of the smaller New England ports, had had no lasting effect on the capital. Strong enough, in fact, to survive the crisis, it prospered with the ruin of so many rivals; and it was attracting more and more the younger merchants of the rural regions who had taken advantage of the decline of shipping, during the years of war, and the boycott of English goods that followed the war, to build up a manufacturing system and supply the American people with native products. Factory-towns were rising on every hand, in eastern Massachusetts and New Hampshire,—Lawrence, Lowell, Fitchburg, Manchester, Lynn. Every village with a waterfall set up a textile-mill or a paper-mill, a shoe-factory or an iron-foundry; and as Boston remained the financial centre, as well for manufacturing as for shipping, the mercantile fortunes of the inland counties were joined with those of the magnates of the seaboard.

Boston was rich, in short, as never before; and, having the means, the leading citizens could not imagine why their little town should not be the finest in the world. No one challenged this prepossession. New England was an isolated region, and Boston had some right to its self-esteem. It had taken the lead in the Revolution, with the statesmen of Virginia, and played a large part in both the wars in which the United States had defeated England. The boast of the Boston poet,—

We have the guns,
We have the ships,—

was justified by the British themselves. All their commentators had asserted that the American cruisers were the best and that the Yankee rifle in Yankee hands had set a new standard of marksmanship. No one could guess what happy fortunes lay before the valiant young republic, and Boston hoped for a special dispensation. The old dream of a Puritan commonwealth, a true city of God, lingered in the New England mind, and it seemed as if the appointed hour had come. Cotton Mather had foretold this hour. Jonathan Edwards, on his lonely rides over the forest hills of leafy Stockbridge, had seen the millennium approaching. Bishop Berkeley, on his farm at Newport, had prophesied the golden age. The hard conditions of life in earlier days had yielded to more propitious circumstances. The time was surely ripe; and what wealth was unable to compass might be left to piety and reason. The Boston people had only themselves to blame, or so, at least, they felt, if the kingdom of heaven, a sober New England kingdom,—not built of the gaudy materials that vulgarized the Book of Revelation,—was not, at last, at hand.

They meant to do their best. The Lowells, the Cabots, the Appletons, the Jacksons, the "codfish aristocracy" and the "Essex Junto,"—the members of which had wished

to break the Union, in favour of their New England
separatism,—the Perkinses, Higginsons, Cushings, the
brothers Lawrence, who had made their fortunes on the
sea, along with the Hong merchants of the Flowery Kingdom, or from the whirring of their wheels and spindles,
united in a passion for the *genius loci*. Some of them
suggested in their faces, faithfully painted by Stuart, the
florid merchants of colonial times, their grandsires and
uncles, in velvet cap and flowered robe, flushed with
wine and generosity. Others recalled the Puritan cast,
the lean, shrewd, nervous Yankee type, cautious, with a
turn for metaphysics, dried by the American atmosphere.
All of them lived and moved, walked and spoke as if
their little town was a holy city and Rome, Paris and
London were their suburbs. For this there were certain
reasons. Boston was only a regional capital, but a Boston
man could say to himself, quite truly, that it was much
more a capital than either New York or Philadelphia;
for the people were more homogeneous. A visitor from
New York, observing the crowd in the streets, exclaimed,
"Why, all these people are of one race. They behave like
members of one family, whereas with us a crowd is an
assembly of all the nations upon earth." As one of the
results of this homogeneity, the institutions of the town
and country had a greater similarity than in other regions,—a fact that was full of meaning for the future.
It favoured the growth of the region in all its parts. For,
while Boston attracted the master-minds and took them
away from the smaller towns, it rendered them more active and efficient; and, precisely because of this concentration of powers, it was able to send forth influences
that were beneficial to the rural districts. It was able to
do so and it wished to do so, more and more as the century advanced. The older patrician families, those that
had come over in the "Arbella," and those of whom it
was said that, at the time of the Deluge, they had a boat

to themselves, possessed a sense of responsibility that sometimes seemed acute. The eminent men who had come from the country, or from the smaller ports and county-seats, and who mingled on equal terms with the patricians, were loyal to their rustic antecedents. One and all felt, as the Boston orators were always saying, in the old "cradle of liberty," Faneuil Hall, that they were the heirs of the Revolution. They were determined to carry out, in every sphere in which their interests lay, their duties as American citizens. They meant to make Boston a model town. They meant to make New England a model region.

Boston was another Edinburgh, with marked variations of its own. It resembled Edinburgh in many ways, as New England resembled Scotland. The bitter climate and the hard soil, the ice, the granite and the Calvinism, yielding to more gracious forms of faith, the common schools, the thrifty farmer-folk, the coast-line, with its ports and sailors' customs, the abundant lakes and mountains, the geological aspects of the region, all suggested the land of Sir Walter Scott, as well as the adjacent land of Wordsworth, whose bareness and simplicity, together with his loftiness and depth,—proofs, as Hazlitt said, that his work was written in a mountainous country,—commended him to the young New England mind; and if, in this mind, there was something cold and hard that recalled the ice and the granite, there were reserves of feeling and perception that were to find expression in the years to come. A well-known Scottish traveller[1] remarked of Boston, "I could scarcely believe I was not in Scotland." One found there, as in Edinburgh, the same wealth, similarly earned, the same regard for manners and decorum, the same respect for learning, the same religious point of view, alike in its antecedents and in

[1] Sir Charles Lyell,—some years later.

its liberal modifications, the same scrupulous conscientiousness, the same punctiliousness and the same pride, even the same prudence. One found the same exactions in matters of taste, the same aristocratic prepossessions and the same democratic feeling underneath them. The golden calf the Bostonians worshipped was a mere pygmy, as Dickens said, a generation later, beside the giant effigies one found in the other American cities.

Not that the Boston people were other-worldly, for all their messianic expectations, except as compared with the profane New Yorkers. Some of them lived in magnificent style. Many of them were accomplished in the art of living. The Cushing house in Summer Street was surrounded with a wall of Chinese porcelain; peacocks strutted about the garden; the Chinese servants wore their native dress. The older folk, sedate, a little complacent, dwelling in the solid garden-houses that stood about the Common, each with its flagged walk and spacious courtyard, filled with fragrant shrubs, shaded by its over-arching elms, were genial and pleasure-loving, as a rule. Here and there one found a Sybarite. Harrison Gray Otis, at the age of eighty, after forty years of gout, breakfasted every morning on *pâté de foie gras*. Every afternoon, at the Otis house, ten gallons of punch evaporated out of the Lowestoft bowl that was placed on the landing. One of the Perkins brothers, challenged by a rigorous pastor, who had come out for total abstinence, doubled his children's ration of Madeira. Even the young girls, in some of these houses, where they maintained the royalist traditions and sometimes toasted "the King," under the rose, read *Tom Jones,* Smollett and *Tristram Shandy,* as if they had never heard of a Pilgrim Father. In every house one found the standard authors, Hume, Gibbon, Shakespeare, Milton, Dryden, Addison, the *Arabian Nights, Don Quixote,* Sir William Temple's works in folio, a set of Hogarth's original plates, perhaps, or two or three first editions of Pope, books that were worthy of their calf bindings, on shelves that might have been carved by Grinling Gibbons, surmounted by marble busts. The children were brought up on Maria Edgeworth and the writings of Mrs. Barbauld and Fanny Burney. Sons who came home from abroad with too many airs were greeted with an almost crushing composure. The Boston people were willing to learn, but only if one recognized how much they knew already. Their minds were closed on certain lines, and they did not like "originality." But, as a generation that knew the world, they were prepared to humour their sons and daughters.

There were many strains in the Boston mind, a warm and chivalrous Tory strain, a passionate strain of rebelliousness, a strain of religious fervour, a marked and even general disposition,—despite the sybaritic Mr. Otis, who, for the rest, was public-spirited,—to sacrifice at other than mundane altars. The town abounded in quixotic souls, "unmanageable" Adamses, younger sons who refused the social uniform, visionaries, *exaltés,* nonconformists. The future was to provide them with their causes. It was true that these idealists, who spoke for "impossible loyalties," found Beacon Hill a mountain of ice. Principle was a reality in Boston. Conscience was a large reality. Everyone knew the story of the merchant who, when one of his ships was overdue, found that he was more anxious about his thoughts than about the money he was losing. Was it possible, he asked himself, that he had really grown to love his money more for itself than for its noble uses? To settle the point in his own mind, he reckoned the value of the ship and cargo and gave the sum to his favourite charity. The story was typical of the Boston merchants who, within a space of thirty years, from 1810 to 1840, established thirty benev-

olent institutions. And yet there were those who said that
Boston had a double intellect and only half a heart.
The prevailing mind was cautious, excessively formal,
singularly obsessed with its own importance, bigoted in
its fear of political change. The mother of "Athenæum"
Shaw enjoined upon him, during his early travels, the
virtues of silence, secrecy and circumspection, quoting
the counsel of an experienced father, that one should
keep one's countenance open but one's thoughts close.
The Puritans had learned this art in their days of perse-
cution, and a trading community had found it useful.
Moreover, the prevailing mind was legalistic. Burke—
with Dr. Johnson, its favourite author—noted that more
than half of the first edition of Blackstone's Commentaries found its way to America. A large proportion had remained in Boston, where it served as an arsenal of logic
against the Jacobins and their bob-tailed crew. For Boston was controlled by an oligarchy, an unofficial caste of
leading men for whom a "republic" and a "democracy"
had next to nothing in common. Hamiltonian Federalists
to a man, Whigs after the fall of Federalism, they had
found that the doctrines of Burke and Johnson admira-
bly supported their property-interests. For the rest, they
had "looked at France," as Fisher Ames had advised
them to do, and witnessed the results of a red revolution,
—anarchy, infidelity, just as Burke had prophesied, with
a lord of misrule, Napoleon, as the end of all things.

Stability at any price! They had had too many wars
and altercations. The first French Republic had gone to
the dogs. They could not believe that their own would
fare much better. In days of debt and disunitedness, it
was a natural assumption that power ought to go with
property. The theory had a special justification in days
when *not* to have property, if one wished it, was almost
a certain sign of shiftlessness. "Where are your poor?"

said Lafayette, when, a few years later, he scrutinized the crowds in the Boston streets. The slum was a thing of the future,[2] and most of the rich men had acquired their wealth by the superior exercise of traits that almost every Yankee shared and applauded. Besides, if their minds were closed in political matters, they were more than liberal in religion. They took a lenient view of human nature. Few traces of Puritanism were left among them. Most of them had seen the world, as supercargoes, merchants, statesmen, students. They had fought with Tripolitan pirates, visited Canton, India and Egypt, bought skins in Canada and sold them in China, carried ice from Labrador to Java, taken the grand tour to Rome and Naples and had themselves measured by London tailors, who continued to make their clothes when they had shrunk within the measurements. The fact that the clothes were made in London was more important than that they did not fit. If their views were not loose, like their clothes, at least they were enlarged, as people said. They no longer looked on their fellow-beings with the eyes of Puritan deacons. Indeed, the human nature they found about them, far from being totally depraved, seemed, in the light of these wider circumstances, compared with Chinese coolies and Italian beggars, singularly innocent and good. Who had measured its capacity? Boston boys believed in themselves. They grew up alert and self-reliant,[3] battling with the east winds, coasting over the frozen snow, convinced that they were able to

[2] There was, however, one region in Boston, on the Cambridge side of Beacon Hill, that is said to have been extremely squalid and vicious. It was filled with crowded, tumble-down tenements where crime ran riot. This region greatly exercised the Boston and Cambridge humanitarians, notably the fathers of Lowell the poet and Charles Eliot Norton.

[3] A rule of the household of Wendell Phillips's father, the first mayor of the city of Boston: "Ask no man to do for you anything that you are not able and willing to do for yourself."

"lick creation." [4] How could they accept the ancestral doctrine of the worthlessness of human efforts and motives? How could they hear themselves described as "vipers"? Were Boston boys "little fallen wretches," even worse than vipers? They were more ready to think that, having succeeded in so many things, they could succeed in everything. In short, they believed in perfectibility.

This change in their religious point of view, gradual, scarcely perceptible at first, signified an emotional revolution as marked as the events of '76. Absorbed as they were in politics and trade, the Boston folk were hardly aware that the old faith had vanished from their horizon. Twenty years before, the well-known wit, Robert Treat Paine, had cursed the "Vandal spirit of Puritanism,"—a levity of the fashionable circles, savouring of the colonial governor's court, that had grown to be a commonplace. In 1809, the most popular preacher in Boston, referring to the creed of the Pilgrim Fathers,— Calvinism, with its "revolting forms,"—spoke of Milton's eyes as having been "quenched in the service of a vulgar and usurping faction." A mild and tolerant Unitarianism had been set up as the State Church. Known far and wide as the "Boston religion," it still possessed a frail dogmatic structure, of which it was only conscious when it was challenged. The ministers were graceful rhetoricians. Calling themselves Arminians or Arians, sometimes Moderate Calvinists, they still believed in the supernatural; and, having "disproved" the Trinitarian doctrine, with most of the other doctrines of their forbears, they clung to the Christian miracles, as the proper evidences of the faith.

[4] All classes in New England shared this assurance. See Emerson's Journal, at sea, 1833: "The captain believes in the superiority of the American to every other countryman. 'You will see,' he says, 'when you get out here how they manage in Europe; they do everything by main strength and ignorance. Four truckmen and four stevedores at Long Wharf will load my brig quicker than a hundred men at any port in the Mediterranean.'"

Negative and pallid as it was, the new religion sprang from an atmosphere that was favourable to the flowering of the mind. The ministers, learned, cultivated men, lovers of music and eloquence, had introduced the literary sermon. Their models were Bossuet and Massillon. They had abandoned the older pulpit methods, the texts, the arguments and the commentaries. Their sermons were glowing essays, dealing with the interests of daily life. Joseph Stevens Buckminster, the melodious preacher, the "Chrysostom of America," as he was called, who had read his Greek Testament at five, had prophesied the birth of a great school of American letters. Poets and historians, he had said, in one of his discourses at Harvard College, were soon to appear, to direct American taste and mould the genius of the young republic, men of whom posterity was to stand in awe. "You, my young friends," he had exclaimed, "are destined to witness the dawn of our Augustan age, and to contribute to its glory,"—a very different note from Fisher Ames's, for this spokesman of the previous decade had never missed a chance to say that the American genius was foredoomed to fail. Buckminster's successor, William Ellery Channing, the great ethical leader of the future, equally sanguine, was more critical. The impassioned little saint with the burning heart, whose intellect was the conscience of New England, felt that the hour had struck for American thinkers. Mind, mind required all one's care! In his youth he had had a sudden illumination, a vision of human nature, which seemed to him a godhead in the making. He ceaselessly preached the gospel of self-improvement. "We want great minds," he said, "to be formed among us. We want the human intellect to do its utmost here."

Boston corresponded to Plato's city, a population that was not too large to hear the voice of a single orator. The people were prepared for these stirring sermons.

With Faneuil Hall as their Acropolis, they were accustomed to public speaking, and oratory had filled them with exalted thoughts. At school they learned to recite the swelling strains of the *Life of William Tell:* "Friends of liberty, sons of sensibility, ye who know how to die for your independence!" Bombast, in a sense, but they believed it. Their fathers and uncles had fought in a similar cause, swept along by a tide of eloquence. Moreover, Plutarch was their second Bible, together with Pope's Homer. Deep in their hearts they cherished the conviction that they could emulate these heroic models and reproduce the deeds of history. The sons of William Emerson, for instance, the former minister of the First Church, who had founded the Philosophical Society, were born with these convictions in their blood, and one of them, a boy of twelve named Ralph, a chubby little spouter of Scott and Campbell, who had recently trundled his hoop about the Common, where he pastured the family cow, was to express them later in his essays. The Emerson boys, "born to be educated,"—the object of a Boston childhood seemed to be to prepare for the Latin School,—were typical of a ministerial household, heirs of a long line of divines and scholars, one of whom had prayed every evening that none of his descendants might ever be rich. Their mother, like all the devout New England matrons, enjoyed her morning hour of meditation. Their aunt, the minister's sister, Mary Moody Emerson of Concord, who despised the new religion, poor, low, thin, as she thought it was, dwelt in the fiery depths of a Calvinism which, although she only half believed it, filled her with a sombre poetry. She prophesied that her nephews were to be called of men Rabbis and Fathers. Ralph already had a mind of his own. He carried the *Pensées* of Pascal to church, to read during the sermon. At night, in his cold upper chamber, covered with woollen blankets to the chin, he read his precious Dialogues of Plato. He associated Plato, ever after, with the smell of wool.

Under its placid surface, Boston tingled with a new ambition. Half the boys expected to go to sea. They hovered about the ships and the wharves, scenting the salt air, the ropes and the tar, listening to tales of Chinese pirates, greeting some cousin, home from Spanish Manila, in white trousers and jacket of sky-blue silk, marvelling over an older brother who, for a lark, on his way back from Cairo, had travelled the length of Italy, in his carriage, dressed as an Oriental potentate. As many others dreamed of a life of letters. Here and there, some poor young man, who could not go to the Latin School, bought his own Andrews and Stoddard's grammar, from which every proper Boston boy supposed the Latin language had been derived, and spent his nights over a commonplace-book, copying his favourite passages from Gibbon. Learning was endemic in the Boston mind, as befitted a town whose first inhabitant, the Cambridge scholar Blaxton,—who had built his thatched cottage, with a garden and spring, on the site of Louisburg Square,—had brought his library with him. There had been books on the slope of Beacon Hill when the wolves still howled on the summit. There had always been some Boston man who could address in Arabic or Persian a merchant or diplomat from the land of Xerxes; and now that the war was over, and the nation seemed to be on a solid footing, the intellectual life grew apace. The clever Frenchmen, with their godless notions, had made all thought suspicious for a while. The Boston people preferred to settle questions by thumping the table, or by whacks and blows,[5] in the manner of Dr. Johnson. But

[5] Not, however, delivered on the person. In spite of the downright ways of the old Bostonians, New England was noted for its mildness. Timothy Dwight reported that he had never heard of a New England man using arms in a private quarrel. Josiah Quincy said that only five duels were known to have taken place in New England up to 1820.

subtlety had grown with confidence. The argand lamp, improved by Jefferson, had furthered the habit of reading. It was observed at once that dinner-parties, formerly lighted by candles, ceased to be as brilliant as of old. Those who had excelled in talking took to their books and writing-desks. It was true that this intellectual life was timid, cautious and derivative. In short, it was still colonial, forty years after Bunker Hill. English culture had a right of way that no one thought of challenging, and every Boston boy was taught to regard Pope and Burke as unapproachable. The literary government of Europe was a more potent yoke than the political government had been. But the ferment of the rising generation might be expected to break it.

As if to provide the future with a proper setting, the Boston people had rebuilt the town. The architect, Charles Bulfinch, the son of a doctor, had appeared with providential promptness. A man of sensibility, he had been moved to tears, on a tour of Europe, when he had entered St. Peter's at Rome. He had been obliged to teach himself. Among so many carpenters and builders, skilful, well-trained craftsmen, schooled in the styles of Wren and Inigo Jones, there was not an architect in Boston when he returned in 1787; and, search as one might, high and low, one could not find a book on architecture. Bulfinch, who had bought some books in Europe and found his taste and talent in demand, soon developed a style,—an outgrowth of the prevailing style, more delicate than the colonial Georgian, quite without the English massiveness,—that caught the temper of the Boston people. It was modestly elegant, somewhat prim, but dignified and simple. He had built the first theatre in the town, as far back as 1793, where all Boston rejoiced in *The School for Scandal*, disguised as a "moral lecture." He had built the admirable State House, which was to serve as a model for so many others. He had filled Boston with his works, houses and blocks of houses, crescents, churches, which, with their grace and propriety, struck the note of an epoch, an outward and visible sign that the new Boston mind had crystallized and found its appropriate form. Various institutions of learning followed in rapid succession, a Library of Law in 1806, a Theological Library in 1807,—in the same year, the Boston Athenæum. Modelled on the Liverpool Athenæum, this was largely the work of Buckminster, who had spent most of his little fortune buying books in Paris. He had sent three thousand volumes home, sets of the British essayists and poets, the Botanical Magazine, topographical works on Greece and Rome that brought the classical world before one's eyes, works in unknown realms, Roscoe's *Lorenzo de' Medici*, Duppa's *Life of Michael Angelo*, Italian and Spanish dictionaries. The first wistaria vine, the first mimosa was scarcely more of a novelty in Boston than some of these intellectual plants and vines that were to scatter their seeds across New England.

Two other institutions, the Handel and Haydn Society and the *North American Review*—founded, both, in 1815—marked the coming-of-age of the Boston mind. For music and for letters, these were of the future. The culture of the immediate past and present found expression through another organ. For several years there had existed, from 1803 to the outbreak of the war, a club devoted to literary interests. The Anthology Society, as it was called, numbered among its members Buckminster, Channing, William Emerson, Dr. Gardiner, the rector of Trinity Church, William Tudor, the merchant, President Kirkland of Harvard, John Lowell and other well-known men. The members met one evening every week to discuss the manuscripts for their magazine, the *Monthly Anthology*, over a modest supper of widgeons and teal, brants or a mongrel goose, with a little good claret. There was too little intercourse, they felt, among

Americans who cared for letters. They even hoped that their review, the first of its kind in the country, which had succeeded many feebler efforts, might foster the growth of a national literature.

The members were not professional men of letters, a species that was still unknown in Boston. Moreover, their expectations were not excessive, or much beyond the pleasures of their task. William Emerson was the editor. William Tudor, who had established the club, had made a small fortune, with his brother, shipping ice, cut from their pond at Saugus, to Martinique and South America. Indeed, the Tudors introduced, throughout the equatorial world, even as far as Calcutta, the custom of using ice in table-drinks.[6] Dr. Gardiner, an Episcopalian, conducted a little school in his spacious study, instructing a chosen handful in Latin and Greek, following the methods of his master, the great English scholar, Samuel Parr. Among the other contributors or members, some of them correspondents from a distance, were the rising Portsmouth lawyer, Daniel Webster, who had not yet moved to Boston, the Reverend Aaron Bancroft, who lived in Worcester, a theologian of the older school and the father of a son who was soon to be famous, Joseph Story of Salem, the notable jurist,—the greatest writer on the law since Blackstone, as the Lord Chief Justice of England called him later,—and two younger men of ample promise, Alexander Everett and George Ticknor. Judge Story, a classmate of Dr. Channing, had published a poem, *The Power of Solitude,* suggested by the writings of Zimmermann. Although he had taken a "lawyer's farewell of the muse," he often entertained himself in court by making his notes of arguments in verse.

The magazine, though somewhat staid in manner, de-

[6] It was to William Tudor, when he was presented to George the Fourth, that the king remarked, "What, one of us?"

cidedly starched and impersonal, was yet an enterprise
that promised much, in days when "Who wrote Junius?"
was still an exciting topic of conversation. In style it resembled the British reviews, not yet irradiated by Lamb
or by Hazlitt, the English Unitarian minister's son who
had spent three years, as a boy, in Massachusetts, who
had seen Boston before he saw London and never forgot
the Yankee barberry-bushes. Far from calling a spade a
spade, it always called a name an appellation. Behind
these traits of Johnsonese, moreover, might have been
discerned the self-distrust that marks the colonial mind,
a mind that has no centre of its own and clings to the
well-tried ways of the mother-country after the mother-
country has thrown them off. It abounded in Addisonian bric-a-brac, playful bits on toast and cranberry sauce,
worthy of a Grandison's hours of ease, accounts of visits
to Dr. Johnson's birthplace, continuations of Collins's
Ode to the Passions, reviews of *The Gamesters: or Ruins
of Innocence,* Beresford's *The Miseries of Human Life*
and *A Wreath for the Rev. Daniel Dow.* It defended
Pope against all comers, especially Coleridge's nonsense.
Even in Boston there were even lawyers who thought its
tone was pompous and said that Dr. Gardiner was a
snob. But this was a little severe. The magazine was
well-informed; it reviewed the museums, the theatres,
the social assemblies, and criticized the state of Harvard
College; it noticed the important publications, Washington Irving's *Knickerbocker,* Aaron Bancroft's *Washington,* Madame de Staël's *Corinne,* Wilson's *American
Ornithology.* It published intelligent essays on Erasmus,
the Carelessness of Dryden, Sir Walter Scott, whose poems stirred the Boston breast and who was supposed to
be writing the Waverley novels: "Who writes the Waverley novels?" was almost as thrilling a question as "Who
wrote Junius?" It attacked Blair's *Grave,* for the mortu-

ary vein was running out.[7] It printed papers on Italian
painters, Luca Giordano, the Caracci, and even a version of the *Sakuntala,* the first Hindu work to appear in
the country. It deplored the backward state of American
letters, the servile imitation of England, the fruits of a
superficial education. Whatever the future might produce, the writers of the review showed that the Boston
of Gilbert Stuart had roused itself out of its ancient slum-
bers.

Some of these writers, in fact, prefigured the future.
Buckminster professed the daring notion that there was
a higher poetry than the "mere language of reason." He
had himself taken as much delight in the ragged splendours of a western sunset, rich, disorderly, indistinct in
shape, as in the seven colours of the rainbow, properly
disposed in a semicircle, as if a good Bostonian had arranged them. This was quite absurd, Dr. Gardiner said.
Heaven could only tell what it betokened, in a world
that persisted in moving and changing its mind.

[7] "Sixty years ago," said Emerson, referring to this period, "the
books read, the sermons and prayers heard, the habits of thought of
religious persons were all directed on death. All were under the
shadow of Calvinism, and of the Roman Catholic purgatory, and
death was dreadful. The emphasis of all the good books given to
young people was on death. We were all taught that we were born
to die; and, over that, all the terrors that theology could gather from
savage nations were added to increase the gloom."—*Letters and Social Aims.*

CHAPTER II

HARVARD COLLEGE IN 1815

ALL ABOUT Boston, to the north, west and south, there still dwelt, in these days of Gilbert Stuart, many a veteran of the Revolution, protagonists, master-minds and lesser worthies. In Cambridge, in Concord, up and down the coast, in every port and village, one found survivors of the stirring hour, with their firelocks over their chimney-pieces. They recalled the brave days of the Roman republic, when the chief men of the State stayed on their farms, awaiting some summons for a public council to call them from their villas to the Senate.

At Pepperell, near the New Hampshire line, Colonel William Prescott had his farm, which he held by its original Indian title. The hero of Bunker Hill, like Cincinnatus, had taken up the plough again where he had left it standing in the furrow. Passing through Dorchester southward, or driving through the quiet lanes of Brookline, where the great East India merchants had their villas, with spreading lawns and airy parlours, filled with plaster casts and Italian paintings, and summer-houses in the Chinese style, one came at last to Quincy, where John Adams lived. There, like Thomas Jefferson at Monticello, with whom he had resumed his correspondence, on his ancient terms of good will,—since all passion was spent now,—the patriarch cheerfully sat for the painters and sculptors and studied the greater art of growing old. Once a year, together with his Bible, he read and pondered Cicero's *De Senectute*. He liked to talk with his friends on subjects suggested by his reading, such as the merits of Alexander the Great; and, as the years passed, he waited calmly for a better world, where he expected to meet all the great and good who had gone before him.

Close by, his kinsfolk the Quincy family dwelt. Josiah Quincy, now in the prime of life, the ancient doge of later times whose mind had been formed in the stress of the previous age, also spent his leisure hours, those he could spare from active politics, either in Boston or Washington, or from the toils of his farm, reading his three editions of Cicero, one for the shelf, one for the table and one, in twenty volumes, for the pocket, along with his Plutarch and his well-conned Horace. For generations, on their ancestral acres, where, with his six servants, the first American forbear of the family had raised his honoured roof-tree, the Quincys had lived as magistrates and squires, loving their field-sports as they loved their country and poring over the Tusculan Disputations: for Cicero, the defender of liberty, stirred a responsive chord in the Quincy bosom, Cicero, the instructor of every profession, the friend of every age! If the present master of the house, a house as ample as those of the Brookline merchants, overflowing with cousins and friends and public men of half a dozen countries,— if the present Josiah Quincy was not himself a man of the Revolution, he might, equally well, have been his father, whose life he had seen mirrored in Pope's Homer. He was the happy warrior who, for a long generation to come, was to fight for all the Revolution had stood for. He was the *integer vitae* who, like the Romans, in his inmost heart, had built twin temples to virtue and honour, so joined that one could enter the temple of honour only by passing first through the temple of virtue. He knew and loved the ancients, as Harvard knew them, not so much because he cared for learning as for their noble patterns of behaviour.

The happiest moments of the Adams household, few

as they were at present, snatched from the busiest life
that America knew, were those that John Quincy Adams,
the rising hope of the old President's heart, was able to
spend with his aging father and mother. Already in train
for the White House, Minister to England, Secretary of
State, almost a popular hero, like Andrew Jackson, thanks
to his work in concluding the recent war, he, too, was a
man of the Revolution. At eight, he had watched the
Battle of Bunker Hill; at nine, he had served as a little
post-rider; at fourteen, he had entered public life as secretary to the Minister to Russia. He had known Washington, Franklin, Jefferson, Jay, as a younger member of
their constellation, and had followed a proud, unmanageable course that had won him the hatred of his own
party and the gratitude of the nation. Against the interests of his Federalist friends, for whom money counted
more than country, he had fought for Jefferson's Em-
bargo, as later, in the teeth of the cotton-interests, he was
to fight the slave-power. For the selfish claims of his class
and breed he cared no more than he cared for his own
popularity; and yet, by the force of his intellect and will,
he had carved for himself a career that every common
politician envied. It was a career that his father understood and Abigail Adams rejoiced in, for he had never
compromised his faith that statesmanship was the noblest
of human callings. And if, at times, his methods were
those of the hedgehog, at Quincy the quills were always
folded in.

There, in the peaceful homestead, where later generations of Adamses were to sit in the old President's chair,
in the quiet upstairs study, and write their memoirs and
their histories, father and son, at these propitious moments, discussed the great problems of their country.
John Quincy Adams, now turning fifty, short, stout and
bald, less florid than his father,—for the English type was
gradually dying out,—had passed his earliest years there,

and there, in later years, still fighting, in the House at
Washington, for justice, for improvement, justice for the
Negroes, justice for the outraged Indians, for science, for
the Smithsonian Institution, with both feet planted on
the Rock of Ages,—there he was to pass his long vacations, always writing, writing, with ink-spots on his fingers, notes on Plutarch, notes on the Book of Leviticus,
speeches, essays, poems, nodding in his chair, wandering
about the garden and the ragged orchard, with hatchet
and saw in hand, pruning his pear and cherry-trees, hoeing and plucking weeds, bending over his plants in their
pots and boxes or using his wife's best tumblers to cover
the caterpillars that were supposed to turn into butterflies but—as his grandsons noticed—never did so. At
Quincy, as a little boy, with his thoughts filled with birds'
eggs and trifles, he had begun his famous Diary, enjoined
thereto by his austere papa, so that he might later be able
to note the stages by which he had advanced in taste,
knowledge and judgment. There he had read his fairy-
tales and revelled in the *Arabian Nights* and Shakespeare. In all the furious years he had passed in Holland,
Prussia, Russia, France and England, as well as in Boston and Washington, since, as a boy, he had gone to
school in Paris, in Amsterdam and Leyden, the charm of
his life had been literature. Rising at four or five, lighting his fire and candle, reading his Bible first, with
English, French and German commentaries, reading his
Homer and his Latin authors, without whom he could
not have endured existence, reading Evelyn's *Sylva* for
his garden, reading all the new books on science, bent on
his own improvement, bent on the improvement of his
children before he undertook to improve his country, he
had mastered Dutch and Russian as well as the tongues
that other people knew. And the summit of his ambition
was to write, to serve his country, at its feeblest point, by
some enduring work of literature.

One work he was to write that served his country, the celebrated *Report on Weights and Measures*. But this was not the work he had in mind. Nor was the Pepysian Diary, incomparable in American letters, the living portrait of his wilful mind, with malice towards all, with charity for none, least of all himself. He had written a volume of *Letters on Silesia* that showed what gifts he had for observation. His *Lectures on Rhetoric and Oratory*, delivered at Harvard College in 1806, revealed his powers of organized reflection. He had heard the greatest orators of the previous age, Fox, Pitt and Burke, as well as their American contemporaries, and Harvard was prepared to hear the doctrine, sanctioned by Cicero and Demosthenes, that, while liberty was the parent of eloquence, eloquence was the stay of liberty. It was a doctrine that Harvard wished to hear, in an age when the art of the pulpit, the art of the forum, the art of the judge and the lawyer, soon to be followed by that of the lecture-platform,—all one art, in its several branches,—was the only literary art that performed a vital function; and Adams, with his experience and his learning, his gifts for perspicuity and order, was certainly the most competent instructor the college could have found. His lectures served as a text-book for the rising generation of public speakers.[1] But this was not the writing he had dreamed of, and dreamed of still, when, on a Christmas morning, he read Pope's *Messiah* to his household, or when he noted that an actor's letter, asking for his analysis of

[1] "When he read his first lectures in 1806, not only the students heard him with delight, but the hall was crowded by the professors and by unusual visitors. I remember when, long after, I entered college, hearing the story of the numbers of coaches in which his friends came from Boston to hear him. On his return in the winter to the Senate at Washington, he took such ground in the debates of the following session as to lose the sympathy of many of his constituents in Boston. When, on his return from Washington, he resumed his lectures in Cambridge, his class attended, but the coaches from Boston did not come."—Emerson, *Letters and Social Aims*.

Othello, pleased him more than all his political honours. Like his own grandson, Henry Adams, who, longing to think like Benvenuto, knew that his instinct was "blighted from babyhood," he longed to think and feel as Shakespeare felt, or as the Germans Wieland and Bürger felt, writers he had read so many years before, as far back as 1800, when he was living in Germany, the first of all Americans to do so. But his instinct also had been blighted by the long winter of Puritanism. The time had not yet come for New England poets.

The time had not yet come, but the time was coming, and Adams, in his pertinacity, represented the chill before the dawn. During those years in Germany, he had translated Wieland's *Oberon.* The poet, to whom his tutor sent the version, compared it with the English Sotheby's version. Adams's was more accurate, he said, but Sotheby's was more poetical. Alas, the more Adams had written since, the more he realized that, with poetry, there was a certain point that one might reach, by means of the virtues that New England knew, beyond which no vigils or vows would take one. But he was under a spell. What was he to do? Riding, walking, musing, he poured the verses forth, odes to Lucinda, Narcissa, Belinda, whose charms he could not refuse to acknowledge, translations of Juvenal's satires, elegiac stanzas, versifications of La Fontaine's fables, versions of the Psalms in rhyme, even a long poem, *Dermot McMorrogh,* a satire in the eighteenth-century mode that filled his mind for weeks and left him, at the end, like a pleasant dream, to dull and distressing realities. What could he do when the rhymes insisted on coming and he found he could sometimes hold in his mind fifty lines at once? Throw his poems behind the fire? Or suffer a few, at least, to appear in print? Certainly one of the greatest statesmen living, he was content to be known as one of the smallest poets of his country. Meanwhile, as a searcher of the skies, who

knew that there are many kinds of stars and who liked
to promote astronomy, he scanned the horizon every day
for other and better poets than himself.

*
* *

Cambridge, across the Charles, was a quiet village, so
quiet that one could hear in Harvard Square the boom-
ing of the guns in the navy-yard in Boston. One even
heard the murmur of the waves breaking on the far-away
sea-beaches. Cambridgeport was a huckleberry-pasture,
with a few wharves and houses. Thence the sloop "Harvard," moored to its dock, a Viking ship in the eyes of
the village boys, sailed once a year to the coast of Maine
to bring back wood for the college.

Through the port, as first through the village centre,
passed the white-topped wagons that brought to the Boston market the wares and products of the inland regions.
They filled the yards of the inns, the Porter House, for
one, beyond the village, and the shouts and oaths of the
teamsters rang through the tranquil air. Around the un-
garnished Common, where the dust and the snow blew
unchecked, a few old houses stood amid their ample gardens. One of them, a gambrel-roofed dwelling, General
Ward's headquarters in the Revolution, was the house
of the Reverend Abiel Holmes, the author of the *Annals
of America,* a work, sufficiently bald, that was yet the first
of its kind. The house next door was that of the Higginson family. On Dana Hill stood the Dana mansion. The
family of Chief Justice Dana, the first American minister
to Russia, had owned their Cambridge farm for six generations. On Brattle Street stood the Craigie house, one
of a line of spacious Georgian villas that were known as
Tory Row. They had been built before the Revolution
by opulent loyalist families, who owned slave-plantations
in the West Indies. In the careless eighteenth-century

days, the great halls and chambers of these houses had echoed with the sounds of music and dancing. Elmwood stood a mile or so beyond, the last house in the row, formerly the home of Elbridge Gerry. It had been occupied for several years by the Reverend Charles Lowell and his household. Widespread lawns encircled these dwellings, covered with wine-glass elms and willows with orchards at the rear. The windows of the Craigie house overlooked the placid meadows to the river Charles.

From these Cambridge windows peered,—one saw them from the street,—the faces of aging women, now and then with turbans on their heads and massive silver spectacles, eyes that had witnessed and remembered the passing of guns and troops in the Revolution. Mrs. Craigie's head was often seen, as she sat at her parlour window. Her house had been Washington's headquarters, in the winter of '76, and there Mrs. Washington had come, with a coach and servants in scarlet livery, to celebrate her wedding-day. The late Mr. Craigie, the Boston merchant, had been famous for his entertainments; and among his guests, in this house, had been Talleyrand [2] and Queen Victoria's father. But the days of Queen Victoria had not arrived, nor the days of a Cambridge poet who was to make the house more famous still. Mrs. Craigie, once a well-known beauty, a widow now, much reduced in fortune, even to the point of taking lodgers, spent her days reading her favourite authors, Voltaire and the British reviewers. Her house was well-stocked with books, like all the other liberal Cambridge houses. Hume, Addison, Gibbon, Swift stood on every shelf, along with Milton and *Evelina,* Richardson, perhaps a polyglot Bible, Casaubon's Polybius, two or three Elzevirs. The library of the Reverend Charles Lowell, who had a church in Boston, numbered nearly four thousand

---

[2] Of whom Miss Mary Moody Emerson said, "I fear he is not organized for a future state."

volumes. Mr. Lowell had exiled to the attic the old prints
that had filled his grandfather's study, heads of the ancient wise men, Plato, Pythagoras, Socrates, Cicero, Seneca; for, without thinking less of the ancients, he thought
more of the moderns. He had studied his theology in
Scotland and had visited Southey and Wordsworth, the
new English poets, whose work he enjoyed discussing;
and facing his chair in the dining-room hung a portrait
of Wilberforce, the symbol of his humanitarian interests.
The Reverend Mr. Holmes, who also made the most of
the art of living, had yet maintained the ancient faith.
Indeed, he was deposed for doing so, although he was
only mildly Orthodox, for the Cambridge people were
Unitarians. They had settled this great question for good
and all, along with the Boston people. They were Unitarians as they were Whigs. Here and there one found a
Calvinist, as here and there one found a Democrat, like
Mr. Timothy Fuller of Cambridgeport. But one had to
be a personage, a Member of Congress or a magistrate,
a man who could afford his coach and pair, to carry off
these odious opinions. The Cambridge people knew what
they believed, and they did not propose to discuss it. But
Mr. Holmes had literary compensations. His house overflowed with books. Amid the lumber in the attic, one
found Erasmus's *Colloquies* and queer old Latin works
on alchemy. Sometimes, in the evening, Mr. and Mrs.
Holmes and their sons and daughters gathered about the
London-made piano, and one of the daughters, who was
the family minstrel, sang the *Irish Melodies* of Thomas
Moore.

All of these ampler houses, those of the ministerial
and legal families, and some of the merchant families,
abounded in family portraits. They were the work of so
many journeyman painters, at ten, twenty or forty dollars a head, that they represented only a decent regard
for fathers and mothers who would have thought them-

selves passing rich on a thousand dollars a year. If one had a Copley or a Stuart, one had the right to lift one's chin a little. On the shelves of the closets lay bundles of mint and catnip, lavender, sweet-marjoram, pennyroyal. Apples were stored there, and peaches spread their fragrance on the darkness, as if waiting to inspire strains and strophes. For little boys were growing up in Cambridge who were to be known as "household poets," and often as something better. Their parents even wished them to be poets. The Cambridge fathers and mothers were not poetic, but they respected poetry. Their gardens were full of marigolds, hollyhocks, larkspurs, with the humbler vegetables of the working kind, carrots, parsnips, beets,—as if to remind the sons of the Revolution that classes were provisional in republics, that a deserving carrot was better than an undeserving lupin, that hollyhocks were only hollyhocks when they were plucky enough to withstand the wind, each on its own stalk (which made them pleasing vegetables indeed), and that the man who had the family portraits must always prove himself on other grounds. One of the "household poets" [3] was to make this clear. The Cambridge flowers had a moral meaning, as good New England flowers ought to have; but they had a poetical meaning that was even more apparent. So did the sounds one heard on summer evenings, the bells of the cows ambling home at twilight, the lullaby of the crickets in early autumn, the hymns of the frogs, in spring, in some neighbouring swamp, not to speak of the creaking of the winter wood-sleds, dragging their loads of walnut over the complaining snow. Every sound and odour had its value. One heard the carpenter smoothing his knotty boards, and the whips of the four-horse coaches rattling by; one heard the ticks in the joints of the old bedsteads; one smelt the salt of the sea in the summer breeze. What a store of allusions and sim-

---

[3] Oliver Wendell Holmes.

iles, drawn from the homely facts of his daily living, a Cambridge boy might pack into his poems! When it came to associations and recollections, such as all New England boys shared in common, buried under the leaves of many summers, the Cambridge boys who were to write their poems were to understand the meaning of Byron's line about "striking the electric chain."

In Cambridge, other facts pressed themselves upon one's attention. There was the village church-yard, where one puzzled over the Latin inscriptions on the grave-stones of old theologians and presidents of the college, the diamond-shaped cavities in the stones from which the leaden escutcheons had been removed to be used for bullets in the Revolution, the graves of ancient scholars, with virtues ending in *issimus* and *errimus*. One somehow acquired the sense that learning was a very distinguished object, which made the scholar a natural leader of men. The spot where Washington took command of the army was near the spot where President Langdon of Harvard had offered prayers, before the assembled troops, and sped them on their way to Bunker Hill. Learning might indeed be quaint and queer, as, for instance, with those living tutors who had so steeped themselves in Latin that their English was a foreign babble, men who said "intramural aestivation" when what they meant was town-life in summer, men who might have written a poem beginning—

> In candent ire the solar splendour flames;
> The foles, languescent, pend from arid rames.[4]

But all the New England statesmen were also scholars, and most of them had come to nurse in Cambridge. There had been set up, in the year the town received its name, the first printing-press in the commonwealth, brought from England in 1638, the press that had pro-

[4] Holmes.

duced for two-score years all the printing in the colonies, including Eliot's Bible and the *Freeman's Oath*. Learning was immemorial in Cambridge. Learning was omnipresent. In a population wholly derived from England, one counted the foreigners on a single hand: two Scotch gardeners, a hair-cutter of nebulous antecedents, one Irishman, the master of a spade. And the Irishman knew his Latin, like everyone else: he had learned his Horace at a hedge-school and was always ready to lean on his spade and test a boy's knowledge of the *Quo me, Bacche*. The shopkeepers around the square added tags of Latin to their signs. The janitor of the newly-established Law School was a notable spouter of Virgil. The height of wit in all the Cambridge circles was a thoroughly sound Latin-English pun.

The schoolmasters in Cambridge, as in Boston, were cut on the ancient pattern. They drove the boys with switch and ferule, and even drove the girls, all the more when the boys and girls were children of the learned families; for everyone in Cambridge was precocious, and only a dunce could fail to be ready for college at fourteen or fifteen. The best-known school, soon to be opened, for Greek and Latin only, was that of William Wells, an Englishman. It was he who had published in Boston the Cicero in twenty volumes, and he had also edited Tacitus. His school was a Gehenna of blood and tears.[5] At Cambridgeport, there was another school where, in the process of flogging the Latin in, and pulling the boys about by the ears, the master almost pulled their ears off. One of the little Dana boys, the grandson of the old Chief Justice, never forgot how his ear had felt. He had his mind made up in regard to floggers, especially when he sailed before the mast and saw the sailors flogged; and in days to come he was to speak his mind. But the boys were

[5] "My dears, it was hell," said Charles C. Perkins, the art-critic of later days.

not without their pleasures. They pitched hay with the hired men, and even with their fathers, on occasion. They knew all the trees by their bark and leaves, and all the birds by their notes and manner of flying. They scoured the country in search of flowers and insects; they fished for pouts and waded for water-lilies; they searched for powder-mills and old redoubts, left from the Revolution. They lay and chattered on the grassy slopes and fought the battles over again. They haunted the Boston wharves, redolent of the ocean and swarming with ear-ringed seamen. Moreover, they had their parties with the Cambridge girls. Strangers who came from less heroic regions sometimes found these parties a little chilly. One of them said that, during the quadrille, his partner touched his hand as if she were feeling for cucumbers in the dark.

Harvard College was the heart of Cambridge. Seven generations before, every New England household had given the college twelvepence, or a peck of corn, or its value in unadulterated wampum peag. But those were the good old days when the Orthodox faith reigned in every mind. Established now on a Unitarian basis,—for the founding of the Divinity School, with Dr. Henry Ware as its chief professor, settled the character of the new regime,—the college was considered, in the country districts, dangerously lax and liberal. West of Worcester, and up the Connecticut Valley, the clergy, Calvinist almost to a man, united in condemning the Cambridge collegians, in the very words of Whitefield, as "close Pharisees, resting on head knowledge,"—the same collegians who had called Whitefield "low." But as for this "head knowledge," no one denied that they possessed it. More than a few of the Orthodox admitted that it was what collegians ought to possess. Harvard still had an exalted prestige. The patrician families of Boston and Cambridge regarded it as more than a family affair,—it was a family responsibility. They sent their sons to the college, as a matter of course. But they considered it a public duty, not only to endow and foster it, in the interests of the meritorious poor, but to maintain its standards and oversee it. They founded chairs that bore their names, the Boylston chair, the Eliot chair, the Smith professorship.[6] They watched and brooded over its progress and welfare. Who would have respected wealth in Boston if wealth had not, in turn, respected learning? And, if the professors' salaries were very small, everyone knew they were partly paid in honour.

It was true that the standard of learning was not too lofty. In this, as in certain other respects, the well-known "Harvard indifference" resembled that of Oxford and Madrid. Intellectual things took second place. The object of study was to form the mind, but this was to form the character; and Massachusetts knew what its character was and took a certain satisfaction in it. Everyone was aware of the best Boston and Cambridge type, the type that Josiah Quincy represented, or the late Chief Justice Dana, formed on the classic models. A clear, distinct mentality, a strong distaste for nonsense, steady composure, a calm and gentle demeanour, stability, good principles, intelligence, a habit of understatement,[7] a slow and cautious way of reasoning, contempt for extravagance, vanity and affectation, kindness of heart, purity, decorum, profound affections, filial and paternal. A noble type, severely limited, which Boston celebrated in its marble

[6] The Boylston chair has been held, among others, by John Quincy Adams, Edward Tyrrel Channing, Charles Townsend Copeland and Archibald MacLeish. The line of the Smith professors is as follows: George Ticknor, Longfellow, Lowell, Bliss Perry. Of Adams, Emerson says: "I have heard that no man could read the Bible with such powerful effect." (*Letters and Social Aims.*) This was a distinction also of Adams's successor, C. T. Copeland.

[7] See Jonathan Phillips's remark about his saintly friend, Dr. Channing: "I have known him long, I have studied his character, and I believe him capable of virtue."

busts. Comparing it, trait for trait, with half of Plutarch's characters, one might have felt that Boston deserved its busts. Moreover, beneath its cold and tranquil surface, burned, though the fires were low, the passions and convictions of the Revolution, ready to flame forth on a fresh occasion. But would the occasion ever recur? That was what a stranger might have asked, face to face with the marble busts. The surface, at least, seemed somewhat tame, suited for the merchant and the lawyer, and the man of God after the Boston fashion.

This was the type, and almost the only type, the curriculum of Harvard contemplated. Whatever studies favoured its formation, whatever were the best ways to form it, these were the ways and the studies that Harvard knew. Whatever studies did not favour it, or favoured the formation of other types that Boston did not like or had never heard of, these were no concern of Harvard, or its concern only to oppose them. Josiah Quincy was not enthusiastic. Why should Harvard be? Mr. Dana was eminently decorous. He had caused the arrest, for contempt of court, of a butcher who, appearing at the bar, had left his coat behind him. Decorum was a Harvard characteristic.[8] Neither Mr. Quincy nor Mr. Dana cared a button for the German language, which had been spoken by the Hessian troops, a half-barbarous tribe of Europeans who had been hired out to the British king. German, from the point of view of Harvard, always excepting John Quincy Adams, who, as everyone knew, was a little queer,[9]—German was an outlandish dialect; and, while it was not improper to speak French, the language

[8] In time, it even became, with Irving Babbitt, one of the many Harvard religions.

[9] Concerning the Adams family, the popular view remained unchanged for four generations. "I think them all . . . exhibiting a combination of talent and good moral character with passions and prejudices, etc. . . . that would puzzle La Bruyère to describe and which has no prototype in Shakespeare or Molière."—Harrison Gray Otis on Charles Francis Adams the first.

of Lafayette, which it was quite improper not to know, more than a few felt that Bonaparte had destroyed its respectability. Greek was esteemed as the tongue of a group of ancient republics that possessed some of the virtues of New England. Greece had produced a number of orators who were more eloquent even than Samuel Adams. Search as one might, however, in Massachusetts, one could not find a play of Euripides; besides, compared with Latin, which everyone drank in with his mother's milk, Greek was a little dubious. The Roman word "convivium" meant "living together." "Symposium" had a similar sense in Greek, but what did "symposium" imply? "Drinking together." Was not this alone enough to prove that the Romans were more respectable than the Greeks? Cicero had made the point, and everyone knew that Cicero must be right.

These were the days of the genial President Kirkland, who, after conducting an examination, regaled the boys with a fine dish of pears. He was an easy-going man, a Unitarian minister, like most of the professors, sympathetic and of the gentlest temper, naturally frank and cordial, with all the delicate feeling for human behaviour that characterized the best New Englanders. It was said that he threw his sermons into a barrel, as the farmers threw their corn into the silo, and that on Sunday morning he fished out enough for a discourse and patched the leaves together. The story had a symbolic truth, at least. It signified the president's "Harvard indifference," which was accompanied by the best intentions and a notably warm heart. He never took the narrow view. Hearing that the flip at the Porter House had proved to be too attractive to the students, he dropped in to see the proprietor. "And so, Mr. Porter," he said, "the young gentlemen come to drink your flip, do they?"—"Yes, sir," said Mr. Porter, "sometimes."—"Well, I should think they would," the president said. "Good day, Mr. Porter." Any sort of illumination, physical or spiritual, might have taken place under his eye. He was kind to the rich young men whose fathers, at their graduation, gave them dinners in a great marquee, with five hundred guests and dancing in the Yard. He was kinder to the poor young men whose black coats were turning green. He was not a man to oppose any important change in the system of studies; and before the end of his long reign certain changes were to occur that were eventually to transform the college. But he could not see why changes should occur. He thought the old ways were good enough, and he played into the hands of firmer men who thought that all other ways were bad. Four hours a day for study and recitation were quite enough for anyone. A library of twenty thousand books was certainly large enough. In fact, the Harvard library was a wonder. No other American library was larger, except perhaps one. A young man with literary tastes could find Hakluyt's *Voyages* there, Cotton's Montaigne and Dodsley's *Old Plays,* as well as the books that he ought to have at home; and the window-sills were broad enough to sit on, if he was too fidgety to keep his chair. What more, in reason, could one ask for? For the rest, the teaching consisted of recitations. No nonsense on the part of the professors, no lectures, no unnecessary comments, no flowery illustrations. One ground in one's Latin and mathematics, under a pair of candles, and the next day one ground them out again. Professors were not nurses, neither were they dancing-masters. One did not go to Harvard to stimulate a dubious fancy. One went to learn to deserve a marble bust.

A few imaginative persons had their doubts. The college was dying of antiquated notions,—so, at least, they thought. Twenty years before, one of the students, who was known later as a writer,[10] had printed certain strictures on the college. He had called it "the death-bed of

[10] William Austin, author of *Peter Rugg, the Missing Man.*

genius." How many immortals, he asked, had Harvard
educated?—and how could it expect to produce immortals? The delicate muse of belles-lettres could never be
induced to visit Harvard. "No, she would recoil at the
sight of our walls." And very properly, the professors
thought. The college was not for ladies, neither was it
meant for men of genius, or any other sort of extravagant creature. For a thorough Boston lawyer, a merchant
who desired a well-trained mind, a minister who did not
indulge in raptures, Harvard had proved to be an adequate nest. It fostered polite, if not beautiful letters, it
sent one back to Plutarch for one's models, it sharpened
the reasoning faculties, it settled one's grounds for accepting a Christian faith that always knew where to draw the
line.

In short, the college was a little realm as fixed and
final as a checker-board. The squares of the various studies were plainly marked, with straight lines and indispu-
table corners. All one had to do was to play the game.
Dr. Popkin, "Pop," was Professor of Greek. Over his
cocked hat he carried a circular canopy that Cambridge
learned to know as an umbrella. The doctor was a sound
grammarian. He found his poetry in the Greek roots; he
did not need to seek it in the flowers. A second umbrella
appeared in the Cambridge streets, in the hands of Professor Hedge, who had written a famous *Logic*. He had
spent seventeen years composing this work, with the aid
of the other members of his household. No Logic could
have been better, and he hoped his students would learn
it word for word. For logic was important. Unless one
knew logic, one could not read Locke; and who that had
not read Locke could ever be certain that his Christian
faith had a solid bottom? Logic was the Golden Calf of
Cambridge, the muse of Theology, the muse of Law. For
Hebrew, one went to Professor Willard; for Latin, to
Brazer or Otis; for Natural Religion, to Professor Fris-

bie, whose taste for the ethically severe was modified by
his love of graceful ease,—he enjoyed Maria Edgeworth
as well as the rigours of Tacitus. Dr. Ware presided over
Divinity. Dr. Ware's favourite phrase was "on the one
hand, on the other hand." He knew he possessed the
truth, but he did not wish to slight its minor aspects. He
was famous for the accuracy of his definitions. No one
could distinguish better than he between "genuineness"
and "authenticity"; and, although he had nineteen children, he never used the rod. He punished infractions of
the household law by the hydropathic treatment.

Towering modestly over the other professors, Andrews
Norton symbolized the *zeitgeist,* a word that he would
have deprecated. It savoured of those antic tricks which
the young men were beginning to play with language (or
were so soon to begin to play),—German barbarisms,
exclamations, inversions, coarse and violent metaphors,
innovations which, to Mr. Norton, seemed both *outré*
and *bizarre,* much as he disliked to use two foreign words
in a single sentence. His own greatest days had not arrived, but Cambridge was prepared for his fortunate marriage. The heir of John Norton, who had proclaimed his
line a "royal priesthood," not himself ordained, was yet
a potent theologian, the Dexter Professor of Sacred Literature. He was more than a match for the daughter of
a Boston merchant who kept a variety-store on Dock
Square and who, after sending his son to Europe, to
make the grand tour in his own carriage, wished his
daughter to live in becoming style. Mr. Norton's father-
in-law purchased Shady Hill for the promising couple,
made a gentleman's house of it and bought the fifty acres
of Norton's Woods, as the domain was henceforth to be
called, an elegant park, unrivalled in homely Cambridge,
where, in time, were to blossom, along with little Charles
Eliot Norton, the handsome daughters whom the college
knew as the "Evidences of Christianity," a reference to

their father's famous book. Shady Hill was to have a notable history long after its first lord, the "Unitarian Pope," as Carlyle was to call him, who, for a generation, was to fight, on behalf of Harvard and common sense, against the Germanizing radicals, the Transcendentalists and their noxious crew, metaphysicians of the wilder sort, —long after the great Andrews Norton had laid his cold head in the colder tomb.

These days were still remote. Professor Norton was not married yet. He was not yet the "tyrant of the Cambridge Parnassus," nor was there an Emerson to call him so. He had not yet edited Mrs. Hemans, although he had written his own devotional poems. He had not visited his English readers; nor had he produced his commanding work, the *Evidences of the Genuineness of the Gospels,* which proved, to the satisfaction of honest men, —whatever the Germans might say, in their so-called higher criticism,—that Matthew, Mark, Luke and John had really written the books that bore their names, a demonstration as clear as Hedge's *Logic.* The four great volumes were still unborn, but Mr. Norton had won his spurs already. His head was long, his head was firm, his mind never wavered or misgave him. In Cambridge, *chiaroscuro,* a word unknown, would have been thought to savour of corruption; and the man who had put the Calvinists to rout, by sheer force of reasoning, was not the man to be upset by any other appeal to the vulgar "feelings," that of the pantheist Schleiermacher, for instance, with his notion that the verities of religion rested, not on the letter of the Scriptures, but on "the soul's sense of things divine." Odious phrase, how German! Mr. Norton's lectures had spread his fame. There was not a lawyer in Boston or Cambridge who could find a crack in his chain of logic. No one could prove that he was mistaken; and, inasmuch as a lawyer-proof religion was exactly what Boston wished for, Mr. Norton's eminence was uncontested. Was he a little petulant and vain? That was beside the point. And if he was called a Pharisee by certain ill-bred persons, that was wholly a matter of definition. Mr. Norton, like Professor Ware, was a master of definition. He was benevolent, he was conscientious. Moreover, he was the only professor,—or he was soon to be,—who had his private carriage. One saw it every Sunday, drawn up beside the president's carriage at the entrance of the college chapel.

Such was Harvard College, as it might have appeared in the eyes of a travelling Persian. It resembled Paley's watch. One found the watch on the seashore and instantly inferred that some intelligent mind must have designed it. One found Harvard College in the village of Cambridge: the evidences of design were also there, the wheels and all the parts in perfect order. The mainspring was useful common sense, based on a thrifty view of Christian ethics; and, if it resembled the watch in other ways, if it was small, cold and mechanical, was it more mechanical than Oxford, where they also put the Apostles in the witness-box while they drowsed over their bottles of port? Oxford was torpid also, droning along in its eighteenth-century grooves, waiting for its great awakening. Harvard was only a more provincial Oxford, as the travelling Persian would have seen at once, and meanwhile a sympathetic stranger, an aspiring student, especially one who had been born in Cambridge, would no doubt have seen it in a rosier light. The Cambridge boy would have known the "Cambridge elm," with its suggestions of the Revolution, the old houses with their charming customs, the gracious lawns, the birds, the luxuriant flowers, stuff for a dozen poets, especially when the naturalist Thomas Nuttall became curator of the Botanic Garden and wrote his books on botany and ornithology, drawn from observations of the local scene. The Cambridge folk were intelligent and kind; and, if it was one of their foibles to put other people in their places, this was an indication, after all, that other people's places were not Cambridge. They were serious, devout, cultivated, stable. They were not given to excesses, even on the side of righteousness. The "ministers' sons" who became proverbial were the sons of the brimstone God of the inland regions. The ministers' sons of Cambridge never knew repression and therefore had no wild oats to sow. Neither in its action nor in its reaction was the Cambridge mind marked by a waste of force. Its only danger was a certain smugness. Its only excess was an excess of caution.

Harvard, moreover, was on the brink of change. Woe to the student, woe to the youthful tutor who counted overmuch on the signs of the times, who interlarded his speech with foreign phrases, sported embroidered waistcoats or even thought that modern languages ought to be included in the course of studies. Harvard was intellectually sound, and the sound intellect makes its changes slowly. But the changes were plainly imminent. President Kirkland might have been indifferent, but he was also liberal in temper. The ethics that Professor Frisbie taught might have been cold and dry, but the warmth with which he taught it,—he was a poet himself, in a modest way,—gave his pupils an impulse to study ethics instead of accepting it on authority. The Harvard philosophy was not exciting,—Locke, Paley, Reid,—but one became excited over it. One acquired a taste for philosophy. One acquired a sceptical attitude that opened the way for other points of view. Even Andrews Norton promoted this sceptical attitude. He had no sympathy with the new ideas that were dawning in people's minds, but had he not demolished the old ideas? One could not, after hearing Mr. Norton, revert to the Calvinist view; and if one had disposed of Nortonism, to one's own satisfaction, at least, one was obliged to go forward to something else.

And Mr. Norton's positive tone aroused the desire for combat in his pupils. They therefore learned to fight in the world of the mind. Their intellectual life was filled with zest.

In a word, the students learned to think. Moreover, they learned to write. Whatever might have been said of the Harvard professors, their taste could not have been impugned. Their taste was as refined as their ethical instincts. Their standards were severe. Their students might have certain limitations, but certain others they could hardly have. Their style was almost sure to be marked by grace and, as often as not, by force. Their scholarship was sure to be exacting, especially when Edward Tyrrel Channing, the younger brother of Dr. Channing, became professor of rhetoric,—two years after the birth of a Concord boy, Henry Thoreau by name, who was to acknowledge, in later years, that he had learned to write as Channing's pupil. In fact, the whole New England "renaissance" was to spring so largely from Channing's pupils, Emerson, Holmes, Dana, Motley, Parkman, to name only a few, that the question might have been asked, Did Channing cause it?—

> Channing, with his bland, superior look,
> Cold as a moonbeam on a frozen brook,
> While the pale student, shivering in his shoes,
> Sees from his theme the turgid rhetoric ooze.[11]

That the rhetoric oozed from his pupils' themes, under his bland eye,—that is to say, the "turgid" rhetoric,—was one of the secrets of his influence; for turgid rhetoric was the bane of letters in the days of the Boston orators, the orators whom every boy adored. He had a remorseless eye for the high-falutin, the swelling period, the emphatic word, morbid tissue to this ruthless surgeon whose Puritan instincts had been clarified by a sensible classical

[11] Holmes.

culture. None of his pupils grew the sort of feathers that required the ministrations of Artemus Ward.

One of these pupils[12] kept his college themes, and a list of some of the subjects that Channing set might go as far as any other fact to explain why his pupils were to go so far. Bearing in mind the careers of his pupils, poets, historians, essayists or whatever, one asks oneself what must have been the effect, on adolescent minds, prepared and eager, of questions like the following,—on which they were obliged to write, and to write with perspicuity, whether they shivered in their shoes or not: on keeping a private journal, the anxieties and delights of a discoverer, the cultivation of the imagination, the pleasures and privileges of a literary man, the duty and dangers of conformity, the superior and the common man. These were the subjects that Channing discussed and urged his little classes to discuss, these and the topics of his brilliant *Lectures*,[13] a writer's preparation, a writer's habits, permanent literary fame. The literary life, as he described it, seemed very important and very exciting. Moreover, he spoke of its problems in a way that brought it home to the rising generation. He referred to the confident freedom of thought and style that comes from a writer's pride in his own people and gives him a fine "bravery and indifference to foreign doubts and censure." He showed how the world in general values most the writers who bear the unmistakable stamp, the pungency and native sincerity, of their own time and place. The early Roman writers—like the American writers of the past—depended on foreign examples and supplies. In Rome, at least, this question had found an answer in the praise the Romans bestowed upon their writers for turning home at last for their themes and their style.

[12] Thoreau.
[13] Edited by Richard Henry Dana, author of *Two Years Before the Mast*.

Judging by the fruits of his instruction, one might almost say that Channing sowed more of the seeds that make a man of letters—when the seeds fall on a fortunate soil—than all the other teachers of composition and all the writers of ingenious text-books that have ever taught a much-taught country. A Harvard student of his generation had certain advantages of an inward kind that were not likely to be soon repeated. One of them was that, reading Plutarch, in this sympathetic atmosphere, he might have understood Cicero's youth,—how, consulting the Delphic oracle, he listened to the pythoness who advised him not to regard the opinion of other people, but to make his own genius the guide of his life.

CHAPTER III

THE COAST AND THE HINTERLAND

IN EVERY corner of this New England country, where the ways of the eighteenth century lingered on, a fresh and more vigorous spirit was plainly astir. On the granite ledges of New Hampshire, along the Merrimac River, in Essex and Middlesex counties, where the spindles whirred, or westward, on the lovely Housatonic, life was filled with a kind of electric excitement. The air resounded with the saw and hammer, the blows of the forge, the bells in the factory-towers. In all directions the people were building turnpikes, hundreds of miles of straight lines that cut athwart the old winding roads. The Green Mountain boys had erected their State House. Dwellings were going up in clearings and meadows, or, being up, were carted bodily off to better sites. Churches grew like snowdrops in early March. Villages, towns sprang from the fields. A current of ambition had galvanized New England. The "era of good feeling" was on its way.

As yet there were no signs of a similar movement in the intellectual life of this buzzing region. No poets, no historians had arisen, none or few, feeble as they were few, to celebrate and record men's thoughts and feelings. The mind of the country, torn, since the Revolution, with other anxieties and preoccupations, was tired and too busy with the present. It had no use for its own imagination. The ways of the folk, the deeds of the past, of the notable sires and grandsires of New England, if surely not unhonoured, were unsung. The seaports, like

47

the inland villages, bristled with their legendary lore, tales of the wars, tales of Indian fights, of painted Indian faces at the farmhouse window, of the war-dance, the powwow and the forest, of great snows in which men had lost their lives, of haunted bridges, buccaneers and red-coats, of Yankee maidens and their Tory lovers, of ship-wrecks and battles,—themes for a New England Scott or Byron. One heard of the "screeching woman" of Marble-head. One heard of "witches' hollows," groves of beech and hemlock, where the Indians had held their demon-worship and burning crosses appeared in a greenish light. There were popular ballads and folk-songs,—"Skipper Ireson's Ride," for one,—sailors' chanties along the coast, ballads of village murders, rockaby songs, sugar-makers' songs, sung by weavers and carpenters, by farm-wives and wandering fiddlers, by hunters, trappers, guides and lum-bermen, snatches and refrains and longer pieces, brought from the old world or natural outgrowths of the Ameri-can soil. But the rhymesters, for there were plenty of these,—the rural colleges and academies were turning them out in hundreds,—the rhymesters, unmindful of Burns, whom they imitated, ignored these rude materials of their art, as they were unaware of the greater themes the history of their country offered them.

They felt, these rhymesters, one and all, as later writ-ers felt,—as Hawthorne was to feel, in his earlier days, —that the American scene was too prosaic. How could one write poems and romances about a world that seemed so spick-and-span?—a country that had no shadow, no picturesqueness, no mystery, no pageantry of the past, none of those romantic associations that gathered like moss about every roof and tree, about every hill and valley of the older countries? A land where everything sprawled on the same dull level, in the broad, simple, garish light of day? It required a vision that no one as yet possessed to detect the stores of poetic interest that lay beneath this commonplace appearance. Among these living poetasters, whose style and tone were so flat and thin, whose only thought was to follow the current fashion, or who were busy translating Horace's Odes, or giving new twists to the Psalms, there was not one who had the diviner's eye. But for two hundred years the New England people had been actively working their minds. They had been striving to educate themselves, thinking, brooding, keeping their journals, reading their Bibles, their classics, their books of sermons; and all this life was preparing to bear its fruit. In the country schools, no doubt, in the grammar schools, even in Boston, Cambridge and New Haven, the masters droned along in their ancient ruts. No business of theirs to produce Virgils and Livys! They made the scholars spell aloud in chorus. One learned, at the rod's end, the longest words in the language, learned them to the last sad syllable, a method which, if it failed to rouse one's mind, taught one that every error meant a rap. One saw the schoolmarm, with her willow switch, pinning the boys and girls to her terrible apron, when they were restless and unruly. One found, in many a village, the methods of some old "Ma'am Betty," who kept school in her bedroom and chewed tobacco and drank from the nose of her tea-kettle. But other, more promising methods were rapidly growing, in the Latin schools about the capital, as well as in the towns along the seaboard.

At Newport, Salem, Portsmouth, where the great square mansions faced the sea or lined the stately streets, with their beautiful gardens, cultivated by Scotch and Irish gardeners, there were notable scholars in charge of the young, Harvard men or Englishmen, French tutors, Italian dancing-masters, the dim dawn of a cosmopolitan culture. There were public reading-rooms in Newport and Portsmouth. Salem, like Boston, had its Athenæum and a Philosophical Library, one of the prizes of the late war, second to that of Philadelphia. In Portland, in the cultivated circles, where many spoke French and a few Italian, they were beginning to criticize Dr. Johnson, whom no one had ever criticized before and who had been so unjust to the poet Gray. Music, so long the symbol of the ne'er-do-well, began to be heard on summer nights. The strains of the harp and the flute had ceased to suggest the danger of a drunkard's grave. Here and there some carver of figureheads, or of pumpheads and wooden urns for gate-posts, some young whittler, fired by a book on Rome, which he had found in the reading-room, dreamed of a sculptor's life. If he could carve these eagles for McIntire doorways, these heads of Galen for the apothecaries, why should he not create a marble group that would fill the portico of the county court-house?

In all these bustling ports, or ports that had recently bustled, where the forests of masts rose at the wharves and Portuguese sailors sauntered through the streets, the wide world was omnipresent. Everyone talked about voyages "up the Straits," or to Hong Kong and Calcutta, towns that seemed closer to Salem or Portsmouth than Hartford or New York had ever seemed. The lofty chambers of the great dwellings, hung with French or English tapestry, adorned with arches and columns and carved Italian mantel-pieces, were papered with bold designs, brilliantly coloured birds and tropical flowers and scenes from the Mediterranean lands. The massive bedsteads in the upper rooms were draped with curious curtains of India linen, covered with quaint pagodas and figures in turbans. Canton shawls and Smyrna silks were as common as linsey-woolsey. There were parrots and pet monkeys in half the houses. The children played with cocoanuts and coral and spent their pennies for tamarinds and ginger, or spent their Russian kopeks and their British coppers, which circulated as freely as American coins. The

men wore Chinese gowns at the Salem assemblies, and
the horn-pipe was taught in the dancing-schools. At the
great merchants' houses there were formal parties, where
the heads of the Federal government came to dine, with
ambassadors from the European countries. One of the
Salem magnates of the previous decade was the largest
shipowner in the world.

All these towns abounded in interesting persons, sometimes droll and quaint, often witty, almost always
learned. At Salem, the most imposing of the seaports,
dwelt a circle of distinguished men who were to leave
their mark in American history. One of them was Joseph
Story, already Mr. Justice Story, who wrote for the
Monthly Anthology in Boston. Judge William Prescott
was another, the son of the old hero of Bunker Hill, who
lived on his farm at Pepperell. Both these worthies were
men of renown and both the fathers of sons who were
famous later. Another was John Pickering, the son of
Timothy Pickering, who had learned Arabic in his youth,
while travelling with his father, and had mastered twenty
other tongues. He had refused, as a busy lawyer, the
chairs of Greek and Hebrew at Harvard and was at work
on a philological project, for the spelling of the American
Indian tongues, that was to lead to a world-wide movement for the study of all the primitive languages.[1] Presently, Rufus Choate joined the circle, the great Boston
orator of the future, a weirdly exotic creature in appearance who might have come over in one of the ships from
Java. All the members of this Salem group,—like Daniel
Webster of Portsmouth, Choate's more famous fellow-
orator, who had already made his mark in Congress,—
were soon to move to Boston, as the fortunes of Salem

[1] John Pickering, the first president of the American Oriental
Society, was the author, among other works, of a pioneer book on
Americanisms.

waned and the capital spread its tentacles through New England.

So was the most illustrious of the Salem worthies, the great mathematician, Nathaniel Bowditch, the author of *The Practical Navigator,* a little, nimble man with burning eyes, with silky hair prematurely white, who darted about, rubbing his hands with excitement. This second Benjamin Franklin, the son of a poor cooper and mechanic, who had learned his Latin as a boy in order to read Newton's *Principia*—in which he found an error—had found eight thousand errors in the best English book on navigation. The book he had written himself, the *Navigator,* had saved countless lives and made the American ships the swiftest that had ever sailed. Everyone knew that, as a supercargo, bound for Sumatra and Manila, Bowditch had mastered astronomy so well— between the stars that he watched from the deck and the books he carried with him in his berth—that he was able to revise Laplace. Everyone knew how, on a Christmas night, in the midst of a blinding snow-storm, when he was captain of his own ship and there was not a landmark to be seen, Bowditch had sailed straight to his Salem wharf, as if it had been a sunny day in June. He had taught all his sailors navigation, and every one of them became a captain. And what a work was this *Practical Navigator,* a work that was still to be in active use a century after his death. The literary circles in Boston and Cambridge blushed over the taunts of the British reviewers, the clever men in London who were always asking, "Who reads an American book?" For they felt helplessly mortified. But here was an American book that every British seaman had to read if he hoped to get ahead of the Yankee skippers. It was a classic in its realm, as stoutly built as one of the clipper-ships for which Dr. Bowditch had prepared the way. If the Yankee mind could produce a work like this, what could not the Yankee mind produce when it turned its faculties in other directions? Even here in Salem, where the Prescotts lived, where a little boy, also called Nathaniel, the son of another skipper, was reading his *Pilgrim's Progress*.

In all these centres of the seaboard life, there had arisen a buffer generation that lay between the hard old Puritan ways and the minds of the younger people. Alive itself to literature and thought, prosperous, interested in a larger world, creative, though only, or mainly, in practical spheres, it was a kind of *cordon sanitaire* against the repressive habits of the past. The lawyers, merchants, ministers and scholars who formed the society of these towns preserved the faith in discipline and standards that had marked the older culture, and yet they encouraged in their sons and daughters a free mind, a knowledge of mundane things, the study of languages, music, drawing, dancing, an education of the eye and ear which, from the point of view of the inland regions, savoured of the frankest paganism. The Unitarian cause had won the day all along the sea-line. The leading families professed the "Boston religion." Their intercourse with other lands and peoples had mollified their mental habits; indeed, almost as much as their wide-flung commerce, a little good Madeira softened the old rigidities. They smiled at the faith of their forbears, when they were not shocked by its consequences. For which of them had not seen, in some neighbouring farmhouse, or even in one of the mansions or beside the wharves, some poor crazy woman, chained to a bed, or held by a staple in the floor, driven mad by some hysterical sermon about some unpardonable sin? Wherever one turned, in these prosperous ports, far more in the towns of the hinterland, one seemed to encounter simpletons, and worse, idiots and harmless lunatics, freely walking about, as if the supply of chains were insufficient; and the young people drew their own conclusions. They respected the old ways and the old religion. But they felt there was something unwholesome in this life from which their own minds had been liberated.

For among the younger folk of all these towns, on the sunny side of this buffer generation, these lawyers and merchants and scholars and experienced skippers, there were boys, growing up in dozens, who were to thrive on these new influences. Newport was already reaping its harvest, for there the Channing family lived. William Ellery Channing, the Boston preacher, had spent half the hours of his childhood wandering about the beach and the towering rocks, listening to the music of the waves, with the wide ocean before him, filled with a sense of awe and rapture; and there he spent all his vacations now, in the house surrounded by the charming garden, which had been laid out by the son of Gilpin, the famous writer on the picturesque. At Newport, on winter days, the air was soft and springlike, tempered by the Gulf Stream. There the northern blizzard seldom came, and the English ivy grew on the old stone walls and covered the well-known Mill. Legends throve in the languid atmosphere, and the British arms still hung in Trinity Church, near Bishop Berkeley's organ. And there, in a setting half rustic, half cosmopolitan, the Southern planters brought their families and mingled with the New York and Boston merchants. One could almost see in imagination the Brighton or Baden-Baden of the future. On the promenade, as if it were Europe, the men took off their hats to one another; and the ships set sail from the strange little wharves for Mozambique, Fayal or Zanzibar. The sailors talked of the East and the West Cape and a voyage to the Indian Ocean, perhaps in some fishing-smack of fifty tons.

Newport, the "American Eden," so like the Isle of Wight, had fostered in Channing a feeling for Wordsworth and Byron, those two romantic poets who had shared his moods. There, as a boy, after some sulphurous sermon, dealing with infant damnation, he had heard his father whistle. That was the end of the old faith for Channing. If his father did not believe in it, life was not so dismal, after all. Mingling with the Southern families, he had come to dislike what he called the avarice of the North, the selfish prudence of his fellow-Yankees. He loved the spontaneous ways of the Southern folk, who took no thought for the morrow, ways that fostered poetry and art. He had spent a year as a tutor in Virginia, and it was the Jeffersonians there who had weaned him away from his Federalist prepossessions, strong enough, at first, in a Newport boy whose father had entertained, as he well remembered, Washington, Jay and the other Federalist leaders. In the South, he had read the French philosophers, Godwin's books and Mary Wollstonecraft, and first conceived those dreams of social justice that were to find a voice in his later years. His health had never been strong since those early days when, with a stoic desire for self-improvement, he had slept on the bare floor, subjected himself to a rigid system of diet and prolonged his studies till two or three in the morning. But the slender, pallid, nervous little man, grave, reflective, fond of lonely rambles, teemed with the new ideas that were slowly coming to birth along the seacoast. All thanks to Newport!—where the South and Europe seemed so close at hand. And if Newport had also sheltered the great, grim author of the *System of Doctrines,* Dr. Samuel Hopkins's views had gradually melted away from people's minds. They were no longer "willing to be damned." All that the Newport people wished to recall was the doctor's prediction that the millennium was bound to occur within two hundred years.

In this little corner of New England, Roger Williams too had lived and toiled for the cause of religious liberty. Channing's brother, Edward Tyrrel Channing, had also spent his childhood there. So had the cousin of the Channing brothers, Richard Henry Dana, the poet and critic, the son of the old Chief Justice. So had Washington Allston, the painter and poet, the child of one of the South Carolina families who flocked to Newport for the summer season. His father and mother, distressed by his early talent, and fearing that he would disgrace a planter's household, had sent him North to cure him of his folly; and at Newport he had fallen in with Malbone, the unrivalled painter of miniatures. Allston, whose first wife was Channing's sister and who was later to marry the sister of Dana, had played as a boy with both of his brothers-in-law, both his friends at Harvard and both the inseparable friends of his Boston years. At Newport, Gilbert Stuart had lived, and there the great Berkeley had dwelt for a while. In his house, Whitehall, near the sea, he had planned his new-world university. He had written his *Minute Philosopher* among the rocks where the Channings, Allston and Dana had dreamed and wandered. One might have imagined that Berkeley's benign spirit still lingered in the gracious Newport air.[2]

Other writers and poets were to draw from Newport the themes of poems and stories. There were themes enough,—the writers had only to pluck them,—in the burying-ground of the Portuguese Jews who had settled there after the Lisbon earthquake, in the Mill, which, as people supposed, the Norsemen had built, in the old black houses and rough-stone mansions, in the anomalous figures, vaguely savouring of the great world, whom one saw on the promenade or behind the curtained windows, one the reputed sister of an English queen, one the heroine of a strange romance, an impoverished lady of title who paid her washerwoman with costly lace. There were

---

[2] Most, if not all of the fashionable American watering-places were first "found" and colonized by writers and artists,—Newport, Bar Harbor, Southampton, East Hampton, Monterey, etc.

themes near by on the Providence Plantations, where lingered, and were to linger for many years, the great feudal dwellings of the rural magnates, households of seventy, eighty, ninety persons, where the master of his twelve thousand acres, his fox-hounds and his four thousand sheep kept twelve dairy-maids at work, each with another girl to wait upon her, and two dozen cheeses, as big as cart-wheels, vanished into the void every day. There were stories enough to the north and west, in the valleys and plains of Connecticut, on the green hill-slopes of Vermont, where the Scottish ballads, on the lips of immigrant weavers and shepherds, bloomed again as in their native air, and the farmers and hunters were building a commonwealth. Themes enough for the novels and the poems, waiting for the novelists and the poets.

But still, or more than ever, in these inland regions, not poetry, or history, or romance, but a more sombre form of exercise possessed the people's minds. They did not care for stories. They thought that fiction was a fraud and worse. Religion was their only poetry. The cultivated few, the "mansion people," those who had seen something of the world, or knew at least Boston or New York, the families of the rural magistrates, the squires, the village notables who had connections in the capitals, made an exception of Scott, whose Waverley novels were in every house. They read Scott for his moral tone, just as they read Richardson's *Clarissa* and the tales of Maria Edgeworth, which all the leading families enjoyed and discussed,—often with the families of the Boston merchants, who, in their travelling-carriages, constantly made tours across New England, to Stafford Springs, through the Berkshire hills, to Round Hill, Mount Holyoke or Graylock, perhaps on their way to Niagara or Trenton Falls, for a little holiday outing, stopping to see their cousins on the way. These novels, so moderate and so elevating, served them as patterns of manners. Scott, who

adorned and beautified all that was growing old and passing away, appealed to their conservative feelings, and
Richardson's Grandison was their beau ideal. Many a
girl said she would never marry until she found his like.
Novels like these were hardly "fiction." One read them
without loss of self-respect, as one read the works of Hannah More, or Mrs. Chapone on the bringing-up of girls.

This was only in the mansion-houses. The mansion
people formed an invisible chain, stretching across the
country, through which the currents of the great world
passed. Outside, the village life continued in its primal
innocence. Even the rural aristocracy, touched as it was
by foreign influences, retained its strong indigenous character. America was the only land it knew, or that its forbears had known for seven generations. In towns near
the seaboard, one found a loyalist family here and there.
A few old ladies lingered on who spoke of themselves
as "eating the King's bread," because their father had
fought on the Tory side and they still received a British
pension. Miss Debby Barker of Hingham, a town that was
much like "Cranford,"—as everyone saw at once when
the book came out,—went into mourning, donned a purple dress, at the death of George the Fourth. There were
many Miss Debby Barkers in Boston and Newport, but
most of the country aristocracy had always opposed the
crown. The village folk in general, mainly of the purest
English stock, carried on their ancient village ways, not
in a spirit of Anglophobia, but rather as if England had
never existed.[3] They formed a self-sufficing Yankee world,

---

[3] Anglomania, in all its forms, social or poetic, was confined to the
fashionable urban classes. The British, from the rural point of view,
were as foreign as any other foreigners, and most of the countrypeople, high and low, deprecated intermarriage with them. Miss
Fortune, in *The Wide, Wide World*, undoubtedly expressed their
attitude: "I wish Morgan could have had the gumption to marry in
his own country; but he must go running after a Scotchwoman!
A Yankee would have brought up his child to be worth something.
Give me Yankees!"

separated by a pathless ocean from the ways of the
mother-country. They were farmers almost to a man,
aside from a few mechanics. Most of the ministers tilled
their own soil. Each village had its Indian population, a
cluster of huts on the outskirts, a few Negroes who had
once been slaves, sometimes two or three Irishmen and
one or two beggars and paupers. The larger towns had
public reading-rooms, possibly a Franklin Institute,
where a few odd volumes of Shakespeare, Hume and Milton, Young's *Night Thoughts,* Thomson's *Seasons,* Rol-
lin's *Ancient History,* filled the shelves with old books of
sermons, Owen's *Indwelling Sin* or *An Arrow Against
Profane and Promiscuous Dancing.*

Every village had its squire and parson, a Deacon
Hart, living on the turnpike, where he raised the golden
squashes, the full-orbed pumpkins, the rustling Indian
corn and the crimson currants that straggled by the
painted picket fence. Further on, dwelt some Abihu
Peters. An Ebenezer Camp contrived the shoes. A Patience Mosely made the village bonnets, hard by Comfort
Scran's general store. There were always two or three
hired men, a handy-andy, usually a fiddler, who had
made his violin from the bole of a maple and strung his
bow from the tail of the family horse. Now and then one
found a village drunkard, who might have been a poet,
perhaps some scalawag of a Stephen Burroughs, the worst
boy in the town, who was often kept in chains in the
county jail. There were a few Yankees of the swindling
kind who found their proper sphere in the peddling business. Sometimes they were caught as counterfeiters. The
Yankee mind was quick and sharp but singularly honest,
as a rule,—as honest as the men of Maine a hundred years
later. Everyone who travelled through the country marvelled that the New England farmers' doors were seldom
locked or barred, even at night; and, while the land

flowed with rum, and even overflowed,[4] the great popular drink was homely cider. The cider-barrel was never
empty at weddings and ordinations, on training-days, at
huskings, at Thanksgiving, when the sounds of chopping
and pounding and baking and brewing rose from the
smoke-browned walls of the farmhouse kitchen. Those
who grew up in these inland regions, looking back on
the old village life, saw it in the light of Goldsmith's Auburn, abounding in mild virtues, faithful swains, rural
virgins, peace and innocence. The goodman's daughters
made his shirts and stockings; his garments were provided by his flocks and herds. So were those of the
women-folk, who, as they spun and knitted, discussed the
weekly sermon.

For religion filled the horizon of the village people, all
that was left by politics and law. On Sunday morning, in
the church, one heard the Psalms repeated, in Sternhold
and Hopkins's version, which some of the old women
believed were the very strains King David had sung to
his harp,—"The Lord will come, and he will not," and,
after a pause, another line, which most of the children
thought was another idea, "Keep silence, but speak out."
The old-fashioned polemical sermon followed, fortified
with texts and garnished with quotations in Greek and
Hebrew, for most of the clergy were still learned men.
Perhaps only the week before, the minister had driven
in his one-horse chaise twenty or thirty miles across the
country to meet some reverend brother and settle some
nice point in theology on which he was writing a treatise:
he could not agree with Dr. Stern that God had created
sin deliberately, and he wished to lay his case before his
flock. Many of the village ministers, whose cocked hats
and gold-headed canes were symbols of their unques-

---

[4] When the Reverend John Pierpont made his pilgrimage to the
Holy Land, the first object he saw, on the wharf at Beirut, was a
hogshead of New England rum.

tioned authority, as shepherds and judges of the people, devoted their lives to writing these treatises. The farmers discussed them over their ploughs, and the farm-wives over their spinning-wheels. For religion was their romance. They named their children after the biblical heroes, and the Bible places, Chimmin and the Isles, Dan and Beersheba, Kedar and Tarshish were stations on the map of their El Dorado. The congregations followed the web of the sermons with a keen and anxious watchfulness, eager to learn the terms of their damnation. And they talked about fate and freedom and how evil came, and what death is, and the life to come, as familiarly as they talked of their crops and the weather.

All New England seethed with these discussions. One heard about "potential presence" and "representative presence" and "representative identity," and Dr. Bancroft's sermon on the fourth commandment. Blacksmiths and farriers, youths and maidens argued about free will and predestination, about "natural ability" and "moral ability" and "God's efficiency" and "man's agency." Sometimes it was a morbid interest, when the children sat on "anxious seats" and wept over their wicked little hearts. The conscience of New England was precocious. Even Cotton Mather had observed that "splenetic maladies" throve among the people, maladies that were scarcely allayed by some of the more emotional preachers. One heard of "sweating" sermons and "fainting" sermons, followed by "convulsion-fit" sermons, in the best tradition of Whitefield.[5] Sometimes, in the frontier settlements, on the borders of the wilderness, in the forests of New Hampshire and Vermont, where men almost forgot that they had voices, and only the axe and the hammer broke the silence, where, on the frozen slopes, the snow fell for days together, strange and terrible thoughts rose in the mind. A Green Mountain boy with an axe in his

[5] See the Reverend Mr. Stoker, in Holmes's *The Guardian Angel*.

hand might sing his happy songs in the busy summer, rejoicing in the Alpine air, scented with fir and hemlock, for the Green Mountain boys had their mountain freedom. But when the snow began to fall, and he sat brooding beside the stove, over his calfskin Bible, in the close, foul air of the farmhouse kitchen, digesting food that was never meant for man, then, as he conned the mystical Revelations and the savage mythology of the ancient Jews, visions of blood-atonement swept his brain. Among the native ballads of the Vermonters, bloodshed was an omnipresent theme. They felt the presence of the God of Vengeance. They heard voices that were not benign. From them was to spring, a few years hence, the cult of Joseph Smith and Brigham Young,[6] where flourished now, as foretastes of the Mormons, the quiet murder and the loud revival.

Sometimes, on the other hand, these wrestlings over sublime abstractions rose, in some lonely soul, to the loftiest heights, where the mind was lost in mystical raptures over the universe and its great Architect, and men conversed with angels. Here and there, in the woods of Maine or among the hills of western Massachusetts, some spinster or some godly man, like Benedict in his solitary cell, seated on the mount of transfiguration, kept his days of appointment with the Eternal. What hopes, what rhapsodies possessed his soul, what meditations on a time and space in which all transient ills were engulfed or muted! He saw the whirling of the puppet-world with the eye of the mounting eagle that faces the sun. What mattered this changing planet with its petty cares, lost in the unfading light of moons and stars? [7] There was a fire in the New England heart, in the intellectual depths of Calvinism, which the cold minds of Unitarian Cambridge possessed no knowledge of, a hunger for righteousness and

[6] Both born in Vermont.
[7] See the journals and letters of Mary Moody Emerson.

a thirst for truth, a passionate dream of perfection. Concord knew this dream, and Concord was to express it. Not for nothing had this vigorous race invested in its flaming ancient faith all the treasures of its thought and feeling. Deep in its mental caverns lingered still the spiritual passions of the Middle Ages. Deep in its mental caverns lingered the passions of the Roundheads, who had suffered and fought for freedom and human rights. Let the trumpet sound again, let the God of Hosts unfurl his banners! New England was prepared, when the time was ripe, for another holy war.

At the moment, the state of mind of these inland regions,—even Connecticut, which faced the sea,—seemed hardly auspicious for the man of letters. It was not quickened by the mental currents that brought new light to the towns of the Eastern seaboard. It was wrapped in an atmosphere of gloom; and its doctrines of total depravity and the utter vanity of human effort paralyzed the literary sense. Whatever mobility this mind possessed was all but confined to the theological sphere.

One could only say that in this sphere its mobility was surprising. The great New England schism had broken out, thirty years later than in Boston. The theocratic Church was giving way. Many of the farmers were moving westward; others were in revolt against the blue laws. The Church had been forced to yield in its main positions, as the democratic movement grew apace, for the democratic movement, with its faith in equality, could and would no longer tolerate the aristocratic doctrine of "election"; and, breaking at the centre, it had begun to branch at the outer edges into forms that were often fantastic. Many of the congregations were held together by the prestige of some ancient minister, who still ruled the village as of old. But as these ministers vanished, one by one, the congregations fell apart in factions, and hundreds of conventicles arose,—poor little ugly scraps of wooden Gothic,—in the shadows of the village churches. The mansion people, up and down the country, had begun to be touched by the Unitarian movement. Some of them, as in Boston, were Episcopalians. All of them had lost their taste for the Orthodox phraseology; and to please them, or to express their own views, which were also rapidly changing, numbers of the Orthodox clergy let down the bars of the old religion. Their sermons wandered from the ancestral standards. The humbler folk, meanwhile, who were breaking away, the farmers, mechanics, factory-hands, were offered a wide choice of isms, some of them brand-new, an assortment as appetizing and variegated as that of any Connecticut pedlar's pack. The more emotional sects, the Methodists, throve on the sudden reaction against the logical sermons of the past. The Universalists promised salvation to all. For the Adventists, Christ was coming at once: they did not have to wait for a far-away judgment. Perfectionism captured some; Restorationism captured others. According to the Come-outers of Cape Cod, the word was written in the human heart, a doctrine that pleased the unlettered who had heard too many texts in Greek and Hebrew. As for the question of punishment after death, one could choose between No Punishment, Eternal Punishment, good for most of one's neighbours, or a strictly limited punishment that stopped after the first million years.

All this represented a movement of mind that was to find expression in other spheres, the practical sphere, the scientific sphere,—for it promoted enquiry and the feeling for action,—but whether in the sphere of literature was rather open to question. At present, the intellect of the rural regions was largely confined to two of these factions: the mansion people, with their broader leanings, and the still potent Orthodox party. The sects, appealing to the simpler-minded, contributed to the Abolition movement, which was to make its appearance presently;

but they had little to give to thought or letters. The Unitarians were still few and scattered. There remained the Orthodox leaders who, to regain their power, as the dissolution of the Church advanced, redoubled their ancient threats of hell-fire. To stop the Unitarian movement, the "icy system," as Lyman Beecher called it, they founded the Andover Seminary and built the Park Street Church in the centre of Boston, fortresses of the old faith, in the heart of the enemy's country, from which to pelt the enemy with their sermons,—"each one fresh, like bullets from a mould." [8] They denounced the "vandal spirit of innovation," as Robert Treat Paine had denounced the "vandal spirit of Puritanism." They reaffirmed the glory of the Pilgrim Fathers. As far back as New England history went, the "Connecticut school" had had its own tone, distinct from that of the "Massachusetts school"; and now more than ever, with Lyman Beecher,—as erstwhile with "old Pope Dwight," Timothy Dwight, the president of Yale, who died in 1817,— the Connecticut school was conscious of its strength. Its efforts to capture the stronghold of Boston were futile, but on its own ground it stood firm. The ancient Puritan faith had been revived in a new and powerful cult.

This energy seemed to promise an abundant life in various other realms. At Yale, for instance, the great centre of learning, the second capital of the New England mind, a notable school of science had arisen, with Benjamin Silliman as its presiding spirit. Harvard, with all its literary prospects, had nothing to show as yet, or for years to come, beside this genius of the laboratory, who formed for Yale its collection of minerals and its physical and chemical apparatus, along with the *American Journal of Science*. Silliman's pioneer work in science might have been expected to offset the obscurantist theology of the college, for Yale, like the other and lesser centres

[8] Lyman Beecher.

of learning, Williams, Amherst, Bowdoin, Brown and Dartmouth, those minor Paley's watches, continued to be stoutly Orthodox. Through Silliman's *Journal,* the science of the world passed into the mind of the nation; and Yale was in other respects nationally-minded, with broader political sympathies than Harvard and a much more all-American student-body. But it was isolated from the great-world interests, outside the field of science, that were so soon to stir Boston and Cambridge; and this, in addition to its religious thinking and the relative poverty of the institution, portended little good for literature. Certainly there was little enough at present. Timothy Dwight, the "last of the Puritans,"—as people had called him once, before they became aware of Lyman Beecher, —Timothy Dwight, Jonathan Edwards's grandson, a mighty man, a prodigy of learning, even a poet himself in earlier times, had frowned on "song" and the "arts of the pencil and chisel." He had made every effort to restore the Puritan modes and methods. Of the New Haven poets of the hour, James A. Hillhouse was symptomatic. The son of a well-known senator, a college-mate of the novelist Cooper, he wrote long poems, correct but decidedly dismal, on biblical themes.[9]

At Hartford, the political capital, the second New England seat of the Federalists, which had grown in about the same proportion as Boston, the literary scene was scarcely brighter. A few of the "Hartford Wits" lingered on. Humphreys, Barlow and Lemuel Hopkins were gone, but Theodore Dwight remained, the "old Pope's" brother. One saw him strolling about the Hartford streets,

---

[9] "Yale has never put its football relish into letters or followers of letters. All that related to rhetoric or composition in my day was most shabbily pursued or methodized; nor, indeed, has Yale ever put its foot strongly in that direction."—Note by "Ik Marvel," in Dunn's *Life of Donald G. Mitchell.* See also President Hadley's remarks in *Four American Universities.* Naturally, all this was changed later.

filled to the brim with anecdote and learning, Dwight who had once pursued the Jacobins with the vigilance of a beagle in the brush. John Trumbull still lived in Hartford, the once-famous author of *MacFingal*, old, small, emaciated, bent, tottering on his cane, his fine little face alive with Erasmian humour. One could not forget that the Hartford Wits, whatever their faults and limitations were, had laughed away the popular taste for bombast, at least for a generation. They had had a vigorous interest in poetry which the Boston of their day could only match in the bilious rhymes of Robert Treat Paine. But their day was already remote. Hartford had lost its tincture of intellectual life, and Mrs. Sigourney and her little *salon* still belonged to the future. A youthful poet[10] who, at this moment, oscillated between Hartford and New Haven, cried to the empty air for someone with whom he could talk. A mere author had no place here. The only society that he could find was a handful of indolent and dyspeptic tutors, one or two lawyers without ambition and the illiterate mistress of a boarding-house.

The Connecticut mind, as travellers often noted, was keen, strong and witty, but usually narrow, educated rather than cultivated. It abounded in prejudices that were often small, like most of the "Yankee notions." It lacked, as a rule, the power of generalizing, which had been marked in New York, in Virginia and in Boston. It was a village mind, in short, that had never breathed a larger atmosphere. It bore few of the fruits that spring from an intercourse and collision with other minds from other mental regions. The only important Connecticut man of letters, a man of great importance, a symbol of his world in many ways, was the famous lexicographer, Noah Webster, who was more concerned with "educa-

[10] James Gates Percival. It was characteristic of these years at Yale that Percival, whose failure as a poet almost became proverbial, was eminently successful as a man of science.

tion" than he was ever concerned with "cultivation," but who was doing more with his education than all the American pedagogues put together. A tall, lean, black-coated man, with black small-clothes and black silk stockings, and with an odd, quaint, old-fashioned air,—if you had met him in China, you would have known that he hailed from Connecticut,—always a farmer's son in his heart of hearts, a busy-body, self-important, vain, but upright and honest, aggressive, enterprising, pertinacious, a schoolmaster, lawyer, journalist, who had written on banking and medicine, and yet, for all these multifarious interests, possessed a vast and accurate fund of learning, he was at work, at New Haven, writing his Dictionary, for which his Spelling-book had prepared the way,—a new Declaration of Independence. His object was to establish a national language as a bond of "national union," for Webster, with his democratic tastes, was an old-school Federalist in politics. Already an elderly man, he had lived through the Revolution; and, filled as he was with patriotic fervour, he had not failed to note that, while the Americans boasted of their freedom, nevertheless their arts, their dress, their customs still aped the ways of the mother-country. Why should they receive, in this supine way, everything that came from a foreign press? A spirit of the blindest imitation stifled all American enquiry, benumbed the intellectual faculties. During the years of war, when the intercourse with England was interrupted and American school-books had to be improvised, he had supplanted Dilworth's Spelling-book with his own popular speller. He saw no reason why American children should learn that the letters "Ast. P. G. C." meant "Astronomy Professor of Gresham College," on the other side of the ocean. He had worked up his own vernacular word-book, based on the common usage of New England. The store-keepers, up and down the country, laid in supplies of Webster's Speller, along with their hogsheads of rum and their kegs of molasses. The pedlars carried it from door to door, until, as the decades passed, fifty million copies had been sold. It had given the population a uniform spelling.

The irrepressible Cobbett, in his will, bequeathed five pounds to Noah Webster to pay for a new engraving of his portrait, so that the children who used his speller might no longer be frightened out of their wits by the grim Websterian visage. But the visage had its work to do. Webster was a fighter. He had fought for an author's copyright law, travelling through the South and the Middle States, working on the minds of the legislatures. He spoke in terms that farmers understood. The copyright, he said, was the "author's soil." Only the products belonged to the purchaser; the soil should be vested in the owner. He fought for his mother-tongue in a similar fashion. He toiled along the road from village to village, visiting every country printing-house, handing the compositor a printed slip, saying, as he did so, "My lad, when you use these words, oblige me by spelling them as here," —*theater, center, honor,* etc. He had such a passion for detail, for the fruits and even the process of enumeration, that he often counted the houses in the village, counting up one side of a street and down the other side. For the rest, he saw no reason why the language should not be spelled as the average man pronounced it, even,—he had his little crothets,—dropping the final *e* in *fugitive;* for he had no use for the formal grammarians. As a patriotic gesture of a wholesome kind, he used, as illustrations in his work, quotations from the American fathers, Hancock, Barlow, Livingston, along with Burke and Johnson. It happened that all his own affiliations, in spite of his prodigious store of learning, had been with the plain people: a fact which, accounting for his success, also in-

dicated his limitations. For he had little literary feeling;
he had no sense, or only a primitive sense, of the flavour
and the history of words, well as he knew his etymology.
He had a somewhat arid emotional nature, and the rela-
tively thin, pale speech that had come to prevail among
the Yankee farmers, who had lost, in the dry American
air, much of their ancestral heartiness,[11] sounded as
rich and full in Webster's ears as the deep chest-notes of
the men of old, whose tones were maintained in culti
vated usage. His temper, as befitted a man of Yale, was
rather scientific than humanistic; and his influence, as a
result of this, was very far from happy. When it came to
the niceties of language, whether in spelling or pronun-
ciation, Webster's work was always to be challenged. But
he did his task so well, within his limits, adding his thousands of words, adding his tens of thousands of definitions, which no previous book had ever contained, that
"Webster," with its countless modifications, was destined
to remain a standard work for the English-speaking peoples of the world.

In short, the great Connecticut Dictionary stood, as a
monument of New England learning, beside Bowditch's
Practical Navigator. Only by courtesy works of literature,
these two solid books rose like a pair of imposing gate-
posts at the opening of an epoch. Indeed, the lonely
scholar, Noah Webster, who, for a generation, prowled
round and round his study-table, shaped in a hollow
circle and piled with dictionaries of Greek and Latin,
Hebrew, Arabic, twenty other tongues, was a highly symbolic figure; for learning, at this moment in New Eng-

[11] Emerson often remarked on this phenomenon, in its various aspects, e.g., "In America I grieve to miss the strong black blood of
the English race; ours is a pale, diluted stream . . . Our American
lives are somewhat poor and pallid, no fiery grain; staid men, like
our pale and timid flora . . . The Englishman speaks with all his
body. His elocution is stomachic,—as the American's is labial."

land, was in a very active state. The new sects paid less attention to it, but there were many country ministers like Edward Taylor of Westfield, who, years before, had taken such delight in Origen's works that, not being able to purchase them, he copied them out in four quarto volumes. One heard of ministers who, rebuked for heresy by a group of others, defended themselves in Latin, Greek and Hebrew, and, when they were cornered in all these tongues, retreated into Arabic, where they were safe from pursuit. Here and there, some secular scholar, dressed in his decent black coat,—old but not untidy, neatly bound at the cuffs,—conned his Christian fathers and his Cave and Stanley while he composed his work on the Universe. The children of the ministerial households,—whose mother, as often as not, read Virgil aloud in the afternoon,—talked about Homer and the ancient myths while they were milking or learning to bake, or, in New Hampshire and Vermont, sugaring-off in the spring. Serving-women were not unknown who read their Latin with the boys and girls and heard them recite, after washing the dishes. Young girls, who rose at five and asked themselves, "What hard good work have I to do today?" began with two or three books of *Paradise Lost,* to give them the proper tone. They talked about Dugald Stewart and Alison on Taste, or perhaps about the *Life of Sir William Jones,* which was spreading an interest in Oriental studies. Older sisters advised their younger sisters, who were filled with the *furor scribendi,* to discipline their minds by studying Butler's *Analogy.* One little girl of seven, who had read a book on the ancient gods, telling how much they had been loved and honoured, they whom no one worshipped any more, felt her heart fill with pity. Entering the woods near by, she built a little altar of stones, decked it with flowers and shells and laid her favourite toys on the summit. Then she apostrophized the god of gods: "Poor old Jupiter, I love you! Nobody else worships you, but I will, dear old god. You shall have my doll, and I will bring you flowers every day."

All over New England, not only in the "Literary Emporium," as Boston was called far and wide, there was a passionate interest in self-culture. Countless households followed Miss Edgeworth's theories, or some other theory of education, and practised on their friends and youthful cousins. All the sons and daughters of the well-to-do were sent to the "literary institutions," the colleges and academies. Children of the poorer families, who could not afford to buy paper and ink, made their own, or used chalk or charcoal, and learned to write on the kitchen floor; and here and there some group of boys and girls, who had read Washington Irving's *Salmagundi*, edited a family magazine. This interest in reading and study, in books and authors, laid trains of feeling in the general mind that were about to burst into expression. Throughout the region, as throughout the nation, there was a widely spread presentiment that a great native American literature was about to make its appearance. Everyone read English books, histories, poems, essays, in which people found the moulds of their minds and manners; but they already felt that these English authors described a world that had ceased to be their own. They read about beggars, in the British novels, just as they read about kings, but few had seen a beggar, no one had seen a king. They read about skylarks and nightingales, but a skylark was as rare as a "pampered menial." Who had seen a pampered menial? Most of the distinctions and conventions which they found in the European writers were foreign to their own experience. They were ready to welcome tales and poems without the kings, the menials and the beggars,— with bobolinks instead of larks, with the blue-bird and the wood-thrush where the nightingale had been, and fresh American flowers instead of the far-away verdure of the British poets,—whenever the authors appeared who were able to write them.[12] They were ready for historians and poets who might prove to be as independent as their statesmen had already been.

Of this frame of mind it was symptomatic that a New England author of the future, describing the generation that preceded his own, wrote a story about a valley in which the people cared so much for greatness that they were watching for the man to come, the child born in the valley, who was to be the greatest of his time. The story of *The Great Stone Face* had its prophetic element. It also had a foundation in fact, which it could not have had a century later; for it was true that the New England air was filled with a sense of expectation.

[12] Within a few years, almost all Americans felt as Hosea Biglow felt:

> "Why, I'd give more for one live bobolink
> Than a square mile o' larks in printer's ink."

CHAPTER IV

GEORGE TICKNOR'S WANDERJAHRE

IN THE spring of 1815, two young Boston men had embarked on a voyage of discovery. Not content with the state of affairs at Harvard, they had made up their minds to go to Germany and investigate the reports that had come to Boston about the prodigious progress of the German scholars. Was the German tongue obscure and artificial, as everyone supposed in Massachusetts? Were the Germans merely a race of barbarous pedants, as almost everyone thought in England also? George Ticknor, a lawyer, a Dartmouth man with a great respect for Harvard, had serious doubts about it. So did Edward Everett, a brilliant young minister of twenty, with whom and two or three other friends, Everett's older brother Alexander, Edward Tyrrel Channing and Nathan Hale,[1] who had married Everett's sister, Ticknor had formed a reading club. At the meetings, they shared their Latin compositions, largely aimed at one another's foibles, and ended up with a hasty-pudding frolic.

These two enquiring spirits had sailed for Liverpool, the first stage for Germany, along with a party of other Boston friends and two sons of John Quincy Adams. George Ticknor was a rich young man, with very engaging manners, vivacious, with a melodious voice, with large, dark, velvety eyes and hair that curled and might have been romantic. He was positive, self-assured in the Boston way, not by any means a man of genius, or he would not have been so self-assured,—that is to say, at

[1] The father of Edward Everett Hale.

twenty-three,—but certainly a man of remarkable talents, and talents of a useful kind. The son of a notable merchant who, before he acquired his wealth, had written an English grammar and who shared his son's scholarly aspirations, the young man was favourably known in Boston as a member of the Anthology Club and the editor of Buckminster's posthumous papers. Everett was even better known. He was an intellectual prodigy. At twenty, he had already preached for a year in the most fashionable of the Boston pulpits. The son of another minister who had composed a famous "Eulogy on Washington," which Everett was to repeat for fifty years, with variations and modulations,—or so his enemies said,—he had been highly praised for his school orations. He was the prize boy as a speaker of pieces and had once interrogated the listening air with a question that was soon to have an answer. Why were there no American poets? Why was not New England what it should be, a "nest of singing birds"? Everett sang in prose. His florid and affluent fancy was greatly admired. He was compared to Massillon.[2] John Adams called him "our most celebrated youth." Moreover, Everett really knew his classics; and, when he was asked to become Professor of Greek,—one

[2] See the comment of John Quincy Adams on a sermon of Edward Everett's: "It was without comparison the most splendid composition as a sermon that I ever heard delivered. . . . His composition is more rich, more varied, more copious, more magnificent, than was that of Buckminster. There were passages that reminded me perhaps too much of Massillon, but the whole sermon was equal to any of the best that Massillon ever wrote. It abounded in splendid imagery, in deep pathos, in cutting satire, in profound reflections of morals, in coruscations of wit, in thunderbolts of feeling."—J. Q. Adams's *Diary*, February 13, 1820.

It may be said of Adams that, while he shared the taste for the rococo that was common among his contemporaries, he knew, by comparison with the best in the world, what oratory was. Boston abounded in connoisseurs of sermons. They knew all the points of oratory, as Haydn's audience knew a fine concerto. They enjoyed it so luxuriously for itself that they were glad to overlook its frequent emptiness of content.

of those Harvard chairs that were almost as important as a seat in the Senate,—he accepted the nomination without reluctance, on one condition only, that he might prepare himself in Europe.

The two friends had much in common. Both were model students. Both had an ample share of the Boston sense of responsibility. Everett was considered the brightest student who had ever passed through Harvard. Ticknor had had less opportunity to show what he was made of; but anyone could see that he was solid, whatever his limitations were, while there were several persons who suspected that Everett might be hollow. This was quite unjust. Everett was a little spoiled, perhaps. How could he not have been spoiled when President Kirkland said that he resembled the bust of Apollo? He was a little vain, but he was unquestionably gifted. He was a little ambitious, in every sense of the word; but he had his own way to make in the world, while Ticknor had been born on the upper crust. If he had abandoned, with little scruple, the career of the man of God, everyone knew that half the ministers were only men of God because the pulpit, which was highly honoured, also gave them time to read and write. No one denied that he was conscientious. He was a helpful friend. Besides, his Greek was really something to boast of; it could only have been more surprising if he had studied in Germany. So, at least, Everett surmised. That was why he had sailed away with Ticknor.

But how had it all happened? Who had put the notion of Germany into the heads of these two exemplary students? Madame de Staël, of course, the lady who owned the land in upper New York, bordering on Lake Ontario. They had read her famous book, *De l'Allemagne,* which had just appeared in an English version. They were predisposed to like the book, since everyone knew that Napoleon did not like it. He had suppressed the book and driven Madame de Staël out of France. Moreover, they had read a remarkable pamphlet defending the university of Göttingen against the evil intentions of Napoleon's brother, the ill-famed King of Westphalia. Everyone knew that a thing must be good, whether a university or a book, if the Bonapartes disliked it. The university of Göttingen was plainly good, almost too good to be true, Ticknor thought, when a travelling Englishman who had actually seen it,—he must have been one of the first,— described the library to one of his friends. Ticknor, having time to spare, set to work to learn the German language. But where was he to find the books he needed? Several young men in Boston had heard of a Mr. Goethe, who was said to have written a few respectable pages. They had even heard of Dante, the Italian bard, who had been almost forgotten even in England.[3] But of either tongue, German or Italian, who possessed a grammar? Everett's clever brother, Alexander, produced a German grammar from his desk, and Ticknor remembered that one of his friends in New Hampshire had spoken of a German dictionary. Then he found that John Quincy Adams had bought and kept a copy of *The Sorrows of Werther*. He puzzled it out and made a translation of it.[4]

[3] The popular knowledge of Dante, among the English-speaking peoples, dates from the publication of Cary's translation at about this moment, 1814.

[4] Carlyle's experience in Scotland, at just this moment,—as related by him to Charles Eliot Norton,—was a parallel case. Having become aware of German thought through Madame de Staël's book, he could find only two persons in Edinburgh who had any knowledge of the German language. There was not a German book to be bought in the city. He finally procured a set of Schiller through the skipper of a trading-ship at Leith. This was about 1815.—See *Letters of Charles Eliot Norton*, I, 480-481.

Although German was so little known in Boston, there were a few students of the language elsewhere in New England. Dr. Bentley of Salem and Professor Moses Stuart of Andover both owned collections of German books.

Whatever Ticknor did was sure to be thorough. Everett was thorough, too, in all these scholarly matters. Much as he might have been thought a Laodicean, in certain aspects of his later life, he was bent on the welfare of Boston and Harvard, as afterwards, no doubt, of a larger world. He was convinced that the scholar had a mission. Going to Germany was not a lark, for such a mind as his; it was a novitiate, to be taken strictly. Ticknor felt this even more profoundly, or had the time and means to appear to do so. His country, he felt, would never lack good lawyers, but it was in urgent need of scholars, not the musty theologues of old but well-trained teachers and men of letters. In this capacity he could be more useful, especially if he had seen the world. And he was well-equipped for seeing the world. In fact, he was a man of the world already, with a shrewd eye for the traits of human nature. He could recognize at sight a man of genius, or, if not genius, animated talent. Real genius might be another matter: the fact that one is actually in its presence "dawns slowly on a Boston mind," as one of the Adamses remarked later. To this rule, Ticknor was no exception. He was to meet several men of genius, both in his own country and in Europe, who never dawned on his mind at all, unless they were his friends or men of high breeding.[5] But his eye for talent served him well. When the famous Francis Jeffrey came to Boston,—the editor of the *Edinburgh Review*,—in pursuit of a young lady of New York whom he had met in Scotland, most of

---

It is odd that Ticknor knew nothing of the four translations of *The Sorrows of Werther* which had been published in America before 1800. Parson Weems sold this book as a colporteur for Mathew Carey, the Philadelphia publisher.

[5] See the remarks in his *Journal* about Lamb, Hazlitt and other English "bohemians," together with his marked indifference to the later movement of mind in Boston and Concord.

the Bostonians disliked him. They did not know what to
make of the stout, little, red-faced man who seemed to
have none of the dignity for which his magazine was so
respected. They thought he was a merry-andrew, frivolous, vain, far too free and familiar, who had obviously
not grown up in a well-bred circle. But Ticknor liked him
thoroughly. Why expect from a foreigner the decorum
that could only spring from an early discipline,—that
is to say, a Boston discipline? Jeffrey's impatience and
abruptness, which wounded the self-esteem of the Boston
people, seemed to him rapidity of mind. It was prodigious. It was wholly pleasing. If this was the sort of torrential eloquence, torrential and yet logical and compact,
that characterized the foreign intellect, Ticknor was prepared to see it twice.

Not, however, before he had taken pains to see what
the American intellect yielded. The American mind had
produced the Revolution; and everyone knew, not in
Boston only, that there was no event in modern times
with which to compare the American Revolution. The
French Revolution, perhaps, but in Boston one did not
dwell on this fiasco. Besides, everyone knew, even in
France, that the French would never have had a revolution unless the Americans had had one first. The men
who made the American Revolution were world-heroes
of the first order. Even in London, nobody questioned
this; and as two or three of these men were still alive,
Ticknor proposed to see them. Adams and Jefferson were
a pair of yardsticks with which to measure any man in
Europe,—for Jefferson had risen in the Boston mind, now
that he had abandoned politics and found his Horace and
his Tacitus much more interesting than the daily papers.
A journey through the other American cities would surely
give a young Bostonian that proper notion of his own
country which Dr. Johnson said a man should have be-

fore he travelled abroad.[6] Moreover, he might encounter a few persons who, having been to Europe, could give him a little useful information about the universities and means of study. With a number of letters that Adams placed in his hand, Ticknor had set out for New York and the South; and before many months or weeks had passed, he could almost have said,—although he would not have said it,—that he knew John Randolph, Madison and Marshall. The old philosopher of Monticello was more than pleased with this ardent neophyte, who offered to purchase books for him in Europe,—the new German editions of the classics,—and who was so ready to discuss his plans for the education of the Southern people. Not since his own years abroad had Jefferson seen such an eager student; and, seated in his beautiful study, surrounded by his seven thousand books, he talked of the days when, on his foreign missions, he had escaped, when he could, from his public business to spend his time with the continental scholars. Twice, a few years later, he was to invite the young Bostonian to teach in the university he had founded, offering him an unheard-of salary. And he gave Ticknor letters to his friends in Europe, scholars and men of affairs, that almost conferred on him the rank of an unofficial ambassador.

Everett, too, had made the American tour and called on President Madison. He, too, was equipped with letters that opened every European door. In fact, amid all the adventures that lay before them, the heads of these two young men might well have been turned. For what young men of any other country,—during this year that followed the Peace of Ghent,—could have had quite their

[6] It was the rule, at this period, for young Americans, e.g., Josiah Quincy, to make the grand tour of the United States, through Virginia and the Carolinas to Charleston, and sometimes Savannah, before they went abroad. This sensible classical custom was later indicated in the well-known tag, "See America first."

opportunities, as the first young scholars, with attractive manners, or, rather, the first after Washington Irving, who represented the new American nation upon which so many hopes of humanity rested? What were they to say and feel when Madame de Staël remarked to them, "You are the advance-guard of the human race," when Lafayette, Chateaubriand, Benjamin Constant greeted them in the same soul-stirring fashion? They were to find in Germany that all the great writers of the previous age, Lessing, Herder, Klopstock, had sympathized with the American Revolution,—which they themselves were felt to represent,—that even the old courtier-poet Goethe, whose name had reached their friends at home, recalled the Boston Tea-Party as one of the symbolic events that had stamped itself on his mind as a child. What was a young man to say when the Pope told him that in a few years the new world would dictate to the old? However it might have been with Everett, Ticknor's head was not to be turned; and he quite agreed with those who praised his country. When the Grand Duke of Tuscany asked him where, among all the nations, he thought a man could live most happily, Ticknor replied, "In America," explaining,—as only a Bostonian can explain such matters,—that America was more elevating than other countries.

These were the fortunate days of the youthful republic, when the good old Anglo-American sang-froid had solid facts to base itself upon,—when young men, heirs of the Revolution, knew they had beaten England twice, although they were too well-bred to mention it. They could feel, moreover, if they were students and men of letters, that they were volunteers in a nobler war, as builders of a great new civilization. If Ticknor, and even Everett, in his way, stood so calmly in their own shoes, and used their heads so shrewdly, during a four-years' tour of observation that might have flattered a diplomat,

—as Ticknor's *Journal* was to prove in time, a picture of the Europe of these years that could hardly have been more full or more discerning,—it was because, with the Revolution behind them, they were serving the purposes of the Revolution. They were serving the cause in their studies and travels, a fact they were not likely to forget, with Washington Irving on the ground before them. For wherever they went, they were to meet Irving, who never seemed to weary of discoursing on the prospects and the duties of their country: he liked to tell his young compatriots that, at their time of life, they ought to set aside all other cares and lay up a solid stock of knowledge. Follow their ends, at any cost; scramble, if they had to scramble; buy books, whatever else they lacked. Learning,— this was the sense of Irving's counsel,—was the first of patriotic duties. The touching letters of Ticknor's merchant-father breathed the same spirit. The old man, who had fitted his son for college, longed to see him in a professor's chair. And how would any son have wished to respond to such a letter as the following, so filled with everything that was good in Boston?—

I can look forward and see you, every week, and every month, employed in some part of Europe, in acquiring something which will be useful and pleasant to you in after life. So long as you continue to be the kind, discreet, wise and dutiful son . . . so long I shall . . . continue, even to the end of my life, to aid and assist you, and make the path of life easy and pleasant to you . . . The great object of your journey I am sure you will keep in mind, and never turn to the right hand nor to the left, viz., to improve in solid science, the arts, and literature, and in the knowledge of men . . . You have not left your home for the sole purpose of describing the lawns, the hills, the valleys, the tops of mountains, the columns of smoke, the villages,—except for amusement, and as shades to ornament your other improvements, which may be often and happily interspersed; but you have left your father to grow wiser and better,—to learn how to be more useful to yourself, your friends and your country.[7]

[7] *Life, Letters and Journals of George Ticknor.*

With a letter like this in his pocket, a letter worthy of a Roman parent, a young man knows how to behave when he meets Lord Byron and Sir Humphrey Davy, when Byron tells him about his love-affairs, tells him the story of his life,—as Englishmen are prone to do, in the presence of a sympathetic stranger,—gives him a beautiful copy of his poems, gives him a letter to Ali Pasha, in case he wishes to go to Greece, and a splendidly mounted pistol with which to defend himself there. And when Sir Humphrey Davy presented Ticknor with another handful of letters, one to Canova, one to Madame de Staël,— to whom he already had two letters,—he might have felt that he was fairly launched. The young men were quite at home in England, which was only a larger and livelier Massachusetts. Indeed, their first celebrity, Mr. Roscoe, the Liverpool banker-scholar, a sound Whig and patron of learning who had been the smith of his own fortunes, had been exactly like a Boston man, one of the founders of the Athenæum. Southey also had a Puritan conscience and the same laborious habits one knew at home; and the grand old Samuel Parr, Dr. Johnson's ancient friend and the master of Ticknor's master, Dr. Gardiner, received the young men as if they had had a volume of introductions. He said he had turned on his heel, in the days of the Revolution, when he heard the Americans described as rebels. He added, in his hearty way, "I was always glad that you beat us."

But Ticknor and Everett had not crossed the ocean to find another Boston, with improvements. As for the English universities, Oxford was only a larger and livelier Harvard, far from having had its own reforms. In Germany they were soon to meet a scholar who had put the English Latinists to the blush. He had pointed out several grammatical errors in the Latin notes of a posthumous work of Porson, the pride of the Cambridge scholars. In fact, these German professors were something new under the sun, as formidable in the field of studies as Frederick the Great had been in the field of arms; and Ticknor and Everett, once in Göttingen, found themselves on their mettle. What a mortification, the grievous distance between an American and a German scholar! At Harvard, they thought they knew how to work, heirs of the Puritans as they were, but it was plain enough that, beside these Germans, they cared for nothing but their own convenience. For they had forgotten the twelve-hour stretch that Cotton Mather called "the scholar's day," and they were more indolent than the English scholars. They thought two years sufficient to make a Grecian, and here was little Dissen of Göttingen who had spent no less than eighteen years, at sixteen hours a day, on Greek and nothing but Greek, and who said that even now he could not read Æschylus without a dictionary. It all depended on what one meant by "knowing." No one who had ever seen a German could ever again call a man a scholar unless he was willing to follow Eichhorn's programme: 5 A.M. to 9 P.M., with half-hour intervals for meals. As for the poor little Harvard library, it was a good half-century behind the times.

All this became painfully evident as Ticknor and Everett pegged away, for twenty solid months, at a typical Göttingen schedule: 5-8, Greek, 8-9, German, 9-10, exegesis, 10-12, Greek, 11½-4, Latin and French, 4-5, philology, 5-7, Greek, 7-8, the drill-sergeant, 9-11, résumé of lectures, varied, perhaps, by Hebrew and Syriac, a little natural history and a four-mile walk. No man ever died of study, Eichhorn often said, though he thought that perhaps for soft young Yankees twelve hours a day might answer, at first. Harvard was a school for ministers, and Harvard men could hardly be expected to know what a scholar was. Who had ever seen an American scholar? While everyone knew that the Yankees were enterprising, the wonder was, not that they studied badly, but that they studied at all. And Ticknor and Everett did not study badly. Full-grown as they were, they were glad to go to school again, with their big portfolios under their arms, just like two boys who fear the birch. So was their friend, Joseph Green Cogswell, another Harvard man who joined them shortly, and who was also to play a historic role: for as Ticknor was to become, in America later, the father of modern-language studies, as Everett was to give an unparalleled impulse to the study of Greek mythology and letters, so Cogswell was destined to become, as head of the Astor Library in New York, a founder of the modern library-system. Cogswell, who was thirty, had already had a varied life. His work as a lawyer had taken him to Marseilles, where he had found himself regarded as an authority on books. In the length and breadth of this great commercial city, one looked in vain for a book that was not connected with trade; and, whenever a stray volume in Latin or Hebrew turned up in the hands of the dealers, Cogswell was asked to examine it. The town was more benighted than New York. It was dangerous to be thought a savant there, as the president of the Marseilles Academy told him, and he might well have died of ennui if he had not happened to fall in with two or three learned Spanish exiles. In Göttingen, along with his other studies, Cogswell pursued his bibliographical work, going over the shelves and catalogues of the university library. On their walking-tours, in vacation-time, the three young men visited and examined the great German libraries and several universities. At Weimar, at various times, they called upon Goethe, who gave them fresh sheaves of letters. The old poet was living much alone. He was glad to hear their news from America and eager for their recent impressions of Byron. Cogswell especially touched him. He thanked the young man for taking an interest in his old age and kissed him with affection. He sent Cogswell several presents after he had returned to his own country.[8]

As for Edward Everett, before he set out for home, Cousin said, that, for Greek, he had never seen his equal. Everett was at least so competent in German that Eichhorn asked him for contributions to the Göttingen magazine. Before his visit to Greece, he had spent several days with Sir Walter Scott, who had neglected his old German studies and was glad to talk them over again. He had given the little Scotts a lesson in Tasso. He had heard Moore and Béranger sing their songs, and he had passed a day with Ugo Foscolo and dined with the Bonaparte family, assembled in Rome. He had taken the first steps of his later life as a diplomat; and, when he went to Greece, with Byron's letters,—for he wished, in his way, to consult the oracle too,—he was received and passed on, from one official to another, as if he had been a diplomat already.

Ticknor's studies, after Göttingen, still lay before him. He had been appointed, in his absence, the Smith Professor of Belles-Lettres at Harvard. He was expected to teach Popular Latin, Old French, Provençal, Spanish and Portuguese, and for this he had to prepare in the southern countries. He had formed certain habits as a student that were to make his teaching influential. One of them was to choose, for his private instructors, in Germany first, then elsewhere, in France, Italy, Spain and even Scotland, scholars who were typical of their nations, men with round, full, musical voices who could direct his reading and share it with him, and give him, along with the grammar and the literary history, the overtones and the intimacies of feeling, a sense of the popular spirit from which each literature had sprung. The scholar Conde,

[8] It was through Cogswell that Goethe presented to Harvard College a set of his works in twenty volumes.

who, for all his fame, was dying of starvation at Madrid, —for Spain was in a sad state, and most of the men of letters were so wretched that they were ashamed to receive a stranger,—Conde was one of these instructors.[9] With him, during a spring and summer, Ticknor spent several hours a day, reading the old Castilian authors. In Rome, for four months, a well-known archæologist was his cicerone. In Edinburgh, he read the Scottish poets with Robert Jamieson. Scott, who was glad to give him several days, walking with him about the countryside and telling him stories of the Scottish border, spoke of him to Southey in a letter as a "wonderful fellow for romantic lore."

All this was to have its effect on the rising generation of American poets, so many of whom were to study under him. For Ticknor was not only to sow at Harvard, in a ground already prepared, the seeds of the modern literatures of Europe; he was to stimulate, in some of his pupils,—by opening up these veins of popular legend, the balladry of Spain, Provence and Scotland,—a feeling that was already half awake for the legendary lore of their own country. Scott had renewed the literature of his people by building on this ancient balladry; and Scott had conceived his idea of doing so by reading Bürger's *Lenore,* which had had the same effect in Germany. Why should not America follow Scott, as Scott had followed Bürger? Washington Irving had already done so. He had shaped, in charming prose, the legends of the Hudson river; and every river-valley in New England teemed with similar legends, waiting for other Irvings, in prose or verse. Ticknor did not need to make the point. Boys

[9] Ticknor visited Spain at a moment when, under the despot, Ferdinand VII, the country, ravaged by the Peninsular War, had sunk to the depths of poverty. It was the depressed condition of Spanish letters that gave Ticknor,—as later his friend Prescott,—an opportunity to make himself a world-authority in things Spanish.

who had grown up among the ballads of the Revolution, the folk-tales of Marblehead and Portsmouth, could hardly fail to draw the inference, especially when Ticknor was able to tell them how interesting Southey had found the New England legends. For, to Southey, Mather's *Magnalia* was enthralling; he knew more about Roger Williams than anyone in Boston cared to remember; he had written a long poem on King Philip's War. This was to mean as much to renascent Harvard, with its instinctive respect for an English poet, even a dull poet, as if New England had produced a Shakespeare. And it was to come with force from Ticknor because of his gift for lecturing. Not for nothing had he observed, in the midst of his other studies, the world-famous lecturers of Paris, Cousin and Lacretelle, with all their art and grace of execution.

In fact, as one followed Ticknor on his travels, one could imagine already how he was destined to stir his Harvard class-room. Although his main concerns were prosaic enough,—philological data, sober facts of literary history,—still the lives that he was to talk about, Cervantes, Lope de Vega, Dante, Petrarch, Froissart, Calderon, the old explorers and soldier and sailor poets, were quite enough to excite a roomful of boys who were able to do their own embroidering. They opened up vistas of adventure, unheard-of prospects for a poet's life. And if, without wishing to spread the peacock's feathers, he dropped, in those years to come, into reminiscence, he could unfold a world-panorama such as few in Cambridge had ever dreamed of. He seemed to have met, and more than met, every famous living personage. He had pleased Byron, on a later encounter, by telling him how Goethe admired his work. He had spent three days at La Grange with Lafayette, and Humboldt had read to him from his book of travels. Chateaubriand had told him again and again about his wanderings in the United States, through the unbroken forests.[10] He had known Canova and Thorwaldsen, the sculptors, and Bunsen and Niebuhr in Rome, as well as he knew Sismondi and Madame de Staël, with whom he had often talked beside her deathbed. He had met the Countess of Albany many times, the wife of the last Pretender, who had liked his frankness when he said that England was better off without the Stuarts. He had travelled about Spain with a band of smugglers. At Naples, he had spent all his evenings at the *salon* of the old archbishop, where a group of Italian cognoscenti read Alfieri and Politian, in the Attic fashion of the Renaissance. With Washington Irving he had gone to Windsor: his pupils had read of this excursion if they knew *The Sketch Book*. He had met, among a hundred others, Lord Brougham's "bare, bold, bullion talent,"—for Ticknor was a master of the phrase, when it came to judging character. He had spent an evening with Godwin's circle, Hazlitt, Lamb and Hunt, and had never seen Sydney Smith's equal,—this was at Lord Holland's house, where he felt more at home, —for floating down the stream of conversation, and, without seeming to influence it, giving it all his own hue and charm.

In days to come, the young men at Harvard were to reap the fruits of Ticknor's *wanderjahre*. Here and there, as they followed his lectures, they were to catch a phrase or an allusion that opened up the picture. What patterns of the literary life the great professor, cold as he was, and distant, placed before them!—Humboldt, with his fifteen hours of study, pursued in the midst of all his social duties; Schlegel, who spent his evenings in the

---

[10] Chateaubriand remarked to Ticknor that, in a hundred years, when all the legitimate sovereigns had vanished, Europe would be full of despotisms. It was as if he had foreseen Hitler, Mussolini, Franco and Stalin.

drawing-rooms but rose at four and worked again till midnight; Madame de Staël, whose pen, lifted against Napoleon, was almost mightier than Wellington's sword. Never before, in America, had anyone invested with such glamour the life of the poet and the man of letters; and Harvard was ready for the new evangel.

CHAPTER V

THE NEW AGE IN BOSTON AND CAMBRIDGE

IT WAS in 1819 that Ticknor returned to America, a youthful master of the grand style. Safe in his father's house, he felt rewarded for all these years he had spent away from Boston. He unpacked his collections of books, acquired at such expense, with the aid of half the booksellers in Europe, especially the Spanish collection, which was later to become so famous. There was no room in his mind for that malaise which, in after times, was to affect so many Americans, newly returned from the old world. The sense of an enthralling purpose dominated all his other thoughts.

It was a fortunate moment. "We are living," said the great Dr. Bowditch, who had come to live in Boston, "in the best days of the republic." He said this in his most impressive manner, and Dr. Bowditch was always impressive, partly because he was Dr. Bowditch and partly because of his reputation, which was already international. He felt obliged to add, as one who was accustomed to calculation, that worse days were bound to follow. But that worse days were to follow, even remotely, few Bostonians were prepared to think.[1] The nation was on the march, moving with equal tread towards unknown splendours; and a young man with a ruling passion, that of

---

[1] Josiah Quincy was one of the few. Always cheerful and hopeful, —insomuch that at eighty-two, in 1854, unable to agree with most of his friends, who thought the world was going to the dogs, he said, "Almost everything at the present time seems to me to be better," even religion and morals,—he yet foresaw, through the "era of good feeling," the great convulsion coming, the Civil War.

reforming Harvard College and making it worthy of the new day, had some reason to be happy. With Daniel Webster as one of his intimate circle,—for Webster, too, had settled in Boston,—with Bowditch as another, and Dr. Channing, with the Prescotts, father and son, Judge Prescott and William Hickling Prescott, Ticknor's younger friend, with Edward and Alexander Everett, recently the minister to Spain, he could watch the wheels of progress turning and even give the wheels a push himself; for all these men, whatever their interests were, had a certain tincture of the statesman in their composition. So did the great East India and China merchants and the men who were building up the factory-system and believed they were building up the country. Their public aims and their known distinction, which carried them into diplomatic posts, attracted to the little capital,— larger in its littleness than it was to be when it was big, —every traveller from the old world; and at their tables one met, from week to week, members of the German and Russian legations, Spanish grandees and Danish princes, Chancellor Kent from New York and Lafayette, scientists and historians from England. The Liverpool packets discharged their passengers in Boston, which, for a while, with the Cunard Line, became the main American port of entry.

Boston was more than ever like Edinburgh, the Edinburgh of the last few decades, when the Scottish metropolis was also in its heyday. Later, in both cases, these days of renown were to pass, when London overshadowed Edinburgh and much of the glory of Boston passed to New York. But the social world of Scott, Gifford and Jeffrey, of the Waverley novels, *Blackwood's* and the great *Review*, was reproduced, and more than reproduced in the New England capital for a generation. The intellectual life was the fashion there, just as it had been in Edinburgh, where university professors and men of letters, judges and learned lawyers, lowland lairds and Highland chieftains gathered for evening routs in the winter season. Chalmers had his counterpart in Channing, the shepherd of the Boston flock; nor was there any lack of superior women, cultivated, witty and devout, enough to meet the exactions of Abigail Adams.[2] The greatest mind that was ever born in Boston was able to feel that the town, in its spirit of emulation, suggested Florence. Everyone with talent was impelled to struggle. Everyone laboured to be foremost.[3]

"I meet in London occasionally," Stuart Newton, the painter, wrote, "such society as I meet all the time in Boston." There were many people in Boston who took this for granted. They did not give the British capital the benefit of a doubt, whether their correspondent had met all London. "The true Bostonian," Henry Adams said, "always knelt in self-abasement before the majesty of English standards"; but this was less the case at the present time than at any time earlier or later. No doubt, in the Boston soul, politically American, there was a substratum of Anglicism that was never to be eradicated; and this grew stronger, rather than weaker, as New England lost its control in politics. The more the centre of gravity of the nation shifted towards the West, the more the Boston mind, thrown back upon itself, resumed its old colonial allegiance. But Boston at this moment was dominant and potent. It was not Persepolis, of course:

[2] "If we mean to have heroes, statesmen and philosophers, we should have learned women."—Abigail Adams.

[3] "What Vasari said, three hundred years ago, of the republican city of Florence might be said of Boston: 'that the desire for glory and honour is powerfully generated by the air of that place, in the men of every profession; whereby all who possess talent are impelled to struggle that they may not remain in the same grade with those whom they perceive to be only men like themselves, even though they may acknowledge such indeed to be masters; but all labour by every means to be foremost.' "—Emerson, *Natural History of Intellect*.

one did not find there, or wish to find, the "courts where
Jamshyd gloried and drank deep." What one did find, or
what the Bostonians found, was a singular situation, together with the will to cope with it. They had received a
nation from their fathers, and they proposed to make it
a great nation. This was a notable school of self-respect,[4]
even of the self-sufficiency for which the Boston people
were celebrated;[5] and, if there were many Pharisees
among them, others deserved the phrase, uttered by Benjamin Constant,—they had all the virtues they affected.
No one spoke of provinciality. The word had not yet
come into use, and there was even no occasion for it.[6]
The word provinciality implies a centre, and nations that
are in process of building themselves are always self-
centred. That "the mind is its own place" no one doubts
when people are occupied with important matters. The
Bostonians were absorbed in public interests, and they
had another centre in the classics, which they shared with
all Western Europe. Moreover, having known great
things at home, they knew a great thing when they saw

[4] Ticknor, to whom Metternich said that he found the present
state of Europe "disgusting" and who discovered everywhere abroad
the seeds of decay and "moral degradation," expressed the feeling
of all his contemporaries in writing, "A man is much more truly a
man with us than he is elsewhere . . . It is much more gratifying
and satisfying to the mind, the affections, the soul, to live in our
state of society."

[5] See the remark of President Eliot's mother, addressed to a friend
who had joined the Episcopal Church: "Eliza, do you kneel down in
church and call yourself a miserable sinner? Neither I nor any of
my family will ever do that."—Henry James, *Charles W. Eliot.*

[6] "Americans of that generation hadn't that snobbish shamefaced-
ness about their country,—and especially if they were well-born as
you represent Wentworth to have been. It is a vice of the *nuova
gente* altogether. The older men took their country as naturally as
they did a sunrise. There was no question . . . as to whether their
country were the best in the world or no—they *knew* it was."—
Letter of Lowell to Henry James, 1878, apropos of the latter's novel,
The Europeans.

it elsewhere.[7] The republic had proved to be a triumphant success, for the clouds had not yet risen in the Southern sky, and the wealth and population of the country were growing at a prodigious rate, most of all, perhaps, in Massachusetts. By virtue of their experience and cultivation, the Boston people saw themselves as leaders in a great forward movement of the race.[8] No wonder their portrait-painters throve. "How rages the Harding fever?" asked Gilbert Stuart, in 1823, referring to Chester Harding, the admirable backwoods artist, who was luring away his own clients. Harding was to know as well as Stuart what Boston was willing to pay for its *amour-propre*. He had so many orders that he could not fill them. The Boston people thronged his studio, sometimes fifty in an afternoon. He had to book them like a racing-tout.

Of this little statesmanly world, of which Ticknor was to be *pars magna*, Webster was the great political figure. A demon of a man, a full-blooded, exuberant Philistine, with a demiurgic brain and a bull's body, a Philistine in all but his devotion to the welfare of the State, his

[7] "A noble school," wrote Channing, in one of his note-books, "is profitable only to noble spirits. The learner must have something great in order to receive great lessons." Today, in many large American cities, a man may enjoy every material advantage, and even the advantages of travel, yet still remain as unconscious of the great currents of contemporary thought as any European peasant. But when, a hundred years ago, the *zeitgeist* penetrated New England, with its train of world-ideas, it found a sensibility prepared for it; and a man like Thoreau, who scarcely stirred out of his little Concord, instinctively understood Mazzini and Kossuth,—the Gandhis and the Trotskys of his time. Those who have in their minds the pattern of greatness recognize this pattern wherever they find it. They belong to the freemasonry of the enlightened, whatever their condition may be or wherever they live.

[8] Emerson expressed the general feeling when, some years later, he wrote: "I do not speak with any fondness, but the language of coldest history, when I say that Boston commands attention as the town which was appointed in the destiny of nations to lead the civilization of North America."—*Natural History of Intellect.*

deep strain of racial piety,—this was the grand thing in
Webster,—with an all-subduing personal force, an eye as
black as death and a look like a lion's, as the farmers in
his native New Hampshire said, almost a foreigner, with
his rustic manners, among these Boston lovers of elegance, he was fighting, in and out of Congress, first for
the Constitution, for the Union, imperilled by so many
factions, and secondly for the manufacturing interests
that lay behind New England's rising fortunes. With an
oratorical gift as great as Burke's, in learning, in unction,
if not in cultivation,—for, while Webster had a feeling
for the sublime, he had little feeling for the beautiful,—
he fought for the solid facts of property and the good old
Yankee motive of self-interest. His politics, his economic
doctrines were those of any sound New Hampshire
farmer who owned a dam and a mill and turned his dollars over to the Boston bankers. These doctrines naturally pleased the Boston bankers. As a lawyer, he was
unapproachable. When he talked about other lawyers,
he made them seem like characters in Plutarch. He could
invest a common murder-case with the atmosphere of an
Æschylean drama.

A hunter, fisherman, farmer, who gloried in his rural
avocations, in which the traits of the backwoods pioneer
were mingled with those of an old border baron, Webster was to become, as the years went by, a legendary figure in New England. In Boston, he was the rock of the
Constitution, as kings had been defenders of the faith.
Throughout the country districts, he was "Dan'l," whose
every word, as a farmer remarked, seemed to weigh a
pound. People said that Dan'l was made of granite, and
they knew he had learned his American history from old
Captain Webster of the minute-men, who had guarded
Washington's tent on the battle-field and for whom Liberty and the Union, far from being phrases, were facts
that represented blood and steel. Everyone knew the

great squire of Marshfield, where he had a farm as large
as half a county. Everyone had heard him on the platform, every boy and girl had seen his picture, the dark
brow that looked like Mount Monadnock, the wide-
brimmed hat and the knee-high boots, the linsey-woolsey
coat and the flowing necktie, the walking-stick that was
said to be ten feet long. There was something elemental
in his composition, something large and lavish. Even his
faults were ample. Webster despised the traditional vir-
tures.[9] He spent money in a grand way, borrowing and
lending with equal freedom. He was far from sober, or
would have been if two tumblers of brandy had been
enough to put him under the table. He could be surly
enough, when he had his moods of God-Almightiness, or
when he wished to insult some sycophant. The thunder-
clouds would gather on his brow and the lightning flash
from his eye, and he would tell a committee that their
town was the dullest place on earth. No one could be
more truculent, especially in the hay-fever season; but
he was always good-natured with the farmers, who liked
to think of him as their man. They knew what Webster
meant when he said that his oxen were better company
than the men in the Senate. They knew all his ways and
the names of his guns and animals, as the Jews of old
knew the weapons of Nimrod, or Abraham's flocks and
herds,—his great ram Goliath, his shot-guns, "Mrs. Pat-
rick" and "Wilmot Proviso," his trout-rod, "Old Killall."
They knew he had written the Bunker Hill oration, composed it word by word, with Old Killall in his hand, wad-
ing in the Marshfield river. They had heard of his tens
of thousands of swine and sheep, his herds of Peruvian

[9] "Thirty years ago, when Mr. Webster at the bar or in the Senate
filled the eyes and minds of young men, you might often hear cited
as Mr. Webster's three rules: first, never to do today what he could
defer till tomorrow; secondly, never to do himself what he could
make another do for him; and, thirdly, never to pay any debt today."
—Emerson, Letters and Social Aims.

llamas and blooded cattle, the hundreds of thousands of trees he had raised from seed. They knew that while his guests were still asleep,—the scores of guests who were always visiting Marshfield,—he rose at four o'clock and lighted the fires, roused the cocks with his early-morning candles, milked and fed the stock and chatted in the kitchen with his farm-hands, quoting Mr. Virgil, the Roman farmer. And at Marshfield, as everyone knew, his horses were buried in a special graveyard, with all the honours of war, standing upright, with their shoes and halters.

From Boston, across New England, across the nation, Webster's fame spread, as the years advanced. Boston men who had seen Garrick and Foote and heard Burke and Sheridan, the masters of the spoken word, were satisfied that Webster was their equal. Countless thousands, bankers, lawyers, farmers, read his orations aloud by the evening fire. They felt as if the woods and the fields and the ocean had found a worthy voice in Webster's words; and Captain Thomas, his neighbour, was not the only man who longed for death when Webster met defeat. This faithful follower, fearing that all was lost, after Senator Hayne's second speech, cast away his boots, saying he would never want them more, and took to his bed for days. New England had never known a public man with such a Jovian personality,[10] whose words, when he chose to deploy them in a diplomatic encounter, had the force of a fleet of battle-ships. He could make the United States appear the mightiest of all historic empires. Who knew better than he, or could say it better, that America was the hope of liberty, as those who had visited Europe could see for themselves, as Ticknor and Everett had al-

[10] "There was the monument, and there was Webster," Emerson wrote, referring to the Bunker Hill oration. Sydney Smith exclaimed, when he saw Webster in London, in 1839, "Good heavens, he is a small cathedral by himself."

ready seen, when the old regime had been restored in force, in Italy, France and Germany, when liberal ideas, even in England, were still in doubtful debate? Who was more the symbol of his country? Were the Boston people, with all their self-possession, still, in a measure, tinged with colonialism? Were they prone to ask the visiting European what he thought of American institutions? Were the countryfolk too ready to protest that they had whipped the redcoats? Were the gentry still English in their customs? Webster was the universal answer. Noah Webster, with his dictionary,—whether for better or worse,—had established American usage in the matter of words. Daniel Webster was equally potent in matters of personality. All his traits, his references, his habits bore witness to the national character and buttressed it with the kind of authority that could not be gainsaid. When he spoke of the Bay State and Bunker Hill, of Plymouth Rock, Lexington and Concord, one felt that to belong to Massachusetts was the noblest privilege of history. *Civis Romanus sum.* "Thank God, I also am an American!"

With Webster as the great political figure, Channing was the great religious figure and also in his way a member of Ticknor's circle,—for Channing had not yet embarked on his later career as a social reformer, which was to divide the Boston household. As Webster spoke for the outer life of the town, its property-sense and a kind of patriotism that largely represented its mundane pride, Channing spoke for the inner life of Boston, with a charm and glow of intellectual goodness that triumphed over its prejudices. Although he was a Unitarian,—the only man of genius in the movement, who had defined the faith and even defended it in controversy when the Orthodox party attacked the "Boston religion,"—he was a poet in his theology, for whom a creed was only a vestibule. He was not at home with the Cambridge logic-choppers, whose ways he found repellent. His fluid mind, suspicious of every dogma, wished to live "under the open sky." The adoration of goodness was his religion. He hungered and thirsted for it; and the great, wide, ingenuous eyes that beamed under his broad-brimmed hat and lighted up the little figure, wasted by so many sufferings, proclaimed his inextinguishable faith in the natural possibilities of men. He detested the jealous caution of New England, the insane love of money that pervaded the trading world, the coldness of the calculating mind, the dullness and timidity of provincial manners. Oh, for a Burns to shock the Boston burghers out of their staid decorum! Under the crust of American life, so frigid on the surface, was to be found, he thought, if one looked for it, the simple, wild stock of human nature, with all its natural feelings and social instincts, the seeds of every noble attribute. It required stimulus, it required affection. Channing was always young for liberty,[11] not the mere terrestrial liberty that Webster represented, but a liberty of the intellect and spirit that tended to form a superior race of men.

In days to come, Channing's ideas, which had their own logic, were to be expressed in certain ways that Ticknor and his circle did not like. These were the days,—one saw them in advance,—when Ticknor, with Everett as his only rival, was the great intellectual and social figure, as potent as Webster and Channing in their spheres, the

[11] George S. Hillard recalled that, at the time of his graduation from Harvard, Channing, to whom he was introduced, remarked: "I see that you young gentlemen of Cambridge were quite too wise to be thrown out of your accustomed serenity by the new revolution in France! I was in college in the days of the first French Republic, and at every crisis of its history our dignity was wholly upset. We were rushing to meetings of sympathy, or kindling bonfires of congratulation, and walking in torch-light processions. But now the young American has come to years of discretion and may not give way to such unseemly excitements." Channing, in spite of his early Federalism, always felt at heart as he had felt in college.

host of every visitor to Boston, the one man who had
seen all the world, where others had seen only portions
of it, and numbered among his countless correspondents
the preëminent minds of half a dozen countries. These
were the days after he had married one of the daughters
of the well-known merchant whose other daughter had
married Andrews Norton, and people spoke of him with
bated breath; for wealth united with learning, and learning with prestige, and prestige crowned with conscientiousness,—all these formed a constellation that would
have dazzled any other town. By virtue of a similar constellation, Andrews Norton reigned over Cambridge; and
Ticknor's great house at the head of Park Street, domi-
nating the Common from Beacon Hill, soon became the
symbol of his renown. There he kept his famous library,
the amplest private library in Boston, housed in the largest and most elegant room, approached through a marble
hall by a marble stairway, about which the butler dis-
creetly hovered. Over the mantel hung the Leslie portrait
for which Sir Walter had sat at Abbotsford, and the walls
of the stately apartment were covered with books, me-
thodically arranged and richly bound. And there, with
his air of the scholar-nobleman, gracious but somewhat
marmoreal, like his hall and mantel, Ticknor dispensed
his counsels to aspiring students. He was ready to give
advice about the various versions of Cervantes, if someone wished to make a new translation. He was happy to
lend his books, as many as two or three hundred, to any
qualified applicant, even in Maine or New Hampshire,
or the South. Everyone knew that, where books were concerned, he knew, as no one else, all the resources of
Europe, from Naples and Spain to Scotland, from Holland House in London to the cabinet of Prince John of
Saxony, where his own portrait hung in later years. He
had seen all the books, even the lumber-rooms of the
Escorial, even the Medical Library at Madrid, where he

had been the first enquiring student for three-and-twenty years to break the rust on the locks and the wire nettings. He knew, or was to know, even the little bookcase that stood near the window in Tieck's parlour; and if, as befitted one whose knowledge of Spanish literature was greater than that of any man in Spain, he was especially rich in Spanish works, he was a great collector in other fields. Under the mantel, beside the fire, he held frequent classes for young ladies, the daughters of his friends, in Dante, Milton and Shakespeare.

This was a type that Boston understood, the magnanimous man who passed its peculiar tests. Correct himself, and willing to diffuse correctness, he was able to correct a duchess, when the case called for correction, without disturbing the poise of a drawing-room. Moreover, in addition to his wealth and learning, he was a faithful adherent of Dr. Channing, as long as Channing did not go too far. His pamphlet on Lafayette passed through three editions in the French translation. But in his teaching he was most the statesman; for, although he continued to live in his Boston house, he had at once assumed his post at Harvard. Jefferson, as everyone knew, had tried to induce him to go to Charlottesville: all he desired was that God might send him two or three Ticknors. But Ticknor was not to be drawn aside. The Harvard library, which had seemed so large, seemed to him now merely a closetful of books. The college could scarcely be called a respectable high school. To turn it into a university, one that could bear the name and deserve the name, and set the intellectual pace of the country, was the Jeffersonian task that lay before him.

Meanwhile, Everett and Cogswell had also returned to Cambridge. Cogswell, the master-bibliographer, took the college library in hand and rearranged the books on the Göttingen plan. Everett began his career as Professor of Greek, a notable career, alas, too brief. The old grammarians, who had taught the classics, might have had warmer hearts than Everett, but they had colder minds. They had no feeling for the Greek myths, no feeling for the poetry of Homer, and Everett was an Abélard of literary studies, or so the Harvard students were convinced. But there were other irons in Everett's fire, as time was soon to show. On his arrival from Europe, he had preached a sermon in Washington, where no one had ever heard such magical words. Senators, justices, cabinet members praised him as the prince of orators and asked him to remain as the chaplain of Congress. He had come back to Cambridge with a halo, but with his mind torn with a new ambition. The incident had unsettled him for life. As the years passed and he carried on his lectures, he watched the rising star of his friend Webster. Webster had risen by oratory, and he was as good an orator as Webster. Why should not he too enter Congress and meet his college classes between the sessions? Why should he not be minister to Greece, as his brother had been minister to Spain?—especially when, like Ticknor and Andrews Norton, he had formed a fortunate marital alliance, with the daughter of the richest man in Boston? Not that he craved the splendid burdens of office! But were not the splendid burdens of office, painful as they were, more in the line of a man's public duty than teaching a roomful of boys? Others who have been known to ask this question have answered it in Everett's troubled way. He complained, in a letter to Justice Story, which he asked Story to burn, that he found the life and duties of a professor far too humble for him. They were not, he said, respectable enough.

The roomful of boys at Harvard knew nothing of the professor's doubts and dilemmas. That he was discontented never entered the head of one of these boys, Ralph Waldo Emerson, who thought of Everett as "our Cicero" and took it for granted that, like his prototype, Everett scorned the opinion of the vulgar, those that held a man in low esteem who, side by side with the politi-

cians, was known merely as a "Greek and scholar."
Everett held the students spellbound. He was severe and
precise in his college class-rooms, eager to impart, in detail, the wealth of the new German learning, Wolf's theory of the Homeric writings, the exegesis of Voss and
Ruhaker, the criticism of the ante-Homeric remains.[12]
Outside, in his public lectures and speeches, to which the
students flocked, he let his fancy soar. His Greek brought
back the days of Pericles, his imagery was opulently Persian. That he was magniloquent they did not know. That
he was theatrical they did not care, for oratory was their
theatre. His elegance, his confidence, his ease stirred their
imagination. What pictures he could present of Scott and
Byron, the reigning British poets, whose Harolds and
Manfreds and Marmions were on every lip, of Humboldt,
Madame de Staël and Lafayette! Standing before the
panorama of Athens, which had been presented to the
college, he discoursed on Greece as one who had seen it.
His multifarious quotations were so apt, his style so fluent and graceful, he uttered such inspiring reflections on
the future of American literature! The fame of his foreign training, the glamour of his adventures attracted
students from the remotest parts, from Georgia and Ten-
nessee.

It was a triumph of fantasy and a triumph of style. In
later years, some of Everett's pupils, seeing how vacuous
his career had been, wondered that he had so beguiled
their minds. Too tender-minded for a statesman,—as
they perceived, looking back,—he had followed Webster
as an understudy. He had been Governor of the Commonwealth, Secretary of State and Senator, but always,

[12] "During the present century, I believe that Harvard received
and welcomed the new learning from Germany . . . before it had
been accepted by the more conservative universities of the Old
Home. Everett's translation of Buttmann's Greek Grammar was reprinted in England, with the 'Massachusetts' omitted after Cambridge,' at the end of the preface, to conceal its American origin."
—Lowell, Literary and Political Addresses.

as one of these pupils said, a "dangler"; and the more he elaborated his outward graces, the more he became a shaken reed within.[13] And yet he had not really beguiled the students. Empty as so much of his rhetoric was, it stirred the adolescent imagination. False, or largely false, it communicated an impulse that was true. A student who imitated Everett's style was sure to be corrected by Edward Channing, who hated a purple patch as he hated the devil; and meanwhile Everett waved a wand that opened up the magical world of Homer. Some of the boys who saw the wand waving were always to have a foot-hold in that world, with all its wild beauty, even while the dour Professor Channing kept their other foot in Yankee-land. And with Ticknor busy, with unsleeping eye, over his new department, that of the modern languages, and lecturing, with all of Everett's verve, on

[13] Emerson said of Everett, in his journal: "Webster has done him incalculable harm by Everett's too much admiration of his iron nature; warped him from his true bias all these twenty years, and sent him cloud-hunting at Washington and London, to the ruin of his solid scholarship, and fatal diversion from the pursuit of his right prizes."

In later times, Everett, in contradistinction to Webster,—the oratorical "Michael Angelo," as Everett was the "Raphael," so called, —became the classic example of all that was bad in American oratory. One marvelled over the bursts of applause that followed his apostrophe to Stuart's portrait of Washington in Faneuil Hall: "Speak, glorious Washington! Break the long silence of that votive canvas!" But Everett's style was the style of his age in all but the greatest men. Italy, France and Ireland, in the eighteen-twenties, afforded similar examples. Even Victor Hugo, and even a generation later, abounded in this vein. Everett was a master of calculation. John Bartlett of Cambridge,—"Familiar Quotations" Bartlett,— saw him drilling a group of old Revolutionary soldiers who were to sit on the platform during his Concord oration. The poor old souls were expected to rise when Everett exclaimed, "Noble men!" and bob up and down in their seats at various other points in the oration. He was once observed in a country book-store asking for a pocket Bible, which he wished to produce dramatically during a speech. As the Bible was not forthcoming, he took a copy of Hoyle's *Games* instead. It served just as well, and nobody knew the difference. In fact, there was so much "theatre" in Everett's speeches that people soon wondered whether there had ever been anything else.

French and Spanish literature, a student might well have found himself alert. For Ticknor was a scholar born, as Webster was a statesman born and Dr. Channing was a born priest, never tempted to stray from his natural sphere. He fought for his reforms. He did his best to substitute thorough teaching for the old sing-song ways the college loved. There was a brief flutter. Then the old system was resumed, except in Ticknor's own field. There he had his way. He gathered together a staff of foreign instructors, French, Italian, German. And there he established a path for the university to follow later.

During these years of change and growth at Harvard, Dr. Channing's mind was also growing. Shortly after Ticknor's return, he too had reappeared in Boston charged with fresh life, the result of a year of travel and rest in Europe. In England, he had found many admirers, for the great Boston preacher's reputation had spread beyond the sea; but the doctor, ill and depressed, had fled from all these kindly ministrations and sought the solitude of the English lakes and the conversation of Wordsworth. He had read the poet's *Excursion* again and again; indeed, he had never read anything but Shakespeare more. Ever since his early youth at Newport, he had shared this mystical sense of the universe as the outer garment of God; and the landscape of New England had prepared him for the charms of the Cumberland country. For Channing was a lover of lakes and mountains. He had studied their contours under various skies; he knew all the effects of atmosphere, of mist and cloud and dry and watery sunlight. The grandeur of New Hampshire, the gentle, pastoral beauty of Vermont had swayed and attuned his feelings. He could form a friendship with a mountain; and he knew the interminable depths of the virgin forest as well as he knew the ocean, beside whose crashing waves he had leaped for joy. These temperamental sympathies had drawn him to the new German *Naturphilosophie*. Through Madame de Staël,

at first,—whom he had read with different eyes from
Ticknor's,—and then through Wordsworth's friend, the
poet Coleridge, he had been introduced to the writings
of Schelling, in whose intimations of a divine life, mani-
fested in nature and the soul, he had found his mental
home. He had been roused as well by Fichte's heroic stoi-
cism, which spoke of the grandeur of the human will.
These prophets seemed to him to corroborate the great
hopes of the French Revolution, which he had shared in
his youth. In deference to the feelings of his congregation, the richest and most respectable in Massachusetts,
practically-minded Whigs, with little taste for nonsense,
he had suppressed his natural sympathies. But he belonged to the race of the older and bolder. He looked
askance at the reigning thoughts of Boston, with its
"scared and petrified" conservatism.

His year in Europe, spent with congenial friends, in
England, among the Alps, in Rome and Florence, had
quickened all his apostolic instincts. Wordsworth had
read to him passages from *The Prelude*. He had com-
muned with Coleridge, who described him later as the
"very rarest character" he had known. He had formed
the friendship with Lucy Aiken that was to result in so
many relations between the old world and the new; and
it was observed, on his return, that a change had taken
place in his mental horizon. The preacher who had delighted everyone with his penetrating discourses on ethical questions, dear to the Boston heart, seemed at once
more literary and more social. Not that he ceased to be a
moralist, one of those rare artists of human behaviour,—
like his own Fénelon, for instance,—who, by virtue of
some inward grace, constantly flowing through the intellect, purge the mind of cant and win the imagination
of untold thousands to the beauty of their own unworldly
goodness. Channing was a poet and a saint; and he
shared and led, as no one else could lead them, the
deeply devout religious conversations that occupied so

many Boston minds. He did not care to discuss theological matters, the question of Particular Providence, the Evidences of Christianity, the Genuineness of the Gospels, all those special, textual, technical problems that exercised the learned men of Cambridge. But he was often present at those reading parties where they talked over a chapter of *Rasselas*, or a passage from Plato or Milton, and the topic set for the evening was the distinction between natural and moral happiness. Whether the performance of one's duty should have any connection with one's self-regard. Whether the moral nature was immortal or would be swallowed up in the divine. Gratitude, personal obligation. If one saw two persons in grave danger, which should one save first, one's benefactor and private friend or the person of most use to humanity? In these Boston parlour-conversations, carried on by scholarly casuists, blue-stockings and others, Miss C. defending Paley, Mrs. S. taking the side of Kant, Channing was a frequent arbitrator.

But the focus of his mind had been gradually shifting, along with the general focus of the Boston mind. The serious atmosphere of these discussions,—so like the discussions of similar circles in England, those that surrounded Macaulay, Mill and Ruskin, the rising generation of British authors,[14]—assumed another aspect as the years advanced. The great problems of the factory-system, which was so rapidly growing, the problems of the poor forced themselves on these conscientious minds. They could no longer ignore the social questions that complicated the ethical point of view. What was the effect of an occupation with wholly mechanical things? What was the moral

[14] Also the discussions of the Jansenist circles of seventeenth-century France. The atmosphere of Geneva, in the eighteen-thirties and forties, as reflected in Amiel's *Journal Intime*, was strikingly similar to that of Boston.

For this aspect of the New England mind, see *Memoir of W. E. Channing*, by W. H. Channing, the *Memoir of Mary L. Ware*, by E. B. Hall and *The Life of Charles Follen*, by E. L. Follen.

difference between workers in mills and those who worked by themselves? How much taste and judgment were involved in making a handsome shoe? What were the obligations of the rich in regard to the education of the poor? Unitarianism, it was noted, had always been accompanied by radical movements. Even in far-away Poland, the Unitarians had been non-resistants and pacifists, conscientious objectors, communists, trouble-makers for the powers that be. The Boston Unitarians, as a group, cared for none of these things. They had made a State Church of their religion, and, with their shrewd sense of the interests of trade and their temperamental self-complacency, they were opposed to any further changes. But the Unitarian leaven that worked in Channing was of a much more fundamental kind. He pondered all these matters in his heart, and, as the years passed and his fame grew, the rift grew wider and wider between the doctor and the respectable classes he represented. Living in his beautiful house, the property of his wife, he slept in a cold and cheerless attic, struggling to solve the problems that weighed upon him. How to destroy the worship of money. How to elevate the depressed classes. How to remove the evils of competition. How to convince human beings that they were parts of a great whole, bound to work for the welfare of this whole. The union of labour and culture. Slavery in the South. He could not please the Abolitionists, for he saw all questions in too complex a light; nor could he please his parishioners, who began to cut him on the street. Only his fame and his saintly character kept for him the respect of the practically-minded.

This was in the future, when his name had travelled round the world and he had readers in India.[15] Now already, in these early twenties, he had begun to play the

---

[15] It was Channing's secular essays, on Milton, Fénelon and Napoleon, that gave him, at first, this larger reputation.

part of a leader in the renaissance that was evidently at hand. Were there not seasons of spring in the moral world, and was not the present age such a season? Could one fail to see on every side the signs of an unparalleled energy? And yet the mind of the nation was still asleep. As a boy, Channing had been a famous wrestler. He had loved adventurous sports and had borne well the name of "little King Pepin." He had climbed the mastheads of all the ships at Newport. For twenty years he had wrestled with himself; and who was better prepared than he to wrestle, in the name of enlightened reason, with all the dark forces, inward and outward, that cramped the spirit of his countrymen? Had not theology laboured without ceasing to cover human nature with infamy, to crush its energy and confidence, so that men had almost ceased to believe in their mental and moral powers? They idolized wealth because they did not know what other and greater goods they were capable of. They looked to what was profitable first and only on second thoughts to what was right, for their natural feelings were masked and petrified by caution, policy, prudence. Their lives were needlessly joyless. For himself, he thought the ancients were too solemn in calling the earth Mother, the earth, so youthful, so exuberant, so living and rejoicing. The first of all the wonder-signs of Jesus was that in which he blessed a wedding-feast and heightened all its pleasures, even its pleasures of sense. Was not the intemperance of New England a signal judgment on the Puritans, who had tried to banish pleasure from the world? To rid society of its sordid vices, music should be taught in the common schools. Dancing should be encouraged and festivals fostered, so that old and young might share in sports and pastimes. There should be picture-galleries and halls of sculpture. Boston should develop the sense of beauty by creating beauty.

Such were the luminous thoughts of the climber of mastheads. Every Sunday morning, he mounted his pul-

pit and poured into the ears of his congregation, willing
or unwilling, large draughts of intellectual day. His eyes
grew wider and wider as he spoke, and the little figure
seemed to grow taller and taller. One saw him in the
streets, at public meetings, ubiquitous, alert, robed in his
blue camlet cloak, a shawl about his neck, with his drawn,
ethereal face almost lost under the enormous hat; or at
Newport, at his summer home, Oakland, surrounded
by its gracious lawns and gardens. There, like Lamennais in his retreat,—for Channing, too, had written his
Paroles d'un Croyant, even his *Essai sur l'Indifférence,*—
he gathered his younger followers about him, discussed
and read philosophy and history, in the summer-house
or on the wide verandahs, Plato's *Timæus,* perhaps, or
Coleridge's *Biographia Literaria,* Schiller, Wordsworth,
Shelley, *Wilhelm Meister,* or led them to some seat
among the rocks, where Berkeley had also talked with
his disciples. He rose at Newport earlier than ever. One
heard his quick step on the gravel walk, as he strolled
among the shrubs, with the dogs gambolling beside him,
or in and out of the green-house, where he studied the
plants and flowers. Often the children joined him, troop-
ing along the paths, for Channing was a friend of all the
children. "A child's little plan should be respected," he
wrote in one of his note-books. To say of a child or a
man, as they often said in Boston, "There is a great deal
of human nature in him," did not mean to Channing
what it meant to so many others. He had a large opinion
of human nature,—so large that people thought he was
romantic,—even when its powers were in eclipse. Every
day, for years, it was known in Boston, he fed with his
own hands two poor old women who fancied that people
wished to poison them and would accept their food from
him alone.

Everyone could see, in after times, that Channing had
been the great awakener. By raising the general estimate
of human nature, which the old religion had despised,

he gave the creative life a prodigious impulse; for, if human nature was a thing so precious,—however enslaved, insane, depraved, degraded,—how could one hesitate to emancipate it? How could one fail to fly to its assistance? How could one fail to offer it the means by which to achieve the beauty that was proper to it? Channing was the father of half the reforms that characterized the Boston of his age.[16] Moreover, he harrowed the ground for literature, first by his harrowing of the ground for life, and also by his intuitive understanding of the function of art and letters. He knew his country and he knew the poets, and he knew what his country and the poets needed. Independence, he was well aware,—the basis of all enduring greatness,—was something that had to be earned, and that could be earned. It was for the poets and thinkers to earn it. "A people," he wrote in one of his essays, "into whose minds the thoughts of foreigners are poured perpetually, needs an energy within itself to resist, to modify this mighty influence . . . It were better to have no literature, than form ourselves unresistingly on a foreign one . . . A country, like an individual, has dignity and power only in proportion as it is self-formed." [17] That the true sovereigns of a country are those who determine its mind, its modes of thinking, that writers are the originators of all those currents of thought by which nations and peoples are carried forward,—this was Channing's constant theme and vision. Mind, mind required all one's care.

[16] Among the many well-known reformers who drew their impulse largely from Channing were Dorothea L. Dix, once a governess in Channing's household, who devoted herself to improving conditions in the prisons and asylums, Elizabeth Eaton, founder of a society to help the poor foreigners who were appearing in Boston, 1830-1840; Elizabeth Peabody, the "grandmother of the kindergarten," etc.

[17] *On National Literature.*

CHAPTER VI

THE NORTH AMERICAN REVIEW:
GEORGE BANCROFT

THE LITERARY mind was astir in Boston. Not like thunder, not with a roll of drums, but with a little chirrup here and there, the dawn had slowly broken. In Channing, in William Tudor's books of essays, in the *Travels of Ali Bey,* modelled on the *Lettres persanes,* Boston had become self-critical. Dozens of minds were asking themselves the questions that had found words in the *Monthly Anthology.* Hundreds issued the demand, —which was to be repeated for a hundred years, on each new frontier of the American mind,—for a literature that was really American, "redolent of the soil," "purged of old-world influences." In later years, when people spoke of the "renaissance" in New England, they spoke with a measure of reason; for in Boston, as in Florence, four hundred years before, there was a morning freshness and a thrill of conscious activity. The New England imagination had been roused by the tales of travellers and the gains of commerce, the revival of ancient learning, the introduction of modern learning, the excitements of religious controversy. After the long winter of Puritanism, spring had come at last, and the earth reappeared in its beauty.

Ever since 1817, the little circle of the cognoscenti knew that something important was in the air. There had been decisive proofs of this. Professor Edward Tyrrel Channing and his cousin, Richard Henry Dana, had been driving from Cambridge into Boston. Channing was the editor-in-chief of the new *North American Review*, and Dana was his assistant. As they drove along, side by side, Channing read to Dana two poems that had just come into his hands by a young man named William Cullen Bryant, who lived in a village in the Berkshires. One of them was entitled *Thanatopsis*. As Channing continued to read, Dana exclaimed, "That was never written on this side of the water!" His excitement, he said later, was natural, considering what American poetry had been up to that moment. The day before, a middle-aged country doctor had appeared at the office of the review and drawn from his voluminous pocket-book these poems by his son, which he had brought clandestinely to Boston and eagerly showed the editor. Dana, hearing that Dr. Bryant was making a speech before the Legislature, went at once to the State House, to have a glimpse of the father of such a poet. The American world had moved a step forward when village poets could produce such verses and country doctors could be proud and happy feeling that their sons were men of genius.

All the circumstances of this event were typical of the moment. First of all, the excited recognition that something of importance had happened: the time and the place were ready for the poet. The feeling of Bryant's father was typical also, for most of the writers of the coming age were actively encouraged by their fathers and mothers, for whom the career of letters seemed as normal as that of the pulpit or public affairs. Not even in Catholic countries, where almost every peasant family aspired to produce a priest, was there a keener wish, in the poorest household, that a brilliant son might have "advantages" and follow the line of his intellectual interests. Still more symbolic was another fact: a magazine existed,—after so many abortive attempts,—that could provide an outlet for the writers who were appearing on every hand. Edward Tyrrel Channing and Dana, at this moment, with George Ticknor, also of their circle, were probably, of all American readers, the best informed on English poetry, from Chaucer to the new Romantic school. The rest of the group who wrote the new review, and followed one another as editor,—Edward and Alexander Everett, Jared Sparks and John Gorham Palfrey, two young students of history, Greenwood, Dr. Gardiner, together with Bowditch, Webster and Andrews Norton,— were all men of the world, more or less, who had kept up with the literary current and knew what living writers really counted. They proposed to meet the sneers of the British reviewers in a tone that was neither provincial nor chauvinistic. They were greatly obliged to Scott, the first of living writers, in their opinion, who had said, in his kindly way, that when people once possessed a three-legged stool they would soon contrive to make an easy-chair.

The new review was the easy-chair in question. It was a little angular, perhaps, but no one could have called it a three-legged stool. Its tone was almost as cold and tame as that of the *Monthly Anthology.* It had the dry simplicity, the hard strength, the timid correctness and those other traits that Goethe said so naturally belonged to the early period of every art. It was like the old New England furniture, re-expressed in words. Modelled on the British reviews, still the foundation of all American thought, it imitated their magisterial air. The editors seemed to be on their best behaviour. But the British reviews also were cold and formal, even when they "stripped and whipped" their victims. The great Romantic critics had not appeared, to take the starch out of their pompous manners; and the *North American Review* had many virtues. It was aware of all the important writers in England, France and Germany. It noticed all the American writers, Cooper, Irving, the poet Bryant, who was soon to settle in New York, the centre of his future

life and work. It was on guard against the colonial note:
one of the writers condemned a Canadian author on the
ground that no colonial government had ever evoked the
nobility of mind that was essential to greatness. Its standard was severe and thorough: some of its reviews represented five months of study, during which the reviewer
went behind the author, read all the works that he had
read and verified all his citations. In short, with a firmer
hand and greater resources,,it carried on the task of the
Monthly Anthology; and, as the years passed and it grew
in strength,—until its conservative policy sapped its
strength,—the public became aware that it had at last
a genuine organ of criticism, one that deserved to rank
with the best reviews in the world.

There was no doubt about its conservatism. If it was
clear, orderly and well-informed, if it possessed all the
scholarly virtues, it was hostile to the forms of feeling,
literary, political, philosophic, that were to characterize
the coming age. It was a Unitarian-Whig review, with all
the temperamental limitations that marked Webster's
class of "solid men." In politics, its aim, as time advanced,
was to keep the tariff up, to keep the Whigs in power for
the sake of the tariff, and to keep on good terms with the
Southern magnates, whose cotton fed the Northern factories, so that the tariff might serve the Boston bankers.
All very simple, like the old curriculum at Harvard. In
literature, it had a marked aversion for the notes of the
new age, enthusiasm, mysticism, rapture. Although it felt
obliged to accept the English Romantic poets, if only because they were English, it still preferred the eighteenth-
century modes. For this reason, the tender-minded Dana
soon broke with his fellow-editors. A Whig, even a Tory
in politics,—in the current American sense of the words,
—a lover of old customs and associations, who wrote
Addisonian "Letters from Town," he was a professional
man of letters, the first of his kind in New England, and

the only one of the group, for the *North American* followed the principle of "all gentlemen and no pay." In
him, the old idea of "polite letters" had given place to
something more profound. He did not think of poetry
as a recreation, for he had taken Wordsworth in sober
earnest; and he thought there were truths beyond the
"understanding" that could not be reached in the usual
Boston way. In fact, he preached the high Romantic doctrine. He had written a series of papers on the British
poets, defending the Lake School.[1] He had said that Pope
was not a poet at all.[2] This was too much for his friends,
and much too much for Boston. A furious hubbub resounded through the town. Out Dana went, and out went
with him any hope that the *North American* would ever
understand the new generation.

Alas for Dana, born too soon, not strong enough to
break his own path and yet the symbol of a rising world
where other poets of a tougher grain were to find their
audience waiting. A sensitive dreamer, diffident, self-dis-
trustful, with all the shy and solitary ways that marked
the romantic poet as a type, he was to become an ancient
Nestor, the only man living, decades hence, when even
the Civil War was growing dim, who could still remember Washington's death. As he strolled through the Boston streets, a forgotten ghost, or basked in the sunshine
of his Cape Ann garden, his silvery curls reaching to his

[1] In the opinion of the Scottish Professor John Nichol, these
essays were the best that had appeared, up to that time, on the
Lake School, either in America or England.

[2] The division of feeling in regard to Pope marked the new age
more clearly than anything else. See Parson Wilbur's comment, in
The Biglow Papers, on the youthful Hosea Biglow's view of Pope's
verse: "He affirmed that it was to him like writing in a foreign
tongue,—that Mr. Pope's versification was like the regular ticking of
one of Willard's clocks, in which one could fancy, after long listening, a certain kind of rhythm or tune, but which yet was only a
poverty-stricken *tick, tick,* after all,—and that he had never seen a
sweetwater on a trellis growing so fairly, or in forms so pleasing to
the eye, as a fox-grape over a scrub-oak in a swamp."

shoulders, he would speak of the British essayists of old and the charm that lingered round their memory; but he had lived his life as a recluse, sending forth shoots of prose and verse that had very rarely grown or flowered. He had written a long poem, *The Buccaneer,* the fruit of his early rambles on the Newport beaches, poems modelled on Coleridge and Byron, verses that were not as good as Bryant's, tales of the "darker passions," after the manner of Brockden Brown, *Tom Thornton, Paul Felton,*—young men doomed to live in a world that cannot comprehend their aberrations. Not one of his poems or tales could have been called conclusive. He had started a magazine, *The Idle Man,* filled with his own musings and his friends' verses, and lapsed into an unembittered silence, hoping that perhaps the day might come when an American author would be valued as much as an argand lamp. Thirty years of writing as a profession had brought him less than four hundred dollars. No man, he said, could go on forever without some little response from the world about him.

The circle of the *North American Review* could hardly have been described as sympathetic. These positive minds, however, had other qualifications. Their interests were historical and political, their gifts of a purely critical order. Dana's ablest work was his criticism, and many essays in the magazine were as good as the best in the foreign reviews of their time. Such, for instance, were the essays of Alexander Everett, whose mind was livelier and more vigorous than that of his more famous younger brother.[3] Criticism, oratory, history,—oratory, the states-

---

[3] As minister to Spain, Alexander Everett had studied the South American republics, which were revolting against the mother-country. In his surveys of America and Europe, translated into German, French and Spanish, he showed a remarkable understanding of the post-Napoleonic political era. His literary papers on *Gil Blas,* Voltaire, Mme. de Sévigné, Chinese manners, etc., lucid, learned, often witty, revealed the *North American* at its best. He

man's instrument, and history, the record of his achieve-
ments,—these were the forms of literary expression in
which, at the moment, America most rejoiced. In the
early days of Rome, with which New England had so
much in common, the orators had come before the poets,
the chroniclers before the dramatists. To the little statesmanly world of the Boston patricians, of which the *North
American* was a spokesman, the noblest, the most honourable career, after making history, was to write it. Or, better still, to speak it. Had not Luther said: "Whoso can
speak well is a man"? [4]

In fact, all over the country, in the Middle States, in
the South, as well as New England, during these opening
decades of the century, the historical mind was extraor-
dinarily busy. Old men who had fought in '76 gathered
the children about their hearths and told them tales of
Lexington and Concord. People thronged to Plymouth
Rock, which Webster had signalized in his great oration.
The neglected chronicles came to light. Growing boys and
girls rediscovered Mather's *Magnalia*, wonderful stories
about their country that made them feel the very ground
they trod on was consecrated by Providence. Hundreds
of local histories, histories of states and counties, histories
of towns and villages, proud of the parts they had played
in the recent wars, poured from the rural printing-presses.
It was a symptom of a world-wide movement, for everywhere Napoleon's campaigns had roused the sense of
nationality. In England, Macaulay, Grote, Carlyle and
Milman, in France, Thiers and Guizot, in Germany,

---

translated Theocritus and Goethe and passages from the *Brahma
Purana*, among the first examples of Oriental studies in America.
Of the other early *North American* writers, one might also mention
Caleb Cushing, the statesman who coined the phrase "man on
horseback." Cushing's *Reminiscences of Spain* compare well with
Washington Irving's writings.

[4] "If ever a woman feels proud of her lover, it is when she sees
him as a successful public speaker."—Harriet Beecher Stowe, *Dred*.

Niebuhr and Ranke were only a few of the notable men who were immersing themselves in historical studies. The archives in the European capitals were searched and brought to light, and tens of thousands of dusty documents were scrutinized and passed from hand to hand, even from country to country. The historians formed a princely brotherhood, forwarding one another's investigations,—like the men of science of the future. Niebuhr had set an example and a standard for critical scholarship in historical writing, first in the search for materials and secondly in the examination of them; and there had never been a time when a new and distinguished contribution to history received such universal appreciation. England, like America, stirred by the great continental scholars, had awakened from its age-old isolation and begun to study the history of other peoples, and the English historians were developing, thanks to the recent revival of classical studies,—at Oxford, as at Harvard,—a new and fresh feeling for composition, for the artistic virtues of the ancients. Upon all the English-speaking historians, Sir Walter Scott had a profound effect. He gave them a sense of local colour. He taught them to reproduce, in their narrations, the atmosphere of the times with which they were dealing.

The American school of history, established in New York by Washington Irving, was one of the phases of this world-movement. For its culmination in Boston there were various reasons. The first large library in the town, that of the Massachusetts Historical Society, founded in 1791 by Jeremy Belknap and others, was almost exclusively stocked with historical works. The Athenæum and the Harvard library were both especially strong on the side of history. Young men with literary tastes were drawn into historical research largely for want of other choices, because there was little else for them to read. This was the "accident," as Palfrey called it, that gave

rise to the New England school, soon to fulfil the proph-
ecy of Horace Walpole that Boston was to produce a
Thucydides. But the circumstance was not an accident.
Everything had prepared the Boston mind to centre its
thoughts on history, as it had chosen theology in the past;
and the general interest that filled the libraries with all
this apparatus of research animated the young historians
and gave their works a sympathetic welcome.

The accumulation of private wealth in Boston, thriftily guarded by the canny Whigs, also served the historians. Prescott, Motley and Parkman were men of large
means. So was George Ticknor. Bancroft, who was rela-
tively poor, found himself obliged, and contrived to
spend, in the preparation of his earlier volumes, almost
three times as much as the President's salary. Ticknor's
History of Spanish Literature cost as much to produce as
a public building. In these formidable bills of expense,
the assembling of books and documents was the largest
item; for the public and semi-public libraries grew very
slowly. Prescott, as late as 1839, said that an American
historical writer had to create a library of his own if he
wished to write even on American themes, much more
if his theme were Spain or Holland. In another twenty
years, all this had changed, and the wealth that had
made it possible for a few scholars to command the means
of study provided the means also for the poor. In 1857,
the German Kohl, describing the private libraries of
Boston, which were largely open to students, spoke of the
American "author-princes" who flourished side by side
with the merchant-princes. Even in London he had
scarcely found such splendid collections of books or studies that were arranged so picturesquely, with busts, paintings and curiosities, spaciously illumined from above.
Many of the merchants were bibliophiles. One of them
owned twelve hundred Bibles, including several that
were very rare. Another collected engravings, hundreds

of fine examples of every school. Another had a collection of Americana, first editions of every known work relating to the early history of the country. Thomas Dowse, a journeyman leather-dresser who, in the days of his poverty, when he did not own a pair of boots, possessed "six hundred books, well bound," bequeathed a great collection to the public. There were many rivals for the distinction of owning the finest library in Boston. No doubt, George Ticknor's outshone them all; but by some the honour was claimed for Theodore Parker, the great preacher of the eighteen-fifties, whose library was a river of books that flooded his house from attic to cellar. The libraries of Everett and Prescott were renowned. The books of Rufus Choate, the Salem lawyer, who settled in Boston in 1834, filled his large house from floor to floor, in spite of all the efforts of his wife to stem the appalling tide.

With all these new facilities, the studies of the historians made rapid progress. For a number of quiet readers, more or less in Boston and more or less in touch with one another, were preparing a series of monumental works,— George Bancroft, the son of Aaron Bancroft, the well-known minister of Worcester, Jared Sparks, William Hickling Prescott, J. G. Palfrey[5] and Richard Hildreth, the editor of the Boston *Atlas*. Rufus Choate's friends thought he was better fitted for history than any of these professional historians. The dream of Choate's life was to write a history of Greece; and, in preparation for this, he made a translation of Thucydides, never choosing a word,—or so he said,—until he had thought of at least six synonyms. But the busy lawyer, whose mind dwelt in Athens, had no margin of time for meditation. There

[5] Palfrey, the author of the *History of New England,* published, in 1821, an article in the *North American Review,* pointing out the use that writers of fiction might make of early American history. The first New England historical novel, Lydia M. Child's *Hobomok,* was written in response to this article.

were plenty of others to take his place. Half the men of letters in New England were spreading out their notes and documents in emulation of Robertson and Gibbon. To be sure, they were few at first. Jared Sparks, even in 1840, wrote home from the British Museum, where he was examining manuscripts, "In the reading-rooms are daily congregated more than a hundred readers and transcribers, of all nations and tongues, plodding scholars, literary ladies and grave old gentlemen with mysterious looks. When shall we see the like in the Athenæum?"

Boston was not London; but at least in the Athenæum one might have seen, even years before, the well-known Hannah Adams, working on her history of the Jews, the lady of whom one heard so many stories, as that they were obliged to lock her in, because it was not polite to lock her out. Living, Miss Adams was the only female who ventured to claim her statutory right to browse in these, to her, celestial pastures. Dead, as she was soon to be, she was the "first tenant" of Mount Auburn, or so her gravestone said, though a Boston lawyer, pondering the inscription, remarked, "She cannot properly be called a tenant." One had seen Miss Adams at the Athenæum; one saw the Everetts, Ticknor, Palfrey, Sparks, the pillars of the *North American Review*. One saw Richard Hildreth, a little later, a tall, thin, aging man in black, deaf, absorbed, sitting at his table in one of the alcoves, with his books and papers before him, rising from his chair only to consult some work of reference. The vogue of historical writing increased day by day, in this still air of delightful studies; and the regular Boston dinner-hour, three or four o'clock, lent itself to long, laborious mornings. In 1840, Charles Francis Adams, the famous diplomat of years to come, brought out the *Letters of Mrs. Adams.* John Quincy Adams, Abigail's son, expressed the feeling of a thousand readers when he said that his mother's letters affected him till the tears streamed down his face; and the editor of the book, Abigail's grandson, already touched to tears by these old papers, exclaimed, "Happy are those who pass through this valley with so much of innocence!" [6] The new generation was engrossed in history, not in American history alone, and not exclusively on the highest level. J. S. C. Abbott, the brother of Jacob Abbott of the Rollo Books, represented an army of popular writers. Of his *Life of Napoleon,* Emerson said later, "It seems to teach that Napoleon's great object was to establish in benighted Europe our New England system of Sunday schools." [7]

In Cambridge, in the middle thirties, the boys and girls of the university circle were permitted to dive and delve, with well-washed fingers, into the great boxes, eight in number, where lay the unpublished letters of Washington. There were forty thousand of these letters, which the great man had written or received, many of them in the spacious study where they were now assembled, in the Craigie house on Brattle Street, Washington's study during a long winter. Jared Sparks had moved out from Boston, bringing with him the famous correspondence, which he was preparing for the press, and had rented a suite of rooms from Mrs. Craigie. Sparks, the "American Plutarch," was working on his "lives," the *Library of American Biography,* a series of twenty-five volumes, written by various hands, including his own, describing a whole Pantheon of American heroes. He was soon to be more widely known as the "patriarch of American history." [8] He was already engaged in his great campaign, along with George

[6] Charles Francis Adams maintained the literary habits of the most articulate of American families. Brought up in the White House as a boy, he kept an Adams diary, like his father, for more than fifty years. He contributed seventeen articles to the *North American Review,* on Aaron Burr, Lord Chesterfield, etc.

[7] E. P. Whipple, *Recollections of Eminent Men.*

[8] After his appointment, in 1838, as the first Professor of History at Harvard,—at any American college,—a date that marked an era in historical studies.

Bancroft and Peter Force, to collect, preserve and publish the documents of the period of the Revolution.

His writings, however useful, were hardly exciting, at least, to later readers; and yet they represented a life as exciting as that of an Arctic explorer. Indeed, Sparks had wished to be an explorer, like the hero of his first "life," —the best of all his lives,—John Ledyard, the old Connecticut Yankee, Captain Cook's corporal of marines. Sparks had risen from the ranks, the poorest of the Connecticut poor, supported himself as a carpenter, walked three hundred miles through northern New York, trying to find a school where he could teach. He had battled his way through Exeter, where he had written an essay on the subject, "Intense application to study not detrimental to health." He had battled his way into Harvard at twenty-two and found a position as tutor at Havre de Grace. His Harvard friends protested. How could a man endure existence hundreds of miles from Boston?—considering that, from the point of view of Boston, civilization came to an end at Worcester. But Maryland was the making of him. The inn where he lived was on the postroad, and half the notabilities of the nation stopped there on their way to Washington.[9] At the time of the War of 1812, he saw the British sack Havre de Grace. They burned the great houses where he worked as a tutor, and the British admiral commandeered the finest coach in the town and sent it aboard his ship. Sparks was prepared to write with feeling when he came to consider the days of '76.

In this wider American world, he soon lost his New

[9] Josiah Quincy, who was then in Congress, stopped at the inn one day with Dr. Channing, who had also been a tutor in the South. Quincy and Channing liked the young man and remembered and helped him later. It was Quincy who, as president of the college, called him back to Harvard, and Channing preached at Sparks's ordination, when he became a minister, at Baltimore, the sermon on "Unitarian Christianity" on which his own fame as a theologian was so largely based.

England particularism. He was appointed chaplain of Congress, and, with an interest already aroused in history, found himself surrounded with those who make it. Reading Mungo Park, he dreamed of exploring Africa. While this plan came to nothing, it led him to discover John Ledyard's papers and remains, including parts of the journal that Ledyard kept, describing Cook's death in the Sandwich Islands. Then, having followed Ledyard in imagination, he turned to the exploration of another world, almost as dark as central Africa, the world of American history. He had had enough experience of public life to know where his materials were to be found. He visited all the Southern States, examining the papers in the archives and those in private hands, as often as not in the old family dwellings of the men he had met in Washington. Then he went abroad, to England, Holland, Germany and France, searching the public offices, with Lafayette's assistance, arranging with Guizot and others to publish translations of his *Washington*. One of his aides was Henry Stevens, the "Green Mountain boy," a bibliophile in London, who introduced into Europe thousands of American books and made the British Museum a world-centre for American historical research.

Now, in his Cambridge study, in Washington's own chambers at the Craigie house, he was engaged in the great work of his life. About his standing desk, on every side, heaps of papers lay, not only Washington's letters but the letters of Jay, John Adams, Gouverneur Morris, the statesmen and diplomats of the great war-years. Simple as a child, with his gentle, winning voice and grave smile, he was the boast and delight of scholarly Cambridge. Everyone knew the story of Washington's letters, how Sparks, having found them at Mount Vernon, had arranged to carry them up by ship to Boston. Everyone knew the story of the other letters, Gouverneur Morris's, Franklin's. Some of them Sparks had been just in time to save. He had found two large trunks of Franklin's letters in a Pennsylvania garret, where they had been lying for forty years. Another mass of Franklin's letters and papers turned up in a London tailor's shop, on a shelf, in loose bundles. One of the manuscripts had already been cut in the form of a sleeve-pattern. One shuddered to think what might have happened if Sparks had not possessed the explorer's eye. Two or three years more, and it might have become forever impossible to write a correct history of the Revolution.

It was true that he "embellished" all these papers. He could not let the father of his country speak of "old Put": he changed the phrase to "General Putnam." He could not allow Washington to speak of a sum of money as a "flea-bite." The sum was "totally inadequate to our demands." In short, he bowdlerized the political fathers, in the spirit of a neo-classic age. He had in mind the marble bust, after the timid fashion of Canova, the bust that later times, too cynical, were to find little better than plaster. For this there were certain excuses. Science had not regulated history. No settled standards existed anywhere in regard to documentation. Quotation-marks had no precise value, and the greatest historians did not hesitate to revise their quotations without comment. There were other local excuses that were not so sound. In the days of Andrew Jackson, those who cherished manners, grace and form had some reason to feel, as the Romans felt in the days of the Gothic invasions, that all the amenities of life were threatened. The amenities received a double sanction, all the more because, in America, there was no prescriptive class to defend them. The famous "genteel tradition," of which one was to hear so much later,—so very much too much, when the phrase ceased to be used with any discretion,—largely dates from these days of Andrew Jackson, who brought the Wild West into the White House; and the high-minded Sparks, who, for the rest, had made his own way in a world that worshipped manners, could hardly have been expected to underrate them. The wonder was that he remained so candid. His Washington had to be a correct example, in harmony with the feelings of the thirties and forties; but he took pains to see that the causes of evil fell on the right heads.[10]

As for the nature and value of his writings, they were excellent *mémoires pour servir*. Sparks preserved the materials for later writers and placed them in a position to correct himself; and those who, in days to come, visited the library at Harvard looked with respect at the carved mahogany chest, modelled after the tomb of Scipio, in which reposed the Jared Sparks papers. The fame of his work showed what an audience awaited the coming historians, and what a social function they fulfilled, a function as vital as that of the orators, the ministers, the scholars and the portrait-painters.[11] For the twelve volumes of his *Washington,* orders came from the remotest hamlets in Georgia, Alabama, Illinois. Two hundred sets were sent to the Red River. The *Franklin* was translated presently into one of the dialects of Hindustani.[12] But Sparks's vogue was slight beside that of Bancroft, whose *History of the United States* began to appear in 1834.

---

[10] Sparks, in his bowdlerizations, followed a general practice of the time. Similiar cases can be found in every European literature. The heroes of the early eighteen-hundreds, conceived by readers of Plutarch, had to be heroes at any price.

[11] The first necessity of a new nation is to believe in itself. To create this self-confidence was the function of the early American orators and historians. "The only nations which ever come to be called historic are those which recognize the importance and worth of their own institutions."—Tolstoy, *Anna Karenina.*

[12] This was the greatest period of Franklin's universal fame. "The Greeks admire the character of Franklin. His name is far more familiar to them than that of any other American, not excepting Washington. Many of the 'sayings' of the philosopher are in the mouths of their instructed men."—Samuel G. Howe, *Historical Sketch of the Greek Revolution.*

Never before had anyone attempted to tell the whole story of the nation, and the poor little dry chronicles and annals, Dr. Abiel Holmes's and so many others, that stood for American history were swept from the shelves by Bancroft's enterprise. There were reasons for Bancroft's renown. He was a conscientious student, laborious, open-minded, enquiring, zealous, with the strong will of an old Puritan settler. He had the imagination to see and present the life of the South and the West, as well as New England. He was learned enough to place American history in the main stream of historical events. His style was often picturesque and moving, irradiated with a solemn glow. It was true that, in the first editions, before Bancroft "slaughtered the adjectives," the book was like a Fourth of July oration, like one of Everett's speeches long drawn out, with the Stars and Stripes streaming from the author's hands.[13] This was the note of the nation in Jackson's time, when, with little reflection or criticism, the "giant of the West," rejoicing in size and numbers, growing, mounting in wealth and population, building its turnpikes, railroads and canals, heaping up its factories, bounded towards its "manifest destiny." For Bancroft, God was visible in history, and history culminated in the United States. No wonder his "epic of liberty," with its solid merits, was also acclaimed for other reasons.

Bancroft was prepared for his task. He had grown up in a scholarly circle, and, when he was six years old, his father, Aaron Bancroft, referred to him a question in Roman history which two friends of the house, one of them Chief Justice Theophilus Parsons, found themselves

---

[13] "Come, children of sorrow! You on whom the Old World frowns; crowd fearlessly to the forests; plant your homes in confidence, for the country watches over you; your children grow around you as hostages, and the wilderness, at your bidding, surrenders its grandeur of useless luxuriance to the beauty and loveliness of culture."
The pruning of these unnecessary feathers of the newly-fledged American eagle was Artemus Ward's special joy and task.

unable to settle. He had known Sparks at Exeter. At Harvard, Edward Everett and Andrews Norton had taken him under their wing. The college had sent him to Germany. Another grand tour, like that of his predecessors. Wherever he went, in England, Italy, France, the first question that everyone asked was "Do you know Everett and Ticknor?"—who had been so diligent and so attractive. Bancroft was prouder than ever of his country; and he was engaging, too, with his black hair and firmly cut features, his eager air and obvious earnestness. Humboldt wrote to a friend, "He belongs to that noble race of young Americans for whom the true happiness of man consists in the culture of the intelligence." With all his exciting adventures, his meetings and visits with Byron and Benjamin Constant, Manzoni, the Princess Borghese, Lafayette, whose house was hung with engravings of American scenes, he never lost sight of his object. At Göttingen, along with his Latin and Greek, he studied Hebrew and Syriac. He met students from every country, Hungarians, Netherlanders, Poles. He learned to waltz, he learned to ride on horseback: one saw in him already the little sprightly man with the Santa Claus beard who, at eighty-eight, two generations later, pranced about the roads at Washington, with a big red rose in his buttonhole. At the same time, as a Christian devotee, a more than passive Unitarian,—in short, as that species of minister, sometimes ordained, sometimes not, under the guise of which so many young New England men of letters made their first appearance before the public,—he preached to the country congregations about the town of Göttingen, always speaking in the German language. He spent much of his time with Schleiermacher, the great court preacher at Berlin, listening to his lectures on education,[14] and made a study of the German schools.

[14] The influence of Schleiermacher was apparent in the mystically religious passages in Bancroft's history.

Bancroft's heart, however, was far from simple. Still less simple was his outward manner. Returning home, as tutor in Greek at Harvard, who wished as much as Everett and Ticknor to introduce the German thoroughness, he found himself thwarted at every turn. This was not merely because of the Harvard indifference that also thwarted Ticknor. Bancroft was a vain young man and even more ambitious than Everett, in the less engaging sense of the term. He had neglected to observe Bacon's admonition in regard to travel, which all good Americans regarded as sound, that one should not change one's country manners for those of foreign parts, but only prick in some flowers of that which one has learned abroad into the customs of one's own country. He had half forgotten the English language. French, German, soft Italian phrases blossomed on his lips, a flaunting of the dulcet strain that was much too much for Brattle Street. Bancroft's apparel and gestures were a scandal. He greeted his old protector Andrews Norton by planting a large kiss on each of his cheeks,—a Cambridge tableau, if there ever was one. It was the beginning of the end for Bancroft. But this young instructor was resourceful. He took himself off to Northampton and founded the Round Hill School with Cogswell, another peacock in the eyes of Cambridge. Indeed, there were anchors on every side of Bancroft's little ship. A diligent scholar, who worked for his school, he worked still harder for his own advancement; and the good Sparks, who welcomed his contributions to the *North American Review,* felt obliged to chide him for his foibles. He urged him not to use too many words like "emotions, love, affection, sensation, feeling," which carried him sometimes "into more soft abstractions." This was the counsel of a severe student with an eye for the rigours of language, who knew, as Bancroft did not know, the perils of a turgid rhetoric. And Sparks, with even greater penetration, told him frankly that he was too greedy after the treasures that the moths enjoy. "After what else, pray, should a man be greedy?" Bancroft had replied, with equal frankness. It was all very well to talk about "filthy lucre." A young man, the son of aged parents, had to be up and doing. "The only way," as the young man said, "to show you are fit for a better world is to show yourself not unfit for this." And Bancroft made the most of all his opportunities. No "musing with unseen spirits" for him, no folding his hands in contemplative indolence. He was ready to risk the chance that this was the way to rival Tacitus.

In short, with motives that his friends suspected, he had joined the Democratic party. He had little to fear from censorious Cambridge and Boston, when he had the growing will of the nation behind him. A Democrat in Boston was a social outcast;[15] but Bancroft had allied himself with powers which, as he well knew, and as Boston surmised, had the future with them. He had transcended the sectional mind of New England. From an equally obvious point of view, he had placed himself in the practical line of advancement; for the Democrats of New England were so few that any distinguished member of the party was sure to be rewarded in the end.[16] This prospect was certain in the case of Bancroft, a practical man with a gift for administration, almost the only scholar in the party, a learned Harvard man who had had the courage to smite the Boston Whigs with his scorn, —the Whigs who had smitten him, in the person of Andrews Norton,—even one who found in the people's

[15] William Henry Channing recorded later that, as a boy, he had heard with utter amazement,—as if such a thing could scarcely be conceived,—the remark of an old Bostonian, "A Democrat may be honest in his convictions."
[16] "A Massachusetts man has little chance of success in public life unless he starts a Federalist; and he has no chance of rising above a certain low point unless, when he reaches that point, he makes a transition into Democracy."—Harriet Martineau, *Society in America.*

hero, Jackson, the "nursling of the wilds," the hand of God himself. Bancroft, visiting Washington, drew his chair "close up" to the powers that were, as he said in one of his letters. Jackson and Martin Van Buren liked a man who could shape their political views in eloquent words, who was "easily first in literary improvements," as the "kitchen cabinet" called him. Bancroft's career in politics followed as a matter of course.

No doubt, his association with politics was useful to a writer of history. Who, moreover, could impugn a man for taking sides against the Whigs? The party that Jefferson founded and Jackson maintained was grounded in the welfare of the nation, as some of the best Whigs had begun to see; and the Adamses had always agreed with Bancroft that Hamilton's aristocratic policy, shaped in the interests of the few, had no base in principle and morals. Bancroft's sympathy with the popular will was honest, beyond all question. Aside from his political associations, most of his European associations confirmed him in his faith that the Democrats represented the all-American cause for which the Revolution had been fought. Byron had sided with the Democrats. The Democratic party upheld the convictions that Lessing, Herder and Klopstock had in mind when they spoke of the "lodge of humanity" in the West; and yet, alike in Bancroft's life and mind, there was that element of self-deception which often dogs the spokesman of popular interests. The sentimentalist was marked in Bancroft. The conservative Prescott detested the Mexican War,[17] as a travesty of American principles. It was the Democrat Bancroft, the voice of the people, by no means including the Mexican people, who, as acting Secretary of War, ordered Taylor

[17] "The impolitic and iniquitous war in Mexico . . . mad and unprincipled . . . The patriot would rather see us go ahead by the arts of peace than war, as better suited to the permanent prosperity of the republic."—Prescott, *Correspondence*, 648, 658, 668.

to march into Texas and gave the command to seize California,—in order to extend the "area of freedom" for
those who did not rightfully own the country. Literary
men indulge in humbug only at a price, and Bancroft
abounded in humbug. "Did he believe what he was saying?" Anthony Trollope remarked in later years, after
one of Bancroft's swelling speeches. Emerson had asked
the same question when he said that Bancroft was a
"soldier of fortune" who would "take any side and defend it." Who can say how much a man believes, when
he has an actor's temperament and a demagogue's faith
in numbers? [18]

And yet Bancroft's work was impressive and made him
"one of us," as Ranke said. All too keen for the cloud
of witnesses, very imperfectly a man of letters,[19] insomuch that, after revising his work, pruning its highly-
coloured feathers, he gave it an effect of truncation and
bareness, he was an indefatigable student, with a grandiosity that was sometimes grand. He had first conceived
the enormous task during his years at Göttingen and had
exercised himself, to prepare for it, in a series of shorter
studies, most of them on historical themes, the Economy
of Athens, the Decline of the Roman People, the Wars
of Russia and Turkey, some of them on German liter-

[18] "Bancroft talked of the foolish *Globe* newspaper. It has a circulation of 30,000, and, as he said, each copy is read by ten persons,
so that an editorial article is read by three hundred thousand
persons, which he pronounced with all deep-mouthed elocution.
I only told him that I wished they would write better if they wrote
for so many. I ought to have said what utter nonsense to name in
my ear this *number,* as if that were anything. Three million such
people as can read the *Globe* with interest are as yet in too crude
a state of nonage to deserve any regard. I ought to have expressed
a sincere contempt for the Scramble newspaper."—Emerson's *Journals.*

[19] His later writings, *The Life of Martin Van Buren* and *The Life
and Character of Lincoln,* are always either commonplace or tumid,
sometimes ridiculously so.

ature.[20] Meanwhile, he had steeped his mind in the legendry of the country, and, as the years went on,—the fifty years during which he was occupied with his twelve volumes, each one emblazoned on the back with the well-known phrase of Berkeley, which summed up the note of the days of Jackson, "Westward the course of empire takes its way,"—he mastered every corner of his field, as far as a contemporary could have done so. He had laid out a plan on the scale of Gibbon. He carried on a voluminous correspondence with every man and woman he could reach, north, south, east and west, who was able to give him any information or any unpublished letters. He opened up veins of tradition, collected half-forgotten anecdotes, travelled up and down the Mississippi, set his agents to work in London and Paris, searching the archives for him. After his first volume had been published, the whole world of scholars was ready to help him; the libraries and manuscript collections of almost every family in Europe that had had associations with America were freely opened to him. No one questioned his thoroughness. After forty years, he was still alert for any new material that he could use in some fresh revision of his work. The hardy old man, at eighty-five, still rose in the night, lighted his fire and candles and read his Gibbon and sometimes toiled for fourteen hours on end.

This was the great life-pattern of New England,[21] and Bancroft's work was not unworthy of it. One still recap-

[20] Printed in the *North American Review*. Jared Sparks, as editor, had spoken up for nationalism in Italy, Greece and South America, and the magazine was widely read abroad. A dozen copies a month were sold in Calcutta, and the Bourbon king, Louis XVIII, caused to be prohibited in France this tribune of popular liberties. Bancroft's essays on Goethe, Herder and Schiller were among the first in America on these subjects. Goethe thanked him heartily for the paper he had devoted to himself.

[21] "For fifty years he rose before the sun," as President Kirkland of Harvard said of John Adams.

tured later, turning its pages, the pride that thrilled the
bosoms of the forbears for whom the glowing historian
first unrolled the panorama of the national epos. The forbears themselves shared Bancroft's fervour. The young
republic shared it; and the republic saw itself reflected
in Bancroft's flattering mirror. There, like a river-system
seen from a lofty mountain, the whole American story
unrolled its length, down to the adoption of the Constitution: the founding of the colonies, the struggles with the
European peoples, the Puritans, the Cavaliers, the Quakers, the red men and their ways, the slave-trade, the early
wars, the wonders of the Western wilderness,—the elk,
the stag, the bear and Daniel Boone, pausing to rest
in the golden thickets,—the savage forests and the great
plantations, the gathering of the forces in the Revolution,
the nation, established at last, rejoicing in its strength.
Happy days when Plancus was the consul, remote as
Rome itself, when the young republic delighted the soul
of Tocqueville and every American morning was a
Fourth of July! Who would smile, in the sweep of such a
vision, at the touchy, self-important little man who served
as its rhapsodist and its hierophant, the leader with the
rose pinned on his coat who called the steps in the barn-
dance of Progress?

CHAPTER VII

PRESCOTT'S *FERDINAND AND ISABELLA*

SUDDENLY, in 1837, out of this throng of historical studies, honest and laborious, some of them fervent, none of them august, a great work appeared, like a wonder of nature, as it seemed to American readers,—*The Reign of Ferdinand and Isabella.* It was a brilliant performance, as any child could see and no scholar was ever to deny. Its limitations were obvious enough. It was not a philosophical history. The author had no great leading views, nor any profound feeling for human motives. There were depths upon depths behind and beneath the story that he had never plumbed. But, as a work of art, a great historical narrative, grounded at every point in historical fact, and with all the glow and colour of Livy and Froissart, it was a magnificent success. Its outlines were as firm as those of a cartoon of Raphael, and its pageantry of picturesque detail was calculated to feed as never before the starved imagination of the country. The book had been planned like a battle and built as stoutly as a Salem clipper, destined to sail through many enchanted minds for generations to come.

It was the work of William Hickling Prescott, Ticknor's young friend, the charming, amusing son of Judge Prescott, who lived in his ample house in Bedford Street, overlooking a beautiful garden. Prescott?—who could believe it? He was partly blind, and he had an extravagant love of jolly parties. He talked with a joyous abandon, running over with animal spirits, laughing at his own inconsequences, with always some new joke or witty sally.

He could be happy in more ways, in spite of his defective eyes, and happier in every one of them, than anyone else his friends had ever seen. One met him in the street, with his rosy air, with his gay blue satin waistcoat, tall, graceful, with light brown hair and a clear and ruddy complexion. He seemed to look younger every day. It was known that, for twenty years, he and a group of his friends,—writers in the *North American Review*,—had carried on a literary club, reading their papers over a merry supper. He had printed a few essays in the review. But this was in a dilettantish spirit, everyone supposed. One of his relatives, meeting him on the street, not long before his book appeared, urged him to undertake some serious task. It would be so good for him. It would be more respectable than leading this unprofitable life.

Every evening the light from his study-window glimmered through the pear-trees in the garden. But only George Ticknor, outside the household, knew that, for at least ten years, Prescott had been hard at work, harder, perhaps, than any Boston merchant. And, if everyone bought his book for a Christmas present, it was only because the author was so attractive. One of his cronies, who was not a reader, rose before dawn, on the day it was published, to buy the first copy; but, while everyone saw at once that it was good, no one was aware how good it was. There were scarcely twelve men living who were able to know. Within a year or two, the electoral returns came rolling in, from England, France and Spain. The book had been born a classic.

It was a conquest of personality. Prescott was a first-rate human being, exuberant, gallant, wilful, firm, devoted, far removed from the clerkly sort of scholar, painstaking but wanting in vigour and sinew, who, in a world in which the most virile types adopted careers of enterprising action, ruled over the sphere of books. He was an artist-cavalier. His temperament fitted him to understand an age of courageous exploits, and yet—as if in his veins flowed in equal parts the blood of the old colonel of Bunker Hill and that of the mild and philosophical judge, his father and his grandfather—he was a just and sensitive referee, whose verdicts could be trusted. Whatever he did was sure to be decisive. For the rest, he was happiest on horseback and might have been a soldier.[1] He did not like to get up in the morning and had to instruct his servant, the faithful Nathan, to pull away his bed-clothes. He did not like to work. He had to make bets with his secretary that he would write a certain number of pages or carry out some other resolution. He was always making resolutions, never too old to make them; and he was never old enough to keep them. He had formed this habit at Harvard: resolutions about the number of hours he was going to spend in study, about the number of times a week he was going, or not going, to theatres and balls. When he broke too many resolutions, he introduced into his reckoning sets of fixed exceptions, amendments on amendments; then he scored them all off and opened a new account. By this means, and others, he made himself a casuist, able to comprehend the Spanish mind.

The refractory horse makes the most mettlesome charger. Prescott had a formidable will, and his gay inconsequence gave it buoyancy. Underneath his mock self-scrutiny, he formed the habit of self-examination; and he had bridled and harnessed his indolent nature. Every morning, in the dead of winter, to wind himself up for the day, he mounted his horse and rode to Jamaica Plain, to see the sun rise from a certain hill. As for his blindness, which was never total, he made an advantage of it. One

---

[1] Several of the New England authors, Bancroft, Longfellow, Parkman, etc., were, like Prescott, excellent horsemen.

"The absolute tyranny of a human will over a noble and powerful beast develops the instinct of personal prevalence and dominion . . . It makes men imperious to sit a horse."—Holmes, *Elsie Venner*.

might have thought that blindness was a blessing. He could not read for more than ten minutes,—an hour or two a day at the best of times. And how could a blind man write a history, based on unpublished documents, in two or three foreign languages?—for Prescott, who was unable to study law, had fixed his mind on history. Dr. Johnson had said it could not be done, a very good reason to prove that it could, as two of Prescott's later friends, two of the great historians of Europe, Thierry and Capponi, were to prove as well. He made his ears do the work of his eyes, with the aid of a friend and a sister and later of a competent secretary. Blindness had always favoured contemplative habits. Had not Malebranche closed his shutters in order to drive the sunlight out? Had not Democritus, as the legend said, blinded himself deliberately to stimulate his thinking? Saunderson, Euler, Huber all were blind. The blind town-crier of Salem, where Prescott had spent his earliest years, had performed most of the functions of a daily paper. Blindness was good for invention, as many poets proved, from Homer to Milton. The blind were famous for their patience, especially for their feats of memory. One lingered later over passages that were read aloud.

By no means a fatuous optimist, Prescott summed up these thoughts in one of his essays. He taught himself to use a noctograph, by means of which, with the aid of an ivory stylus, pressing on a sheet of carbon-paper, he took his notes and wrote his manuscripts. The secretary copied the notes in a large round hand, which Prescott was sometimes able to read himself. Meanwhile, he had learned to memorize, composing in his memory to such an extent that he could often carry in his mind as many as three chapters of one of his books, seventy-two pages of printed text. He could hold this there for several days, turning it over and over, remodelling every sentence. One chapter he thus remodelled sixteen times, before committing a word to paper. His blindness had another effect. No reader of his histories ever imagined that, however he dealt, perforce, in a wholesale fashion, with the butcheries of the Spaniards,—"the Inquisition dogs and the devildoms of Spain,"—Prescott himself was impassive or callous in his feelings. He had sat at the feet of Channing, for whom no sparrow fell to the ground in vain. His blindness increased the sensitivity that lay behind the judgments he conveyed—as an artist ought to convey them—by subtle modulations of tone and style. He spoke of the careless indifference with which men who would never abuse a dog crushed, without a thought, insects whose bodily agonies were imperceptible to the naked eye.

He had first acquired these mental habits when, as a young man with failing eyesight,—the victim of an accident in college,—he had been sent abroad, to London and Paris, to consult the doctors there, and had spent a quiet winter in the Azores, where his mother's father, Mr. Hickling, was consul at Saint Michael's. People were surprised, in later years, that Prescott, who had never visited Spain, or Mexico or Peru, knew so much about these tropical scenes and was able to fill his books with such glowing pictures,—Spanish gardens, myrtles, laurels, lemons, the box-tree and the rose, mountain vistas, wildly picturesque, the Cordilleras and the Sierra Nevada, with convent-bells ringing in the valleys. Through his writings, to the very last, even to the final portrait of Charles the Fifth, dying in his garden-monastery, breathed the fragrance of the orange-trees, flowering in the southern sunshine. A young man who had grown up in Boston, under cloudy skies, lashed by the east wind, would have had little imagination if he had not received vivid impressions during these June-like months at Yankee Hall, on the outskirts of Ponta Delgada, with a grand old patriarch like Mr. Hickling, as warm-hearted and merry as his grand-

son, and a gay brood of half-Portuguese cousins. And suppose this young man, surrounded by so many marvels,—
castellated country-houses, gorgeous churches, crumbling
nunneries,—passing enchanted hours in mule-back rides
over the volcanic mountains, had yet been obliged, in his
blindness, to spend half his time in a dark room, walking
scores of miles from corner to corner, throwing out his
elbows to feel the walls till he wore away the plaster, till
he knew what a dungeon felt like and might have been
himself, even he, one of the victims of the Inquisition,—
would he not have preserved these impressions of what
his eyes had beheld? One takes a good look when, for all
one knows, it may be a last look. One takes two looks at a
tropical scene when one has lived in New England. It was
in this dark chamber, singing as he walked, to keep his
courage up, that Prescott learned the art of memorizing.
He composed a long poem for one of his friends.

The rest of this European journey also had its consequences. A young historical student, one who is going to
write about soldiers and statesmen, cannot see too soon,
at close range, a few good specimens in the flesh, not to
speak of the scenes of which the Romans had written.
In Italy, with his Livy and his Horace in the net of his
travelling-carriage, he crossed the great battle-fields, those
of the Gran Capitan, which he was to describe in *Philip
II*. In Paris, he paid his respects to Lafayette, like all the
other good Americans, some of whom, alas, were eating
their hero out of house and home.[2] There, in his dark-
ened room, where, at a crisis of his illness, he seemed to
be at the point of death, he renewed the friendship with
Ticknor that was never to lapse for forty years. And in
London, face to face with the Elgin Marbles, images of

[2] Lafayette collected a fund to restore to their own country various
penniless Americans who overran La Grange. Thus early the new
world began to turn the tables on the old. See John Neal, *Wandering Recollections*.

classical form that left long traces in his mind,—traces a little too long, perhaps, for there was too much marble in Boston already,—he spent his days with John Quincy Adams, who was acting there as minister. It was in Adams's private library, the great collection of books which he had deposited in the Athenæum, that Prescott had browsed as a boy, the turbulent boy who could not control his laughter and who had infected one of his sober professors, insomuch that, when the professor rebuked him, the more he looked at Prescott the more he laughed, till the class dissolved in tears. In those earlier days, Prescott, who had the run of the Athenæum, had spent half his time reading books of adventure and romances, like Southey's *Amadis of Gaul*, wishing that he could have been a knight-errant. He read French, Spanish and Italian; and he and a friend played at mimic battles, first with bits of paper and then dressed up in old fragments of armour, which were kept as relics in the Athenæum. On their way to school, they told each other stories, improvising epics of adventure, in the manner of Ariosto. Prescott's head was full of the wildest fancies.

At that time, the Peninsular War had been raging over Spain. The newspapers were full of it; and Prescott, as a grown man, could not recall a day when feats of arms amid Spanish scenes had not filled the foreground of his mind. Now, restored to Boston, after his taste of the Azores, and with his feeling for history quickened and sharpened, he was to find another stimulus to follow up this interest of his boyhood. His friends rallied about him in his blindness and read to him aloud, six or eight hours at a time, especially the inseparable Ticknor, absorbed in the study of Spanish literature, on which he was lecturing at Harvard. Ticknor, to amuse him, read his lectures to him, three or four afternoons every week, along with his favourite classics and historical works and the old English romances; and, together with an exiled Italian scholar, who was spending a year in Boston, they read the Italian poets. The friends wrote to each other in Spanish. On a snowy day, when they could not meet, Prescott defended his belief that Petrarch's Laura was a real woman. Ticknor was more sceptical, much as he loved Petrarch, whom he had read at Vaucluse, on a spring day beside the fountain. Ticknor was almost the only friend one had, in this bustling, money-getting American world, who, having the means, had the time, as well as the passionate zest, for these enchanting studies.

Prescott was reading for pleasure, with Ticknor's Spanish library as his hunting-ground. He had in mind no scheme for a composition, but he was planning a literary career, after the manner of Gibbon, for which he proposed to lay a firm foundation. This was one of the solid Boston customs. As John Quincy Adams had laid a foundation for the statesman's life, based on blocks of good political granite, so Prescott put his blocks together, first clearing the ground with a thorough study of the English tongue. Let the suitable subject find him ready, even the suitable field of concentration. He had made up his mind that the age of thirty-five was soon enough to put pen to paper. English grammar first, as if he had never gone to school or college. For style, Sidney, Bacon, Browne and Milton. One hour a day for the Latin classics, Tacitus and Livy for elevation: he knew them virtually by heart already, but this was quite a different matter. A year devoted to French, from Froissart to Chateaubriand. A year for Italian, another year for Spanish. There he paused, there he felt at home, too much at home to carry on with German. His eyes were not equal to the Gothic script.

Meanwhile, for practice in composition, he wrote an annual essay for the *North American Review*. On one of these papers, *The Arabs in Spain*, which he decided to save for his first book, he spent seven months of close work: two hundred and fifty foolscap pages of notes, all carefully indexed. The review had set a pace for scholars. These essays, which he continued to write and later collected in his *Miscellanies,* dealt with themes suggested by his reading, Molière, Cervantes, Scott, Irving, Bancroft, Scottish Song, Italian Narrative Poetry, the Poetry and Romance of the Italians. It amused him to note that Corneille's friends, like his own friends in Boston, had sat with him for six months at table without suspecting that he was at work on a *Cid.* He wrote a short biography of Charles Brockden Brown, who had found so much of poetical and human interest under the prosaic surface of American life. Brown had attracted him, perhaps, because he had planned to write two epics on the conquests of Peru and Mexico. As for the general quality of these essays, they were such as one found in all the reviews, the "Old North," as it was called already, as in those of England, Scotland and France; they were neither better nor worse than Southey's or Lockhart's. They were scholarly books in miniature, learned, lucid, rather like Macaulay's, without the prejudices and without the genius,—for Prescott's genius was for story-telling. They showed his temperamental limitations, those of the Boston Whig point of view, in its most attractive form,—positive, somewhat obtuse, clear, just, full of romantic feeling, with scarcely a shred of intuition. Prescott did not like the idea of looking for mystical meanings in *Don Quixote;* and for him, as for all his school, the French Revolution had been fought in vain. His essays were best when they touched upon Scott, and Ariosto and Tasso. Prescott understood, no one better, these poet-story-tellers of chivalrous times. He belonged to the same family of minds.

Out of these related studies, his great theme rose with a sort of inevitability. For a while, he thought of writing a history of Italian literature. Then it struck him that an Italian subject would not be new: Sismondi had covered the ground too well. He wished for a theme that was new as well as great, for he was not planning a history to please unlettered readers who had not kept up with the progress of research. He meant to write for the world, for the guild of historians, first of all, who formed a super-nation, just as he wrote for the pure love of letters. If one pleased Irving, Southey, Thierry, and conquered, for literature and science, a realm that no other mind had conquered, one's work would be good enough for the popular taste; and Spanish history, if it was not unknown, had not been explored at its most vital point, the reign of Ferdinand and Isabella. Theirs was the momentous reign during which the scattered kingdoms had been brought together,—the age of the conquest of Naples, the age of the subversion of the Spanish Arabs, the founding of the Spanish Inquisition, the opening of the Western hemisphere. It was an age of great men, Ximenes, Gonsalvo de Córdoba, Columbus, an epoch that contained, for better or worse, the germs of the modern political system; and, thanks to the present government of Spain, call it liberal, call it anarchistic, the archives had been thrown open to Spanish scholars. They were busily publishing documents, chronicles, memoirs. But the decrepit kingdom, humbled by the loss of its foreign empire, rising from its ancient lethargy, was yet in too chaotic a condition to foster any vigour of expression. Spain, with all its historiographers, had not produced a master-mind who could assimilate for a greater purpose all these documents that had come to light.

The great theme was at Prescott's disposal. For the books and manuscripts that he required, he could count upon Alexander Everett, the minister at Madrid, who had aroused Irving's interest in Spain. In order to feel sure-footed in the language, he went over his Spanish grammar again. Then he began to read all round the subject, beginning with the general laws of nations, the constitutional history of England, the histories of the continental countries, France, Italy, Germany, Portugal, the general history of Spain, before he settled on his special field. For a few weeks, each summer, he went to Nahant, where his father had a cottage, Fitful Head, perched on a wild sea-cliff. Strolling under the chestnut groves, and among the silver poplars that throve in the salt sea-breezes, he often met the muse of history there. But this old resort of Boston fashion, about which Willis had written his sparkling stories, was full of mundane souls. He worked better at Pepperell, in the plain old salt-box farmhouse, the home of his Prescott forbears. There he had always spent his best summers, close to the "Fairy Grove," with its woodland streams. Behind the house, looking towards Monadnock, a shady path wound beside a pond, where he composed many of his chapters, sauntering back and forth. Sometimes he composed on horseback, especially when he wished to describe a battle, shouting his favourite ballad along the wood-paths, to rally his impressions,—"O give me but my Arab steed." He felt as he had felt, years before, dressed in fragments of armour at the Athenæum.

Many were the bets he had to make, and the forfeits he had to give, to keep his wits screwed up to the proper pitch. The book was a ten-years' task:[4] three and a half years of study before he wrote the opening sentence, three months for chapter one, seven months for the final chapter, two years for condensing and abridging. He had the text set up in type and caused four copies to be printed, for his friends to correct and criticize. But who would

---

[4] "If you wish to be happy, always have ten years' work laid out before you,"—a phrase of Prescott's father that Ticknor was fond of quoting to his classes. No doubt, the phrase had its effect in the lives of many of Ticknor's pupils.

have dreamed that a book on such a subject could have been received with such hosannas? Not Prescott, who, as he painfully scrawled his chapters, writing the lines twice over in his blindness, never guessed how hungry his countrymen were for the brilliant glow and colour that he gave them, the pageantry of kings and queens and battles. This was the romance that America longed for, as if the tapestry-makers of Bayeux had suddenly reappeared in sober Boston. Nor had Prescott guessed how eagerly the English, who had won the Peninsular War and were keenly interested in Spain, welcomed tales of soldiers and empire-builders.

The book was a universal triumph, one that even grew, as the years advanced, as the progress of historical research proved that Prescott's skill and documentation had left him the master of his field. The freshness and the freedom of the descriptions, the unity and proportion of the structure, the quiet and modest authority of the apparatus, the lustre of the language were new notes in American history-writing, different indeed from Jared Sparks's bareness and Bancroft's grandiosity. The author's style was a little over-formal, in the good old Boston way, and Prescott presently took this in hand. He knew that American writing was archaic, as colonial and provincial writing tended to be, and he knew that the style of the new generation in England had grown more personal and more familiar. He wished to write the "prose of the centre," of which one was to hear so much; and, in preparation for his future work, he searched and reviewed his own prose, to make it the natural vehicle of his mind. The sympathy with which he presented his heroes, always judging the action, not the actor, was even more of an innovation, although he had certainly pictured Isabella somewhat in the guise of a Boston lady, in whom a Boston man could find no blemish. Or, rather, a Boston boy, for whom a lady could not be a bigot. For

Prescott was a boy, from first to last, a charming, virile and romantic boy, with a scholar's conscience and an artist's genius. One might well ask for different things, but one could scarcely ask for anything better.

CHAPTER VIII

LONGFELLOW IN CAMBRIDGE

THE CRAIGIE house in Cambridge had grown accustomed to distinguished lodgers when, in the summer of 1837, a young man of thirty, Henry Wadsworth Longfellow, the new professor of modern languages, applied at the door for chambers. Jared Sparks had lived there, Edward Everett had brought his bride there. Dr. Joseph Worcester, the lexicographer, was living there at present, working on his *American Dictionary*. Dr. Worcester had recently moved from Salem, where he had been a schoolmaster and had had among his evening pupils the new professor's friend and Bowdoin classmate, the young Nathaniel Hawthorne. The dictionary on which he was working now was a counterblast to Webster, his fellow Yale-man, who had removed from the language, in the interest of American independence, so many of its ancestral elegances. In matters of quantity, numbers of words and the like, together with the excellence of his definitions, the utilitarian Webster had won the day, even against the English dictionaries. In matters of quality, he was much at fault. Dr. Worcester saw no reason why the speech of his countrymen should lose its inherited succulence and fullness. In the name of Massachusetts, he wished to protest against the Connecticut school, with its thin and calculated rigours.[1]

[1] Worcester remained for a generation the dictionary of the best New England writers. See Holmes, *The Poet at the Breakfast Table:* "Mr. Worcester's Dictionary, on which, as is well known, the literary men of this metropolis are by special statute allowed to be sworn in place of the Bible."

Early as one rose in Brattle Street, Dr. Worcester was up and out already. One saw him on his black horse, jogging along in the shadows of dawn. Then he vanished into his cave of notes. The new professor was equally unobtrusive. It was true that he had a rakish air. With his rosy cheeks and china-blue eyes, he wore his hair in curls. He was fond of colour in his raiment. His neckties and his waistcoats were open to question; so were his gloves and his cane. Mrs. Craigie, much as she loved Voltaire, regarded him with suspicion. But she had read the extravagant *Sorrows of Werther;* moreover, she had read a recent book, *Outre-Mer* by name, the work of the young professor, a sort of all-European continuation of Washington Irving's *Sketch Book.* She liked the book, she liked the young man. It was plainly another case, like Bancroft's, of having studied abroad, and the new professor, unlike Bancroft, was willing to live it down. He got his own tea and toast for breakfast, quietly went about his college duties and buried himself in his rooms. And he soon exchanged the garments of his heart for a broad-brimmed black hat, a black frock-coat and a black walking-stick.

Change his skin as he might, the young professor could not change his spots. He was a romantic soul. He was a born poet whose every fancy clothed itself in images and rhymes as naturally as an apple-tree in May clothes itself with blossoms. He was a poet like those Troubadours, those early-morning "finders" of poetry, who found it on every bush and sang as the vireo sings in summer, about whom he was lecturing to his classes. For he was also a scholar, the man in all America best fitted to fill Professor Ticknor's vacant chair. Ticknor, who wished to resign, in order to visit Europe again and write his history of Spanish literature, had virtually appointed his successor. He had seen some of the young man's translations; and eleven years before, when Longfellow had set out for

Europe to fit himself to teach at Bowdoin College, he had given him letters to Southey and Washington Irving, advising him to study at Göttingen. Longfellow had spent three years wandering over the continent, taught at Bowdoin six years more and gone back to Europe for another year, in Germany and Scandinavia, in preparation for his new position. He had shown the practical sense that makes the professor, worthy of the son of a Portland lawyer who had been Dr. Channing's Harvard class-mate. He had formed an acquaintance with various eminent men in every corner of Europe, Lafayette in Paris, who remembered his family pleasantly in Portland, the Swedish poet Nicander, whom he met at Naples, Thomas Carlyle in London, Grillparzer at Salzburg, Bryant, already known as the "father of American poetry," with whom he shared long walks at Heidelberg. Taking a leaf from Sir William Jones's letters, he had learned not only the usual languages, all that Ticknor knew, but also Finnish and Swedish, and he had published several text-books, French and Italian grammars, and a Spanish reader. But he was a poet all the time. As a boy, he had written ballads of the Revolution, songs of the Maine woods, elegiac verses about Indian hunters whose race was falling like the withered leaves when autumn strips the forest. He had planned a series of poetic sketches dealing with aspects of New England life, the taverns, the village customs, the parson, the squire, the husking-frolics and the Indian dances, the French-Canadian peasants. And in Europe, where others were to be so conscious of all that America lacked,—the castles and cathedrals and ivied ruins,—he had recalled the corn-fields of New England, garnished with yellow pumpkins, the green trees and orchards by the roadside, the bursting barns, the fences and the well-poles, the piles of winter firewood, the fresh, cheerful, breezy scenes of home. Everywhere, the Europe that he witnessed,—the Europe of the "Romantic Reaction,"

—had gone back to its national origins, and the poet
had become the skald again, the bard, the singer and the
story-teller, the moulder and hierophant of the national
life, the people's aspirations. Longfellow had felt this
world-impulse.

Settled now in Cambridge, in the gracious mansion, so
like an Italian villa, the young professor, who was always
ready to draw forth some scrap of song or story to entertain some fair Angélique, found willing ears also in his
classes. Beside the round mahogany table in University
Hall, he sat among his pupils, discoursing with a silvery
courtesy,—how different from the harsh, monastic fashion of most of the older professors,—in a style that was
far too flowery, the older professors thought, but with a
feeling for the romance of letters that was much more
intimate than Ticknor's. In Ticknor one felt the glow of
a marble surface. This lecturer was a painter and a poet.
All the tones of his voice were soft and warm. He was a
master of the pastel shades, whose mind was suffused
with the light of Claude Lorrain. The facts, the details,
the philology he left to his large corps of young instructors,—for the university, having abandoned itself to
these degenerate modern languages, wished to do it hand-
somely. His task was to provide the general outlines, to
give the aroma, the bouquet; and in what corner of the
house of song was there a chamber where he had not
lived? From the mouldering walls of the Anglo-Saxon
bards, weather-stained and ruined, he passed to the courts
and gardens of the French Trouvères, *en route* for the
Minnesingers and the Mastersingers. (One had to use
these French words now and then, silly as they seemed no
doubt in Cambridge ears.) He told again the ancient
Frankish legends, the Chansons de Geste, the story of
Reynard the Fox, souvenirs of far-off springs and summers that seemed to have a sort of occult relation to these
early-morning days of the young republic. One heard the

New England birds in the old French gardens, the songs like cherry-blossoms, drifting through an air of dawn, notes of expectation. Were some of the ballads rather grim and ghostly for a bright May morning in the college yard? The lecturer knew how to win his pupils . . . How joyously this ballad opens! It is the Feast of Pentecost. The crimson banners wave on the castle walls. You see how well-arranged the contrast is. The knight appears in his black mail, the mighty shadow trembles in the dance, the faded flowers drop. However, this ballad tells its own story. It needs no explanation. Here is something in a different vein, *The Castle by the Sea.* A somewhat sombre piece. Would you like me to read it? . . . Grim as the poem might be, it was inviting beside the Paley, the Locke or the mathematics one heard in the other class-rooms.

Warmly, too, with what a gift for colour, the young professor spoke of his life in Europe. This was not the cold, old classical Europe that everybody knew or had read about, the Europe that one crossed in a travelling-carriage, on grand tours, with letters of introduction. It was a garden of memories, songs and tears, softly bright as a spring bouquet, tinted with rose and apple-green, pale canary-yellow and the palest blue. One followed the professor on his travels, whether one had read his book or not, shared his pipe in homely Flemish inns, floated with him in a Dutch canal-boat, through meadows laden with tulips, played on his flute, like Goldsmith, on the Loire, among the peasants busy in the fields. One stopped for a month or two in a Spanish village, ambled through Tyrolese valleys, over the blossoming carpet, lay beside him on a flowery ledge, drenched with a summer silence that was broken only by the sound of evening bells. One walked through the still Swedish forests, heard the hemlocks murmuring, watched the sunlight on the waterfalls; one saw the yellow leaves drifting over Denmark. One

called upon old Dannecker, Goethe's friend, the great
Canova's pupil, the sculptor of the charming "Ariadne,"
and shared the young man's thoughts on his homeward
stroll,—whether he too might not accomplsh something,
bring something permanent out of this fleeting life, and
then, serenely old, seat himself in his garden, like the
artist, wrapped in a flowered morning-gown, and fold his
hands in silence.

The young professor often spoke of Goethe. Once he
dreamed that Goethe came to Cambridge. The professor
gave him a dinner at Willard's Tavern and told him he
thought Clärchen's song in *Egmont* was one of his best
lyrics. The god smiled. He liked to speak of Heidelberg,
where, to the music of the nightingales that flooded the
castle garden, he had filled his heart with the old German
lore. His friends there dwelt in a land of fancy where
brooklets gushed and hemlock-trees were faithful, where
maidens' bosoms were not always faithless, where graves
were the footprints of angels and all things that lived
sang together, the roses, the tulips, the birds, the storms,
the fountains. The flowers melodiously kissed one another, keeping time with the music of the moonbeams.
Many were the talks the young men had about fame and
the lives of authors. Where should the poet and the
scholar live, in solitude or in society, in the green stillness
of the country or in the grey town?—urgent problems to
be passed along to the young men at Harvard. There
were admirable examples at Heidelberg, students with
their sixteen hours a day and men of letters with retired
habits: Thibaut, poring over his Pandects, and that wild
mystic who spent his nights reading Schubert's *History of
the Soul,* while his own soul dwelt in the Middle Ages.
There, with his German Minna, lived the French poet,
Edgar Quinet, who, having helped to revive the long-
forgotten Chansons de Geste, had written his fantastic
Ahasvérus, with its Holy Roods and Galilee-steeples, its

arabesques and roses, hoping to do in words what Stras-
bourg Cathedral had done in stone. Lives of great men
to remind one . . . toiling upward in the night. One had
to learn patience, especially in the world that surrounded
Harvard, where the pulse of life beat with such feverish throbs. At Heidelberg, one heard tales of Richter,
of Goethe, Hoffmann, Schiller, who loved to write by
candle-light, with the Rhine wine always on his table.
What more could a professor do, for his aspiring pupils,
—and who was not aspiring at Harvard?—than to picture all these French and German scholars, toiling, in
want, in pain, sickness, sorrow, familiar with the weep-
ing walls of dungeons, to carry out their noble purposes?
But for them, who would have kept alight the undying
lamp of thought? But for them, the flapping of some con-
queror's banner would have blown it out forever.

Thus the professor discoursed, beside the mahogany
table, while the shadows of the elm-trees in the Yard
danced on the white pilasters of the class-room. His mind
was like a music-box, charged with all the poetry of the
world.[2] Ballads that rippled with the River Neckar.
Ballads of summer mornings and golden corn, blossoms,
red and blue, leafy lanes and hedge-rows. Spanish, Swedish, Danish ballads. Epics and fragments of epics, like
Frithiof's Saga, by the mad Scandinavian bishop, Esaias
Tegnér, half pagan Viking, half Lutheran priest, who
had revived the chants of the ancient skalds in the pastoral setting of a Swedish Wakefield. Sagas of ships and
sea-craft and laughing Saxons, dashing their beards with
wine. Songs of Norwegian chieftains, proud of their flowing locks, night-songs, songs of childhood, Christmas car-
ols, stately Italian sonnets. The music-box unrolled its
coloured stream; but the lecturer was not an antiquary.
He was a poet and teacher of poets who spoke with a

[2] For the range of Longfellow's knowledge of poetry, see his prodigious collection, *The Poets and Poetry of Europe*, 1845.

mildly apostolic fervour. He had published an essay defending his vocation. Poetry did not enervate the mind or unfit the mind for the practical duties of life. He hoped that poets would rise to convince the nation that, properly understood, "utility" embraces whatever contributes to make men happy. What had retarded American poetry? What but the want of exclusive cultivation? American poetry had been a pastime, beguiling the idle moments of merchants and lawyers. American scholarship had existed solely to serve the interests of theology. Neither had been a self-sufficient cause for lofty self-devotion. Henceforth, let it be understood that he who, in the solitude of his chamber, quickened the inner life of his countrymen, lived not for himself or lived in vain. The hour had struck for poets. Let them be more national and more natural, but only national as they were natural. Eschew the skylark and the nightingale, birds that Audubon had never found. A national literature ought to be built, as the robin builds its nest, out of the twigs and straws of one's native meadows. But seek not the great in the gigantic! Leave Niagara to its own voices! Let the American poets go back to the olden time, studying not the individual bard but the whole body of the world's song. They could only escape from their colonial heritage in this all-human testament of beauty.

Sufficiently mild words with which to announce an era. Twenty other poets and orators were saying the same things. Longfellow spoke for them all and only spoke with more authority because, with his chair at Harvard, he had an ampler sounding-board behind him. He represented the new school. But what was the older school? Who were the living poets of New England, most of whom were destined to fade and vanish within a score of years? Who were those poor "self-deluded" creatures, pictured by the disappointed Dana, "seated, harping, on some weedy knoll, and fancying it the mount of all the

Muses"? Self-deluded or not, their name was legion. The bolder talents, Bryant, Halleck, Willis, had gathered round Washington Irving in New York, but enough remained in New England to constitute a timid air of springtime. Pale, shy little books of poems blossomed on every hand, like the anemones of an April woodland. Connecticut had most to show, for the best-known Boston poet, after Dana, Charles Sprague, author of the "odes," —odes in the marmoreal style, which he produced for every Boston "occasion,"—was a survivor of the days when Pope and Dryden were the reigning writers.[3] Connecticut had its little school, with Lydia Huntley Sigourney at Hartford and James Gates Percival at New Haven. John Quincy Adams, watching the skies, wrote in his Diary: "It would take nine such poets to make a Tate."

In fact, there was not a poet in New England, except perhaps Maria Gowan Brooks, who could have written a stanza of the translation with which the Cambridge professor had shown his mettle. Longfellow, in days to come, might have been thought, by some, tame and faded; but the beautiful tone of the *Coplas of Manrique,* the old Spanish funeral ode,—an act of high talent, if there ever was one,—sounded like full summer, in its music, beside the pallid poems of the thirties. Mrs. Brooks, who had lived in Boston, although she had, decidedly, not been read there, had written with this bell-like depth of tone.[4] It was true that her poem, *Zophiël,* partly composed in Cuba, where, on her coffee-plantation, Mrs. Brooks had built a Grecian temple, over-abounded in the female

---

[3] Sprague had the luck to see one of his odes published in Calcutta, a few years later, with its American names cleverly altered, and afterwards reprinted and praised in London, as the work of a British officer.

[4] So well that Charles Lamb, when Southey showed him a copy of *Zophiël,* said that there had never lived a woman capable of anything so fine.

vein. This lady's personal charms, as the reader gathered, —as the reader, in fact, was virtually told in Mrs. Brooks's story, *Idomen*,—had not been appreciated by her Boston husband, a cold-blooded merchant. She had redoubled the spell, in consequence, ransacking half the libraries of Paris, plunging into the Talmud and a Persian grammar for perfumes, precious stones and passion-flowers, for the irritated comments of monks and saints on the secrets of the toilet, on women's hair, lutes and bridal bowers, serpents and fallen angels. Her notes were an armoury of exotic learning. Her fancy, like a Cuban jungle, rioted with Byron and Thomas Moore. But Mrs. Brooks possessed an energy that triumphed over all these fripperies. The good-hearted Southey, who gave her a lift—and opened himself to the vulgar levity that always pursues relations of sentiment—never wearied of quoting the lines that began, "And as the dove from far Palmyra flying." Of *Egla's Song*, he said again and again that it was "far superior" to Sappho. The poem as a whole had a glow and movement that made it one of the best of a short-lived school, on either side of the ocean. The song was destined for a longer life.

Energy was the one desideratum of all this poetry of the New England thirties. Longfellow's *Coplas* possessed it, Mrs. Brooks's *Egla's Song* possessed it. Where could one find it in the other poets, especially in the other "female poets"? For these were the days of the female poets, that soft and sprightly brood. These were the days of "Peter Parley" Goodrich, the Jack who built the house of the female poets, the Tokens and Ladies' Portfolios, the Souvenirs, Albums, Pearls and Caskets of Gems, a family of magazines more fecund, as one of the critics said, than any of the animal tribes. Connecticut knew them well, the annuals and the female poets, almost as well as New York, better than Boston, the home of Katherine Ware's "Bower of Taste"; for none of the brood mildly raged to the tune of Mrs. Sigourney, whose writings filled fifty-seven volumes. Mrs. Sigourney's little coterie abounded in the balmier mental graces, soft as the breath of gazelles; but among the virtues of their "moral pieces" energy was not preëminent. Mrs. Sigourney's poems, as a critic said, were "more like the dew than the lightning"; and Sarah Edgarton, Hannah Gould, Sarah J. Hale,[5] and Eliza Townsend, shadows and shades of shadows, blossomed in other corners as if to prove that "annuals" were not perennials. Nor was Percival's masculine vigour of a hardier kind. This man of prodigious learning, who versified in thirteen languages and who thought that he might have been happy if he had got a cell in Tasso's mad-house, whose life and personal attributes, like Poe's, fulfilled the romantic pattern, wrote as if to prove another fact, that masculine vigour is not energy. If the pattern, not the poems, made the poet, Percival, like Poe, would have been immortal; but all his vigour ran to commonplace.[6] Fluent commonplace engulfed the rest, John Pierpont,[7] John Neal,[8] who was so desperately anxious to "show" the British. Pierpont's odes

[5] Author of "Mary had a little lamb."

[6] Percival is the classic American example of the almost-good in poetry. A typical "manic-depressive," whose life was a mass of pathetic oddities, he was an admirable geologist and died as State Geologist of Wisconsin. He was one of the most remarkable American philologists of his time, and, as a linguist, a rival of George Borrow and Burritt, the "learned blacksmith." He wrote a report on the Basque tongue and spoke and read Sanskrit, Gaelic and six of the Slavonic languages. He made interesting experiments in Greek and German metres. The small house he built for himself at New Haven had no door or windows at the front.

[7] The grandfather of John Pierpont Morgan, a Connecticut man, a minister in Boston, an admirable reformer, who pawned his family spoons to pay the printer of his well-known *Airs of Palestine*.

[8] The Portland "Down-Easter," John Pierpont's partner for a while in business, a shop-keeper, clerk, teacher of drawing and fencing, auctioneer, merchant, editor, lawyer,—in short, a typical Yankee handy-andy,—a journalist in England, for a time, who tried to show the British what the Americans were made of by

and songs, in the manner of Moore and Campbell,
shouted and stamped by schoolboys,—

> Stand! The ground's your own, my braves!
> Will ye give it up to slaves?—

filled the air at public ceremonies with a sound as of
horns and trumpets. But these poets came and went as
the orators came and went: not one of them left an enduring line.[9] It was their unconsidered dash and go that
carried them all into the void together.

What they needed was not praise, alas, but a more
stringent kind of criticism, a lack which the Boston mind
had begun to repair. They were overpraised, as a rule,
as Poe remarked. Many of them passed through three
editions, and the magazines that published their work
rose like the waves of the sea.[10] The good "Peter Parley"
befriended them all.[11] Pierpont's *Airs of Palestine* had

---

talking about the "charter of greatness" written on their cataracts
and mountains. Neal was a good-hearted soldier of fortune who
"bounded" with the bounding years of Jackson. His once well-
known poem, *Niagara*, was described as a "swash of magnificence."
He wrote many slapdash novels, one of them, *Seventy-Six*, in three
volumes, which he composed in twenty-seven days. His only book
of value, *Wandering Recollections*, contains amusing glimpses of
the American Grub Street of his time, together with a description
of Jeremy Bentham, with whom he lived for three years in London,
1824-1827.

[9] Some of Pierpont's lines lasted as long as the nineteenth century.
There were schoolboys in 1898 who knew *Warren's Address to His
Soldiers at Bunker Hill,* although they never guessed who wrote
the poem.

[10] One student has counted 137 periodicals "of a literary character"
—and he knows of others—established in the United States within
two decades of the War of 1812.—W. B. Cairns, *On the Development
of American Literature from 1815 to 1833.*

[11] "Peter Parley," Samuel Griswold Goodrich, the tireless book-
purveyor, the reformer of juvenile literature, an honest, courageous,
simple-minded man, has left, in his *Recollections of a Lifetime,* the
best account of many of these early minor writers. He was kind
to Percival and Brainard; he published Trumbull's *Poems* and
paid the author $1,000 for them, about the sum of his own ultimate

an honest vogue among the devout. Numberless readers looked for Percival's "P" in the newspapers and magazines. Brainard's *Niagara,* written in twenty minutes, sped through the country. If there was nothing decisive in their work, nothing or so little,—Brainard's *Connecticut River* was a good poem,—what was to blame but a national frame of mind that rather welcomed hasty composition, the strained voice, the high key, the midnight fervours of the adolescent? Even in Boston itself, where the angel of intellect had stirred the waters, criticism was only half awake. One found cases in point on every side, in Cambridgeport, for instance, across the river, where Washington Allston wrote his poems and nursed his dreams of Titian under a cold and distant sky. Allston was idolized as a human being. Everyone loved the silvery old man in the red-lined velvet robe. He was a charming talker, with his great, soft, luminous, dreamy eyes and the white curls that clustered about his neck, so vehement, so gracious, so refined,—for the rest, so well-bred and well-connected. The Boston people liked to stop and see him, in his painting-room at the port, an awkward-looking house with a great north window. They read his poems, they sometimes bought his pictures, usually hanging them in a cramped back-parlour between a

---

loss. While his other books have no intrinsic value, the *Travels, Voyages and Adventures of Gilbert Go-Ahead*—who "wasn't made a Yankee for nothing"—reflects the Connecticut popular mind of the time. The hero, a pedlar of clocks in China, Java, Siam, etc., suggests Mark Twain's "Connecticut Yankee." His adventures enable the author to unfold an "educational" panorama of travel like that of the Rollo Books. In his *Sketches from a Student's Window,* Goodrich enumerates, as the works in demand, in a typical book-store of the eighteen-thirties, *Thaddeus of Warsaw, The Scottish Chiefs,* Young's *Night Thoughts* (of which thirty editions were published, in a generation, in the United States), *Sanford and Merton, Paradise Lost, The Mysteries of Udolpho, Caleb Williams, The Lady of the Lake, Cœlebs in Search of a Wife,* and *The Castle of Otranto,* along with Webster's Spelling-book and a large assortment of hymn-books and Bibles.

deadly cross-fire of lights; they marvelled over the dust on his studio floor, thick as a heavy snow-fall, just as it ought to be in an artist's den. They never came back from Europe without a higher opinion of his genius, they were to lecture about him when he was dead. But anyone might have seen with half an eye that Allston's great talent had run to seed. Cambridge was a depressing place for painters.[12] Even more to the point was the want of criticism, or rather the quality of the criticism, along with various other deprivations. The people who adored poor Allston's genius said that he made his women much too plump. These intimations of carnality disturbed their quiet minds. They did not like their limbs to be flesh and blood, they liked their limbs to be metaphysical, though how one was to be another Titian *without* the carnal reminder,—and they wished to think that Allston was another Titian, they wished to think that Boston had produced the last great man of the Renaissance,—might have puzzled even the metaphysicians. This would have mattered less if Boston had given Allston a few carnal models; but, wherever he turned for a model, he only found another metaphysician. Everyone talked metaphysics, everyone praised the artist because his work was metaphysical,—"etherealized and sublimed by religious fervour." [13] His mind, bathed in the fluid mist, grew thinner and thinner every day.

Allston was the case in point that later generations best remembered. A painter, a man of letters,—a man of energy, beyond a doubt,—he had planted himself at the cross-roads, midway between Boston and Cambridge, where everyone was aware of his existence. Hundreds of young men passed his door, drank the enchantments of his conversation, took him for a symbol. He was the

[12] "Cambridge is like Kaulbach's pictures. It is all literature."— William Morris Hunt.
[13] James Russell Lowell.

"eagle tied to the roost," over whom Horatio Greenough mourned. That he was an eagle no one questioned. The only question was about the roost, and this question loomed as the years advanced. He was a man of high talent. His portrait of Coleridge was enough to prove it, aside from his beautiful drawings. His prestige and his legend were imposing. The first enquiry every foreigner made—unless he asked for Channing—was, Where is Allston's studio? All the friends of his European years, Irving and Fenimore Cooper, Thorwaldsen, Vanderlyn, Leslie, Turner, Coleridge, whom he had known in Rome, —walked with them under the pines of the Villa Borghese, talked out the nights at the Caffè Greco, the haunt of the northern barbarians,—cherished and honoured his name and his work. He had praised the greatness of Turner when everyone in England laughed it down. He had taught Leslie to see Titian's colour, when people laughed at Titian as they laughed at Turner. The traits which the American mind revealed, at the very first encounter, in Allston, as in Bulfinch and Washington Irving, were a congenital sense of style and form, refinement and elevation. But something had gone amiss, the young men gathered. Allston had never ceased to paint and write,—fine sonnets on the old masters, grand letters to his brother-artists. His talk was enough to fire anyone's brain. And yet he had spent twenty long years trying to paint a picture he could not finish, the baleful "Belshazzar's Feast," the nightmare of his life. He had brought the picture back from London, in the far-off days of his youth, thinking it needed only a few touches; and Gilbert Stuart had shown him, all too plainly, that his perspective was not right. He had never outgrown those first misgivings. The picture had been bought in advance, he had mortgaged his life to finish it, and he had grown feeble with his doubts and fears. All the fault of the roost, the young men thought. All Boston's fault. A generation

later, Henry James, puzzling over the unfinished masterpiece, "the mask of some impenetrable inward strain,"
was to draw his own deductions from the painter's nostalgia, "the grim synthetic fact of Cambridgeport." William Wetmore Story drew them first, the young poet, the
sculptor of the future, Justice Story's son, a student of
law in Cambridge, who, as he watched the eagle moult-
ing, made up his own mind to fly to Europe. Allston had
been starved, he wrote in one of his letters,—the rich
and beautiful nature, he in whose veins the South had
run so warm, born to have grown and spread such fragrance. With nothing congenial outside him, he had
been forced to feed upon himself. He had drained his
memory dry.

At Longfellow's very door! Times had changed when
tragedies like this pressed themselves on one's attention.
The younger generation was making demands which the
older generation had never dreamed of. What were the
right conditions for artists and writers? The portrait-
painters, the orators, the historians had had no occasion
to ask such questions. The young republic had given
them their conditions, given them freely and fully, in the
very fact of its existence. It wished for oratory, it wished
for history. The statesmen wished to have their portraits
painted. Oratory, history, portrait-painting were all connected with statesmanship; they had a *raison d'être* in
politics and throve in an age of nation-building. But art
and letters of an absolute kind, the kind that has no
mass-demand behind it, had always given birth to the
subtlest problems, problems of the artist's life, influence,
environment, education. In two thousand years, the human mind had scarcely attacked or begun to solve these
problems; and now they had risen before the American
mind, portentous, all but insoluble, alarming. Young
men who could see that Allston's failure had aspects that
applied to painters only, or workers in the plastic arts,

asked themselves if writers were not involved. For if Allston had gone astray, as the young men saw, how about
the poets?—Allston himself as a poet, Neal, who had scattered his talents beyond redemption, Brainard and Carlos
Wilcox, broken reeds, Percival, the walking suicide, feast-
ing on his Connecticut moonshine, "brooding over the
wrecks of celestial longings"? [14] No doubt, they had
natural disabilities. They were victims of persecution-
mania, Percival, at least, Brainard and Wilcox in a less
degree. Were they not also victims of a social order that
was still too immature for poets? Was not even Dana such
a victim, Allston's brother-in-law and special crony, always announcing projects, even planning the famous
book on Allston, after Allston's death, which, like all his
plans, came to nothing? Dana had lost heart. For years
his mind had been dying of inanition. Were writers and
painters in the same plight? Allston's friends in England
had besought him not to return to America, where there
was no "antagonism of talent" to make him toe the mark;
and what American artist had ever lived, aside from the
portrait-painters, to prove that their advice had been
mistaken? But Bryant, Irving and Cooper seemed to
show that writers were in a different case, with human
nature everywhere to study, with books as aids in the
study of human nature, books, the only instructors in
style and form. The question rested on a few examples.[15]

Great talents largely create their own conditions. At
least, they may be said to crystallize tendencies that exist
in the air about them,—tendencies that have gradually
come to exist,—of which lesser talents have been unaware. Cambridge, like all New England, like New York,
was ready for its poets and its tellers of tales. Cambridge
was ready for literature, and Cambridge men were ready

[14] Preface to Percival's collected poems.
[15] These doubts and dilemmas of the younger generation are indicated in several passages of Emerson's early *Addresses*.

to provide it. The world had flowed their way. Allston's disabilities were as nothing,—the metaphysics and the want of models, the poverty under the pressure of which, he said, his pictures crumbled away,—beside the fact that he had lost the world, his world, the world-current of painters and painting. He had followed the wrong tune, as Stuart might have told him, Stuart who saw the dangers of "elevation" and ridiculed Benjamin West's "tenacre pictures," filled with apostles and prophets. A painter's business, Stuart always said, was to paint what he saw with his eyes and leave the elevation to the poets; and Allston had followed West, against his eyes. No one doubted his elevation. It was his painting that had gone to pieces, and anyone in Paris could have told him why.[16] *There* was the fault of the famous "provincial conditions" of which the future was to hear so much. In painting, Cambridge and Boston were out of the world. In literature, they were in the world, even a little too much, it might have been thought, by those who disliked the world of the thirties and forties. Whether or not one liked this world, the world of Alfred Tennyson and Tegnér, of Lamartine and Ferdinand Freiligrath, was a matter of time and taste. Whether one liked or rejected all its poets was a matter of time and taste. But no one was able to doubt beyond a decade that Cambridge and Boston wrote for the world, or that the world was represented in Cambridge as it was represented in Rome and Oxford.

For Cambridge had ripened, in these few short years, as a well-tended garden ripens in June. All in a mist of

[16] Even Delacroix, who continued to paint historical canvases but who knew that the time for this *genre* had long passed. See his comments on the case of Gros, so strangely parallel to that of Allston. (Delacroix, *Œuvres Littéraires,* II, 195 *et seq.*) Gros, like Benjamin Robert Haydon, the English painter of "ten-acre pictures," tried to carry on the grand style in a world that had ceased to be "grand," and both, in despair, committed suicide.

birds and honeysuckle, the literary mind had put forth
shoots. Thoughts were growing, books were growing under the quiet boughs of the ancient elm-trees, in the fragrant shadows of the locusts, the perfume of the daphne
and the lilac. Robins darted down the leafy paths, orioles
swung on their nests; one heard the murmur of bees and
doves and the bobolink's song in the meadows along the
river. The scent of the syringa filled the air. These were
the scholastic shades that poets had always loved; and
books, whether in verse or prose, were springing from
the Cambridge mind, thick and fast as the grass in
the Cambridge door-yards. The old guard clung to its
chimney-corner. Allston and Dana put their heads together and talked about the Waverley novels. Allston
had written a novel of his own, *Monaldi*, full of Italian
souvenirs,—artists, bravos, convents, jealous husbands,—
with a few charming pages of description. The hero was
a painter, like himself, whose mission was to revive the
grand style, in its Raphaelesque roundness. Allston had
pencilled on his studio-walls various "texts for reflection." [17] At Shady Hill, the redoubtable Andrews Norton rejoiced in his gladiatorial Indian summer, playing
out his game of "evidences," which left him leisure for
a little whist. One saw Dr. Popkin in the square, with
his great caped coat and his ruddy visage, looking like
an eighteenth-century beadle. Dr. Popkin's historic umbrella was a symbol of the old regime, the Harvard whose
severity and simplicity seemed to be rapidly passing.

Everyone in Cambridge appeared to be writing a book.
The Holmeses, the Lowells, the Channings, the Wares,

[17] These sentences were preserved by Anna Jameson, who called
upon Allston in 1838 and copied them, with the painter's permission. Some of them deserve to be remembered, e.g.:

"The most common disguise of envy is in the praise of what is
subordinate."

"Fame . . . is only known to exist by the echo of its footsteps
through congenial minds."

"The only competition worthy of a wise man is with himself."

the Danas were turning into literary families, expanding like rivers as they advanced. Dana's young son, Richard Henry II, who had spent two years before the mast, was assisting Edward Tyrrel Channing as instructor in English. Jared Sparks and his friends of the *North American* trudged back and forth between Cambridge and Boston, with bags under their arms stuffed with papers. Henry Cleveland was editing Sallust and writing a life of Hendrik Hudson. George S. Hillard was editing Spenser, with elaborate annotations. Cornelius Conway Felton, the jolly giant, the new Professor of Greek, who had edited Homer, with Flaxman's line-drawings, was making a translation of Menzel's *History of German Literature*. Felton was one of Longfellow's special friends. Another was Charles Sumner, Hillard's partner, a lecturer at the Law School. The all-attractive Sumner,—the son of the grim old sheriff who hanged his murderers with his own hands "because it was disagreeable,"—dazzled even Boston with his legal learning. Only the other day, on a visit to England, invited to sit with the judges in Westminster Hall, he had settled a point that arose in the course of the trial. The Lord Chief Justice, at a loss for a precedent, had asked him if any American decision bore on the point in question. Sumner had answered that he knew of none, but that the point had been settled in his lordship's court, and he had given the citation. The incident had echoed through the world of lawyers.

With Sumner stretched on the sofa at the Craigie house, reading Politian or Bossuet, the Funeral Orations that he loved,—for Sumner, like Hillard, was an orator, —with Felton to discuss the German poets, with Dr. Beck and Roelker, the young instructors, to sing German songs and share his hock, Longfellow had his Heidelberg in Cambridge. Sometimes, on a sunny morning, Prescott rode up on his horse to the door, handsome, gay, a little over forty, astonished to find himself so famous. Sometimes, Longfellow walked into town, to stop at Ticknor's house or stroll on the Common, lingering on the bridge to talk with Prescott and watch the kelp and the seaweed floating by. But the great event of the week was Saturday evening, when his rooms beheld a gaudy, worthy of a parcel of good-natured monks. Much as the young professor dreamed of Europe,—villas by the margins of lakes, city-casements looking on sun-swept squares, when the perfume, streaming in at his open window, brought Switzerland back, Italy, the Tyrol,—his mind rode quietly at anchor. He had his own name for the malcontents who, having tasted the old world, talked of nothing else. They were Frondeurs, difficult as the Fronde of Louis XIV. Even while he shared their homesick feelings, he was immune to the virus. He had a shield and buckler in the doctrine that Europe itself had taught him: a poet was the poet of his country. It was easy to believe in this pleasant Cambridge, with the city across the bridge and the village about him, tokens of Europe on every hand, ample chambers, filled with books and pictures, with all the sights and sounds of the young republic, the cheerful hammer and the hopeful saw, a population that was up and doing. And when a poet had friends like Samuel Ward, his old Heidelberg crony, who greeted him with a German kiss,—for Cambridge was losing its rigours,— drew a bottle from each of his pockets, gave him all the gossip of New York and carried off his poems to Fitz-Greene Halleck, who liked to see him "resplendently coruscate" in Park Benjamin's paper, how could he not rejoice in his native land? His native land rejoiced in him, and, if it liked his poems all the more, the more they suggested Europe, that was the most "native" thing about it. "Europeans" never thought of "Europe." And anyone could see that Longfellow's poems, whatever their subjects were, expressed the young American state of mind.

For softly, without effort, as he sat in the vast shadow at his open window, the poems rose in his mind, like exhalations,—*Voices of the Night*. The black hulks of the trees rode at their moorings on the billowy sea of grass. The stars glistened through the heaving branches, the silver Charles gleamed across the meadow. Stanza by stanza, the poems came, sometimes all at once, songs, reveries, echoes of German verses, mingling with the whispers of the summer wind,—youthful regrets, youthful aspirations, psalms of a life which, on such an evening, might well appear a dream, though far from empty: *Footsteps of Angels, The Light of Stars, The Reaper and the Flowers, Hymn to the Night*. On these very evenings, at their open windows, thousands of young men in Hollis Hall, at Bowdoin, Yale, Princeton, in Cincinnati, up and down the Hudson and the Mississippi, in England, Scotland, Holland, in far-off Russia, beside the Neva as beside the Danube, heard the trailing garments of the night, shared these reveries of the New England springtime that Longfellow was putting into words, with such a lucid, natural, velvety sweetness,—verses drifting through the poet's mind as the yellow leaves drift from the trees in autumn and silently fall to the ground.

In later days, when other fashions came, when the great wheel of time had passed beyond them, one saw these poems in another light. They seemed to lack finality and distinction, whether in thought or phrase. But no one could quite forget their dreamy music, their shadowy languor, their melodious charm, their burden of youthful nostalgia; and the world of the Age of Revolutions, which knew the Romantic poets, shared this poet's mood of exaltation. A day was to come when a Chinese mandarin transcribed *The Psalm of Life* on an ivory fan, and a dying soldier at Sebastopol repeated the stirring lines. When *Excelsior* appeared in a German version, the students of Innsbruck, meeting the translator, thronged

about him and embraced and kissed him, with such joy
and transport, as he said, that he always looked upon
that moment as the happiest of his life. These were the
days when to be "up and doing, with a heart for
any fate," seemed, after the drought of Calvinism, the
drought of monarchism and reaction, in the continental
Europe of '48, when people had thought they were pow-
erless, a miracle and a sudden inspiration; and Longfellow spoke for the youth of all the world. He spoke for
the young in his verses, even in his prose *Hyperion,* the
romance of the American student who looked like Har-
old the Fair-hair and bore the name of an old German
poet. This was his own romance, more or less, in the
high-flown style of Jean Paul Richter. Many and many a
reader, as the years went by, readers in English, Swedish,
Dutch and French, followed in the footsteps of the hero,
sought out the inns where Paul had slept, the Star at
Salzig, the White Horse at Bingen, turned aside for a
Sunday at St. Gilgen, lingered, book in hand, under the
lindens and wept over the night at Heidelberg when the
lovely star, Elizabeth, fell from heaven.

Such were the "voices of the night." The voices of the
day were firmer and clearer. On these summer mornings
at the Craigie house, when the birds were carolling in the
trees, when insects chirped in the grass and the sunlight
and the perfume of the flowers poured through his open
windows, Longfellow's mind went back to Sweden, to the
still Scandinavian woodlands, carpeted with blossoms at
this balmy season, where, in a simple, primeval world,
like that of his own Maine, the leaves and ribbons
streamed from the lofty May-poles, and the old pagan
gods awoke once more, and one heard the hammers of
the Vikings, so like the hammers that one heard in Portland, building their oak-ribbed ships. That was his great
discovery, after all, that was the brightest feather in his
cap: other American writers and scholars were rediscov-

ering Italy and Spain, recapturing France and Germany. He was the first who had visited, amply, at least, with a living imagination, the lands of the skalds and the sagas, where one found traces of one's forbears, in the days of the Danish invasions, forests like one's own New England forests, builders of boats with masts of the lordly pine, the Baltic dashing on the northern strand, desolate as one's own North Shore, village ways like the New England ways, houses of hewn timber, white-painted churches, maidens with flaxen hair, brown ale worthy of King Olaf, apples such as a village blacksmith loved, poets, too, like the mad Esaias, scarcely concealing under his bishop's gown the robe of the chanting gleeman, chanting now not the deeds of blood but the wild freedom of the days of old. There, in those northern lands, the ballad, like the ancient yeoman's life,—the life that was fit for free men and simple, fishermen, farmers, sailors, fit for Nantucket men and Portland men, as for the men of Gottland and Malmö,—there the epic and the story-poem still played living parts in human lives, not as mere survivals and revivals, as they were in the rest of Europe. One of the best of Longfellow's translations,— perhaps, like that of the Spanish funeral hymn, it could not have been better,—was *The Children of the Lord's Supper,* in which Tegnér had revived for Swedish ears, as Goethe had revived it for German ears, in *Hermann und Dorothea,* the metre that Homer had used and Longfellow was to use in *Evangeline.* He had passed into this northern mind by such a line of sympathy that the old poet-bishop found his versions of *Frithiof's Saga* the only ones that fully satisfied him.

In Sweden, or in Scandinavia,—for he found in the Finnish *Kalevala* the form he was to use in *Hiawatha,*— he had gone to school to better purpose than elsewhere in his multi-coloured Europe. Before his eyes waved, and were to wave, the mingled shapes and figures of the past, the myths and scenes of European legend, like a faded tapestry, faded then, how much more faded later. The Scandinavian world had given him something far more vital, rhythms that signified a secret kinship, deeper than a student's acquisitions, between the pastoral children of the Vikings and the child of Maine for whom the sea and the forest possessed an unfailing magic. The Scandinavians had given him a feeling for the value of the forms, —the ballad, the folk-poem, the epic fragment, vehicles of the national sentiment that had come to life in America, as it had come to a second life in the North,— through which his mind was to flow with its greatest vigour. All his evocations of feudal Europe, of the mediæval world that haunted him, of the biblical world and the world of the Renaissance, what were they ever to mean, —these incidents of an endless panorama, which the patient and facile showman unrolled for a generation before the eyes of his enraptured public, a panorama of Athens, such as they had set up in Cambridge, extended over the history of the world's culture,—beside a handful of ballads and two or three narrative poems, redolent of the vast American woodlands, the prairies, the prodigious Mississippi, the sylvan solitudes of Canada, the gusty New England sea-coast, poems fragrant still with hemlock, fir and balsam, the salt breeze of the rocky shore, the wild-brier, the rose and the syringa, breathing a tonic piety, as of paternal altars and forest gods?

Such were the voices of the day, which the poet heard, with a soft excitement, as he took his morning walk at sunrise, or, when evening came, lighted the long candles on his upright desk.

CHAPTER IX

THE YOUNGER GENERATION OF 1840

THESE WERE the days of the "march of intellect." The movement started in England by Lord Brougham "to promote useful knowledge" found the tracks laid for it in Boston. In a comedy produced at the Tremont Theatre, Master Burke, the "Irish Roscius," played the part of a professor who taught every subject known to man. The comedy was meant to satirize the much-talked-of march of intellect, and the Boston people saw the point and smiled. But, if their hearts had been opened, there would have been found, engraved within, the talisman Education. Education was the word in Boston, as a generation later the word was Culture.[1]

Whatever could be done by education, Boston proposed to do; for this was the age of "internal development," mental as well as commercial. The merchants had largely relinquished the maritime commerce that had created so much of the city's wealth and turned their energies to manufacture; and the effort of the Southern and Western magnates to build up what they called the "American system," at the expense of New England, drove the Boston mind all the harder. The wheels of the cotton-factories revolved at a furious pace, and the Southern slave-drivers plied their whips to feed the Yankee mills with Southern cotton. The more the prosperity

[1] "We are all becoming cultivated up to the eyes . . . *tiers état* and all. A daughter of an old servant of ours, whose father is an Irish bogtrotter that works on the roads, told me yesterday, 'she had nearly completed her English education, was very well in her French, and should only give one quarter more to her music and drawing.' "—From a letter of Prescott, 1840.

of New England came to depend on cotton, the closer the propertied classes drew to the Southern planters, with whom they felt obliged to ally themselves, yielding to them in all political matters. At the same time, to compete with the South and the West, they developed a system of closer communication between the capital and the hinterland. A network of railroads spread over New England, binding the six States together.[2]

This material growth was reproduced in the intellectual sphere. The rise of the Lyceum lecturing system, in 1826,—the work of the enthusiast, Josiah Holbrook, who went about the country lecturing on geology and natural history, urging the villages to form collections,—was only one of the educational movements that brought Boston and the rural centres into closer touch with one another. Webster, Edward Everett and Nathan Hale established the Useful Knowledge Society. Various other institutions followed. The Natural History Society, the Mercantile Library Association, the Mechanics' Apprentices' Association, the Lowell Institute diffused their currents of intellectual impulse. New England soon acquired the lecture-habit, the fruit of Edward Everett's enterprise, for Everett's public lectures on Greek antiquities were the first of their kind in America. There were constant courses in every town and village,—where Rollo and Lucy sat at the feet of Jonas,—on chemistry, botany, history, on literature and philosophy; and almost every eminent man in New England joined in the general effort to propagate knowledge.[3] A season-ticket for a course, ten to fifteen lectures, usually cost two dollars. In Boston,

[2] This development came quite suddenly. About 1831, Nathan Hale, the father of Edward Everett Hale, was considered a fanatic as a railroad-prophet. He suggested in a speech at Faneuil Hall that, if people could come from Springfield to Boston in five hours, an average of nine people would come every day. This was regarded as a preposterous statement.

[3] It was a practice of Dr. Holmes, after an evening lecture, to write a poem that was suggested by it.

all the boys and girls went to the Lowell lectures. As many as five hundred at a time learned that acids were not alkalis and that Homer did not write the Iliad.[4] It was quite the rage. The boys invited the girls, and after the lecture they walked home together, ending the evening with an oyster-supper.

Boston, all New England respected learning. No New England boy was allowed to question that he was destined to succeed in life, provided he knew enough; and Boston was determined that the boys and girls, and the blind and insane as well, should have an opportunity to know enough,—schools based on the best current theories, reform-schools that really worked reform, schools for the blind that caused the blind to see. Was not Dr. Howe's famous pupil, the blind, deaf and dumb Laura Bridgman, a proof that education was the mother of wonders? Boston had taken Channing at his word and really believed in perfectibility. It was true that at first the Boston pedagogues resented the assaults of Horace Mann, who had no use for their old-fashioned ways. But no one could resist this human cyclone, the tall, humourless man in the long frock-coat, so anxious, so exacting, so dogmatic, with the will of a battering-ram, who founded the State Board of Education in 1837. Having closed his law-office with the reflection, "Let the next generation be my client," Horace Mann found Boston thoroughly roused to a sense of the vital importance of public instruction. But what could be done with the country common schools, the merest "dormitories," as he called them, at least in comparison with the Scottish schools, which he had visited on a tour of study? The administrative features of the Prussian system seemed to

---

[4] The "Wolfian theory," long since exploded. "Poor old Homer was relegated to the world of myth. As a schoolboy, I used to hear the belief in the existence of such a poet derided as 'uncritical' and 'unscholarly.' "—John Fiske, *A Century of Science.*

him the best, and he adopted them largely, much as he detested, in the Prussians, the "blind acquiescence" that enslaved the mind. For eleven years he travelled night and day, stopping in every hamlet in Massachusetts, forming conventions of teachers and school-committees. To make an impression on Berkshire County, he said, was like battering down Gibraltar with one's fist, and the Cape Cod mind was solid sand. Nothing new would grow there. But he knew how to deal with sand and granite, having so much of both in his own composition. He counted on the instinct of a people who thought there was nothing odd in asking a stranger if he was "learned in roses."

A Boston man had to be learned in something, and the passion for learning on the upper levels soon spread through all the other strata. Harvard set the pace. Thomas Wentworth Higginson was not unique as one who, at the time of his graduation, read French, Spanish, Italian, Latin and Greek, who later acquired German and Portuguese, Hebrew, a little Swedish, and always hoped for a chance to study Russian. Theodore Parker, the minister, somewhat older, the Roxbury Friar Tuck, the Lexington farmer's son who was able to carry a full barrel of cider, read Dutch, Danish and Russian, along with the others, Coptic, Chaldaic, Arabic, Ethiopic, and was found by one of his friends deep in a grammar of Mpongwe.[5] Here and there, some workman followed suit. Elihu Burritt of Worcester, the "learned black-

[5] Theodore Parker's learning was famous in New England. T. W. Higginson related that he wished to find a certain reference in the Salic, Burgundian and Ripuarian codes before the codification of Charlemagne. Neither Sumner, Justice Gray nor Chief Justice Shaw could assist him on this occasion, but Sumner said, "Try Parker." Parker said at once, "Go to the Harvard Library, and on the fifth shelf in the fourth left-hand alcove you will find a small, thick quarto entitled 'Potgeiser: de Statu Servorum,' which will give you all the information you want." Higginson found his question answered there.—Chadwick, *Theodore Parker.*

smith," was a typical figure of the moment. This well-known self-taught linguist who, as an apprentice, had kept a Greek grammar in the crown of his hat to study while he was casting brass cow-bells, who made a version of Longfellow in Sanskrit and mastered more than forty other tongues, toiling at the forge or in the evening, after a full day's work, affected no singularity, as he said. His aim was "to stand in the ranks of the workingmen of New England and beckon them onward and upward to the full stature of intellectual men." The noble-hearted Burritt[6] was not the only man of his kind. Many a boy walked thirty miles to Cambridge to feast his eyes on the sight of the college; and many a farmer's son, like Burritt, might have walked to Boston, a hundred and twenty miles, from New Britain, with two or three dollars and a silver watch tucked away in a handkerchief, hoping to catch a ship for India, where he could study Sanskrit. Sir Charles Lyell and Agassiz were surprised, when they arrived in Boston in the forties, by the universal interest in education. Lyell had never seen such crowds of workmen listening on winter nights to learned lectures on geology and zoology, Shakespeare and Milton. Agassiz was present at an assembly of three thousand mechanics, brought together to form a library and listening for two hours with rapt attention to a lecture on the advantages of reading. Dickens was impressed by the interests of the factory-girls of Lowell, a public that he knew so well in England. There were joint-stock pianos in their boarding-houses; the walls of the mills were covered with their

[3] A passage from Elihu Burritt's diary, 1837: "*Monday,* June 18, headache; forty pages Cuvier's Theory of the Earth, sixty-four pages French, eleven hours forging. *Tuesday,* sixty-five lines of Hebrew, thirty pages of French, ten pages Cuvier's Theory, eight lines Syriac, ten ditto Danish, ten ditto Bohemian, nine ditto Polish, fifteen names of stars, ten hours forging. *Wednesday,* twenty-five lines Hebrew, fifty pages of astronomy, eleven hours forging. *Thursday,* fifty-five lines Hebrew, eight ditto Syriac, eleven hours forging. *Friday,* unwell, twelve hours forging," etc.

poems; they subscribed to the British reviews; they had classes in German; they all seemed to know *Paradise Lost* by heart and talked about Wordsworth, Coleridge and Macaulay in the intervals of changing bobbins on the looms. Flocks of these serious girls, described by Lucy Larcom in her *Idyl of Work,* afterwards went West as school-teachers and founded "Improvement Circles" on the prairies. The fame of the *Lowell Offering,* which contained their writings,—humorous and pathetic tales, fairy-stories, poems,—travelled round the world. A volume of selections, *Mind Among the Spindles,* was later published in London, and lectures were given at the Sorbonne on this portent of the times.[7]

In Cambridge, nobody was surprised to hear that the youthful Dana,—before the mast,—had kept his crew of sailors from going ashore, on the California coast, by reading aloud all day from Scott's *Woodstock.* Rough as the sailors were, most of them were Massachusetts sailors, and everyone took it for granted that in Massachusetts reading had a sovereign right of way. At Harvard, the young men read too much, or so it seemed to those who had frugal minds. They were hatching very strange ideas. They sat at their open windows on New Year's Eve and spouted the *Midnight Mass for the Dying Year.* Thomas Wentworth Higginson, the bursar's son, took a vow of poverty: he spoke of putting himself on equal terms with the vast army of the hand-workers. Marston Watson talked of raising pears, a better occupation than raising dollars. George P. Bradford, a brilliant scholar, a descendant of Governor Bradford, was bent on setting up a market-garden and trundling his own wheel-barrow

[7] These lectures were given by Philarète Chasles. Recent writers on the Lowell mill-girls, tending to slight their accomplishments, dwell solely on the pitifulness of their wages. Their wages were pitiful indeed,—about three dollars a week. It is to be noted, however, that these wages were more than three times higher than the average corresponding wages in Europe.

through the streets. William Ellery Channing, the doctor's nephew and namesake, refused to go to chapel. Determined to be a poet at any price, he absconded from college with his clothes and took refuge in a lonely farmhouse. All these notions were very disturbing. The young men said that terrestrial love was only a reflection of celestial love. They spoke of "bathing in a sea of thought." They went off mooning in the woods. They refused to talk about railroads, banks and cotton. They had no use for Blackstone and Justice Story. They were unwilling to be "mere" lawyers,—heaven save the codfish in the State House! They laughed when their fathers quoted Dr. Johnson. They smiled when their uncles quoted Burke, who had become a very old story. Goldsmith and Pope, to them, were as flat as stale beer. They spoke of the president of the college as President Littlego of Triflecut and referred to Cambridge as "Doughnut." They sneered at Doctor Phosphorus and Lawyer Smealmin and Swippens's Wholesale Grocery concern. They remarked that "the great art of being a merchant is to look wise and ride in a carriage." [8] Poetry was the only life for them, or painting, or contemplation, if they had to starve in a garret or a hut. And if all this was not the result of reading, where, pray, had they acquired their notions? The mothers and aunts and cousins of young New England,—not to speak of the fathers, who carried on the wholesale grocery business, the cotton-factory and the firm in State Street,—were filled with alarm and dismay.

Not that the fathers and mothers and aunts and cousins were opposed to books and reading. Some of the Boston merchants were authors themselves.[9] The solid men believed in education. They heartily favoured the great

[8] See W. Ellery Channing, *The Youth of the Poet and the Painter*, in *The Dial*.

[9] See Nathan Appleton on *Original Sin*, and the miscellaneous writings of Thomas Handasyd Perkins, Abbott Lawrence, William Sturgis, Robert Bennet Forbes, etc.

educational movement. It fitted the young men, their
sons and nephews, not to forget the meritorious poor, to
make the most of all the dazzling chances, legal, tech-
nological, commercial, which the expanding republic
offered them. But books of a new kind had begun to
appear, French and especially German books, even books
by Englishmen and Scotchmen, who should have known
better, filled with the wildest sort of metaphysics. These
were the books that addled the minds of their sons,
as Everett and Ticknor quite agreed,—for Everett and
Ticknor, who knew the Germans, shared the opinions
of the men of State Street regarding all these "follies
of form and style." [10] The young men who read the
new writers,—Thomas Carlyle, George Sand, Jean Paul,
Schleiermacher,—saw the matter in another light. If they
were drawn to these writers, who spoke of the inner life,
it was because the outer world repelled them. They could
not share the current of ambition that galvanized the
tougher-minded spirits,—the "forth-putting" types, as
they said in New England, those that had "faculty," those
that knew how to "take hold." What if trade and politics
were advancing? Even if they had cared for politics, was
it not evident that, with Jacksonism, the noble type of
the trained statesman had yielded to the tricky politician?
Politics had certainly lost the glamour which the great
age of the statesmen had given it.[11] And commerce, too,

[10] The *North American* group as a whole was invincibly opposed
to the new school, the Transcendentalists and all their works. See
Prescott's remarks on Carlyle's *French Revolution*,—"a shower of
twaddle . . . new-fangled words . . . ridiculous affectations . . . perfectly contemptible . . . both as to *forme* and to *fond*."—Ticknor's
Life of Prescott.

[11] This was the standing complaint of Henry Adams, a generation
later. Many fine minds anticipated Adams. Josiah Quincy wrote in
1834 that the new race of politicians "steer the ship of state by the
winds of popular favour, before which they run, which they never
seek to stem, which they dare not resist."—Edmund Quincy's *Life
of Josiah Quincy*.

The *Letters of Major Jack Downing*, popular in the thirties and

had lost its grand role. The old China trade was a statesman's business. The factory was dull and small beside it.
And who could ignore the abuses of modern business?—
the fraud and perjury at the custom-house, the bribing
of foreign officials, the sweating of the workers in the
mills, the hideous oppression of the sailors? Worst of all,
slavery. Was not half the wealth of the Northern mills
drawn from the whips of the Southern overseers? Was
it not true that in Cuba one slave out of every ten died
every year in order to give the Americans their sugar?
The ways of trade were unfit for a chivalrous man, unless he could reverse the whole system.

In short, the more sensitive minds of the younger
generation, the imaginative, the impressionable, the perceptive, those who characterize a generation,—for the
practical people never change, except in the cut of their
clothes,—were thoroughly disaffected. The shape of the
outward world had ceased to please them. The Fourth
of July orations had ceased to convince them that "freedom" had any connection with freedom of mind or that
"liberality" in religion had any connection with religious
feeling. The aristocrats of trade were essentially vulgar,
the "rational" Unitarians were materialistic. The young
people were radicals and mystics. They had no interest
in size, numbers and dollars. They had begun to explore
the inner life, the depths of thought and sentiment.
They had returned, on another level, to the mental habits of their Pilgrim forbears. Those who were socially-
minded allied themselves with the various cults and
movements that were breaking out all over the country,
the temperance and non-resistance societies, the vegetarian movement, the no-money movement, the Abolition
movement, which was rapidly rising, the Socialist move-

forties, added to the general disillusion. That American politics had
returned to the Stone Age was a very natural deduction from this
picture of Jackson's "husking frolic" around the Washington "crib."

ment, which had come to stay. The Chardon Street Convention gave them a platform.[12] They sympathized with "Wandering Jew" Taylor, who roamed about the roads and country lanes and whom one saw, at street-corners in Boston, standing, bare-headed, offering prayers for the city. They sympathized with old Father Lamson, with his long beard and white habiliments. They sympathized even with Abby Folsom, the well-known "flea of conventions," who ended each remark with the shrill refrain, "It's the capitalists!" Those whom a dream had possessed!—mad, no doubt, but God-intoxicated. The young people whose interests were social wished to "do good," they wished to be "of use,"—like the young people in Germany and Russia, in England, Italy, Hungary and France. For in these late thirties and early forties, at Harvard, as at Oxford, as at Warsaw, at Heidelberg, Toulouse and Salamanca, the young people spoke the same language. And not at Harvard only. At Yale, Princeton, Williams, in New York, they grieved over the sorrowful disproportion between their faculties and the importunate work which the state of the world so patently placed before them.

For, whether their minds were social or poetic, they all agreed regarding the state of the world. It was a cold, unfeeling civilization, bred by commercial interests and isolation, a negative moderation, an excess of prudence, compromise, provincial good taste. It cast a censorious eye on human nature, on all the free flights of the picturesque, the goodly growths of fancy. It offered employment to no one but the decorous and the complacent. It was timid, imitative, tame; worse, it was mean and cruel.

[12] The Convention of Friends of Universal Reform, 1840. The Chardon Street Chapel, the haunt of the reformers, was remodelled from the Parkman family's barn. Dr. Parkman, Francis Parkman's father, who did not like reformers,—although, as one of his eulogists said, he was "particularly kind to the unattractive,"—always referred to the chapel as "my mother's barn."

It taught the mind of the young to aim at low objects,
—and never had the young been so unsubmissive. They
did not care a button for common sense. They were
bored by the ideal of the marble statue as a pattern of
social behaviour. They did not wish to "get," they wished
to "have." They did not wish to "do," they wished to
"be." As one of them said, in a burst that amused their
elders,

> Greatly to Be
> Is enough for me,
> Is enough for thee.

To reaffirm the senses and the soul. To exist, expand,
feel, to possess their own uniqueness.[13] To have, when
it came to "having," a flute, perhaps, a little telescope
with which to study the tree-tops from Wachusett, a book
of Tennyson's poems to sing and recite on long walks
over the Andover hills. For Tennyson had just appeared
in Boston, a little later than Keats, who represented the
purest cult of beauty. If one parted one's hair in the middle and let the locks flow down over one's shoulders, if
one wore a blouse or a frock on fitting occasions, one
could forget, at least for a day or two, the brutal, monk-
ish regimen of the college.

Here was a "newness" for the New England fathers.
They had known ten younger generations who had accepted without sighs or murmurs the yoke of the farm
and the counting-house and gladly sought the pulpit and
the Senate. All of them had been stable and well-teth-
ered. These boys and girls of the new age were as distinct
from their predecessors as young Italians were from the
people of Iceland. They had a mania for the "natural."
They detested conventional ways. They chose to wander

[13] "I want my place, my own place, my true place in the world,
my proper sphere, my thing which Nature intended me to perform
when she fashioned me thus awry, and which I have vainly sought
all my life-time."—Hawthorne, *The Intelligence-Office.*

alone, like so many madmen. Stearns Wheeler, a tutor in Greek at Harvard, built a hut in the woods and went to live there. Two young clerks in Boston counting-houses also spent a winter in the woods, reading and writing in their cabin, in imminent peril of an Arctic death. Jones Very, the poet, another Greek tutor, the son of a Salem skipper, lost his mind for a time and had to be placed in the McLean Asylum. A few fled frantically to Europe, where they could lose for a while their sense of oppression. Others committed suicide. Young women indulged in fantasies, one of them about a *femme fatale* who ran through the woods half-naked, bathed under the moon in icy pools, enticing men in order to repel them. The *mal du siècle* was in full career, although it usually assumed the most innocent forms. A "band" of aesthetic youths and maidens gathered in Cambridge and Watertown. They read Keats and Tennyson together, copied their own poems in manuscript-books, which they passed from hand to hand, and talked about women's rights and socialism. The girls composed flower-pieces and painted in water-colours. The young men read Saint Augustine and Plato, traversed the cycle of religious faiths and thought they would like to join the Catholic Church; and, between a winter in Rome and a summer in Paris, they echoed the Plymouth tutor, Robert Bartlett, who said that they should make their own country "classic to themselves": the American mind should cease to replenish itself with the mighty wonders of Europe and find its fire within. When they could not meet, they corresponded, enclosing an anemone or a mallow-blossom. How swiftly, like magic, the spring was advancing!—every dry twig bursting forth, covering itself with beauty. Why should not the dry hearts of men burst forth in a similar way? Some new and hidden fount of life was about to revivify existence. The young girls read the young men's characters by holding the young men's

letters against their foreheads,—with a certain bashful-
ness, however, a certain indirectness, as if they were
ashamed to confess that they were interested in these
mundane matters. They marvelled over their sensibility.
One of them read character by the form of the letters, another by the merest "contact with a person." They made
all sorts of discoveries, as that sometimes words came
into one's mind that had a deep meaning for oneself,
although they conveyed nothing to anyone else. Their
thoughts seemed to come too fast for expression. They
asked one another questions: "Has your impressibility
returned?"—with a sort of breathless virginality, as if
they were on the brink of some great secret. The strange,
dire planet called Human Nature, hitherto so dark and
almost baleful, had swum into their ken. It seemed to
portend an age of novel-writing.

In Boston, these new feelings had a focus in the various institutions of art and music that were appearing now
on every hand. The C-Minor Symphony of Beethoven
was played in the Odeon in 1840, a flowering of the Handel and Haydn Society, which had put to rout the old
psalms and glee-tunes. The young men walked in from
Cambridge, in parties of three or four, deliciously
thrilled by the darkness of the road and the chance of
meeting a footpad. The Athenæum displayed its collection of casts, the gift of Colonel Perkins, the Brimmer
collection of Italian drawings, collections of gems and
engravings, Stuart's florid merchants, Allston's dreamy
women, Copley's grim ladies, clad in satin, landscapes by
Cole and West, an Annibale Caracci, a Murillo, a few
half-fabulous Raphaels and Luinis. The galleries became
a rendezvous, where art and love blossomed under the
skylights. One could almost feel, in the tranquil air, that
one had embarked for Italy, with a best-beloved companion. Sometimes in a single day a little group of youthful
amateurs enjoyed a double wonder, a glimpse of "Bel-

shazzar's Feast" and an hour of Mozart. Sometimes they met at the rooms of the *cognoscente* who had upon his door a blazing sun, with gilded rays running in all directions, bearing the motto, "Universal Unity,"—for the young man was a Fourierist,—and underneath the black-and-white inscription, to bring one's mind back to Massachusetts, "Please wipe your feet." Sometimes they found aid and comfort at Dr. Channing's "Club of the Jacobins," in Jonathan Phillips's rooms at the Tremont House, where the two old friends liked nothing better than to greet a Harvard man who was not "indifferent." Or they spent an afternoon of early summer on the spreading lawns of one of the Brookline merchants, with music and a game of battledore, a punch-bowl and a bowl of plum-like cherries, a Reynolds and a Ruysdael to look at, and possibly Prescott in the middle distance, or Daniel Webster sitting under an elm-tree. At night, beside their argand lamps, they pored over albums of engravings, Piranesi, Raphael Morghen, discussed the German poets and read the springtide writers, Chaucer, Boccaccio, Dante. They talked about spiritualism and mesmerism, phrenology and animal magnetism, all the dark problems of the human mind over which the sun of hope seemed to be rising.

Across the hinterland, through the rural centres, the new mood spread like the flowers of May. One heard the flute in the fields. Farmers and village tailors stopped to watch the birds building their nests. They went on woodland walks. They recorded the days when the wild-flowers opened. They observed the little tragedies of nature that no one had noticed before, a cat springing on an oriole and marching proudly off with her golden booty projecting in all directions from her mouth. They gathered the first hepaticas, the trailing arbutus that had bled unseen under the boots of their fathers. In hundreds of hamlets the neighbours assembled awe-struck while the night-blooming cereus opened its petals, standing hushed in the presence of the marvel, as the connoisseurs of Florence had stood in the presence of a new Botticelli. It filled them with romantic associations to think of these splendid flowers opening in the night of the Mexican jungle, where there were no eyes to look at them but the agate eyes of lizards and serpents. The cereus was their Boston Athenæum, and all the airs of Mozart sang in its petals; and the young men and women, like those of Boston, graduates of the female seminaries, of Middlebury College, Dartmouth, Williams,—where Mark Hopkins sat on the end of his log,—also wrote their poems and their meditations. It was true that the country ministers still preached on the Dangers of Beauty. Hiram Powers, the sculptor of the future, attracted crowds with the panorama of hell which he exhibited in the villages, an orgy of sulphuric flames, the livid faces of children and devils with pitchforks,—a sermon such as one might have heard in Rome. The old faith survived in force, and here and there some youthful minister, seduced by the Boston Unitarians, felt like a Hindu who has lost his caste and moaned through his house, "Oh, where shall rest be found?" He found his rest by "aiming at the stars" or writing a parable about the boy who climbed the Natural Bridge. For the old faith, like the new, contributed to the mood of exaltation. Life ought to be consecration, labour, worship! All the young aspired who had read *The Psalm of Life* and knew the meaning of the "strange device" that Longfellow might have invented for Ibsen's Brand.

Poetry spread like fox-fire through the woodlands. Every village had its Gifted Hopkins, author of *To Myrtle Awaking* and *To Myrtle Retiring* or *Contemplations in Autumn,* after Pollok. Many a village had its youthful sculptor, who modelled figures of "Innocence" in snow, and a Pantasophian Society that served as a medium of exchange for minds that would otherwise have blushed unseen. Over his native Connecticut hills and meadows scudded the haggard Percival, the poet, with a wild glitter in his eye, startled at the approach of a fellow-creature, wrapping his rusty camlet cloak about him, silent, never smiling, the "old rock-smasher," as he was called by the farmers; for the poor rhymester-vagrant, with his sinister air, had taken to studying minerals and was to do in geology, in the end, what he had failed to do in poetry. Other and younger poets, destined for a happier flowering, or a happier life, at least, dreamed under the stars, perhaps in a hammock, swung between two elm-trees,—a boy who longed to be a Marcus Curtius and leap into a gulf to save his country, a girl, born in India, on a voyage, in the midst of tropical scenes that returned to her with the breeze of her sandalwood fan. They were to have their say, they were to have their hour at the Tourney of Poets, when New England began to reveal its "portfolio" writings, the Thoughts on Art and Thoughts on the Scholar's Calling, the Musings of a Recluse, the "rapture-feelings" that were to fill *The Dial*. Here and there, a judge or a factory-owner, the great man of the village, touched by the note of a beauty-loving day,—a little confused as regards the fundamentals, though not more confused than the city-people,—built the Greek temple with the green shutters that was to be known as the "house on the hill."

For this was still the day of the Greek revival. Grecian dwellings rose on every Main Street, Parthenons of painted wood, churches and banks vaguely suggesting Athens, with variations in the Egyptian vein. Everett's lectures had borne fruit at Harvard, Byron had contributed a strain. The Greek struggle for independence had caught the imagination of the people, and Dr. Howe's romantic adventures in Greece,—whence he had returned with Byron's helmet,—appealed to the general

mind.[14] The casts in the Athenæum played their part;
so did the writings of Walter Savage Landor. A school
of American sculptors had appeared and found a home
at Florence, where they carried on the tradition of
Canova: Horatio Greenough, who, as a boy, had learned
to cut his chalk in the Athenæum, soon to be followed by
Thomas Crawford, the carver of mantel-pieces in New
York, and Powers, who came from Vermont, where the
ridges of the hills were of solid marble and marble pig-
sties rose on lonely farms. The children, brought up on
Flaxman's outlines, knew their mythology as they knew
the Bible; they were prepared for Emerson's Platonism
and the *Wonder-book* and *Tanglewood Tales* of Hawthorne. Everyone talked mythology, as everyone had begun to discuss the history of religion; and the best New
England novels, at the turn of the forties, those of William Ware, *Zenobia, Probus, Julian, or Scenes in Judea,*
presupposed a feeling for ancient Greece, as they also
took for granted a circle of readers who were steeped
in the Bible and the Latin authors. Classical stories ran
side by side with the realistic stories of New England life
that Catherine M. Sedgwick was writing at Stockbridge,
Hope Leslie, Redwood, A New England Tale, truthful,
simple, sometimes too-too simple, after the fashion of
Maria Edgeworth, in praise of the duties of home and
the virtuous poor. Miss Sedgwick was a highly intelligent
woman, a friend and correspondent of Sismondi; she was
cultivated, bountiful and good, and her household was
the centre of the Berkshires. The naturalness of her style
was a kind of triumph, and she prepared the way for the
writers who followed by stimulating the interest of her
readers in their own landscape and manners; but no one
could have supposed that her work would live. Her fel-
low-philanthropist, Lydia Maria Child, the editor of a

[14] See *Historical Sketch of the Greek Revolution,* by Samuel Grid-
ley Howe, 1828, a vigorous and memorable book.

magazine for children, the author of a novel of Puritan times, of the first important anti-slavery book, of *The Progress of Religious Ideas,* of lives of Madame de Staël and Madame Roland, produced a classical novel among the rest. *Philothea* followed *The Frugal Housewife,* a feminine *Poor Richard's Almanac,* a treasury of New England household lore that showed, with an abundance of homely detail, how one could live on less than a dollar a day. *Philothea* was a dream of Greece, of Pericles, Plato and Phidias, in which a New England maiden in a peplus tries to reform Aspasia. It was a virginal vision, like Powers's "Greek Slave." But William Ware's novels were well-wrought and solid. This Unitarian minister, the son of Dr. Henry Ware of Cambridge, who had visited Greece and the Holy Land, well knew the world of which he wrote, the Roman Empire of the early Christians, and had the imagination to relive it. If his heroes and heroines savoured a little too much of Dr. Channing's circle, Ware was an artist notwithstanding. His novels were to remain for those who enjoy a style that reproduces, with their scenes and subjects, the enchanting rhythms of the ancient authors.

The interest in modern languages, meanwhile, had thriven under the influence of Coleridge. Professor James Marsh of Vermont had published editions of Coleridge's prose writings, but long before this the poet Dana had introduced his critical ideas, and the increasing numbers of American students who flocked to the German universities were spreading them far and wide. The doctrine of "following nature in variety of kinds" had led to an intellectual revolution; for, if nature was inexhaustible in variety, so were the possible forms of the human mind. This key had opened the worlds of letters that lay behind the modern languages. It had destroyed the "rules" that measured everything by the classical standards. The critic was no longer in a position to sit

on a lofty throne and send to Gehenna authors who did
not conform to these obsolete rules. He had to yield to
times and circumstances. He was obliged to submit to
other tests than the tests of the "savage and tartarly"
Jeffrey and Gifford and the strip-and-whip school of the
previous age, with its arrogant insularity. The critic had
to "characterize" the author, to understand him and in-
terpret him, asking, From what point does he look at life?

These catholic and supple views of Coleridge, derived
from the writings of A. W. Schlegel, whom Ticknor had
known in Paris, marked the new era in criticism. All the
American writers of the future who had any claim to
be considered central shared these views as a matter of
course; and the writers of the *North American* group,
learned but narrow in their range of feeling, dry, mechanical, timid, subservient to the abstract laws that had
governed the eighteenth century, children of Burke and
Johnson, gradually lost influence as they spread. In the
dialect that Coleridge propagated,—also the fruit of his
German studies,—the old school was the school of the
"understanding," the new school was the school of "reason." These were the Transcendentalist categories for
which the New England mind was so well prepared, for
they corresponded with the generations, the older and
the younger generations, or, rather, the temperaments
of these generations, which were at open war with one
another. The "understanding" was the faculty that observed, inferred, argued, drew conclusions. It was the
Lockian faculty; it assumed that everything in the mind
was drawn from the experience of the senses. In short,
it was the lawyer's point of view that governed conservative Boston, the cold, external, practical notion of life
that guided the merchants in their counting-houses and
the Unitarian ministers in their pulpits. The "reason"
was the faculty of intuition, warm, perceptive, immediate, that represented the mind of young New England.

It assumed, it actually *knew*, that the mind contained powers of its own, not derived from the senses. In the theological sphere, Transcendentalism was a reaction against both Unitarianism and Trinitarianism, neither of which possessed any belief in the self-sufficiency of the human mind outside of revelation. It spoke for an order of truth that transcended, by immediate perception, all external evidence. "God becomes conscious in man," as Fichte said, "the philosopher man, the man of reason, in whom the absolute being recognizes himself. The reason gazes immediately on the eternal realities." This was the gist of Schleiermacher's teachings, which shocked Andrews Norton,—the phrase, "the soul's sense of things divine." Herder, in the *Spirit of Hebrew Poetry*, translated by Dr. James Marsh, had extended the conception to literature. Writing of the Jewish prophets, he had abolished the distinction between the sacred and the secular, transferring to the credit of human genius all that had been ascribed to the divine. In the bards of Israel, all bards were glorified, a notion which, to the candid mind, far from drawing angels down, raised mortals to the skies. It recognized the creative powers of man. Coleridge had prophesied that a golden age, in letters, art, religion, social ethics, would follow the spread of Transcendentalism; and from various German thinkers, Jacobi and Fichte, the new generation in New England was receiving special impulsions, towards heroism and towards mysticism, that appealed to the youthful mind.

For the influence of Germany grew apace. It had passed quite out of the hands of the earlier students, Everett and Ticknor, Longfellow even, who scarcely shared the Transcendental impulse. It raged through other students and translators, some of whom, like Frederick Henry Hedge, the Unitarian minister in Bangor, the son of Dr. Hedge who had written the *Logic*, had studied in the land of Kant and Herder. To the hesitant

North American Review, Bancroft contributed essays on
the German writers. He also helped to popularize the
sympathetic writings of Victor Cousin, the French eclec-
tic philosopher, for whom all systems were true in what
they affirmed, false in what they denied.[15] Felton, the
anti-Transcendentalist, translated Menzel's history; Mrs.
Lee of Brookline wrote a life of Jean Paul Richter;
Charles T. Brooks, the minister of Newport, began the
long series of German translations that was to include, as
time went on, works by Goethe, Schiller, Jean Paul,
Rückert. A collection of minor poems by Goethe and
Schiller, in the version of John Sullivan Dwight, appeared as one of a number of similar works. All the
young men and women read the German authors. They
echoed Schiller's great command, "Keep true to the
dream of thy youth." They pondered Novalis's *Heinrich
von Ofterdingen:* several Harvard students spent a summer rendering this "apotheosis of poetry" into the language of their own hearts. They "longed for Italy" after
Wackenroder. They believed in the gospel of *Lucinde*
that poetry and life should be one and the same, and
shared the despair of the heroine over the discord which
they could by no means harmonize. They read the tales
of Tieck, Musæus, Hoffmann. They yearned for the "blue
flower." They dreamed of Jean Paul's Titan, Roquairol,
who longed for an enterprise for his idle valour, the hero,
torn by passions and hopes deferred, who did not possess
the power to mould his world. They felt within, like
Manfred,—

> an awful chaos—light and darkness—
> And mind and dust—and passions and pure thought
> Mix'd, and contending without end or order.

[15] In the earlier volumes of his history, Bancroft appeared as a
champion of the new philosophy, which he identified with Quaker-
ism, the gospel of the Inner Light. See his discussion of Locke and
William Penn.

They felt that men should be true and wise, beautiful, pure and aspiring. They worshipped heroism, they worshipped genius. And they believed,—the thought was in the air,—that the way to greatness was through books, not battles. Thomas Wentworth Higginson, who seldom yielded even to moral excesses, said of Mrs. Lee's *Life of Richter* that it set before him, just at the right time, the attractions of a literary life, carried on in an unworldly spirit. "From that moment," he added, "poverty, or at least extreme economy, had no terrors for me, and I could not bear the thought of devoting my life to Blackstone."

Much of this German influence reached New England through the medium of a greater man than Coleridge, greater, at least, in energy, greater as a moral force, Carlyle. The readers of the British reviews,—and every well-instructed student read them,—had long been aware of the author of *Characteristics*, the essay entitled *The Signs of the Times* and the series of papers on the German writers. Carlyle,—the name began to emerge from a Scottish mist of anonymity,—Carlyle, the "Germanic new-light writer," was, in fact, the perfect middleman for this new movement of ideas. One thought of New England and Scotland as almost interchangeable terms. There was an occult relation between these regions, with their immemorial Calvinist past and their instinct for the heroic.[16] The greatest foreign influence in New England had been, for a generation, Scott, who had also been stirred by the German poets; and Carlyle was to find in New England his first large circle of readers, even a publisher for *Sartor Resartus* before the book appeared in

---

[16] New Englanders have often felt more at home in Scotland than in England. It is significant that little Ellen, in *The Wide, Wide World*, when she inherits her paradise, inherits it in Scotland, not in England, though the paradise is properly qualified as a "Scottish discipline" and she returns to America, with equal propriety, in the end.

his own country. He represented the romantic spirit on its ethical and religious side, where the New England mind was most at home; and for twenty years, down to the Civil War, his influence was to remain almost despotic. This was before the brutality of his later years grew upon him with his indigestion, till the splendid dreams of his youth were all but lost in the spoiled peasant's worship of lordship and power.

Over the rising school of New England writers, even over the toughest-grained, Carlyle and Carlylese were to leave their traces. Even the style of Thoreau was to be tinged faintly here and there with the rhythms and locutions of a writer whom lesser minds could not resist. Lowell was deeply affected by them. The eighteenth-century style of his Homer Wilbur, the intransigent parson of *The Biglow Papers,* was wrenched, by Carlyle's influence, even to the extent of whole pages, out of its normal channel.[17] Margaret Fuller wrote Carlylean essays. Theodore Parker's *Historic Americans* might almost have been written by the man whom Thackeray, Dickens and Ruskin called their master. Sylvester Judd's *Margaret* bristled with the dialect.[18] The picturesque historical style of Motley was almost as much affected as Dickens's *Tale of Two Cities* had been by Carlyle. This was the greatest magnetic force of an age that was much concerned with animal magnetism; and writers who seldom wrote greatly rose above themselves when they wrote of Carlyle.[19] He vindicated, they felt, their celes-

[17] "On whirls the restless globe through unsounded time, with its cities and its silences," etc.—Lowell, *The Biglow Papers.* See also Mr. Wilbur's sermon, First Series, No. VI.

[18] See the exclamations of Margaret, in the scene after the trial: "My poor murdered brother! Fades the cloud-girt, star-flowering universe to my eye! I hear the screaming of hope, in wild Merganser flight to the regions of endless cold!"

[19] See Bronson Alcott's description of the "British Taurus" in *R. W. Emerson: His Character and Genius:* "Curious to see him, his chin aloft, the pent thunders rolling, lightnings darting from

tial birthright, showed them that the current ideals were shams, ridiculed the respectable, the "gigmen," the heroes of a mechanical age; he taught the "science of Dynamics," the "primary, unmodified forces and energies of men, the mysterious springs of love and fear and wonder." He gave them faith in their own endeavours. He told them to quit their paper formulas and know that they were alive and that God was alive. "Did the upholsterers make this universe? Were you created by the tailor?" The old ideal of manhood had been forgotten. To young valour and the thirst for action, a calculating age of profit-seekers was deaf, dumb and blind; and yet the Invisible still existed, and opened itself to the inward eye, and fought on the side of the seeker of it. That every man had his own task, his own peculiar inlet into the sea of Divinity, which, once found, destroyed the canker of doubt: this was an open-sesame for young New England. According to the Arab saying, "Every people has its own prophet." Was Thomas Carlyle this prophet? So it appeared, for a while. Then it became apparent that Carlyle was only a part of the atmosphere. The real New England prophet was another man who dwelt in the little town of Concord.

---

under the bold brows, words that tell of the wail within, accents not meant for music, yet made lyrical in the cadences of his Caledonian refrain, his mirth mad as Lear's, his humour as wilful as the wind."

CHAPTER X

EMERSON IN CONCORD

RALPH WALDO EMERSON had lived in Concord since 1834. The former pastor of a Boston church and a son of the Reverend William Emerson, he had withdrawn from the ministry. Having a little income, he had bought a house on the Boston turnpike, surrounded with pine and fir-trees. There was a garden by the brook, filled with roses and tulips. In the western window of his study, he placed an Æolian harp. It sang in the spring and summer breezes, mingling with the voices of the birds, fitfully bringing to mind the ballads that he loved, the wild, melodious notes of the old bards and minstrels.

He had been writing essays and giving addresses that grieved and vexed most of his older hearers. Dozens, even hundreds of the younger people, thinking of him, thought of Burns's phrase,

> Wi' sic as he, where'er he be,
> May I be saved or damned.

But, although he had his followers in Boston, he was anathema to the pundits there. Everett sneered at Emerson's "conceited, laborious nonsense." John Quincy Adams and Andrews Norton thought he was an atheist and worse. The Cambridge theologians reviled him: he was a pantheist and a German mystic, and his style was a kind of neo-Platonic moonshine. The Concord prophet smiled at these accusations. He had the temerity to think that the great Cambridge guns were merely popguns. There was nothing explosive in his own discourse. He was a flute-player, one who plucked his reeds in the Concord river. But when he began to play, one saw a beautiful portico, standing in a lovely scene of nature, covered with blossoms and vine-leaves; and, at the strains of the flute, one felt impelled to enter the portico and explore the unknown region that lay beyond. It was an irresistible invitation. As for the smiling musician, he was a mystery still. One thought of him as the man in Plutarch's story who conversed with men one day only in the year and spent the rest of his days with the nymphs and demons.

Everyone had heard of him in Boston, where he was giving lectures. His birthplace there was a kitestring's distance from the house where Franklin was born and the house where Edgar Allan Poe was born. But, although he belonged to one of the oldest scholarly families, with countless names in the college catalogues, most of the signs had been against him. Tall, excessively thin, so thin that, as Heine said of Wellington, his full face looked like a profile, pale, with a tomahawk nose, blond, with blue eyes and smiling, curved lips, he had none of the traits, aggressive or brilliant, that marked his brothers in various ways. At moments, on the platform, he spoke with a tranquil authority, but his usual demeanour was almost girlishly passive. He had not acquired the majestic air, as of a wise old eagle or Indian sachem, that marked his later years. He appeared to be easily disconcerted, for his self-reliance was a gradual conquest. He had drifted through many misfortunes, drifted into and out of tuberculosis, drifted into teaching and out of the Church, maturing very slowly. He had known dark hours, poverty, pain, fear, disease. His first wife had died; so had two of his brothers. The trouble with him was, his elders thought, that he seemed to like to drift. He had no sort of record as a student. At Harvard, even three generations later, when people spoke of Emerson's "education," they put the word in quotation-marks.[1] It was not that he did not know his Greek and Latin, but that he was never systematic. He had read, both then and later, for "lustres" mainly. He had drifted first to Florida and then to Europe, and finally settled at Concord, the home of his forbears, where he had often visited at the Manse. The minister there, Dr. Ezra Ripley, who was Emerson's step-grandfather and very fond of the young man, felt that he was obliged to warn the people against this leader of the Egomites, those who "sent themselves" on the Lord's errands, without any proper calling. As for the lectures that Emerson was giving in Boston, on great men, history, the present age, the famous lawyer, Jeremiah Mason, when he was asked if he could understand them, replied, "No, but my daughters can."

To the outer eye, at least, Emerson's life was an aimless jumble. He had ignored all the obvious chances, rejected the palpable prizes, followed none of the rules of common sense. Was he pursuing some star of his own? No one else could see it. In later years, looking back, Emerson's friends, remembering him, thought of those quiet brown colts, unrecognized even by the trainers, that out-strip all the others on the race-course. He had had few doubts himself. He had edged along sideways towards everything that was good in his life, but he felt that he was born for victory. He had not chosen his course. It had sprung from a necessity of his nature, an inner logic that he scarcely questioned. In college, he had consulted the *Sortes Virgilianæ,* opening at the line in Dryden's version,—

Go, let the gods and temples claim thy care.

It seemed to suggest the ministry, and he had followed the suggestion, as his fathers had followed it before him.

[1] See President Eliot's *Harvard Memories.* The true Cambridge mind could never accept such cavalier remarks of Emerson's as that "books are for the scholar's idle times."

But Unitarianism could not hold him. The walls of this temple, he thought, were wasted and thin, and at last nothing was left but a film of whitewash. Then, gradually, another faith possessed him. Channing, who had helped him with his studies, had mentioned some recent writer who said there were two souls in the human body, one the vulgar, waking, practical soul, the other a soul that never suspended its action and guided the involuntary motions. This hint of German Transcendentalism, savouring of the Neo-Platonists and the sacred books of the East, with which his Aunt Mary Emerson was familiar, lingered and grew in his mind. What was this involuntary soul, this "absolute being" of the German thinkers, but the "inner light" of the Quakers, with whom he had talked at New Bedford, that indescribable presence, dwelling in every being and common to all, which the contradiction of all men could not shake and which the consent of all could not confirm? Every religion had known it, the Holy Ghost, the Comforter, the Dæmon, the still, small voice, the light, the seed, Channing's moral sentiment, the One of Plato and Plotinus, the Universal Mind of the Yogis and Sufis. One felt this presence at moments only,—Emerson had felt it a thousand times, in the woods and fields at Concord; but there was a depth in these brief moments that gave them a strange authority. He felt a sudden influx of power; the currents of the universal being seemed to circulate through him. Was not all nature saturated with deity, and was he not himself a part of nature? He seemed to see in a flash the laws of life, justice, truth, love and freedom. Why should he not explore these wonderful realms? Why should he not proclaim this Joyous Science?

It was to confirm these intuitions that he had visited Europe. He wished to escape from theological problems, which seemed to him the soul's mumps and measles, and meet the living writers, Carlyle, Coleridge, Wordsworth,

Landor, who, having nourished his own vigour, seemed to say that men were of tunable metal. He spent a few weeks at Rome and Naples and studied for a while at the Collège de France. In the zoological gardens in Paris, he underwent a strange experience that was the greatest lesson of his journey. Observing the rocks, the grasses, the fishes, the insects, the lions, vultures and elephants, he felt a conviction stirring in him that all these forms of life expressed some property in himself. He felt the zoophyte in him, the centipede, the fox. He was moved by mysterious sympathies, such as he had felt in the woods at home. Was he not one with all these creatures? Nature was indeed a living whole, a spiral ever ascending. He had been struck by Lamarck's ideas. What Plotinus said, that all beings, even the plants, even the soil that bore them aspired to attain conscious knowledge, seemed to be confirmed by modern science. He had conceived, in his way, the theory of evolution, which he was to express in all his writings; and he felt that the new age of science represented a further ascent. Men would rise above their conventional notions, emerge from their belief in mere prescription, their blind and ignorant following of custom, as science more and more increased their insight into the laws of nature. They would learn to trust themselves, the universal soul within themselves, casting off their "old clothes," walking the earth at last as supermen,—for this was Emerson's notion before it was Nietzsche's. It was Carlyle's belief as well, and Emerson had visited Carlyle. He had spent a day and a night at Craigenputtock. He was "the one of all the sons of Adam" who, as Carlyle wrote later, "completely understood what I was saying and answered with a truly human voice."

In no haste to publish his reflections, Emerson, settled in Concord, "put his ear close by himself," as Montaigne had done before him, and held his breath and listened.

He liked the phrase of Simonides, "Give me twice the time, for the more I think the more it enlarges." Was not America full of puny scholars, clamorous place-hunters and village brawlers, whose talents were only for contention? Was it not a country of small adventures, short plans and daring risks? For patience, for great combinations, for long, persistent, close-woven schemes, where could one look in all this fuss and bustle? Was it not true that Americans lived on the surface, a poor, thin, plausible existence? Their vice, their national vice was imitation; they copied foreign forms in their manners and writing, forms that were merely capricious, as if these were permanent forms of nature. The scholars and the thinkers and the writers, as shallow and as frivolous as the rest,—able as they might be in special tasks,—had no advice to give in vital matters, and the public disregarded them. For the public had its own public wisdom: what it asked of the thinker was something else, the private, the universal wisdom of which it had been defrauded by its own dwelling in the street. Was it not time to be dumb for a while, to sit with one's hand on one's mouth, a long, austere, Pythagorean lustrum? Inner independence was what the thinker needed, and the life of the cottage and the woods,—insulation of place,—only had value as an aid to this. But in solitude, Emerson found, his faculties rose fair and full within, like the forest trees and the field flowers. He did not wish to print his thoughts until he had something to say that men would be obliged to attend and hear.

He knew and would know no such thing as haste in composition; and he was determined to keep his freedom, even at the risk of uselessness. A course in which clear faith could not go might well be worse than none. Besides, although he did not know his way, he felt that the current knew it. There was a pilot within him, and, when he did not know how to steer, and dared not hoist a sail, he had only to drift. He lectured here and there, in

Boston, in the neighbouring towns, in Concord, in order to supplement his little income. He travelled further and further from home, until he was known as a lecturer throughout the West. He joined in the village life and served on local committees, and he gave the memorial address when Concord celebrated its second centennial. In the village Social Circle he found a suggestion of the well-known society in *Wilhelm Meister,* in which every member was a master of one of the arts of life, mechanics, agriculture, medicine, law. He liked to talk with farmers, millers, tailors, with carpenters and coopers at their work, horse-trainers, geologists, physicists, chemists, whom he visited in their laboratories, astonished by their feats of skill, their powers of observation and endurance. He watched with awe the life of his farmer-neighbours. Were not the men in the cities who were the centres of energy, the driving wheels of trade and the practical arts, the sons and the grandsons of farmers? And were they not spending the energies their fathers had accumulated in poverty, necessity and darkness, in their hardy, silent existence, in their frosty furrows? He looked to life for his dictionary. He wished to master in all these facts a language by which to embody and illustrate his own perceptions; for the thinker was a man for whom all men worked,—geologist, mechanic, merchant, chemist, king, painter, composer,—and a thousand men looked through his eyes. And why should he travel for his illustrations? Was it not the secret of the gods that they came in low disguises? Real kings hid away their crowns and affected a plain exterior, as Odin dwelt in a fisherman's hut and Apollo served Admetus as a slave. In the legends of fairy lore, the fairies largest in power were the least in size. It was the magic of genius to lift the curtain from the common, showing us the divinities that were all about us, disguised as gypsies and pedlars, as farm-hands and clerks.

With all this active social life, Emerson guarded his

solitude. He bought a woodlot by Walden Pond, a wild, rocky ledge, with a grove of chestnuts, oaks, maples and hemlocks sweeping down to the shore. He trimmed the old path around the pond that had been worn by the feet of Indian hunters. He cut vistas over the water, where he bathed on summer afternoons; and there he strolled and lingered, sitting on the bank, reading Plato or Goethe, writing in his journal. There he was "adjacent to the One." He had always felt like a king in the woods, walking through tents of gold and bowers of crimson, garlanded with flowers, vines and sunbeams, surrounded with incense and music. An active enchantment seemed to reach his dust there, as if he had the keeping of a secret that was too great to be told, as if a god dwelt near him in a hollow tree. Every light from the sky, every shadow ministered to his pleasure. He seemed to dilate with the wind. He felt the blood of thousands in his body, and his heart seemed to pump through his veins the sap of all this forest vegetation. It was as if he had left behind all his human relations and become one with carbon, lime and granite. The frogs piped, the leaves hissed, the far-off waters tinkled, the grass bent and rustled, and he seemed to die out of the human world and enter another existence, a life of water, air, earth and ether. He passed into the trances of the Yogis and Sufis, the mystical state of Samadhi, in which the mind works without desire, objectless and bodiless, superconscious, and one feels free, omnipotent, immortal. In this state of elevation, elation and joy, shared by all the mystics, one feels that one belongs to another species, and the vision of a superhuman race becomes more real than reality. Nietzsche felt so at Sils-Maria, and so Emerson felt in the woods at Walden. There was a god in man, an angel in disguise that played the fool! The millions that called themselves men were not yet men. They were half-engaged in the soil, pawing to get free, and they needed all the music that one could bring in order to disengage them. They seemed to be on the verge of all that was great, and so they were, indeed, were they only aware of the faculties that slumbered within them. Emerson's own path lay clear before him. It was to look within himself and report his own perceptions and reveal the powers that lay in the soul of man.

He had brought out a little book called *Nature*, the germ of his later essays; but he seemed to be more eager to further his friends than his own interests and ventures. He arranged with Stearns Wheeler, the Harvard tutor, who had built the hut in the woods and had edited Herodotus with notes, to copy out from *Fraser's Magazine* the pages of *Sartor Resartus*, which no British publisher would issue; and he had the first edition published in Boston. Far from shrewd in financial matters, he gathered money shrewdly for Carlyle.[2] He also edited Jones Very's sonnets. This excellent Greek scholar, a tall, spindling ghost of a man, was one of the new group of Harvard mystics. As a boy, he had voyaged in his father's ships, outward bound from Salem, and he had taken flight, in after years, to realms that Salem ships had never reached. In the McLean Asylum, where he dwelt for a while, he had written an essay on Shakespeare, which had been "told" him by the Holy Ghost. He believed that he had risen from the dead, that he had ceased to live in the physical world and had passed beyond earthly realities; and indeed his voice seemed to come from the tombs, and his face with its web of skin suggested a skull. He valued his sonnets not because they were his, but precisely because they were not, because, as he supposed,

[2] Emerson told Edward Everett Hale that the first money he received from any of his own books was a cheque, in 1850, for *Representative Men*. He called on his publishers, Phillips and Sampson, and asked them if he was free to use the cheque. Mr. Phillips showed him how to endorse it.—E. E. Hale, *Memories of a Hundred Years*.

God spoke through him. Emerson selected and revised
these sonnets, among them *The Stranger's Gift* and *The
Barberry Bush*. There was little magic in them. Mono-
tones in silver-grey, sober as a dove's breast, they were
true poems, none the less. They had a sort of solemn
incandescence. They were like frosted orbs of electric
light. One caught their dim glow of religious feeling
three generations later, partly thanks to Emerson's revisions; for no one knew better than he the importance
of skill. He had a passion himself for rhetorical studies.
He had aped the styles of various authors, Chateaubriand, Montaigne, Bacon, Browne, during his years in
college, and had been drawn to the styles that were
"rammed with life," in Ben Jonson's phrase, those that
were pregnant and laconic, unlike the starched or flowing styles that were popular and current in his youth.
His own prose diction suggested the seventeenth-cen
tury authors who had never stooped to explain their
thoughts. In his verse he avoided the conventional forms,
drawn from English poetry, which all the other American poets accepted, the sonnet, the romantic tale, the
song. He liked to write gnomic lines, epigrams and rules
of life, conveyed in a lively image, after the Greek or Persian fashion, sometimes contained in a single stanza,—

> Though love repine, and reason chafe,
> There came a voice without reply,—
> ' 'Tis man's perdition to be safe,
> When for the truth he ought to die.'

Occasionally he wrote some longer poem,—the magical
Give All to Love and *Bacchus*,—in a free-verse style of
his own invention. But most of his poems were composed
in the couplets of Milton's *L'Allegro,* which he filled with
a sunny sublimity.

The poet Very was one of the neophytes who felt the
fascination of the Concord prophet. Emerson's address,

The American Scholar, followed by his Literary Ethics, The Method of Nature, Man the Reformer and others, appealed to the younger generation more intimately than Carlyle and the German writers. These speeches and Emerson's essays, appearing at the same time,—History, Self-Reliance, Compensation,—were filled with their problems and dilemmas, which Emerson seemed to have shared. Unlike the professional orators, he addressed himself to the thinking classes, especially to students and beginners in life; and, instead of preaching the popular virtues, of which they had heard so much, and the value of conforming to the world about them, he spoke to the individual in each of his hearers. Popularity was for "dolls," he said; and the "bloated vanity called public opinion" should have no weight against the private will. He spoke of the "maxims of a low prudence" which they would hear every day, suggesting that the first of all their duties was to get land and money, name and place. They should turn a deaf ear to these base counsels, knowing that the search after the great was the proper occupation of youth and manhood. All young persons thirsted for a real existence, for something they could do with all their heart. And was it not true that each had his own vocation, some bias or talent or special executive skill, by feeling and obeying which alone he could rightly find his place in the world? Every man had his magnetic needle, which always pointed to his proper path, with more or less variation from other men's. He was never happy or strong until he found it, and he could only find it by trusting himself, by listening to the whisper of the voice within him. Was it not the chief disgrace in the world not to be a unit, not to be reckoned one character, not to yield that peculiar fruit which each man was created to bear, but to be reckoned in the gross, in the hundred, or the thousand, of the party or the section to which one belonged? If one paid no attention to the world's opinion, but followed one's own *proprium,* as Swedenborg called it, if one lived wholly from within, planting one-self on one's instincts and standing firm, the world would come round to one at last; for one's inner voice was the voice of the "collective psyche," as later writers called the Over-soul,—the term that Emerson used,—which imparts a common rhythm to all existence.[3] One would be acting in harmony with the laws of life, to which the phenomenal world is obliged to bow.

Emerson was proclaiming in these speeches and essays the doctrine which, according to William James, has marked all the periods of revival, the early Christian age and Luther's age, Rousseau's, Kant's and Goethe's, namely, that the innermost nature of things is congenial to the powers that men possess. That everything that ever was or will be, as he said in his essay, *Self-Reliance,* is here in the enveloping now, that he who obeys himself is a part of fate,—this challenged the natural faculties of his hearers. It stirred them to take life strivingly in full belief that what man had done man could do, that the world was all opportunities, strings of tension waiting to be struck, especially perhaps by thinkers and writers, to whom Emerson spoke most directly. Why were young Americans so imitative, so timid, tame, compliant? Why did they so easily lose their aims? Why did they look backward and renounce their hopes and yield to the conventions that turned them to stone? Why did they care so much for foreign opinions?

> Who bides at home, nor looks abroad,
> Carries the eagles, and masters the sword.

[3] See C. G. Jung's description of the "artist" as a type: "We see that he has drawn upon the healing and redeeming forces of the collective psyche that underlies consciousness with its isolation and its painful errors; that he has penetrated to that matrix of life in which all men are embedded, which imparts a common rhythm to all human existence, and allows the individual to communicate his feeling and his striving to mankind as a whole."—C. G. Jung, *Modern Man in Search of a Soul.*

Could they not see that the near was as great as the far, that every drop of water was a little ocean, that the clay with which the Persians and the Greeks moulded their noble symbols was common lime and silex, the clay that one held now in one's foolish hands and threw away to go and seek in vain in sepulchres and mummy-pits in Europe? It was the deep today that all men scorned, the poverty that men hated, the heaving of the lungs and the heat of the blood. All art was yet to be created, all literature yet to be written. All nature was new and undescribed. America had listened too long to the muses of Europe. It had met the expectations of mankind with little but the exertions of mechanical skill. Why should not Americans enjoy an original relation to the universe? A poetry of insight and not of tradition? A religion by revelation to themselves? Did the discontented souls who flocked to Europe expect to find anything essential there which they had not found at home? Wherever they went, they could only discover as much beauty or worth as they carried with them. America's day of dependence, its long apprenticeship to other lands was drawing to a close. The millions who were rushing into life could not always be fed on the sere remains of foreign harvests. Events were arising that had to be sung and that would sing themselves. Who could doubt that poetry would revive and lead in the continental America of the future?

The effect of these essays and lectures on the younger people was like that of the sound of a trumpet. It was a high and solemn music that dissolved the knots in their minds, roused their wills, enlarged their affections, filled them with a new illumination. It seemed to justify their glittering dreams, even as it brought to their support the authority of their own unconscious natures. They felt themselves no longer "pinched in a corner," as Emerson described their former state, but potential benefactors and redeemers, advancing on chaos and the dark. For

Emerson pictured America in a way that made them feel how much the scholar counted. This careless, swaggering, shallow nation of theirs, this great avaricious America, boasting of its crops and the size of its cities, indifferent to the kind of men it bred, heedless of its liberty and other people's, gambling away the charters of the human race for a petty, selfish gain, this country needed them to calm and guide it, to see the right done, to check self-interest, to give it repose and depth. The feats it bragged about were of no great moment, telegraphs and steam, gas and ether. Its immense mechanical apparatus turned out little more than Nuremberg toys. But who doubted what the mind could do, seeing the shock given to torpid races by Mahomet, by Buddha, or by Newton or Franklin? All that was requisite, at any time, was a few superior men to give a new and noble turn to things; and Emerson summoned his hearers to the task. The path was a difficult one that lay before them, but in stressing this he won them all the more. They must be ready for bad weather, poverty, weariness, insult and repute of failure. The ease, the pleasure of treading the old paths they must surrender in making and walking their own, with the self-accusation and the faintness of heart, the uncertainty and loss of time and effort that always entangle the feet of the self-directed. Their reward would lie in exercising the highest functions of human nature, raising themselves from private considerations and breathing and living on public and illustrious thoughts. They would be the world's eye and heart, resisting the vulgar prosperity that retrograded to barbarism.

Such was the word of the Concord seer who had thought of calling his essays "Forest Essays"; for he had scarcely ever had a day-dream on which the breath of the pines had not blown.

CHAPTER XI

HAWTHORNE IN SALEM

WHILE BOSTON and little Concord were moving forward, Salem, like most of the other seaports, stricken by the War of 1812, had lapsed into quietude and decay. Beside its dilapidated wharves, where grew the fat weeds, the windlass chanty and the caulker's maul no longer broke the silence. The water-side streets were no longer thronged with sailors, "all right" for shore, with their blue jackets and checked shirts, their well-varnished hats and flowing ribbons, with bundles under their arms from the cannibal isles, or from India or China. One seldom heard the lively "Cheerily, men!" while all hands joined in the chorus. The grass choked the chinks of the cobblestones over which the drays had clattered. An occasional bark or brig discharged its hides. One saw some Nova Scotia schooner, drawn up at Derby's Wharf, unloading a cargo of firewood. A few idle seafaring men leaned against the posts, or sat on the planks, in the lee of some shabby warehouse, or lolled in the long-boats on the strand. But the great days of the port were a tale that was told, over and over, by the ancient skippers, who dozed away their mornings at the custom-house, with their chairs tilted against the wall.

Salem had an immemorial air, the air that gathers about a town which, having known a splendid hour, shrinks and settles back while its grandeurs fade. But Salem was old in spirit, aside from its faded grandeurs. The past that hovered there had much in common with that of the ancient ports of northern Europe, where the

Gothic fancies of the Middle Ages have not been dispelled by modern trade. Salem was still Gothic, in a measure. In its moss-grown, many-gabled houses, panelled with worm-eaten wood and hung with half-obliterated portraits, dwelt at least the remnants of a race that retained the mental traits of a far-away past. In its isolation from the currents of world-thought and feeling, it seemed to be only a step removed from the age of the Dance of Death. In the mansions of Chestnut Street and Federal Street, one found the traces of a livelier culture, the books that were read in Boston, together with the Oriental spoils brought home by the Salem navigators. But over the quiet lanes and leafy side-streets, where the graveyards lay, brooded the hush of many generations. Queer old maids with turbaned heads peered from behind the curtains, quaint old simple-minded men hobbled along under the sweeping elms, "pixilated" creatures, many of them, as they said at Marblehead,—bewildered by the fairies,—half dead and buried in their houses, or buried in the morbid family pride that flourishes where life runs low.

There was vigour enough in Salem, there were plenty of stout merchants and politicians. One saw swarms of boys and little girls, in blue, yellow, green and crimson dresses, bursting from church and school-house, like garden-beds of zinnias or water-colours of Maurice Prendergast. It was only in comparison with Lynn and Lowell, those near-by towns whose enterprising burghers, faced with the decline of shipping, had built their factories for internal trade, that Salem seemed somehow grey and sad. The Prescotts, Story, Pickering, Choate and Bowditch, the great circle of earlier days, had long since departed. At a stone's-throw from the Essex Institute, one almost heard the silence. One caught the tinkling of the bell at the door of some little cent-shop, even the quiver of the humming-birds darting about the syringa bushes. The rattling of the butcher's cart was the only event of the day for many a household, unless perhaps one of the family hens cackled and laid an egg. Spiders abounded in these houses, eluding the vigilant spinster's eye. Indeed, there were so many cobwebs that it might have occurred to a doctor,—some old Salem doctor, as odd as the rest,—to gather the webs together and distil an elixir of life from the dusty compound. In the burying-ground in Charter Street, where the Gothic emblems flourished, —death's-heads, cross-bones, scythes and hour-glasses, such as one found in Dürer's woodcuts,—the office of grave-digger passed from father to son. Just so passed the household legends, behind the bolted doors, grimmer with each generation. Beside the kitchen fires, old serving-women crouched as they turned the spit and darned the stockings, always ready to tell the children stories. Some of them seemed to remember the days of the witches. Their stories were as dusty as the cobwebs.

For Salem, like the whole New England sea-coast, bristled with old wives' tales and old men's legends. No need to invent stories there: one heard them in the taverns, from the sailors, from charcoal-burners who looked like wizards, from the good-for-nothings on the water-front. One heard of locked closets in haunted houses where skeletons had been found. One heard of walls that resounded with knocks where there had once been doorways, now bricked up. One heard of poisonous houses and blood-stained houses, old maids who lived in total darkness, misers who wallowed naked in heaps of pine-tree shillings. One even heard of Endicott's dreary times, when the stocks and the pillory were never empty. One heard of the magistrates who awoke each morning to the prospect of cropping an ear or slitting a nostril, stripping and whipping a woman at the tail of a cart, or giving her a stout hemp necklace or a brooch in the form of a scarlet letter. One heard of the grey champion who emerged from nowhere to rebuke the tyrannies of the British king, of children who had sprung from the loins of demons, of the wastrels of Merry Mount and the grizzled saints who had stamped out their light and idle mirth, clipping their curls and love-locks. Would they not have stamped out the sunshine and clipped all the flowers in the forest in order to clear a path for their psalms and sermons? In these quiet towns, where nothing happens—except an occasional murder—to agitate the surface of existence, history is ever-present, lying in visible depths under the unstirred waters; and who could have known in Salem what to believe or not? However it might have been on Chestnut Street, the fringes of Salem society were superstitious. If the ring that Queen Elizabeth gave to Essex had appeared in a collection-box on Sunday, it would not have seemed surprising to some of the people. There were plenty of old souls in the lanes and side-streets who never knew where to draw the line. They half believed the tales they told the children. Were there not hollows in the hills close by where the Devil and his subjects held communion? Were there not ill-famed men in the western mountains who were condemned to wander till the crack of doom? All these tales had their truth, and so did the Indian legends, which the farmers repeated. There was an element of fact behind them. Was there a carbuncle in the Crystal Hills that gleamed like the westering sun, as the Indians said? Or was it the sun itself? There were men still living down in Maine who had never settled the question. Carbuncle or not, they had certainly seen it. At least, they had caught its radiance, far up the valley of the Saco.

Salem was a centre for these legends. The mediæval mind had lingered there, in the absence of recent enterprise; and, while the town as a whole was sufficiently modern, there were odd corners and shadowy households where symbols and realities seemed much the same. The

young men and women knew the difference, but sometimes it amused them to ignore it. They did not believe
in ghosts, but mesmerism had become the fashion: they
let their fancies play on the border-line. They sat up at
night and told tales of ghosts, largely in default of mundane gossip. Occasionally, they even thought they saw
one. The Hawthornes, who lived in Herbert Street, under the shadow of a family curse, were often troubled
by an apparition that seemed to haunt their yard. The
only son of the household, Nathaniel Hawthorne, who
lived like a ghost himself, haunting a little chamber
under the eaves, appearing only at nightfall, could not
count the times he had raised his head, or turned towards the window, with a perception that somebody was
passing through the gate. He could only perceive the
presence with a sidelong glance, by a certain indirection;
if he looked straight at the dim thing, behold, it was not
there. As no one ever passed through the Hawthornes'
gate, it may have been Elizabeth, his sister, who also appeared only when dusk had fallen. In fact, one could live
for two years under the same roof with this spectral sister and see her only once. That was the way with the
Hawthornes. The father, a Salem skipper, had died of
yellow fever, years ago, in far-off Surinam; and no mor-
tal eye had penetrated, or was to penetrate for forty
years, the Castle Dismal on the second floor where the
mother of the family had taken refuge on the day she
heard the news. Her meals were brought up and left
outside the door, as they were at Elizabeth's door, and
Louisa's door,—at least, as often as not,—and, one flight
further up, at Nathaniel's door. When twilight came,
one heard the sound of footsteps echoing on the stairs,
and a door that must have been opened was certainly
shut. Elizabeth went out for a little walk. Then Nathaniel went for a walk, alone, in another direction.

All day long, every day, or almost every day, for twelve

years, he had sat in his flag-bottomed chair in his little room, beside the pine table, with a sheet of foolscap spread out before him. He was writing stories that rose in his mind as mushrooms grow in a meadow, where the roots of some old tree are buried under the earth. He had no love of secrecy or darkness, uncanny as he seemed to the handful of neighbours who knew that he existed; he was merely following the household pattern. His family, prominent once, had been almost forgotten, even in Herbert Street. No one came to see him. He had few friends, aside from the circle of his Bowdoin class-mates, with whom he had almost ceased to correspond. As a boy, he had often said he was going to sea and would never come back again; and he sometimes remarked to an acquaintance that he thought of disappearing, changing his name, escaping from the orbit of the postman, as if he had not sufficiently disappeared merely by staying at home. He had lapsed into this solitary life, half through a kind of inertia, and half,—he had always known he was going to write,—as if to protect a sensibility that was not yet ready to yield its fruits. His nickname had been Oberon at college, a reference to his shy, elusive ways. He had a massive head; his eyes were black and brilliant; he walked with the rolling gait of a sailor; he had a somewhat truculent voice and presence. Standing, he could leap shoulder-high. He liked to look at himself in the upright mirror and make up stories about the image he found reflected there. This image was dark and picturesque, tall and rather imposing. There was something vaguely foreign in its aspect.

He felt like a man under a spell, who had somehow put himself into a dungeon and could not find the key to let himself out. He had seated himself by the wayside of life, and a dense growth of shrubbery had sprung up about him, and the bushes had turned into saplings and the saplings into trees. Through the entangling depths he could find no exit. His style, his personality, his habits had been formed as far back as he could remember. At six he had read *The Pilgrim's Progress*. The first book he had bought was *The Faerie Queene*. To see the world in terms of allegory, or in the light of symbols, was second nature with him. At twelve, in a note-book his grandfather had given him, urging him to write out his thoughts,—a few every day,—he had described a child named Betty Tarbox as "flitting among the rosebushes, in and out of the arbour, like a tiny witch,"—phrases that might have occurred in the tales he was writing now. At sixteen, he had written a poem, precisely in the vein of some of these tales, about a young man dying for love of a ghost. He had certainly not acquired from Godwin's novels, however they intensified the taste, the feeling for romantic mystery that had sprung, for him, out of the Salem air. The novels of Scott had only excited further what seemed to be an inborn predilection for the history and the scenery of New England. All he knew was that these habits of mind, already formed in Salem, had been fostered in Maine, where he had spent a year, during his boyhood, on a lonely farm in a border hamlet. He had heard all sorts of stories from the farmers, tales of the supernatural, tales of ghosts, legends of the old colonial wars. He had heard the story of Father Moody of York, who had worn a black veil over his face. In summer, he had seen the Indians, on the Penobscot River, in their birch canoes, building their wigwams by the mill-dams. Round about stood the pine forests, bordering the northern lakes. He had skated all winter in the moonlight, alone and silent. He loved the black shadows cast by the frozen hills.

He might well have been thought uncanny. He was certainly "deep," as the country people said, deep as a night-scene by Albert Ryder. His mind was bathed in a kind of *chiaroscuro* that seemed to be a natural trait;

and yet it was a trait that he cultivated, half by instinct, half by deliberation. He had a painter's delight in tone. He liked to throw a ghostly glimmer over scenes that he chose because they were ghostly. It was a taste like Claude Lorrain's for varnish. He liked to study chimneys in the rain, choked with their own smoke, or a mountain with its base enveloped in fog while the summit floated aloft. He liked to see a yellow field of rye veiled in a morning mist. He liked to think of a woman in a silvery mantle, covering her face and figure. A man's face, with a patched eye, turning its profile towards him; an arm and hand extended from behind a screen; a smile that seemed to be only a part of a smile, seen through a covering hand; a sunbeam passing through a cobweb, or lying in the corner of a dusty floor. Dissolving and vanishing objects. Trees reflected in a river, reversed and strangely arrayed and as if transfigured. The effects wrought by moonlight on a wall. Moonlight in a familiar sitting-room, investing every object with an odd remoteness,—one's walking-stick or a child's shoe or doll, —so that, instead of seeing these objects, one seemed to remember them through a lapse of years. Hawthorne could never have said why it was that, after spending an evening in some pleasant room, lighted by a fire of coals, he liked to return and open the door again, and close it and re-open it, peeping back into the ruddy dimness that seemed so like a dream, as if he were enacting a conscious dream. For the rest, he was well aware why he had withdrawn to this little chamber, where there was nothing to measure time but the progress of the shadow across the floor. Somewhere, as it were beneath his feet, a hidden treasure lay, like Goldthwaite's chest, brimming over with jewels and charms, goblets and golden salvers. It was the treasure of his own genius, and it was to find this precious treasure that he had sat at his desk through summer and winter. The snow-flakes pelted against the

window-panes, the casement rattled in the December
gusts, clouds of dust blew through the open window.
Seasons and years rolled by. He had his doubts. Was he
tearing down the house of his mind in order to find the
treasure? In the end, when the house was destroyed, for
all he could say, there might be nothing in the chest but
rubbish.

Sometimes, in summer, on a Sunday morning, he stood
by the hour behind the curtain, watching the church
across the way. The sunrise stole down the steeple, touching the weather-cock and gilding the dial, till the other
steeples awoke and began to ring. His fancy played about
this conversation carried on by all the bells of Salem. At
twilight, he would still be standing there, watching the
people on the steps after the second sermon. Then, as
dusk set in, with a feeling of unreality, as if his heart and
mind had turned to vapour, he ventured into the street.
Sometimes, he was out all day, for the sake of observation. He would spend an hour at the museum, looking at
the black old portraits that brought back the days of Cotton Mather. These portraits explained the books that
he was reading, histories of Maine and Massachusetts,
the *History of Haverhill*, Felt's *Annals of Salem*. Or he
walked over to Marblehead and Swampscott, where the
old salts gathered in the store, in their red baize shirts
and oilcloth trousers, enthroned on mackerel barrels. He
felt a natural bond with all these Yankees, fishermen,
cattle-drovers, sailors, pilots. Some of them could steer
with bandaged eyes into any port from Boston to Mount
Desert, guided by the sound of the surf on every beach,
island or line of rocks. He liked to sit with them in
the bar-rooms, alive with curiosity, over a steaming hot
whiskey-punch. He studied the coloured prints on the
tavern walls. He noted the gateways in the crooked
streets, the whales' jaw-bones set like Gothic arches, the
bulging windows in the little shop-fronts, filled with nee-

dles, fishhooks, pins and thimbles, gingerbread horses, picture-books and sweetmeats. He stood at the toll-house on the Beverly bridge, watching the procession of carts and sulkies that rolled over the timber ribbon under which the sea ebbed and flowed; or he strolled on to Browne's Hill and traced out the grass-grown hollows, the cellars of Browne's Folly. Occasionally, he spent a day in Boston, haunting the public-houses in Washington Street. He penetrated behind the sober shop-front that masked the old Province House. Oftener, setting out at dawn, he rambled over Endicott's Orchard Farm, over the witchcraft ground and Gallows Hill, or perhaps Phillips's Beach, exploring the coast from Marblehead to Gloucester. He would bathe in a cove, overhung with maples and walnuts, pick up shells on the water's edge, skip pebbles on the water and trail the seaweed after him, draw names and faces in the sand. He would sit on the top of a cliff and watch his shadow, gesturing on the sand far below.

Occupations worthy of a poet who knew the value of reverie. These idle, whimsical movements absorbed his body while his mind pursued its secret operations. One had to be bored in order to think. Passivity was Hawthorne's element, when it was not curiosity. Usually, in the summer, dressed in his blue stuff frock, he undertook a longer expedition, to Maine or the Berkshires, perhaps, or to Martha's Vineyard, or along the Erie canal, as far as Detroit, where the old Connecticut poet, John Trumbull, was spending his last years. Nothing escaped him then; he had resumed his habit of keeping a note-book. He would stop for commencement at some country college, at Williams, so like his own Bowdoin, and mingle with the sheepish-looking students, half scholar-like, half bumpkin, fidgeting in their black broadcloth coats. He would spend a day at a cattle-fair, among the ruddy, round-paunched country squires who, with their wonderful breadth of fundament, waddled about, whip in hand, discoursing on the points of the sheep and oxen. He fell in with big-bellied blacksmiths, essence-pedlars chattering about their trade, old men sitting at railway stations, selling nuts and gingerbread, oblivious of the rush and roar about them, wood-choppers with their jugs and axes who had lived so long in the forest that their legs seemed to be covered with moss, like tree-trunks, pedlars of tobacco, walking beside their carts,—green carts with gaily painted panels,—conjurors, tombstone-carvers, organ-grinders, travelling surgeon-dentists, the queer confraternity of the road. He would exchange a word with a tavern-keeper, reading his Hebrew Bible with the aid of a lexicon and an English version. If it was a rainy day, the toddy-stick was in active use and the faces gleamed about the bar-room fire. He would stop at a farm for a glass of milk or linger in the market-place at Pittsfield, among the buckboards and the farmers' wagons, while the stage-coach discharged its passengers. Opening his note-book in the evening, he jotted down his observations. He had seen a tame crow on the peak of a barn. A half-length figure had appeared at a window, with a light shining on the shrouded face. A little boy had passed him on the road, lugging a basket of custard-cups. An intrusive reader, looking over his shoulder, might have wondered why it was worth his while to record such trifling items. To Hawthorne they were anything but trifling. Every one of these notes possessed for him a golden aureole of associations. Traits of New England life, aspects of New England scenery: a stone wall covered with vines and shrubs and elm-trees that had thrust their roots beneath it, a valley like a vast bowl, filled with yellow sunlight as with wine, the effect of the morning sun on dewy grass, sunlight on a sloping, swelling landscape beyond a river in the middle distance, an afternoon light on a clump of trees, evening light falling on a lonely figure, perhaps a country doctor on his horse, with his black leather saddle-bags behind him. Dark trees, decaying stumps, a cave in the side of a hill, with the sunlight playing over it. How like the human heart, this cave, with the glancing sun and the flowers about its entrance! One stepped within and found oneself surrounded with a terrible gloom and monsters of divers kinds.

Once, before turning homeward, he pressed on to Franconia Notch. This was the artery over the mountains through which the groaning wagons from the seaports carried the goods of Europe and the Indies to northern New Hampshire and Vermont. There stood the Great Stone Face. One dined on bear's meat in these northern woods, echoing with the notes of horn and bugle. Under some avalanche an ambitious guest, a young story-teller, for example, might have been crushed at Franconia Notch. Who would ever have heard of him then, his history, his plans, his way of life? Or suppose this young writer had frozen to death on the summit of Mount Washington? The mountain would have been a pedestal, worthy of a story-teller's statue. Hawthorne roamed up and down the Connecticut Valley. He fell in with a group of vagabonds, on their way to the camp-meeting at Stamford, a book-pedlar with the usual stock, —a handful of gilded picture-books and ballads, a Life of Franklin, Byron's Minor Poems, Webster's Spelling-book, the New England Primer,—a degenerate Indian with his bow and arrows, willing to turn a penny by shooting at it, an Italian conjuror with a merry damsel attired in all the colours of the rainbow. A travelling puppet-show had joined the troupe. The grave old show-man, in his snuff-coloured coat, turned the crank of the organ, and all the little people on the miniature stage broke into lively movement. The blacksmith's hammer fell on the anvil, the tailor plied his needle, the dancers whirled about on their feathery tiptoes, the soldiers wheeled in platoons, the old toper lifted his bottle, the merry-andrew shook his head and capered. Prospero entertaining his island crew! It was a masque of shadows that seemed as real as any other world that Hawthorne lived in. Would it not have been a good idea for a young story-teller to join this group and become an itinerant novelist, like the Oriental story-tellers, reciting his extemporaneous fictions at camp-meetings and cattle-fairs, wherever two or three were gathered together?

Most of Hawthorne's journeys, to be sure, were journeys *autour de sa chambre*. He was never away from Salem long. His note-books, however, filled along the road with incidents and casual observations, were precious memorabilia. They gave his ideas a local habitation. One saw this in the stories he was writing, sketches of actual life, historical tales and allegories. He thought of these as "twice-told" tales because, in several cases, he had heard them first before he had worked them out himself. How did he feel about his compositions? It seemed to him easier to destroy them than to court an indifferent public. He had thrown into the fire the *Seven Tales of My Native Land,* for which he had failed to find a publisher, and he had burned every available copy of his little published novel, *Fanshawe.* There was a devil in his manuscripts! He saw it laughing at him as the sparks flew upward. As for his recent stories,—the annual magazines had begun to accept them, the *Souvenir* and Peter Parley's *Token,*—they seemed to him to have an effect of tameness. They had, he felt, the pale tint of flowers that have blossomed in too retired a shade. If they were read at all, they should be read in the twilight in which they were written. They had been concocted from thin air; but it was this that gave the tales their magic. Some of them were really insubstantial, dim as ghosts basking in the starlight; in others, the apparently insubstantial was a new and original substance.

In Tieck's and Hoffmann's Germany, where the Gothic mind had reawakened, in harmony with this mood of spectral Salem, even in Poe's New York, one found similar tales of the listening dead, of graves and flitting shadows and lovers knocking at each other's tombs. Processions of mourners passed with measured tread, trailing their garments on the ground. One saw figures melting in mist. Black veils, boys with bandaged eyes, bridegrooms dressed in shrouds. Pools paved with marble and mosaic. Images shimmering in water. One heard the cries of children lost in the woods. Young men slept in the roadside shade, oblivious of the fates that might have been theirs if they had been awake; for fortune, crime and love hovered about them.

They were tales like evening moths or butterflies, light as clouds or flowers of early May, blooming in a woodland solitude. Out of them rose, when they were gathered together, an opalescent world that was strangely old, yet fresh and unfamiliar; it was like Prospero's island, half terrestrial, half an ethereal fabric. It was a new creation, this world of Hawthorne, with a past in Merry Mount and the Province House, in Howe's Masquerade and Esther Dudley, a present in pedlars and Shakers, in vagabonds and white old maids, in sunny Connecticut valleys and forest hollows, in snowstorms and ambiguous lime-burners, a future in little puckish boys and girls at play in the flickering sunshine. All very simple, it appeared, simple as the brightly coloured leaves that drift over a sedgy stream, only that too often, before one's eyes, the stream sang its way out of the meadow and carried its bright burden into the forest, where all grew dark and baleful.

Such was Hawthorne's world, as it rose in the minds of his readers. No other American writer had revealed such a gift for finding his proper subjects; no other had more consciously pursued his ends. Hawthorne had jotted down four rules of life: to break off customs, to meditate on youth, to shake off spirits ill-disposed, to do nothing against one's genius. He had shaped a poetic personality as valid and distinct as Emerson's; but the "spirits ill-disposed" were not easily conquered. He was drifting towards a cataract, he felt. "I'm a doomed man," he wrote to a friend, "and over I must go." He was threatened with melancholia, and he knew it. Out of this fear had sprung, or were to spring, the themes of many of his other stories, *Wakefield, The Man of Adamant, Ethan Brand,* tales of the unpardonable sin that consists in losing one's hold of the human chain. The Man of Adamant turns to stone, Ethan Brand forfeits, in his lonely bleakness, the key that unlocks human nature, Wakefield, who leaves his family and lives for twenty years in a neighbouring street, makes himself an outcast from the world without being admitted among the dead. Hawthorne repeated this note in twenty stories, tales of minds and hearts like chilly caverns, hung with glittering icicles of fancy. Tales of hypersensitive recluses who find themselves in white-washed cells. Tales of diabolical intellects,—*Rappaccini's Daughter* and *The Birthmark,*—which, in the name of some insane abstraction, destroy the life that they have ceased to feel. Tales like that of Lady Eleanore who, wrapped in pride as in a mantle, courts the vengeance of nature. Tales of diseased self-contemplation, of egoists who swallow serpents and sleepers who have missed their destiny. What traits, or, rather, what predicament, what fears did these tales reveal in the mind that conceived them? Hawthorne had lived too long in this border-region, these polar solitudes where the spirit shivered, so that the substance of the world about him hung before his eyes like a thing of vapour. He felt as if he had not lived at all, as if he were an ineffectual shadow, as if, having stepped aside from the highway of human affairs, he had lost his place forever. One night he had a dream that told him this. He seemed to be walking in a crowded street. Three beautiful girls approached him and, seeing him, screamed and fled. An old friend gave him a look of horror. He was promenading in his shroud.

Luckily, Hawthorne had another self, a sensible double-ganger. This other Hawthorne, this prosaic Hawthorne, the son of a Salem skipper, was interested in his own self-preservation; and, while he would never have taken too much trouble to keep himself afloat, he was glad to listen to his friends in matters of worldly wisdom. Twelve years were enough in a haunted chamber, filled with thoughts of suicide and madness. In 1836, this other Hawthorne entered the publishing house of "Peter Parley," wrote his *Universal History* for him and edited his *American Magazine.* Then, having broken the spell and gone to Boston, this matter-of-fact, substantial, physical Hawthorne accepted a position at the custom-house.

To the end of Hawthorne's life, these separate personalities dominated his destiny in turn. When one of them came to the front, as fishes, in pursuit of oxygen, rise to the surface of the water, the other vanished or concealed himself behind the nearest curtain. The story-teller scarcely knew the practical man of business who worked on the steaming docks, amid the coal-dust. Was this resolute, forcible being really himself, or was it someone who assumed his aspect and performed these duties in his name? Which was the true Hawthorne, which the phantom? The story-teller lived in a trance as long as the automaton carried on. His writing was accomplished in the happy seasons when the automaton was packed away, in the box where he belonged, when custom-houses, ships and offices lay like dreams behind him.

Both these personalities, meanwhile, had focussed themselves on a single object. Hawthorne had fallen in love. One saw him at the Boston Athenæum, where the ghost of Dr. Harris shadowed him, or moving silently through the Salem streets, enveloped in the cloak with its high-cut collar that almost concealed his features. It was a vain disguise, for life had reconnoitred him and love had tracked him out. He had become involved with the Peabody family, whose house in Salem overlooked the grave-yard where, among so many bones, the dust of ancestral Peabodys and Hawthornes mingled under the trees. Dr. Peabody's daughters believed they were descended from Boadicea. Whether it was true or not, the sisters possessed a store of nervous energy; and this, like youthful and impassioned nuns, they were devoting to the "higher life." Elizabeth, the oldest, the genius of the American kindergarten, was already known in Boston, where she was teaching, as the inexhaustible friend of all good causes. She was Dr. Channing's literary assistant, she was the confidante of Washington Allston, she was Bronson Alcott's aide at the Temple School. Of all these adventures of the mind she was to leave descriptions in her books.[1] The second sister Mary was engaged to Horace Mann. Sophia, the youngest, was Hawthorne's inamorata. A neurasthenic invalid, waiting on her couch for the magician who would command her to arise and walk, Sophia was witty and charming, as well as a clever linguist. When her sister married Horace Mann, she said that no doubt the first Peabody grandchild would open its mouth at once and utter a school-report. Her own avocations were artistic. Sometimes, while plying her needle of an afternoon, she would read a little Fénelon in French, a little Isaiah in Hebrew, a dozen pages of St. Luke in Greek and two or three scenes of Shakespeare. When she was not otherwise occupied, she spent her days modelling and painting. She had a pretty studio at the top of the house, and there she had made a medallion of

[1] *Reminiscences of William Ellery Channing, Last Evening with Allston, Record of Mr. Alcott's School.*

one of Emerson's brothers,—for the Emersons knew the Peabodys and sometimes came to visit them,—and a bust of Laura Bridgman. Her work had been warmly praised by Allston and Channing. Meanwhile, she had passed three years in Cuba, in the hope of reëstablishing her health.

It was Elizabeth Peabody, on one of her visits from Boston, who had disinterred Hawthorne from his living grave. With her unfailing scent for remarkable minds, she had followed his work in the magazines. A new and unique style united these often anonymous tales and sketches. Miss Peabody, who had caught this thread, wondered who the author was; and, behold, the clue led straight to a door in Salem. She drew Hawthorne out, induced him to see Sophia, inveigled him into the Transcendental circle that met on Saturday evenings at Miss Susan Burley's. Miss Burley was an amateur of antique gems and the cleverest hostess in Salem. She had even drawn Jones Very, that other Salem solitary, out of his shell. Hawthorne, caught at last in a drawing-room, stood motionless, not knowing what to do, his face pale and stricken. He picked up a knick-knack that lay on the table, to soothe his agitation. His hand trembled so that he almost dropped it.

No matter, he was "out," and out to stay, in a sort of low relief, like Sophia's medallions,—for no one was ever to see around him; and the Peabodys were determined to keep him out. The ever-active Elizabeth, who had introduced Jones Very to Emerson, called upon her friend George Bancroft, the historian-collector of the port of Boston, and obtained for him the post at the customhouse. Meanwhile, Sophia drew pictures for one of his stories, in the style of Flaxman's outlines. These delicate line-drawings of the English sculptor, so cool, so pure, so rhythmical, so graceful, were to leave long traces in American art. The Peabodys and their friends spent

many an evening poring over the drawings for Dante
and Homer, which they had borrowed from Professor
Felton. Sophia had a passion for them, and Hawthorne's
stories seemed to lend themselves to the treatment that
she knew so well. It was a happy augury that Flaxman's
genius, with which Hawthorne had so much in common,
presided over the fate of this pair of lovers.

CHAPTER XII

ALCOTT, MARGARET FULLER, BROOK FARM

JUST AT this moment, the Peabodys moved to Boston. They rented a house at 19 West Street, which soon became a rendezvous for the younger intellectuals, those who were conscious of the "new day." In one of the rooms on the ground-floor, Dr. Peabody opened a shop for the sale of homeopathic remedies. In the front room overlooking the street, Elizabeth and her mother sold foreign books. Mrs. Peabody was herself at work translating Goethe's *Hermann und Dorothea*. "God takes care of us" was her constant motto. She saw no reason not to be high-minded "even in selling a book."

Along with *Blackwood's* and the *Edinburgh*, which everyone read religiously at the Athenæum, they sold the German and French reviews and the writings of the continental authors whose thoughts were in the air. Miss Peabody, with her multifarious interests, chiefly in the "gardening" of children, who, she felt, should be "artists from the beginning," was publishing juvenile books on her own account, among them the three little volumes of *Grandfather's Chair*, which Hawthorne contrived to write in the intervals of measuring coal at the custom-house. There Margaret Fuller was giving her Conversations; and there, on occasion, Jones Very read his sonnets aloud to a chosen few. Eager school-girls flocked into the shop and bought more pencils than they could use for a chance to see Miss Peabody or Miss Fuller. And there, on almost any afternoon, one saw some of the new illuminati, Emerson, Alcott, Frederick Hedge, who had studied in Germany with Bancroft and had settled as a minister at Bangor, John Sullivan Dwight or George Ripley. Hawthorne came often to see Sophia.

This shop, so called, though most of its frequenters were bent on "reforming out" the principle of commercial enterprise, this intellectual caravansary was the liveliest spot in Boston. As a matter of course, the literary Tories, George Ticknor's circle, for example, called it the Hospital for Incapables. It was, in fact, a nest or kindergarten where newly-born thoughts were received and fostered. Thence they merged as books or social movements. Miss Peabody's second Bible was Gerando's essay, *On Moral Perfection and Self-Culture,* and no one was admitted to the circle who did not accept its teachings,—that life was a process of education, of which perfection was the proper aim. Miss Peabody exemplified this faith. Her sister Mary had founded a kindergarten in the very year when the German Froebel opened the first school that bore this name; and she herself wrote text-books and lectured on the history of religions. In her paper, *The Dorian Measure,* she urged the importance of dancing, not the sort that one learned from Signor Papanti but the mystical Grecian ballet, the folk-dance, the rhythmical allegory. This dancing would give the Bostonians a feeling for the customs of other nations. The Dorians had a message for enlightened Boston: severe without austerity, simple and dignified in their private relations, they yet dressed the festival of life, worshipping Apollo in the sunshine, with garlands of flowers and leaves. Perfection in all its forms was Miss Peabody's vision, and at present she busied herself in supplying wants that seemed to indicate a desire for it. The want might be Kraitsir's Lectures on Language, or Bern's Historical Chart, some of the artist's materials that she kept in stock, at Washington Allston's suggestion, a book on the new philosophy, or something more conclusive,—a plan for a desirable social system; for this was a magical shop, the kind one read about in the fairy-tales, where, in the guise of a book or a lecture-ticket, they sold Aladdin's lamps and rings of Gyges. James Freeman Clarke, another frequenter, a Unitarian minister in Louisville, who had come back to Boston for a summer visit, was astonished at the "state of fermentation" he found among his friends. "New ideas," he wrote, "are flying high and low." The centre of the whirl was the shop in West Street.

Miss Peabody was Channing's Eckermann. As a child she had heard the doctor preach, and she had never forgotten her mother's words, "It takes genius to reach children," words she had pondered for years until she learned their meaning from Froebel's writings. She had applied for a post as Channing's secretary; and the doctor, in order to test her, read to her aloud from Plato, raising his devouring eyes to make quite sure that she understood it. All had gone well after this. She dined at Channing's table every evening; she copied his sermons for the press. He had been greatly struck by Emerson's lectures, which seemed to set the young men on fire; and almost every morning he appeared at the book-shop, sometimes bringing Washington Allston with him. He wished to keep in touch with the new ideas, although he had his doubts about socialism, the Fourieristic notions that flourished there; the trend of life, he thought, was towards individuality of expression, and individual property expressed this law,—it was the "lowest expression," but still an expression. The doctor was solicitous about the future, and the West Street shop represented the future. As for Miss Peabody's future, one could see it already. One pictured her, forty years hence, drowsing in her chair on the lecture-platform or plodding through the slush of a Boston winter, her bonnet askew, her white hair falling loose, bearing still, amid the snow and ice, the banner of education.[1] If, perchance, you lifted her out of a snowdrift, into which she had stumbled absent-mindedly, she would exclaim, between her gasps, "I am so glad to see you! Can you tell me which is the best Chinese grammar?" Or she would give you the news about Sarah Winnemucka. "Now Sarah Winnemucka"—this was the maligned Indian princess who was collecting money to educate her tribe. Or she would ask if you had read your Stallo. She took down every lecture she heard, although she seldom wrote what people said: most of her reports were "impressions."[2] She was known to have lived in Europe for two years on $200, passed on with the utmost dignity from one enlightened household to another, invariably losing the railway ticket that found itself, by a miracle, in her hands. She had mislaid the ticket in somebody's *Reminiscences,* but what conductor or purser could disbelieve her?

This was a generation later, but already Miss Peabody was the salt of Boston. With Margaret Fuller as a fellow-worker, she had been assisting Bronson Alcott, another leader of the West Street circle, the Socrates of the Temple School. Alcott, for calling in question the gods of the city, for corrupting the minds of the young with the "new ideas," had had to drink his hemlock. A tall, mild, milky, passionless man, with a singular gift for understanding children, he had had five years for his ministrations. Then

> straight a barbarous noise environed him
> Of owls and cuckoos.

The red-faced sheriff knocked at the Temple door. In vain, Alcott's daughter, little Louisa, striding across the

---

[1] "Miss Peabody is the most dissolute woman in Boston," William James remarked in his sprightly youth. Henry James denied that he had the "grandmother of Boston" in mind in drawing Miss Birds-eye in *The Bostonians,* but the likeness was unmistakable.

[2] "I saw it," Miss Peabody said, when she walked into a tree and bruised her nose. "I saw it, but I did not realize it."

room, assailed the Vandal: "Go away, bad man, you are making my father unhappy!" Down from the walls came the pictures, the maps and the blackboard, Guido's "Flight into Egypt" and the portrait of Channing; the busts came down from their pedestals, Plato, Socrates, Milton; the comely desks, the charming cast of Silence, the dozen or more of Johnson's dictionaries, all these appropriate emblems, so carefully chosen to stir and elevate the dawning mind,—down they came and vanished. And Alcott, leading a child in either hand, followed them down, with mournful steps and slow.

He might have been crushed, if anything could crush him. But the school, that Academe for nascent Boston, was only one of Alcott's paradises. Sheriffs with flaming swords might drive him forth, but who can expel a man from the Garden of Eden that blooms behind his own brow? Not for nothing had he schooled himself as "one of the last of the philosophers." One of the last? He meant to be one of the first. He had, indeed, a philosophic mission, to restore the fabled innocence of man and root it in the soil of Massachusetts. He had never doubted the doctrine of pre-existence, the lapse of the soul from its primordial state, with its native creative powers, never since the days when he had first read Plato and found that Plato's cloud-land was, for him, far more solid than the United States. Coleridge had shown him clearly that the elements of the human consciousness were not to be sought in impressions of external nature, but rather in the self-existent spirit, spontaneous and outside of time and space. "Before time was, I am"; and birth was but a sleep and a forgetting. Then wherefore not awaken and remember? Why not recover what the race had lost, fatuously exiled in the realms of sense? Such were the views upon which his school was founded; such was the faith that he had cultivated, watching over the growth of his little daughters. They had a natural pleasure in beautiful things, a happy trust and affection, free and direct as they were. In them the avenues to the Over-soul were all wide open. How dim were the perceptions of most of their elders! How cold their sympathies were, spoiled and spotted by their mundane interests! How had they fallen from their high estate! They could not become as little children. And Alcott meant to see that the little children did not become like them.

Such was Alcott's theory of education. Every great man of Greece and Rome had had a philosopher as a teacher, and his own purpose in teaching had always been, not to inculcate knowledge,—at least by the method of the pump and bucket,—but to develop genius. Was not every well-born child a genius? By the Socratic method, as it seemed to Alcott, by posing the proper questions, one could elicit from a group of children all the thoughts of Plato. He tried to reach his pupils from within. No forcing, no cramming, no rod or ferule. He had made the schoolroom gracious and attractive and devised recreations and amusements, plays, physical exercises, even a system of self-government. He encouraged the keeping of journals. Children must know themselves to become themselves and escape from the tyranny of custom. With his own little Anna, aged four, he had held intellectual conversations that seemed to him not unworthy of Plato's disciples; and Louisa had been writing her daily journal before she was able to join her letters. He had begun himself when he was twelve, making his own ink out of maple and oak-bark, steeped in alum and indigo; but he had had to fight for his education. A poor farmer's son, like Horace Mann, he had learned to write in a copy-book, forming his letters after the master's phrase, "Avoid alluring company." He had spent his youth as a pedlar, travelling through Virginia with his horse and wagon, with his tin trunk full of Yankee notions, pins, scissors, combs, thimbles, puzzles, with a self-respect presumably unknown to the silken sons of pride and dissipation,—always on the lookout for a school where he could exercise his theories. He had learned his best lessons along the road, from some of the Southern planters, who had taken him into their houses and taught him manners. He had fallen in with the Philadelphia Quakers, whose "inner light" he soon identified with the Brahma of the Oriental Scriptures. Among them, for a while, at Germantown, where his daughter Louisa was born, he had conducted a school, before he opened his great campaign in Boston.

What matter if the Temple School had failed? He had other careers ahead, this Indra of the seven incarnations. He knew that future times would vindicate him. There were plenty of closet-philosophers: Alcott was a philosopher in action for whom the object of life was to be oneself. Be what you were meant to be! If you were a crooked stick, go through the world as an oddity, to your own merriment, at least, if not to that of your contemporaries. Character was a fact, and that was much in a world of pretence and concession. If Boston was not ready for such a teacher, so much the worse for Boston. Was he going to repine and hedge and distrust the powers that always upheld the virtuous and the wise? When a confidence-man asked him for five dollars, and Alcott gave him ten, the groundlings laughed at his simplicity; but the confidence-man, stricken with remorse, sent the money back. One could trust the law of compensation.

The school was a misadventure, though more for the children than for Alcott. So was the fate of his book, the enlightened *Conversations on the Gospels,* most of the copies of which had been sold to be used for trunk-linings. This book had largely caused the trouble. It was a record of Alcott's dialogues with the little sons and daughters of patrician Boston, in which, in connection with the sacred story, he had tried to replace with clear ideas the fabric of traditional association. The parents were alarmed, but the children, most of them eight or nine years old, were entranced with these religious dialectics. Little Josiah Quincy spoke like an infant prophet. Rapt attention had reigned in the beautiful class-room, as the master sat in his pulpit, his pupils gathered in an arc before him, in the soft light that streamed through the Gothic windows. There were special classes for Latin, for sums and spelling, and the children of three and four had desks in the corners. They drew on their slates and learned the art of silence. Sometimes the poet Dana appeared and gave a quiet reading from Coleridge or Wordsworth, for an audience of children pleased him best. If the day was cold, the master read aloud Thomson's *Winter* and analyzed the poem on the blackboard. A dialogue might ensue on winter sports, on the nature of coasting and skating, or the master divided the words he had just been reading into their various classes, as the names of objects, qualities and relations. Or perhaps he would read one of Northcote's *Fables,* or a chapter of *The Pilgrim's Progress,* or a passage from *The Castle of Indolence.* What did it represent? There were passages that excited the moral feelings, fear, pity, courage; others called into play the intellectual faculties, reason, perception, judgment. The master followed his readings with suitable questions. Language had to be picturesque and lively to clothe these thoughts in words. What was the purpose of going to school? To learn good behaviour? What was behaviour, what was the purpose of manners? What was the purpose of the imagination? What was the meaning of a definition? One had to use one's wits at the Temple School.

Boston, hitherto so cold and formal, had begun to receive the gospel of Conversation. This was the message of the Temple School. It was the message also of Margaret Fuller, who, with Elizabeth Peabody, assisted

Alcott. Miss Peabody kept the log-book of the school,
reporting its operations word by word, while she was
reading Greek with Dr. Channing. Margaret Fuller also
assisted Channing: she spent one evening of every week
reading aloud to him in German. But the doctor was too
restricted to suit the impetuous Margaret. He was always
looking for the moral in works of creative genius. She
preferred the abandon of the poet. She liked to duck,
dive and fly for truth. Besides, as an impassioned feminist, she wished to minister to the minds of women.
What woman ever had a chance, among the few men
who enjoyed this fortune? What were the legitimate
hopes of women? Why should they all be constrained to
follow employments for which only some of them were
fitted? While men were called upon, from their earliest
youth, to reproduce everything they learned, women
never reproduced their learning except for the sake of
display. It was partly the fault of society, and partly their
own, because they were so unconscious, victims of domestic preoccupations. Better to have one's curtains and
carpets soiled than to soil one's mind with such paltry
thoughts and feelings! Better, the fragrant herb of wit,
and a little cream of affability, than all the pretty tea-
cups in the world! As for American men, they were tame
enough, with their everlasting business, their little games
of local politics, with only two or three tunes in their
music-boxes. One wound them up, and they tinkled
about "the office," they tinkled again about the next election, and that was the end of their music. They never
added a new tune after five-and-twenty. No spirit, no variety of depth and tone! Why should American men and
especially women be satisfied with the common routines
of living? Why should they not be capable of such relations as those of Landor's Pericles and Aspasia? They
should look for their hidden gifts. They should be satisfied with nothing less than Goethe's "extraordinary gen-

erous seeking." Genius, Margaret thought, would be as common as light if men and women trusted their higher selves. She had never questioned her own vocation, and she was just on the verge of thirty when, towards the end of 1839, she opened her Conversations in the West Street house. It was on a Saturday, at noon, her regular weekly hour. She appeared, with a regal air, with various books of reference on her arm and a huge bouquet of chrysanthemums. The lorgnette was much in evidence.

An electrical apparition was this "queen of Cambridge." She had seen men "bristle," as she said,—the foolish little creatures, youths of untouched heart, shallow, as yet, in all things,—when she crossed the threshold of an evening party. She frightened them with her magnetic powers, the depth of her eye, the powerful onward motion that announced the presence of the mysterious fluid. So, at least, she felt. But most of these men had nothing to fear,—the dry, cold, sordid money-getters,—for Margaret knew at a glance the minds that belonged to her, and she was "sagacious of her quarry." So she wrote in her journal. As the daughter of Timothy Fuller, member of Congress, who had surrendered his income and profession in order to write a history of his country, she had lived in a great house in Cambridge, surrounded by the cleverest Harvard students, who had never seen a girl of her complexion. Her father had taught her Latin as soon as she could speak, and her infant prayers had begun, "O God, if thou art Jupiter!" Occasionally, she had prayed to Bacchus for a bunch of grapes. She thought of herself as a princess, who had been left by mistake on a Cambridge door-step. At boarding-school, at Groton, she had first revealed her insatiable will-to-power. Unable to rule by affection, she had ruled as the demon of discord, swooning at tactical moments, setting the girls by one another's ears, striking her head against an iron hearth, falling into fits of melancholy, until, by one method or another, she had reduced the school to servitude. The girls raved about her. She was the "bandit's bride" of the trashy novels they read behind their desks. No one had such hair as hers, dressed with a tropical flower, such wild, strange, lively ways, such flashes of the eye. There was always something odd in the way she wore a sash or a necklace. Her simplest frock had an air of fancy dress. The girls delighted in paying her homage. They placed wild flowers beside her plate, and they felt that she was born to be misunderstood by everyone but her lover. As for the unhappy teachers, not one of them, as Margaret said, had ever asked herself an intelligent question about the nature of her earthly mission. Margaret's own mission was to "grow." She felt that her impulses were disproportioned to the persons and occasions she encountered and rightly carried her beyond the reserves that marked the appointed lot of women. She looked with envy at Flaxman's picture of Hesiod sitting at the feet of the Muse. Where could she find an intellectual guide? At fifteen, she rose at five, walked for an hour and practised on the piano; then she read philosophy and French. From half past nine till noon, she studied Greek, practised again, lounged for half an hour, read for two hours in Italian, then went for a walk or a drive; in the evening, she played or sang and wrote in her journal. As between Madame de Staël and the useful Miss Edgeworth, patterns that one might follow, she had no difficulty in choosing. Over her head, as over Madame de Staël's, had risen the sun of Goethe. She, too, would have liked to provoke an emperor's wrath.

She had passed through dreams of romance, hours of yearning and passion. She threw herself into Goethe's life. Should he have given up his Lili? She lived through the rapturous days of the heroines of mythology and drama, Iphigenia, Antigone, the Scandinavian world-mother Frigga, George Sand's Consuelo and Corinne, invoking them in her diary: "Antigone, Iphigenia, you were worthy to live! . . . Iphigenia, I was not born in vain, if only for the tears I have shed with thee." She saw herself as the goddess Isis, dazzling the eyes of her votaries. She might have been the Countess Emily Platen, the Polish Joan of Arc. Among her chosen men were Alfieri, the Countess of Albany's lover, and George Sand's Count de Rudolstadt, aristocratic democrats who shared the culture of the fortunate classes but longed for the welfare of all. Carlyle's was the grand method of education!—idolatrous hero-worship of genius and power. She did not expect to be happy. How could a woman of genius conform to the world about her, or find her mysterious impulses understood? She remembered how as a child she had stood at a window from which she could see an eagle chained, on one of the neighbouring balconies. She had seen people poking it with sticks, and her heart had swollen with indignation. The eagle's eye was dull, and its plumage was soiled and shabby, yet with what a mien the monarch-bird endured these paltry insults. In its form and attitude, all the king was visible, even though degraded and dethroned. Such was the fate of genius in a world of pygmies. They censured her in Boston because she filled the girls, who flocked about her, with her own romantic nonsense. She made them wish to marry Alfieris, as if State Street lawyers were not good enough,—not to mention cotton-merchants and codfish-packers with an eye on the Legislature. They laughed at her superstitions, her faith in demonology, omens, foresight. They smiled when she said that "Margaret" meant "Pearl," the gem that is cradled in slime, in disease and decay, like all that is noblest in the human soul. Only the experienced diver knows the pearl.

Who could comprehend her aspirations, the demands she made upon life, her struggles and conflicts? She would lie all day on the shore at Nahant, with the waves washing about her, looking up at the turrets and jagged cliffs bathed in prismatic light. Prometheus, or Promethea, among the rocks, or perhaps Andromeda chained, waiting for her unknown Perseus. Beethoven, at least, would have understood her. She wrote him a midnight letter. With the Boston girls, her pupils,—for she was obliged to teach, to pay for the education of her brothers and sisters, the father's death having left them in distress, —she read her beloved Goethe, Schiller and Lessing, together with Petrarch and Tasso in Italian. With her chosen friends, meanwhile, James Freeman Clarke, with whom she had first studied German, Frederick Henry Hedge, Samuel Gray Ward, and Emerson, her last and greatest conquest, to whom Harriet Martineau had introduced her as the most brilliant talker she had known, she gathered the spoils of culture,—a little meagre still in frosty Boston, but amplified by her enthusiasm,—portfolios of drawings and engravings, designs from Raphael, architectural sketches, the Athenæum casts, the Brimmer collection. In each of her friends she seemed to divine the law of his own interior growth. She gave them to themselves, or so they felt, drew out their unsuspected faculties. Many of these friends, in later years, traced to some conversation with her the moment when they had seen their way before them, when they had formed some resolution from which their careers had sprung. It was true that she had an influence in hundreds of lives. Long after her death, the painter William Morris Hunt saw on a table in Florence a copy of Mrs. Jameson's *Italian Painters*. Margaret had written on the margin, beside a passage on Correggio, "And yet all might be such." Hunt said, "These words struck out a new strength in me. They made me set my face like a flint."

She aspired to write, dry as writing seemed beside the excitement of conversation. The six historical tragedies she had planned had all come to nothing, and she could

not afford the time to finish the life of Goethe for which
she had gathered a mass of notes and sketches. Meanwhile, she translated the *Conversations with Eckermann,*
Bettina von Arnim's *Günderode* and hundreds of pages
of Uhland, Novalis and Körner, with poems of her own
as commentaries. But conversation was her medium. She
liked to see the effects of her mental efforts, and the Saturday classes in West Street were responsive. Half the
feminine *élite* were there, Elizabeth Hoar from Concord,
Lydia Maria Child, the three Peabody sisters, Mrs. Emerson, Mrs. George Bancroft, Mrs. Theodore Parker, Maria
White, who was engaged to James Russell Lowell. The
subjects were Greek mythology, "What is Life?", the history of art, the meaning of the various dances. Margaret
had the true Boston passion for pigeonholes and categories, for putting everything in its proper place. Wordsworth was the "poet of reflection," Jupiter stood for "the
will," Bacchus for the "terrene inspiration." It was all
sharp and clear, like so many definitions from a legal
treatise, ready to be gathered in a note-book. Margaret's
ideas had good square corners, like building-blocks that
fitted at the edges. Set side by side, in just the right arrangement, they formed a solid architectural structure, a
true temple of culture, as unmistakable as a Boston bank.
One of the ladies kept the class in order with her un-
swerving eye for Christian morals, which might have
been lost in aesthetic divagations. Sometimes the Gothic
genius seized the reins of Margaret's fancy, and she
would ride like a Valkyrie over the clouds of German
metaphysics. Then, before the eyes of her worshipping
hearers, the cold New England landscape melted into a
dreamland of romance. One dwelt for a moment in Val-
halla, among the Scandinavian gods and heroes, as erstwhile in Athens of the violet crown.

In West Street, one could buy over the counter, in
exchange for a little good will,—or a thousand dollars,

in case one happened to have it,—a share in the Utopian community that was rapidly taking shape at Brook Farm. This was George Ripley's contribution to the educational movement of Massachusetts. For fourteen years, with no great zeal for the Unitarian cause, Ripley had been preaching in a Boston pulpit; and now, having resigned, he was already living at the farm, at West Roxbury, nine miles out of town. He was a cheerful, hearty, faithful soul, ready for any task, for whom the opinion of the world was but a "puff of empty air." He had always expected to be poor and rather preferred obscurity to fame. "Give me philosophy!" was all he asked. He had heard the call of "association," of the communists and Christian socialists, the Owenites and the Fourierists, followed by the Icarians and Cabet, who were establishing their communities in every corner of the young republic. Almost every month the port of New York welcomed some new boat-load of Europeans who had come to found a "Harmony" or a "North American Phalanx." Ripley, while planning the farm, was editing a work in fourteen volumes, *Specimens of Standard Foreign Literature,* translations of Cousin, Jouffroy, Goethe, Menzel, Benjamin Constant and others. He had recruited many of his translators from the West Street circle. In the winter of 1840-41, the whole group discussed Ripley's project.

It came into existence in the spring, and building was added to building, the Hive, in the shade of an ancient sycamore, the Eyrie, the Nest, the Cottage, the Pilgrim House, and member was added to member, until, at the end of six years, there were more than a hundred and forty associates. Of the circle of the Transcendentalists, most of the ablest members remained aloof, as benevolent neutrals and visitors. "Doing things in crowds" seemed to them too youthful; they were self-sufficient. As Margaret Fuller put it, in her somewhat airy dialect,

"Why bind oneself to a central or any doctrine? How much nobler stands a man entirely unpledged, unbound?" This was Emerson's feeling. For Alcott, the plan was not austere enough. All three dissented from the idea behind the association, "As the institutions, so are the men," preferring to think, with Goethe, "As the men, so are the institutions." But Hawthorne, who had no theories, hoped to find at the farm a practical basis for his married life. John Sullivan Dwight, who had translated for Ripley the *Minor Poems of Goethe and Schiller,* and Charles A. Dana, fresh from Harvard, later known as Dana of *The Sun,* were members for a longer period. So was Isaac Hecker, of the "Hecker's Flour" family of New York, the German-American priest of the future, who founded the order of the Paulist Fathers. George William Curtis and his brother Burrill and George P. Bradford were other members. Bradford, whose *Selections from Fénelon* was another volume of Ripley's series, later moved to Plymouth to realize his dreams of the simple life. In the intervals of teaching Greek, he carried on a market-garden, selling his own vegetables from the cart. This was the charming and sensitive Bradford whose New England conscience was such a nuisance. Once, during one of Webster's out-of-door speeches, he was swept up to the front of the crowd. "I have no ticket," he exclaimed, "I have no right to be here"; and, much to the discomfort of the crowd, but much to the comfort of his conscience, he shoved his way back to the outermost rim. Charles King Newcomb, another member, was an individualist of a different sort. In his high room with the French window, this young Providence mystic kept a wooden crucifix on his table, between portraits of Xavier and Loyola, with freshly gathered flowers at the foot. One often heard his voice, in the midnight hours, chanting the litany or reading Greek. Newcomb lived a strange, secret life, prolonged for half a century in Paris, devoted to the writing of a private journal, as long as Amiel's journal, or even longer, that lay unpublished in a Rhode Island attic fifty years after his death. There were farmers and artists among the members, working-men and Brahmins, girls with hazel eyes and extravagant moods, several Harvard students, an English baronet's son, a Spaniard, two Filipinos, the son of a Louisiana planter, "Omniarch" Ryckman, "Camilla" and "Sybilla,"—for nicknames were in vogue,—"Chrysalis" List and "Old Solidarity" Eaton.

In the broad entry of the Hive, Ripley's library filled the shelves until, to raise more money for the venture, the master sold his books to Theodore Parker. Ripley, the ever-faithful "Archon," steered the unsteady ship with unwavering eye. He was up before the dawn, dressed in his blue tunic and cow-hide boots, milking, cleaning the stalls, blacking the shoes of some member who was going to town, carting off the vegetables to market, directing the field-operations, writing diplomatic letters, giving a Sunday lecture on Kant or Spinoza, or, on a winter evening, when the stars were bright, gathering the members about him in the snow, while he discoursed on the constellations. His wife, Sophia Ripley, Richard Henry Dana's younger sister, who was soon to join the Catholic Church, cheerfully toiled beside him, ten hours a day in the muslin-room, washing, scrubbing the floors, much to the annoyance of her kindred. The school was more than admirable. Ripley taught philosophy and mathematics. Mrs. Ripley had a class in history and a class for Dante in Italian. Charles A. Dana had classes in Greek and German. The bashful, slender, beaming little Dwight, the dictator of musical Boston in later years, carried on the classes in music. He, too, had once occupied a Unitarian pulpit, though he had a way of forgetting to write his sermons. He had a "want of fluency in prayer," for his mind was entirely filled

with Mozart and Haydn. He started his "mass clubs" at
the farm. There were classes in botany and geology, carried on among the rocks and trees. All the studies were
elective; the rule was to "follow one's attractions." The
young men wore blouses and hunters' frocks, belted at
the waist, of plain brown holland or a gayer chintz, with
little tasselled caps; the girls wore muslin dresses, with
flowers and ribbons. The single men lived in Attica, the
garret of the Hive; and the vegetarians had a Gra-
ham table. George William Curtis trimmed the lamps;
Charles A. Dana was the griddle-master. There was
much sitting about on stairs and floors, and the conversation,—analytical often, bristling with the new philosophy, with "intuition" and "the analogous," the objective,
the creative, the receptive,—sometimes assumed those
painful forms of wit that flourish among the intelligent-
sia. There were many jokes about "affinities," puns of
the frostier kind that make one feel so sorry for the punster, animadversions on "morbid familism," *clichés* of a
dire facetiousness: "Is the butter within the sphere of
your influence?" But there were merry dances every
night, picnics on Cow Island or in the grove, boating
parties on the Charles, close by, Shakespeare readings,
Elizabethan pageants, tableaux, charades, plays, scenes
from Byron's *Corsair* and Sheridan's *Pizarro*. Occasionally, in the evening, little groups walked or drove to Boston, to a Beethoven concert or an Emerson lecture,—the
interest in Beethoven seemed to flourish in minds that
had been quickened by Emerson,—or an anti-slavery
meeting at Faneuil Hall. They filled the big farm-wagon,
or Jonas Gerrish's stage, which, twice a day, plied between the Hive and Scollay Square. Their favourite
rendezvous in the afternoon was Elizabeth Peabody's
book-shop. At night, they gathered in Mrs. Harrington's
cake-shop, and the younger men and the girls walked
home under the stars.

The stage from Scollay Square brought visitors, a few, at first, those of the inner circle, then hundreds and even thousands of "civilisees," as the farmers called the rest of the population. Margaret Fuller came to conduct a Conversation on Education, on "What can we do for ourselves and others?" Impulse was the subject on one occasion, an appropriate theme at the farm, where spontaneity was so much in order. Throwing oneself on the floor was not so bad, but yawning, as Margaret said, was a little too impulsive. Georgiana Bruce burned pastilles to perfume Margaret's room and brought the morning coffee to her bedside. For Margaret had become another Pauline Wiesel, the heroine of the German Romantics, whom Humboldt walked thirty miles to see.[3] Emerson often came to lead the talk; sometimes Bronson Alcott. Theodore Parker, who lived close by,—he had a church at West Roxbury,—walked over often for a chat about philosophy or farming. Orestes Brownson dropped in, shouted and pounded on the table and strolled with Isaac Hecker in the grove. They were both on the road to Rome, like Mrs. Ripley; and Brownson's coming always occasioned a talk on Catholicism, Pascal or Port Royal. This was a theme that pleased Charles Newcomb, whose favourite author was Saint Augustine. Brownson, the rustic giant from Vermont, who had passed through so many religious phases, was not a welcome guest. That there was method in his truculence, no one had any reason to suppose; and he had taken up his Greek and Latin, to satisfy his Catholic advisers, at a time when his mental bones had set. He made sad work of his spondees

[3] One of Pauline Wiesel's friends wrote of her, in the vein of Margaret's friends, "I look upon her in the light of a phenomenon of Greek mythology." She herself had written, much in Margaret's vein, "Every means, every possible preparation for living, and yet one must never live; I never shall, and those who dare to do so have the wretched world, the whole world, against them."—George Brandes, *The Romantic School in Germany*.

and dactyls, which the patient George Ripley would not have minded if Brownson had not appeared to be showing off, but George Bradford, the ever-gentle, who had learned his Greek and Latin in the cradle, could not sleep for the misery that Brownson caused him. False vowels and wrong measures were as painful to him as a saxophone would have been. He dreamed one night that he was a Catholic convert and that Brownson, appointed his confessor, obliged him to repeat, after himself, a Latin psalm from the Vulgate. Bradford awoke in agony.

This was a pity, for Brownson, who was honest as the day, was a man of really imposing gifts. He appeared to be unstable enough. He had passed from sect to sect, changing his ministerial coat as many times as the Vicar of Bray, although always in response to a new conviction. Every thinker he read, Lamennais, Jouffroy, Comte, Saint-Simon, Owen, overthrew all his previous views, and he rushed from one position to another, with a headlong, headstrong vehemence, telling the world each time how right he was. With a vigorous, enquiring mind that was anything but sensitive or subtle, he had a warm and generous imagination. He had founded the "Society of Union and Progress," chiefly for the advancement of the workers, and he had preached class-warfare, the death-struggle of rich and poor, as a step towards the "Church of the Future," after the Comtian pattern, of which he saw himself as a John the Baptist. He longed for a new Catholicity until he found a home in the old one. To further his ideas and reflect their changes, he carried on a quarterly review, first the *Boston Quarterly*, afterwards *Brownson's Quarterly*. In this he "aimed to startle," as he said, taking pains to be paradoxical and even as extravagant as he could be; and this method was rather accentuated after he had joined the Catholic Church. The Bishop of Boston lamented the timidity of the

Catholic population, most of whom were recent immigrants, of the depressed classes, in a society that was hostile to them. The Bishop urged Brownson not to hide his light under a bushel. As well urge a bull not to pretend to be a lamb. The rugged, fiery Brownson was happy to learn that truculence had an apostolic value. On ferry-boats between Chelsea and Boston, in barber-shops, in butcher-shops, wherever he happened to find himself, he engaged all and sundry in religious discussions. Once at an inn at Andover, where he was giving a lecture, he loudly commanded the waiter to send for the landlord. "Landlord," he exclaimed, in a voice that was meant for all the guests, "why don't you have something in your house that a Christian can eat? Why don't you have fish? No Christian eats meat on Friday."

This was one of the little things that people seldom did at Andover. They kept a special corner of hell-fire there for travellers with Brownson's views. But Brownson was a courageous man, in the Church as well as out of it, whom the Brook Farmers learned to respect in the end; for, having been too Catholic for the Yankees, he was too Yankee for the Catholics, at least for the Church as he found it, and he stormed against the Irish domination. He wished to make the Church an American Church, to counteract the powerful influence that tended to make it Irish; and no one spoke more forcefully than he against the corruptions of Tammany. He was under a cloud in Dublin as well as in Boston, and Cardinal Newman was forced to withdraw the invitation he had sent to Brownson to lecture at his new university there. He was the first lecturer that Newman invited, and he was asked to choose his own subject, geography or "opossums," if it suited him best; for Brownson's multifarious writings on history, sociology, religion, on politics, art and philosophy had given him a world-name. His standing was high in the Catholic world,[4] and his gifts, from the point of view of any school, his versatility and his breadth of knowledge, his energy and lucidity, were those of a first-rate publicist. Something more than a journalist, something less than a sage, Brownson was a Catholic Theodore Parker. In one book, *The Convert*, the history of his religious life, he left the best account that has ever been written of the spiritual cross-currents of the forties and fifties.

Of the other guests at Brook Farm, two were especially welcome, William Henry Channing, the doctor's nephew, a minister, albeit with many scruples, better known as a Christian socialist, and the tall, slight, graceful Christopher Cranch, with the picturesque head and curling hair, the son of a judge in Washington, who, having ample means and mundane tastes, had gradually "sunk the minister in the man" and followed the call of the muses. He was a landscape painter and a poet; he sang and played the flute and violin; he was a clever actor on occasion and the cleverest caricaturist in New England. In fact, he was the victim of too many gifts, no mere Janus with a double head but a sort of accomplished Hydra. He had taken Emerson at his word and planted himself on his instincts, wherever they led him. They had led him into the pulpit and out again; they led him to Louisville, Kentucky, where he took the place of James Freeman Clarke as editor of *The Western Messenger*. With his flute as his constant companion, he had drawn there his comic illustrations for some of Emerson's essays, such as the "Man expanding like a Melon." These drawings, suggesting Thackeray's, shocked some of the Transcendentalists. In years to come, he was to use this talent in

---

[4] "You alone can prepare us for the great controversies by founding among us a school and arming it with the principles of a sound philosophy."—Letter of Lord Acton to Brownson, 1854. See also the long correspondence with Montalembert in the *Life of Brownson* by his son.

the pictures for his charming books for children, *The Last of the Huggermuggers* and *Kobboltozo*,—years during which he lived as a wandering artist, in London, New York, Paris, Rome and Cambridge. What could an artist do, he would write from New York, in a money-getting world? People rushed in from the streets and stopped for a moment in his studio, only to hurry-scurry out again, eternally driving, driving. In Cambridge, he found a congenial circle, and there he translated the *Æneid;* but whenever he came back from Italy he was struck by the look in people's faces, the hard, weary expression about the mouth, the quick, shrewd eye, the anxious air. Everyone seemed to be worried; and back he would go to Rome, to join the circle of William Wetmore Story, write a few more poems and paint from the costume-models.

His painting was nothing out of the way, but some of his poems had a firmer touch. There are poets who survive in a single line. Cranch was destined to survive in two, from the poem called *Enosis,*—

> We are columns left alone
> Of a temple once complete,—

which hundreds of men have quoted in their later years. At Brook Farm, where he came to visit his friend and fellow-lover of music and German, his Harvard classmate Dwight, he was the all-attractive entertainer. He drew amusing pictures of the Harvard mill grinding its grist of ministers. He performed astonishing feats of ventriloquism. William Henry Channing was more austere. He was a self-tormented creature, earnest, hypersensitive, torn by doubts, a "concave man" who was always retreating, as Henry Thoreau remarked, like a fair mask swaying from a bough. For the rest, he was a man of the world, as all the Channings were, and a preacher unexcelled when the spirit moved him. In later years, he was to live in England, where his daughter married the author of *The Light of Asia*. At the moment, he was editing in New York a magazine called *The Present*, to propagate his socialistic views. What to do for the race? was his constant question; but he was involved in metaphysics, of a sadly tenuous kind, and he was convinced, as a friend remarked, that "Christ did not understand his own religion." He had spent a season in Rome, vainly hoping to get himself converted, and the engravings on his study wall were arranged in the form of a cross. He wrote an occasional poem and various tracts and had recently translated Jouffroy's *Ethics;* but the great project of his life was a work on Vittoria Colonna, a study of the Italian Renaissance. He meditated this for many years, enthralled as he gathered his memoranda, until the enormous task of preparation became a life-work in itself. He never began the book. A mystical enthusiast, like Dr. Channing, but without his uncle's will, irresolute, introspective, the victim of innumerable intentions, a talker and taker of notes who longed to be "useful,"—such was the "evil times' sole patriot," as Emerson called him in a well-known poem. Of all the Brook Farmers, guests or members, William Henry Channing was the symbol, as later times recalled the enterprise. Whatever the facts might be, whatever happened, he could never persuade himself that the world's salvation did not lie just around the corner. He always felt, when he rose from his bed, that the "one far-off divine event" might well occur before he sat down to breakfast.

CHAPTER XIII

EMERSON: WOOD-NOTES

IN THE days of King Philip's War, the Indians had spared the town of Concord. They burned the neighbouring settlements, Sudbury, Chelmsford, Stow, but one of their chieftains said, as they glanced over Concord from a hill-top, "We shall never prosper if we go there. The Great Spirit loves that town." This was an Indian legend, and one could well believe it. Plain, low, quiet, the village had no obvious distinction. The enterprising Yankees passed it by. It had no port, no trade, no water-power, no gold, lead, coal, oil or marble. The granite was better at Fitchburg, and even the Concord ice had bubbles in it. As wood and grass were its only staples, Emerson advised his fellow-townsmen to manufacture school-teachers and make them the best in the world.[1] The village air favoured this, as it favoured meditation and contemplation. The hills and woods, not too exciting, afforded a gentle stimulus to genial and uninterrupted studies. One recalled in Concord the words of the old Chinese painter: "Wherein do the reasons lie that virtuous men so love *Shan-shui,* landscape? Landscape

[1] A staple for the South and West. Edward Everett Hale relates that a certain French investigator, sent by Napoleon III to study American education, found that virtually every teacher in the West and South had come from one small corner of the country, either Connecticut or Massachusetts. He asked Hale to explain this fact, which he said was unique in history. Hale, to settle the question, enquired of a leading citizen of Massachusetts how many young people of his town, when they left school, began as teachers. "He heard me," says Hale, "with some impatience, and then said, 'Why, all of them, of course.'"—E. E. Hale, *Tarry-at-Home Travels.*

is a place where vegetation is nourished on high and low ground, where springs and rocks play about like children, a place that woodsmen and retiring scholars usually frequent, where birds cry aloud their joy in the scene."

Concord abounded in *Shan-shui*. One found peace there and the flourishing days in which minds are high and joyous, the days that Kakki desired for the landscape-painter. There one could have good feeling and beautiful taste; one could create the *Yu*, the wonderful and mysterious. Emerson found it so, in his woodland walks. Once he had left his study, once in the fields, with the lowing cattle, the birds, the trees, the waters, the satisfying outlines of the hills and the ponds, he seemed to have come to his own and made friends with nature. He found health and affinity there,—no petulance, no fret, but eternal resource, a long tomorrow rich as yesterday. The stems of the hemlocks, pines and oaks gleamed like iron on his excited eye. The thrilling leap of the squirrel up the long bough, the softness and beauty of the summer clouds that seemed to enjoy their height and privilege of motion, the millions of sheeny fliers with green body and crape wing that overhung the grasses and the waters, the chickadees in the piny glen filled him with cheerfulness and courage. He was embosomed in beauty and wonder. The very cattle lying under the trees seemed to have great and tranquil thoughts. The songs of the birds, the sunlight full of gnats, the crickets in full cry, the goldfinches eating the seeds of the thistle, scattering the leaves in their excitement, the hedges of barberry, whitethorn, woodbine and ivy were a cornucopia of golden joys. Out upon scholars, he said to himself, with their pale, sickly, etiolated indoor thoughts! Give me the out-of-door thoughts of sound men, thoughts all fresh and blooming.

Much as the village meant to him, it was in the woods and fields that he knew the joy of the Brahmin. Concord, indeed, was a school for the study of human nature. One learned all the trades and professions by talking with the blacksmith, the grocer, the plumber. All history repeated itself in Concord. The wealth and goods of the Indies and China streamed through the village in the trucks and wagons that carried the wares of Boston to Vermont and New Hampshire. One had only to mix a little imagination with all these sights and sounds of the common life: then one found the whole world in any least corner of it, one found Asia and Europe, past and future, within the circle of one's daily walks. The large mind in small conditions, the high mind in low conditions, everything in leasts: why should not Concord be one's Rome, one's world? A tent, a little rice and asses' milk, or, say, the farmer's scale of living, plain plenty without luxury or show; for the rest, health, the south wind, books, old trees, a boat, two or three friends,—what could a poet wish that life did not shower on him there? His sunshine was Susa; Ecbatana, his shade; and he could rest assured that, if he asked them, every one of the gods would honour his feast.

It was for no private ends that Emerson sought privacy. His ends were universal, his ends were public, like those of Michael Angelo, like Dante's, who seldom dined in company. Swedenborg's best of angels, those that dwelt in the midst of heaven, did not live consociated, but separate, house and house; and Ossian's Cathmore lodged in the wood not only to avoid the voice of praise. If the seeker of truth needs solitude, and almost a going out of the body to think, should a poet apologize for the isolation that breeds Olympian thoughts? Steadily to prefer one's native choices, against all argument and all example, defending them against the multitude, even as much or more against the wise, was not this the burden of Emerson's teaching? Should everyone be busy and useful? Was it any merit in a man to make his own stove, or boil and bake his dinner, when others could do it better than himself? His virtue was to carry into action his own dearest ends, to dare to do what he believed and loved, were it only the carving of a cherry-stone or the forwarding of a handful of friends. How much more was it a poet's virtue to solve his own questions, though he died, even if he died of lotus-eating! Therefore, for the poet, idleness, as others chose to think it, leisure for meditation and contemplation. He who could hope to catch the wingéd thoughts that thrilled and agitated humankind, restored youth and sanity, dissipated the dreams under which men reeled and staggered and gave heroic aims to the nations was not required to explain his means. Emerson paid his way by lecturing. For the rest, he abandoned himself to his own caprices. The writer, like the priest, had to be exempted from secular labour, for his work demanded a frolic health; he had to be at the top of his condition. Anyone who challenged Emerson's freedom would have discovered that his village mildness masked, like any woodland creature's, a sharp retractile claw.

He scarcely had a *modus vivendi*. His moods were too variable for this; and he did not wish merely to write. He wished to say only essential things, the things that could not be omitted, the things that his genius uttered,—he did not care to cultivate his talent; and his genius ebbed and flowed and ebbed again. Yesterday, Caesar had not seemed so great; today, he was a dunce. The fruit of his brain was abortive, cramped or mildewed. He was as torpid as a clod. He felt like a ship aground, and suddenly some tyrannous idea, emerging out of heaven, seized upon him. The rigid fibres relaxed; life returned to a finger, a hand, a foot. A river spread over the shoals where the ship lay aground, uplifting the timbers on its waters, and the ship put forth its sails and turned its head to the sea. Were these moods in any degree within con-

trol?—for the fruits of these moods alone were all he
wished to gather. Were there any tonics for the torpid
mind? The electric machine would not work, no sparks
would pass: and then the world was all a cat's back, all
sparkle and shock. A flash of light, a long darkness, then
a flash again. Where was the Franklin with kite and rod
for this celestial fluid?—he who could command it and
convey it into the arts of life, inspire men and take them
off their feet, withdraw them from the life of gain and
trifles and make the world transparent. For to Emerson
nothing seemed incredible, nothing, neither miracles nor
magic, when he had experienced an insight. He longed
for the consecutive, not the single glimpse but the panorama. A fuller inspiration, as it seemed to him, would
cause the point to flow and become a line; it would
bend the line and complete the circle.

To experience this genius and communicate it, to detect and watch the gleam of light that flashed across his
mind from within, was Emerson's dream and hope; and
this alone governed his method of living. Not by fore-
thought, not by calculation, had paradise ever been
gained. The "stairway of surprise" mounted thither, and
this was not to be compassed by rules. To live in the
hour, extempore, free as an Arab, was the only way to be
ready when the gods arrived. All measures of economy
were ugly: the manners of the bard should be above
them. And yet was there not a kind of prudence that had
its negative value? He who respected his ends had to respect his means, however he cloaked and screened them;
and, if all high states of mind were transient, like every
other form of inspiration, still, there were methods of
inducing them, and prudence lay in making use of these.
One had to have a measure of worldly wisdom in order
to keep one's freedom; and no one was shrewder than
Emerson, when it came to this. Well he knew what crip-
pled and untuned him, and his stimulants and purgatives

were many: the fire, as it burned in his chimney,—a kind of muse,—air, landscape, exercise, a page or two of Proclus or Plotinus. He passed into the Elysian Fields the moment he opened these authors; the grand and pleasing figures of gods and demons sailed before his eyes. These rare, brave words filled him with hilarity and spring; his heart danced, his sight was quickened, he beheld shining relations between all things; he was impelled to write and almost to sing. Proclus was his opium. But solitary converse with nature was his special *modus* of inspiration. On spring days, at summer dawns, in the October woods, by flood or field, in natural parks of oak or pine, where the ground was smooth and unencumbered, he heard sweet and dreadful words that were never uttered in libraries. The hills began to dislimn and float in the air. The atoms of his frame began to dance. He came into new circulations; the marrow of the world was in his bones; the opulence of forms poured into his intellect; he seemed to be dipping his brush into the paint-pot with which birds, flowers, the living rock, the landscape and the eternal sky were painted.

Away with prudence then! Allah never counted the days the Arab spent in the chase. The one real prudence was concentration, as the one evil was dissipation. One's work would take care of itself if one lived enough; and as long as one's genius bought the investment was safe, although one spent like a monarch. To be profligate was not to spend, but to spend off the line of one's proper life; and to fill the hour was Emerson's life, to fill the hour and own the day. Him to whom works and days were offered, no god could ever rebuke for taking works. The days came and went like veiled and muffled figures, sent from a distant friendly party; but they said nothing, and, if one did not use the gifts they brought, they carried them as silently away. What fairy or what demon possessed such power as he who used the gifts?—

Bread, kingdoms, stars, and sky that holds them all.

It was in search of this power,—call it the poet's madness,—that Emerson set out for the woods and pastures. He was an abandoned lotus-eater. All he asked was that the days should be, for him, as full as centuries, loaded, fragrant. He had various favourite walks, from the Manse down the river to Peter's Field, to the Estabrook farm, with its straggling orchards, where the apple-trees strove to hold their own against the encroaching forest, to White Pond, a little Indian basin, where one could almost see the sachem paddling his canoe in a shadowy cove, to Walden, where he had his own pine garden and the chickadees flitted through the branches and the waterflies seemed full of happiness. There, as he sat on the bank, he had read most of Goethe,—to please Carlyle,—fifty volumes or more. Sometimes the warm south wind drew him to the summit of the ridge above the Boston turnpike. Sometimes he rose before the light and waited for the dawn over the forest, sitting on a course of dark rock that had been worn by a glacier. Often he went for walks at night, when the moon was making amber of the world and every cottage pane glittered with silver and the meadows sent up the rank smell of all their ferns and folded flowers in a nocturnal fragrance. The little harlot fireflies of the lowlands sparkled in the grass and in the air, and he heard the voice of the wind, so slight and pure and deep, as if it were the sound of the stars revolving.

How many were there who could see the charm of close, low pine-woods in a river-town? Was Walden anything more than a "prettyish pool," as a travelling poet remarked? One had to have musical eyes to see what Emerson saw in these meadows and streams, in the waving rye-fields and the quiet hemlocks. He saw what others heard: all the soothing, brisk or romantic moods that corresponding melodies awoke in them, he found in the carpet of the wood, in the margin of the pond, in the shade of the pines, in the infinite variety and dance of the tree-tops. To him, a skiff on the water was a piece of fairy timber, which the light loved, the wind and the wave. When he struck the water with his paddle, he fancied he had never seen such colour, the hue of Rhine wines, jasper and verd-antique, topaz and chalcedony, gold and green and chestnut and hazel, in bewitching succession and relief. In the hard clouds he saw what sculpture!—what an expression of immensity in the dotted and rippled rack, firm and continental, then vanishing into plumes and auroral gleams, all without crowding, boundless, cheerful, strong. On Indian summer days, he saw the Indians under the trees in the wood. In his neighbour Edmund Hosmer's oxen, the beasts that ploughed his fields, he saw the camels of the faithful Hassan, beside whom even Tamerlane seemed a slave. The railroad at Walden, prosaic enough to others, seemed to him a shuttle, shooting across the forest, the swamp, the river, over the arms of the sea, binding city to city. In an apple-tree, he saw the sun painting itself in glowing balls and leaves,—in apples, the social fruit, in which nature had deposited every flavour. Whole zones and climates were concentrated in apples, barrels of wind and half-barrels of cider. In the oaks and pines, he saw vessels of health and vigour. They were imperfect men, groping upward, bemoaning their imprisonment, rooted in the ground. Beside these plants, hardy in their weakness, he had a sudden sense of relief and pleasure, observing the mighty law of vegetation.

On evenings when the moon shone, the thrifty Concord folk turned out the street-lamps. Emerson did not need even the moon; he could see well enough in the dark. He saw honour in scamps and justice in thieves. He could see energy in beggars and elegance of manners in a peasant. He could see benevolence in misers and grandeur in porters and sweeps. Why this was, he could never have told; for he who had leisure for everything else had no time for introspection. Besides, if he saw in the dark, he preferred the sunlight. None of his moments ever seemed empty in which he had given heed to some natural object, a gentian, a wild apple-tree with fruit that hung like berries, a thorn-bush with its red fruit, the musical, streaming south wind that turned all the trees into wind-harps, the fall of snow-flakes in the still air, the blowing of sleet over a sheet of water. He felt that he was emerging from an egg-shell existence when he saw the great dome that arched above him. An everlasting Now reigned in nature, which hung the same roses on his bushes that charmed the Chaldeans in their hanging gardens.

Often, as he walked, he hummed or whistled the rhythm of some ballad, some song of Herrick's, a fragment of Taliessin, the old Welsh bard, or a strain of Persian poetry, Hafiz or Saadi. It struck him that these metres were organic, derived from the human pulse, beating with the beating of the blood, and therefore natural and universal. There was a charm in the cadences, heroic, pathetic or plaintive, that seemed to set him searching for the words to fill these vacant beats. Rhymes enchanted him, too, in a way he could not explain but had always felt. They suggested the correspondence of parts in nature, acid and alkali, body and mind, character and history, action and reaction. These iterations in the natural world, as in the world of art, had always given him pleasure: the doubling of rocks and trees reflected in water, the repetition of pillars in a colonnade, in a row of windows, or in wings, the symmetrical contrast of garden beds and walks. Rhymes to the eye, such as shadows, explained the charm of rhymes to the ear; and the inner life also had its rhymes, perception and expression, ebb and flow. Rhyme and rhythm measured for him the latitude and opulence of poets. If they were limited and unskilful, one saw it in the poverty of their chimes. But Spenser, Marlowe and Chapman flew far and wide for their weapons: there was no manufacture in their rhymes and rhythms, but a vortex, a musical tornado that whirled the materials of their minds into the same grand order that planets and moons obeyed, and seasons, and monsoons.

He loved rhyme and return, period and musical reflection, rhyme that suggested not restraint but rather the wildest freedom. At Walden, on a winter day, he would stand on the edge of the pond and throw stones across the frozen surface. It charmed his ear as the stones fell and fell again on this crystal drum, repeating the note with just the right modulation. The rhyming and the chiming of this ice-harp filled him with exultation. Well he could understand why poetry had been called the *gaie science,* why sailors worked better for their *yo-heave-ho,* why soldiers fought better for the drum and trumpet. He could understand the building power of music, as the ancient myths described it. He could feel how the walls of Thebes had risen to the music of Amphion's harp. The excitement which the Persian bards produced exceeded that of the grape: they had driven warriors to combat, like Taillefer, who rode out at Hastings, singing the *Chanson de Roland,* challenging the Saxons. Well he could understand why bards and minstrels had been taken for makers and givers of laws, they who had stood for liberation, for courage, freedom, victory. In the myths, they restored the dead to life; they met the approbation of Allah in heaven. They made men, they added and affirmed. They set the intellectual world in action. They sang old ideas out of people's heads and sang new ideas in. They introduced fresh images and symbols that built up the world again in thought. They threw down the walls of circumstance. They awakened in other men the sense of universal relation and power.

Emerson thought of the poet as Adam in the garden again, new-naming the beasts in the field and the gods in the sky, calling aloud to the children of morning that all creation was recommencing. Among partial men, he stood for the complete man. All the forms of life were in balance in him; he saw and handled that which others dreamed of, the whole scale of experience. He was the representative of man, having the largest power to receive and impart. Were not most men like the shepherd who, lost and blinded in the snow-storm, perished in a drift outside his door? Were they not like minors who had not come into their own and did not know what wealth was rightly theirs? They clung to the wearinesses of their daily life, their trivial forms and habits, their petrified social scale of ranks and employments. They were inferior to their proper selves and did not use the powers they possessed. Who but the poet could redeem them from all these routines and idolatries? Their money was a second best, their alcohol, their politics. Which of them would not give his lands and houses for a touch of the perception that stirred the will? Life was a dance, as Plotinus said, in which the bodies were moved in a beautiful manner, as being parts of the whole. But most men could not sustain this order. They were too lumpish and opaque, for their souls had not been awakened. There lay the poet's province. For him the world was always virgin soil; for him all men had their sovereign moments, as every clod contains its germs of life. It was the poet's office to unfold them. He was the master of the dance of life, who knew that every man would begin to move when the music reached and touched his imagination.

The poets who had shown this power most clearly were

the great religious awakeners, Zoroaster and Plato, the bards of the Vedas, of the *Vishnu Purana* and the *Bhagavad-Gita.* For Emerson, these came first, or such as these; they were never out of his mind, and he judged other poets in the light of these commanding oracles. In his reaction against the Church, and all that savoured of official goodness, he seldom thought of the biblical writers. But, even more than the givers of laws, he liked, or at least he liked to think of, the Norse and the Cymrian bards, Taliessin and the mythical Ossian and Merlin, together with Hafiz and Saadi, the Persian poets. It was evident that his notion of these was coloured by his reading of the Eastern scriptures; but even as they were, —as they survived in fragments,—he found them inspiring and tonic. They spoke to him of the vast, of health and courage. The rude strains of the Northern bards, struck out white-hot with love or grief, pleased him all the more in his own recoil from all that was academic in the English classics; and the cheerfulness and force of the "fortunate" Saadi were the fruits of a situation like his own. For Saadi and Hafiz, in Persia, had escaped from Mohammedan fatalism, just as he had escaped from Calvinism. Their joy was a joy of liberation. He liked to think of the Persians and Arabs. In the absence of other intoxicants, as travellers often noted, poetry and flowers were their wine and spirits: a couplet was equal to a bottle and a rose to a dram. Poetry had its highest effect among them. It was also in his wish to escape from the sway of European tradition that Emerson cultivated the Persian poets, who left so many traces in his writings. The luxuriance of their imagery, the breadth of the Eastern modes of thinking refreshed his New England imagination. The bold Oriental muse had an electric power that animated and unbound his mind.

Much as he loved poems of every kind, it was these poets of the early ages, the springtime bards and seers that he loved the best, they who spoke with authority and not as the scribes, who spoke of the morning of the world, whose words stood for things, for the simplest feelings,—not gifted men who sang, but the children of music, whose scope did not lie in exhibition, whose aim was to serve the gods. "Thus saith the Lord" began their songs. Their utterance was large and their language final, as if it came from the Eternal mind and had not been arbitrarily composed by the writer. The Greek Gnomic poets, the Persian poets, whose words might have been engraved on sword-blades, Pindar, with his grand strokes, firm as the tread of a horse, and, among his own contemporaries, Landor, whose epigrams recalled the Greeks: these were his special favourites. They seemed to him the result and the justification of the ages in which they appeared: they made him think lightly of histories and statutes. In their verse, the iron lids of Reason, usually heavy with slumber, were unclosed for a moment. The individual mind became in them the vent of the mind of humanity.

For the rest, Emerson asked that the poet should omit whatever was not important. Was not everything in Shakespeare important?—Shakespeare, who was like Damascus steel, hammered out of old nails. Interested in genius, Emerson was not interested in talent. He loved the charm and skill of execution that he found in Herrick, Collins, Gray and Landor, the elegance that suggested health, the ease that went with mastery. But for external graces he had no use. He thought with Heraclitus that "harmony latent is of greater value than that which is patent"; and Wordsworth's great design, the plan of *The Recluse,* the *Ode to Dion,* pleased him better than all the enamelled poets. None of your parlour or piano verse! None of your carpet poets, content to please! None of your sonneteering, your bookmaking and bookselling; none of your cold spying and authorship! The muse should be the counterpart of nature, exuberant and tranquil. True poetry, Emerson thought, betrayed in every word miraculous presence of mind, quickness, perception of relations. One found it seldom in current letters, even in the history of letters. In a dozen alcoves of English poets, one found only nine or ten who were still inspirers of their race. For literature warped away from life, and the power to transubstantiate the world was the test and measure of poetry. Its mark was contemporary insight, in one's own America as in Pindar's Greece. Easy enough to repaint the mythology of the Greeks, the mediæval Church, the feudal castle, the martyrdoms and crusades of former times. To point out where the same creative power worked in one's own dwellings and public assemblies, to convert into universal symbols the energies acting at this hour in New York, in Chicago and San Francisco, required a subtle and commanding thought. Could one read the poetry in affairs and fuse the circumstances of today? Could one take the hour, with its cares and fears, and hold it up to a divine reason, until one saw that it had a purpose and beauty? Then one would be doing what Pindar did, and Shakespeare and Milton in their times. The dry twig would blossom in one's hand.

Poet that he was in all his prose, it was this other harmony that he longed to compass. He toiled unremittingly over his verses; and, in fact, he had developed a style of his own, as marked in his poems as in his essays, a lean, spare, quick, intellectual style that could only have emerged, one felt, from Concord. In his more flaccid verses, one caught here and there glints of Shakespeare, Collins, Gray and Wordsworth; but the Emersonian style at its best had none of the derivative Cambridge note, nor any of the smooth and facile charm of most of the other American writers. In his preference of the "latent" to the "patent," as a protest against the sort of jingles that, as he said, one "put round frosted cake," Emerson sometimes purposely roughened his verses, throwing in a dissonance or an ill-matched rhyme. Anything rather than rhetoric, for himself. As a matter of fact, with others, he was easily pleased. For all the severity of his conscious standard, anything in rhyme was apt to catch him, provided the feeling was noble. He never took the word for the deed, in the work of other poets, but he sometimes took the deed for the word. The anthology that he published, *Parnassus,* a large collection of his favourite poems, showed the inequality of his taste. In choosing his own poems to publish, he revealed a similar weakness; for at his own worst his work was bad as no merely talented writer's could be. Even the *Threnody* was not really good, and the commonplace or doggerel of much of his writing would never have passed muster with the Cambridge poets. One wondered at the childlike innocence that could have led him to publish some of these verses, for his work was only good when it was great; but he who could write pages of artless lines, with nothing but their sincerity to redeem them, fairly shook the stars when he wrote at his best. One turned the page of *The Adirondacks,* smiling at his ingenuousness, and caught one's breath at his sublimity,—for *Brahma* lay on the next page. So it was with the poet of *Merlin* and *Bacchus,* of *Uriel, Terminus* and *Give All to Love.* At best, he had an intensity like nothing else in American verse. Then, as the Emersonian stars shone forth, over a world peopled with gods and heroes, he seemed like the god of wealth himself, opening power in everything he touched; and one saw that he was one of his own immortals,—

> Olympian bards who sung
> Divine ideas below.
> Which always find us young
> And always keep us so.

Emerson's poems were *sui generis.* They were like
Poe's in this, however remote from Poe in their lonely
whiteness. Of Poe's melodious magic, Emerson had
scarcely a touch. Of colour, he had none, or next to none,
except when at moments, behind his verse, one seemed
to catch a sort of polar splendour, as of an aurora bore-
alis. There was something bleached and dry, in the best
of this verse, like that of an age-old wisdom, exposed for
thousands of years to sun and wind, and one felt as if a
bracing mountain air had somehow blown upon it. Emerson's, at these moments, seemed

> the pen
> Which on the first day drew,
> Upon the tablets blue,
> The dancing Pleiads and eternal men.

CHAPTER XIV

CONCORD: 1840-1844

AT EMERSON'S house, from time to time, the so-called Transcendental Club assembled. Never a club, in the proper sense, never calling itself Transcendental, it was a group of men and women, interested in the new ideas, who met now and then to discuss them. The first meeting had taken place at Ripley's house in Boston, and Ripley, Dwight, Miss Peabody, Margaret Fuller, Alcott, Jones Very, Orestes Brownson, James Freeman Clarke and Theodore Parker were among the occasional members.

Sometimes it was called Hedge's Club, because Frederick Hedge, who lived in Bangor, where he preached to the Penobscot lumber-merchants, made sudden descents upon Boston that resulted in calls for a meeting. Hedge, with Sampson Reed, the Boston druggist, had introduced Swedenborg's writings to his friends, and meanwhile in his snow-bound study in the north he smoked and read his German. He was preparing there his *Prose Writers of Germany.* Many of the members, like himself, like Emerson, Everett, Ripley, Dwight and Cranch, beginning their lives as ministers, were settling down as simple men of letters. Their vocations were fading out like daguerreotypes.[1] Others, ceasing to be Uni-

[1] This was a general symptom of the time. "When I lived in the West, there came a phrenologist to the town, and examining the heads of all the clergymen in the place, found us all deficient in the organ of reverence. More than that, we all admitted that the fact was so; that we were not, any of us, specially gifted with natural piety or love of worship. Then he said, 'You have all mistaken your calling. You ought not to be ministers.' "—James Freeman Clarke, *Self-Culture.*

tarians, had become the same thing without the name. But James Freeman Clarke and Theodore Parker, whatever their doubts or deficiencies, were never to abandon the priestly calling. Clarke's *Self-Culture*, written years later, was a characteristic expression of the West Street circle. His *Ten Great Religions*, a standard book, also published after the Civil War, was an example of the comparative method that Agassiz had popularized in Cambridge. Another warrior of the pulpit who came to meetings of the club was the hallelujah Methodist, Father Taylor. This was the scarred old prophet who walked his quarter-deck at the Seamen's Chapel, where the gay blue flag flew from the roof,—"bounding like a roe over the hills of spices." The greatest natural orator in Boston, who had adopted all the sons of the ocean, the pleading, grieving searcher of souls, so tender and so volcanic, whose rebukes were like broadsides from a frigate, he was a master of unconscious style. Everyone flocked to hear him, Webster and Channing, Dickens, Jenny Lind; for, although, as he said, he sometimes lost his nominative case, he was always on the way to glory.[2]

Father Taylor was ready for any discussion of the lukewarm spirit of the day. This, in its hundred aspects, was the leading topic at the club: the American genius, the causes that hindered its growth, the indifferentism at Harvard and the like. But the talk was often wiredrawn and misty. What was the True, the Beautiful, the Good? What was the Highest Aim? What could be done with an artist who was not an artist? Could sculpture express as well as painting the notion of immortality? Emerson found it rather unrewarding. One did not learn to use one's tongue in a lonely country parsonage, and the mental hinges of some of the members fairly creaked with

[2] "I have never heard but one essentially perfect orator," Walt Whitman said, referring to Father Taylor. He and his preaching are reproduced in Father Mapple's sermon in Melville's *Moby-Dick*.

rust. Not by words like these could one captivate the great American Lilliput, great in land and resources, in coal and corn, but all a village littleness, as Emerson thought. Most of the members were better at writing than talking, though this was far from true of Theodore Parker. If there was any man in the Boston pulpit,—for Parker had begun to preach in Boston,—who added cubits to the Lilliputians, it was this poet-preacher, reformer, scholar, who found fifty hours a week to spare for other than parish work.

It was for Parker's essays on manual labour, on Pharisaism, on German thought that readers bought *The Dial*, the new review with the lilac covers. This was the mouth-piece of the West Street circle, a product of Miss Peabody's shop, and Margaret Fuller was the editor.[3] Dr. Channing was so excited when he heard the news about *The Dial* that he lay awake for three nights. He rejoiced in all these signs of life that represented reforms on his reform; and in fact *The Dial* was a gallant venture. It rallied the younger poets and writers and gave them an adequate focus, as the *North American Review* had rallied the historical students and critics. Margaret, —for so she was called, as one spoke of Bettina or Corinne,—was in her element as the guiding spirit; for the new illuminati were all her friends and she had correspondents all over New England, younger men and girls, aspiring students, lovers of Goethe and Schiller, most of them neophytes and shy beginners. They felt that Margaret carried a hazel twig, for she seemed to divine their hidden springs. They spread their portfolios out before her. Had some young man, who wished to write, watched Stearns Wheeler at the Athenæum transcribing

---

[3] The editor's salary, which was never paid, was $200 a year. The number of subscribers never exceeded three hundred. Miss Peabody's later venture, *Æsthetic Papers*, which had only fifty subscribers, was discontinued after the first number.

the magical chapters of *Sartor Resartus?* Margaret had seen the young man watching. She knew he had something to say for *The Dial;* and Wheeler, who had gone to Heidelberg, was glad to send her letters on German affairs. She appealed to Emerson, Alcott, Theodore Parker, Hawthorne, Cranch and Newcomb. Dwight contributed essays on music, others on archæology, Boccaccio, Shelley, notes on architecture, travel-sketches, voyages to Jamaica and Porto Rico. There were essayists of a single essay, poets of a single poem, sometimes composed at Brook Farm, where the poet plucked weeds to the rhythms of Keats and Browning. Some of the poems were obscure, for Transcendentalism had ways of its own. Others suggested Mary and her lamb. Ellen Sturgis Hooper wrote:

> I slept and dreamed that life was beauty,
> I woke and found that life was duty,—

lines that later readers sometimes recalled as embroidered on their grandmothers' pillow-cases. Little remained of *The Dial* that pleased these readers, for where it was not too simple it was often vague. Much of it was green and immature. But it stood for a moment of history. It even stood for certain frames of mind, certain ideas and convictions that were to mark Americans for an age to come.

Meanwhile, Bronson Alcott had settled in Concord. If the world was not ready for him, be it so. It was no mean subterfuge, no ignoble surrender. He trusted in the majesty of goodness and called no man master. What did Bacon say?—"Overt and apparent virtues bring forth praise, but there be secret virtues that bring forth fortune." These were the virtues that they knew in Concord, —"certain deliveries of a man's self" that have no name or fame. Alcott was not to be embittered if the lottery went against him. A blank was as good as a prize, if one

had the equanimity to take it without whimpering or
discontent.

It was true, he had no material resources, which made
it hard for his wife and the little Alcotts. The Emersons
suggested that the Alcotts should live with them, forming a double household, even as Fichte planned to live
with the brothers Schlegel. But the wives of the brothers
Schlegel had not been congenial. Would the wives of the
Concord philosophers have been more so? The Alcotts,
at least, had plenty of apples; and a basket of pearmains
or golden russets, standing on his table, was almost all
that a sage could ask for. Snatch as one might wildness
from the woods, shrewdness from cities, compliments
from courts, one best betook oneself, for sovereign sense,
for subtlety of thought and the joy of colour, for the
graces of diction and behaviour,—

> Where on all sides the apples scattered lie,
> Each under its tree.

And, to fill the little mouths of the Alcott household, to
provide their bread and potatoes, their boiled rice and
grated cheese, Alcott resorted to the spade and saw. He
worked for his neighbours by the day, delved like any
farm-hand, chopped their wood. Wise and friendly eyes
looked on. There was something emblematic in these
labours. They suggested the annual ploughing of the
Emperor of China, and Dr. Channing, who had longed to
witness the union of labour and culture, remarked that
Alcott at the chopping-block was the most inspiring object in Massachusetts. As for Mrs. Alcott, after a good
talk and a crying spell she recovered her usual cheerfulness. Her husband's tatters, she said, were the rags of
righteousness, and there were others in a sadder plight.
Her cousins, who came for a visit, were obliged to bring
their own tea and pepper; but, as soon as the Alcotts
could count on their rice and turnips, they cut their meals

down to two a day to provide for the neighbour with the drunken husband. There were those who laughed at Alcott. They said that his intemperate love of water made his mind hazy and cloudy. If he had eaten a little meat or fish, it might have had more marrow and substance. But Emerson, who knew his foibles well, loved Alcott for his copious peacefulness and for the mountain landscape of his mind, with its darting lights and shadows.

He was preordained for the philosophic life, a life which, hospitably taken, was a very simple affair. What did he ask for his wealth and estate? A fireside and a spring, a stream to stir one's blood in the morning, the "frequent cold water" of Agathias, a web of cloth, friends and books, a chosen task, health and peace of mind. For thought, the study; for metaphors, a walk; hills for ideas; for force, a glimpse of the ocean, and over and through all the changing seasons, surcharging mind and body, rendering them primitive and elemental. Fields, streams, groves and country houses, rustic recreations, farmers to talk withal, whose wits were level with the world they worked in. Woodlots, the pleasing homestead, forest paths to foster meditation, alleys and graceful gates opening into a wood. Trees of ancient standing, vines like firm friends and royal neighbours. Orchards of Academe, suggesting the ripest learning of accomplished Greece. A garden, first of all.

> Who loves a garden still his Eden keeps,
> Perennial pleasures plants, and wholesome harvests reaps.

An occupation friendly to every virtue, the freest from covetousness and debasing cares. For the rest, a solar diet. Let the groundlings laugh as they might, they had not heard the word of the Samian sage, "A cheerful and a good heart will have a care for his meat and drink"; and who knew better than Pythagoras how to preserve one's powers of divination, one's purity and sweetness of dis-

position, one's grace of form and dignity of carriage?
Cherish the justice that animals claim at thy hands, nor
slaughter the cow and the sheep for thy food or profit.
Shun the succulent flesh that beclouds the soul. Preserve
thy taste for wisdom and elegant studies. Good humour,
flowing spirits, a sprightly wit, and diffidence as the flower
of the rest,—these were the virtues of the Orphic life,
nourished by fair water and fragrant fruit, by grains,
next in the scale, and medicinal herbs, and roots as a last
resort. Nor should one forget the loyal lettuce, by choosing which for a name one of the great families of ancient
Rome raised itself to nobility.

The candid Alcott almost wished at times,—pleased as
he was with Concord,—that he had lived in the days
when groves were temples, when sylvan priests and chaste
philosophers, clad in robes of linen, wise in the pastoral
arts, plucked their learning from the golden bough or
sauntered in the Grecian portico. Towards what was civilization tending? Had it improved upon the state of
things described by the rural poets, Virgil, the sweet bucolic, the friend of every honest husbandman, Herrick,
Izaak Walton? Were not the fading customs of the Yankee forbears, generous, hearty, pious, better, a hundred
times, than these modern ways? What was to be the end
of all this pother about steam-boats and telegraphs and
railroads?—inventions that ought to be dropped or made
short work of, as a squirrel dispatches a nut, that the intellect might be won to worthier occupations. For himself, Alcott proposed to live as if the golden age had come
again, or, rather, as if it had never ceased to be. Let other
men follow other patterns, the English gentleman or the
Roman statesman. His was another model, better drawn
by Iamblicus than Plutarch. Virgilian Concord afforded
a setting for it.

It was true, he had done his best, with ill success, to
fabricate a more extensive Eden, the colony at Harvard

village, Fruitlands. Cheering news had come to him from
England, as he toiled away at the saw and the scythe. His
educational theories, abhorred in Boston, had found sup-
porters in that older world. A school had been established in his honour, Alcott House, near London. The
masters had invited him for a visit, and Emerson had
gladly filled his pocket with a purse of golden sovereigns.
But what could anyone expect of England, choked as it
was with smoke and cynicism? The school had died in its
cradle; and Emerson's friend, Carlyle, had behaved like
an angry peasant in the presence of the man of herbs and
onions. Alcott, with potatoes for his breakfast, mixed his
strawberries with them, till the juices ran together on
his plate, and the sage of Chelsea dropped his knife and
fork and stormed about the table in disgust. Alcott,
blithe as ever, had brought the "English mystics" home.
One of them, Charles Lane, had a little money, enough
to buy the land at Harvard village, and he brought his
library with him, in all a thousand volumes, a notable
collection of mystics and poets, Pindar, Alcæus, Quarles,
Spinoza, Behmen. They planted their Eden with high
hopes, to restore the Orphic life in its pristine beauty.
Austerity was to be the note of Fruitlands, though not
without a touch of continent mirth. Persons fit and few,
twelve at the outset. At early dawn, the silent reveille.
Libations, baths, morning walks alone, music,—for Lane
had brought his violin,—melodies to subdue the passions,
anger, despondency, complaint, dancing of a composed
and Doric order, to pacify distempers of the soul, rural
rites, repasts of native grains, water, herbs and fruit, to
the end of edifying the healthy body. Labour, attractive
labour, after the fashion of the *Works and Days,* with
the spade and the glistening sickle. For raiment, canvas
shoes and linen tunics. Conversation of an interior kind.
A life that knew no indurating toils, but such as Adam's

family might have known, with a little advanced instruction.

Seven beautiful months, of mingled leisure, labour, recreation,—the whole of a grasshopper's lifetime, as the plodding ants made haste to say. For ants and busybodies have no love for these green isles in the sea of platitude. Then the December blasts swept through the paradise lost. Charles Lane took refuge with the Shakers. Alcott turned his face to the wall. For three days he refused to eat; then he arose, new-born, and went back to Concord. Was he going to waste his life, that fine essence housed in the handsome dust? He who possessed the richest gift of heaven, the power of contemplating eternal things? And the joys of earth as well,—the names of the herbs, for instance, that so refreshed him, mint, fennel, sweet-cicely, celandine, dill, caraway, lavender, thyme? He could make poverty interesting, with Mrs. Alcott's highly skilled assistance. His journal was a resource. For income, he could count on Conversations, at Emerson's house, later perhaps in Boston. For ennobling and refining the manners and senses, there was no discipline to be compared with the Socratic dialectic, under the wise care of a thoughtful instructor. The dollars, few enough, were yet sufficient to enable him to refuse to pay his taxes,—$1.50 a year,—to a government that protected slavery and was plainly misbehaving on the Mexican border. Alcott was overseeing the children's lessons when Sam Staples, the constable, his neighbour, regretfully came to say that he would have to carry him off to jail. "Very well, Samuel," said Alcott, "if you will wait a moment till Mrs. Alcott can put some food in a basket." For the prison fare was too rich for him. Mrs. Alcott brought the basket, and down they walked slowly to the jail. At the door the matron met them and said she was very sorry but Mr. Alcott's cell was not made up yet. "Very well, Samuel," said the sage. "I will go back and resume the children's lessons, and when you want me you can come for me." In the meantime, Squire Hoar paid the taxes, with no regard for principle whatsoever.

One might have supposed that in Concord the philosophic life would be understood. But, no, these Roman fellow-citizens were as hard-headed as the other Yankees. They smiled at Cranch's drawing of the indolent magus, lying on the sofa, with a copy of *The Dial* on the floor, and his wife sitting beside him, blacking his boots. But suppose they had seen Alcott,—who did not wear boots but canvas sandals,—on the steps of the Boston Courthouse, when the mob attempted to seize Anthony Burns. There he stood, at ease, cane in hand, calm as Plato in his portico, another Grey Champion, come from nowhere, to vindicate the honour of the State. No one, indeed, denied his courage, he who had been the first, with Samuel May, to shake the hand of Garrison, lodged for the night in the jail in Leverett Street, with the marks of the rope about his neck. And there were Greeks in Concord along with the Romans, who, for the rest, prized the antique virtues. For one, besides Emerson, there was Hawthorne, who had rented the old Manse from the Ripley family,—although Hawthorne had the darker temperament which Alcott regarded with suspicion. Alcott had a passion for the blond complexion worthy of those who, in times to come, were to preach the mystical virtues of the Nordic race. Blue eyes and fair hair, he thought, were signs of the angelic type, determined in a former state of existence, while the dark eye and the swarthy face betokened the demonic, a remnant of the brute in human nature. But Hawthorne, who had married his Sophia, was obviously, by disposition, friendly, the helpless victim of his twilight mood, with a tender and hesitant voice: and Alcott soon forgave his dusky air. He, too, had come to Concord by a natural attraction that seemed to reside in the tranquil atmosphere. He was like the wise man of Plato, who resolves to stand aside under a wall, shielded from the wind and storms of dust, and keep still and mind his own business.

He, too, had his Eden at the Manse, under the silvery mosses, where he was writing—living as he wrote—*The New Adam and Eve*. Sophia, with her ever-busy paint-brush, had worked a miracle there. The dim, dusty, dismal priestly dwelling had vanished at her touch, under the yellow-papered walls, behind the bronze jar filled with ferns, the gift of Margaret Fuller, the vases of dewy rose-buds, the dishes of golden apples and purple grapes, the floods of morning sunlight. At night, in the soft rays of the hanging lamp, the lovers read their Shakespeare or gave each other lessons in German; or, if the evening was mild, ran races up and down the drive, in the light of the moon streaming through the ash-trees. They were up at sunrise to watch the dawn. Then Sophia painted for an hour or two. She decorated the beds and chairs with outlines after Flaxman,—Endymion, Venus rising from the sea,—while Hawthorne groaned in his study. They dined on bread and milk, with a little fruit, and Sophia danced beside the music-box.

Now and again, Sophia went away, to spend a few days with the Peabody household, and Hawthorne gladly took the vow of silence. He trudged through the snow and slush, with his rolling sailor's gait, never speaking a word to man or dog, perhaps on his way to the village reading-room. Sometimes the snow on the drive was untrodden for weeks by any foot but his. He read the tales of Tieck, Voltaire for the sceptical note, the dash of salt one's fancy had to have, in a world so full of reformers, Rabelais for a little well-fed humour. The ghosts had followed in Hawthorne's wake and sometimes forced themselves on his attention. He had no use for these apparitions, but they were a part of his aura, provided for the pleasure of his guests. It was Mrs. George Hillard, not himself, who, as they sat together on a Sunday morning, felt the touch on her shoulder, and Hillard who heard the rustle of the silken robe passing through the room. Hawthorne was the ghost himself, at times. More than one caller at the Manse, charmed by the gay Sophia, saw him gliding swiftly through the entry, with his hat over his eyes. He was not unwilling to be thought uncanny. It served him as a shield and palisade.

As he went for his early swim across the meadow, beyond the flags and rushes, or strolled in the winding wood-paths, or worked among the crook-necks in the garden, admiring their graceful shapes, happy visions coursed with airy tongues through his enchanted brain. The summer days were full of bright conceptions, tinged and streaked with darker hues, gleaming in his mind like the butterflies that danced in the air about him. He was writing stories of a larger sweep than his earlier tales and sketches, and some of them were equally sombre, filled with a pervasive sense of evil, the snake that lurked even in Concord gardens. The more he had seen of reformers, and saw them still, drifting about the village, moths attracted by the Concord Pharos, the Emersonian beacon, the more aware he was of the pestilent serpent that ate the very eggs of Reform itself. The human heart, —there was the sphere wherein the original wrong subsisted of which the crime and misery of the world were merely outward types. Reform from within, in Goethe's sense: that was the only kind he understood. Was not any plan, ignoring this, destined to prove a chimera, a masquerade, as Brook Farm itself was, dissolving before one's eyes like a summer cloud? Not that he was hostile to the reformers. He had joined the Brook Farmers in all good faith. He had worked at the farm in a practical way. Hawthorne was not the man who hoed up the corn and carefully formed the hills about the burdocks. It was

another member,—no doubt, some executive genius,—
who milked with one hand, while he held the cow's tail
with the other. Hawthorne had the common sense that
men of imagination usually have, when they deal with
these affairs of Caesar. He had toiled like a dragon, as
Ripley said, until he had begun to ask himself what part
in his own economy these feats of the barn and dung-
heap represented. He had not become a vulgar sceptic.
He did not think that what the socialists wished was to
change the ocean into lemonade. But he had brooded,
brooded, sitting by himself in the hall of the Hive, after
the day's work, holding a book before him, while the
young people gossipped in the moonlight. He had been
meditating at the picnics, under the maple-trees, watching the masques of Comus. There was a worm in the
rose-bud of life, a grub, unseen by the others, at the root
of the tree, as at the roots of all these touching endeavours to perfect the social man. If the human heart were
purified, then, and then alone, the evil shapes that
haunted the outer sphere, and seemed almost the only
realities, would vanish. They would vanish of their own
accord.

There was the poet's function. Who but he could reach
the heart? His task was to rouse the imagination, creating magnetic images of the nobler world in which his
own imagination dwelt. As for the world that lay without, the system against which the reformers protested,
what could it mean to Hawthorne? No one had less faith
than he in the gods that his countrymen had set up for
worship. In *The Hall of Fantasy*, for instance, he ridiculed the god of machines. He pictured a great world's
fair where all the new machines were shown, one for dis-
tilling heat from moonshine, one for condensing mist
into building granite, one for transforming the sunset
clouds into dyes for women's dresses. Hawthorne was not
deceived by Feathertop, the citizen his countrymen ad-

mired, the solid man of politics and business, living in good repute, never seeing himself, never seen, as what he was, a scarecrow. Hawthorne's were the eyes that satirized, in *The Procession of Life*, the shallowness and falseness of the classifications imposed on men by society, the artificiality of the badges the world considers genuine characteristics and that hide the true relations of human souls. No one knew better than he the failure of a man like Everett who, misled by vanity, acclaimed by all, had abandoned the scholar's vocation in order to become an empty name that brawling parties bandied to and fro. No one said more clearly that the individual seizing of land and gold, of benefits that all enjoy and all should have their share in, was a trait of undeveloped intelligence. No one was more ready than he to rid the world of its trumpery. This was the point of his tale, *Earth's Holocaust*, retold a dozen times by H. G. Wells. The Titan of Innovation was Hawthorne's invention. The earth groaned under its burden of rubbish, and the titan set a match to the pile. He threw into the bonfire all the old title-deeds, the royal crowns and robes, the bonnets and faded finery, the guns and battle-flags, the headsman's axe, the guillotine, the gallows, even the marriage-certificates and the Bibles, certain that, after the holocaust was over, everything would be found among the ashes that really deserved to survive.

Hawthorne was ready for any change, in social customs, politics, modes of worship, trusting that better systems might result. He had the American taste for innovation that characterized the reformers themselves, as he had the American habit of restlessly moving, wandering to and fro like the palmer-worm that knows no single diet or abode. Old houses and antiquated customs charmed his imagination, but he dwelt on the poisonous influences that gathered about them. That towns should be purified by fire every fifty years was one of his fixed opinions; and who delighted more than he in the fresh paint that covered the walls of the Manse? But of what importance, after all, were Hawthorne's views and habits? He scarcely thought of the world as real, either to be seen or touched or lived in, or, for the rest, altered or improved. It was a film on the breast of Maya, the goddess of illusion. No plummet could ever sound the depths of Hawthorne's scepticism. He felt that, in so far as the world existed, it should wish not to exist. It should recline its vast head on the first convenient pillow and take an age-long nap. For himself, he was happy enough, living as if in eternity, happy as Drowne, who made the wooden image, in this brief season of excitement, which had been kindled by love.

The music-box at the Manse belonged to Thoreau, Henry David Thoreau, the pencil-maker, Emerson's *protégé*, who had gone to Staten Island for a visit, to tutor the children of Emerson's brother William. It was a gift of Margaret Fuller's brother to the youthful poet-naturalist who, as one of his friends said, was "getting up a nose like Emerson's." Hawthorne had skated with him on the river, wrapped in his long cloak, and marvelled at Thoreau's dithyrambic dances and Dionysian leaps over the ice, while Emerson pitched along in the weary rear. Hawthorne had bought from Thoreau the fisherman's dory, green with a border of blue, the "Musketaquid," in which Henry and his brother had spent a week on the Concord and Merrimac rivers. Thoreau had changed his name. Dr. Ripley had christened him David Henry, and he had reversed these appellations, after the Concord fashion. For Emerson had altered the name of his wife from Lydia to Lidian, Alcott had revised his native Alcox, and Hawthorne, years before, had inserted the *w* in his father's "Hathorne." This practice of the Concord authors symbolized their love of independence and, better still, their love of euphony; for all these Concordians were Pythagoreans, and the followers of Pythagoras have a taste for pleasing and musical names.

The green dory, moored among the reeds, lent itself to other excursions. Hawthorne loved to drift in the indolent river, watching the reflections in the water. They were composed, like pictures, far more lovely than the stark and upright landscape. The leaves of the overarching boughs attuned his thoughts with their quiet sound. Sometimes he drifted further, on a little rowing journey with Ellery Channing,—William Ellery Channing, the poet, another of the doctor's nephews,—who dropped in at the Manse, now and then, with an armful of novels and reviews. For Ellery Channing, too, had come to Concord, drawn there by Emerson's presence. He had married Ellen Fuller, Margaret's sister, and taken the red cottage off the turnpike, on Ponkawtassett Hill. Ellen had opened a school for little children, and Ellery, half in earnest,—for he was "chiefly engaged in doing nothing,"—made shift to cultivate his acre of land. He preferred to smoke his pipe, read his seventeenth-century folios, stroll with his dog and write an occasional poem; for this racy talker, this lover of landscape-painting, this woodsman second to none, this learned farmer, who exchanged quotations in Greek while others did the ploughing and the planting, had sworn that he would never desert the Muse. He was a professional poet or nothing, and he had contributed to *The Dial* more than anyone else. Some of his poems, *The Woodman, The Swallow is Flying Over*, the *Epithalamium* of later years, *The Field-bird's Nest, The Spider*, were among the best of the Concord school. Light in touch, natural and lucid, with passages that were worthy of Cowper or Wordsworth, they were touched with magic here and there. Everyone remembered Channing's line,—

If my barque sinks, 'tis to another sea.

The Lonely Road was a fine poem. Native wood-notes wild, in every sense, these poems were the despair of Channing's friends, who felt that if he had only taken pains he might have been able to write immortal verses. Emerson edited his first collection, as he had edited Jones Very's sonnets. Channing was to be known in later years not so much for his poems as for a prose volume of the rarest charm, *Thoreau, the Poet-Naturalist*.[4] He had struck up a friendship with Thoreau, the best Greek scholar in Concord, and had soon become his only crony. He made himself agreeable to Hawthorne.

This Ellery Channing was a moody soul, erratic as the sky in early spring, gay as a troubadour, full of salty gossip, then suddenly reserved and enigmatic. He had always been a problem, and was to be, during the sixty years he lived in Concord, with various "disappearances," outliving all the other Concord worthies. A typical Boston eccentric, quite unlike the usual crooked stick one saw in the village streets, he was perverse and unstable enough. He was a thorn in the side of the Channing clan. He had refused to take his degree at Harvard and had wandered off to the West. He lived in a log hut, which he had built, in northern Illinois, on the prairie. He had studied law and flitted East again and flitted back again to Cincinnati, where he had met and married Ellen Fuller. Margaret was much disturbed, for she had little hope that her sister would ever be happy. Why had he come to Concord? He laughed at the "gigmanity" of Boston, but he laughed still more at the rustic village ways. He would rather have settled, he said, on the icy peak of Mount Ararat. He would have liked a villa in the Euganean Hills, or in Florence, or in Malaga or Cuba. He swore at the cook and damned the butcher. He fell into dark rages that lasted for days, passing one on the street

4 Properly to be read in the final edition, 1902.

with a stony look. Nobody dared to question him; one had to deal with him at arm's length; he seemed to take pleasure in hurting his friends. Then the sun would break and Ellery nodded and smiled again, smoking away and joking as he smoked. He came and went like the summer clouds, professing not to know where he had been.

Ellery Channing and Hawthorne went fishing up the river, sometimes turning into the Assabet. There, in a silent cove, they drew the boat up under a leafy bower, kindled a fire with pine-cones and driftwood, spread their supper out on a moss-grown log and tired the sun with talking. For Hawthorne liked to expand at times and fly away on the wings of speculation, and Ellery's whimsical prattle broke over the stillness of the wood like evanescent spray.

CHAPTER XV

THOREAU

IN EMERSON'S white house on the Boston turnpike, Henry Thoreau had taken up his quarters. He occupied the room at the head of the stairs, a little room, but he was a little man: his nose and his thoughts were the biggest things about him. Emerson, and especially Emerson's children, had formed a warm affection for their difficult Henry, difficult, that is, for the rest of Concord but a treasure for the household of a sage. He was short, lean, frail, although nobody guessed it, he was so tough and muscular, with a meagre chest, long arms falling from the collar-bone, a workman's hands and feet, a huge Emersonian beak, rather like Julius Caesar's, bright blue eyes and flaxen hair. He walked with the swinging stride of an old campaigner. His manners were of the homespun sort, different indeed from Emerson's. But, after the first encounter, one perceived that, if Henry Thoreau was a thorn-bush, he was the kind that bears the fragrant flowers.

He was the son of the pencil-maker, who had his little house and shop on Main Street: "J. Thoreau and Sons." The Thoreaus were a mercantile family of small pretensions who had seen better days. They were well-connected in the Channel Islands, where the French Thoreaus were prosperous wine-merchants. Their other forbears in Maine, the Scottish Dunbars, had taken the royalist side in the Revolution. As a barefoot village boy, Henry had driven the turkeys and the cow to pasture, and Emerson had vaguely heard of him as a poor student at Harvard. He had written to President Quincy, suggesting Henry's name for a scholarship. Later, Henry walked in to Boston, eighteen miles from Concord, to hear Emerson speak, and walked home again after the lecture. Emerson, touched by this, was still more touched when, after one of his Concord lectures, his sister-in-law, who was boarding with Mrs. Thoreau, said to him, "Henry Thoreau has a thought very like that in his journal." A friendship had soon sprung up between them, and when, one day, the Emersons went on a picnic, to the Cliffs on the Concord river, they asked Henry to join them and bring his flute. The village people looked askance at him because he was so pugnacious. He had queer ideas about teaching school, refusing to use the ferule; for with children and simple folk he was always gentle. With others, he was obstinate and harsh. He liked to administer doses of moral quinine, and he never thought of sugaring his pills. He had withdrawn from Dr. Ripley's church with a thesis more defiant than Martin Luther's. He liked to speak of a cold spot as "sultry," and he had a way of calling the woods "domestic." But at boating and camping he was a master-woodsman, skilled as Ulysses, shrewd as any fox. The redskins had forgotten the arts he knew. Arrowheads and Indian fireplaces sprang from the ground when he touched it. He charmed the snakes and fishes. Wild birds perched on his shoulder. His fingers seemed to have more wisdom in them than many a scholar's head.

This young Briareus of the hundred hands was something more than Emerson's factotum. There was nothing he could not do in the matter of painting and papering, building walls, repairing chicken-houses, pruning and grafting fruit-trees, surveying, tinkering, gardening. But these were trifles in his bag of tricks, useful to pay his way in the world and justify his creed of self-reliance. He was a master of other arts that Emerson also knew,

and a scholar of unusual distinction; and he wished to
be a philosopher, not a mere thinker of subtle thoughts
but one who, loving wisdom, lived a life that was simple, magnanimous, free. In fact, he recalled those ancient
sages who, when an enemy took the town, walked out of
the gate empty-handed, without a care for the morrow.
Why should one be burdened with impedimenta? Henry
liked the soldier's life, always on the stretch and always
ready for a battle. Each of his mornings brought its strenuous sortie. He lived "for to admire and for to see." He
had spoken his mind in his college themes about the
"blind and unmanly love of wealth" that actuated most
of his fellow-beings. The order of things, he said, should
be reversed. The seventh should be man's day of toil,
wherein to earn his living by the sweat of his brow; he
should keep the rest of the week for his joy and wonder.

These views delighted Emerson. In fact, the two agreed
on so many subjects, always with an edge of difference,
that one might well have supposed the relation between
them was that of master and pupil. Emerson was fourteen years the elder; and it was true that Henry had
acquired some of his traits and mannerisms: his hand-
writing, his voice, even his nose seemed to have gone to
school to Emerson. There was something contagious in
Emerson's aura; everyone was affected by it, nobody
seemed able to resist it. Alcott was more than a little
Emersonized; and as for Ellery Channing, what did the
lady say who heard him lecture?—that his gait, his inflections, the very turn of his eyebrow were Emerson to the
life. Henry Thoreau had felt this influence, as he had
felt the influence of Carlyle. He had his own form, none
the less. Emerson and he had grown in Concord, as two
flowers grow in a common bed, one of them larger and
more luxuriant, the other with a much more pungent
odour; but they stood in different corners of the bed,
with an ample space between them, so that the breeze

could blow upon each of them freely. They were different enough in temperament, as in their personalities; and Henry phrased their common points of view with a sort of acidulous accent that was never heard on Emerson's lips.

They were of one mind in a dozen matters, not least in regard to the reformers. "As for these communities," said Henry, expressing their joint opinion, "I had rather keep bachelor's hall in hell than go to board in heaven." Much as he liked Alcott, the "best-natured man" he had ever met,—"the rats and mice make their nests in him," —he turned up his nose at Fruitlands as well as at Brook Farm. He meant to bake his own bread in heaven, and wash his own clothes there. And suppose, he said, these grievances do exist? So do you and I. And the universal soul prefers the man who sets his own house in order first. A foul thing, this "doing good," observed the contemptuous Henry, instead of looking after one's own life, which ought to be one's business, taking care to flourish, and taste and smell sweet, refreshing all mankind. He had had encounters with reformers that filled him with abhorrence. They would not keep their distance. They tried to cover him with a slimy kindness that fairly took the starch out of his clothes. These "lovers" of their kind were almost more injurious to their kind than the feeble souls that met in drawing-rooms, fabulating and paddling in the social slush, and going to their beds unashamed, to take on a new layer of sloth.

Henry had plenty of acid in his composition. He had taken a few suggestions from Zeno the Stoic,—for one, that he had two ears and a single mouth, in order to hear more and speak less,—as Alcott had followed Pythagoras and Emerson, largely, Plato. Emerson, older and riper, with a fund of sunny benevolence, the fruit of a happier culture and a fortunate bringing-up,—Emerson deplored this hedgehog's posture, the spikes, the spines, the quills that made his Henry a John Quincy Adams of the village. But time would certainly soothe and rectify him. Meanwhile, he was a living illustration of all his own ideas, endowed with hands and feet. Henry described himself, or his hope for himself,—"stuttering, blundering clodhopper" that he said he was,—in words that seemed to have their truth already. He was prepared for a glorious life; he had laid out an avenue through his head, eight rods wide; he had got the world,—much more, the flesh and the devil,—as it were by the nape of the neck, and held it under the tide of its own events, and let it go down stream like a dead dog, till he heard the hollow chambers of silence stretching away on every side and his own soul expanded and filled them. He could not help taunting his fellow-Yankees. Seek first the kingdom of heaven! Lay not up for yourselves treasures on earth! What does it profit a man! Think of this, Yankees, think twice, ye who drone these words on the Sabbath day and spend the other six denying them! "Doing a good business!"—words more profane than any oath, words of death and sin. The children should not be allowed to hear them. If most of the merchants had not failed, and most of the banks as well, Henry's faith in the laws of the world would have been sadly staggered; for what was the sweetest sight his eyes could see but a man who was really fulfilling the ends of his being?—maintaining himself, as he could, if he wished to do so, paying the price in terms of simplification, by a few hours a day at manual labour. Was he a little impatient and a little narrow? If there was anything wrong with his angle of vision, there would always be plenty of others to correct it. For himself, he wished to live deep. He wished to suck out all the marrow of life, to cut a broad swath and shave close, to put to rout all that was not living. If the days and the nights were such that he greeted them with joy, if life emitted a fragrance like herbs and flowers, if it was more elastic and more starry, that was his success and all he asked for.

No use to pretend that, for Emerson, he was a balm, however much a blessing. No, but he was medicinal,—as a gadfly, good; as a goad for an indolent writer, who felt that he ought to dig in his own garden, Henry was even better. As a teacher of natural history, for a lover of nature who, as a matter of fact, scarcely knew a robin from a crow, Henry was better still. Best of all, as a fellow-seeker of wisdom and a man of impeccable taste, competent to help him with *The Dial,* which Margaret Fuller could not wrestle with and had asked her Concord friends to carry on. Henry was a capital editor. He had a sharp eye for the faults of *The Dial,* the phrases,—well one knew them,—that had to be pulled open, as one opens the petals of a flower that cannot open itself. For the rest, the usual style of *The Dial* annoyed him as much as the bombast of the politicians. He liked to see a sentence run clear through to the end, as deep and fertile as a well-drawn furrow. If only writers lived more earnest lives, their minds would pass over the ground like ploughs, pressed down to the beam, like rollers that were loaded, not hollow and wooden,—they would drive in the seed to germinate. It was the height of art, in his opinion, that, on the first perusal, plain common sense should appear,—a law that gave short shrift to much of *The Dial;* truth on the second perusal, beauty on the third. One had to pay for beauty.

The two friends had much in common, in spite of all their differences. Emerson had never built a boat, nor had he shared the Argonautic life that Henry had enjoyed with his brother John,—the John who had built Emerson's bluebird-box,—rounding the capes and sailing before the wind on the Concord and Merrimac rivers, with their cotton tents and buffalo-skins, bringing back their unexpected news of the foreign folk who lived on

the upper reaches. Nor had he roamed over the moors
and meadows, with the fishing-rod and gun that Henry
loved before he perceived that it was not for him, as a
follower of the Brahmins, to "effect the transmigration
of a woodchuck." Emerson was not at home in the wilderness. He could never have whittled a wooden spoon,
better than the factories made, to eat his rice with. He
could not make a fork from an alder-twig, or a Wedg-
wood plate out of a strip of birch-bark. Nor, in the matter of teaching school, had he known such good fortune
as Henry, who had kept the Concord Academy with his
brother John, profiting by Bronson Alcott's methods, taking the children walking, rowing, swimming. But they
both liked to lecture at the Lyceum, where Henry acted
as secretary, and every citizen who had something to say
was expected to give his lecture. Moreover, they loved
the same authors. Henry had a preference of his own for
works of a local kind, ancient gazetteers, State and county
histories, histories of New England towns, farmers' al-
manacs, agricultural pamphlets, out-of-the-way books on
birds and flowers, chronicles of old explorers, the Jesuit
Relations, reports on Indian tribes. His mind bristled
with antiquarian lore. But when it came to Froissart's
bold beauty or Bacon's bolder terseness, to the voyages
of Drake and Purchas, to Raleigh and the earlier English poets, there they were both at home. Nothing had
attracted Emerson more than Henry's manifest knowledge of Drayton, Daniel, the Fletchers, Cowley, Donne,
poets, little known in the eighteen-forties, whose naturalness and vigour Emerson cherished, and who, as Henry
said, were as verdurous as evergreen and flowers, rooted
in fact and experience, unlike so many florid modern
poets who had the tints of flowers without their sap.

They agreed that in literature only the wild was attractive, and that dullness was only another name for
tameness,—the wildness of the Iliad or of *Hamlet*, with

something fresh and primitive about it, something am-
brosial and fertile. All the Greek poets had this trait,
wild in their elegance, wild in their conciseness. Henry
had studied Greek with Jones Very, for a time his tutor
at Harvard, as he had studied German with Orestes
Brownson, with whom he had spent a winter in a Boston suburb, tutoring Brownson's sons. Greek was his second language. He had translated *Prometheus Bound* and
The Seven against Thebes, with many pieces of the minor poets, Anacreon, Simonides, ivory gems of an ethereal beauty like that of summer evenings. One could
perceive them only with the flower of the mind. How
still and serene life seemed amid these classical studies!
Often, walking along the railway tracks, he listened to
the harp of the telegraph-wires, putting his ear to the
posts. Every pore of the wood was filled with music, and
he could find a name for every strain, every swell and
change or inflection of tone in one of the Greek poets.
Often he heard Mimnermus, often Menander. Emerson
had the same impressions when he listened to his ice-harp
at Walden; and Henry, as much as Emerson, delighted in
the Oriental scriptures, which he read in the French and
German versions. The Bible had lost its bloom for both;
but the Vedas, the Bhagavad-Gita came to Henry like
desert winds, blown from some Eastern summit. They
fell on him like the light of the moon when the stars
are out, in the furthest reaches of the sky,—free from
particulars, simple, universal, uttered with a morning
prescience in the dawn of time. What rhythms, what a
tidal flow! Beside these ancient Asiatic books, with their
truths like fossil truths, clean and dry, true without reference to persons, true as the truths of science, the literatures of the European countries seemed to him partial
and clannish, presumptuous in speaking for the world
when they spoke only for corners of it. Henry liked to
remember that the barnyard cock was originally the wild

Indian pheasant, such as the poets of the Upanishads knew.

As they worked over *The Dial,* Emerson, with Henry's concurrence, took pains to include some of these Eastern writings. Emerson chose a group of passages which he called *Ethnical Scriptures.* Henry, who had translated for his own amusement *The Transmigration of the Seven Brahmins,* selected some of the Laws of Manu. Emerson also insisted on printing some of Henry's own writings, which Margaret Fuller had had doubts about. Henry was indifferent to publication. The only audience he really cared for was his own taste and judgment. He wished to write well, to warrant every statement and each remark, till the earth seemed to rest on its axle in order to back it up. Hold the bow tight! was his motto. He longed to write sentences that would lie like boulders on the page, as durable as Roman aqueducts. Sentences kinked and knotted into something hard and significant, which one might swallow like diamonds, without digesting. Sentences nervous and tough as the roots of the pine, like hardened thongs, the sinews of the deer. He wrote best when his knees were strong, when the juices of the fruits that he had eaten, ascending to the brain, gave him a heady force. Margaret Fuller had not liked *The Service,* his manual for the spiritual soldier, suggested by the talk about non-resistance of the mealier-mouthed reformers. But his essay, *The Natural History of Massachusetts,* was beyond cavil or praise. Into *The Dial* it went, with *A Winter Walk.* Henry revised and revised, until his page was a mass of blots and blackness.

Into *The Dial* went also some of his poems, the verses that he had ceased to write. These poems were of a homespun kind, well-woven, but indifferently cut, like Henry's raiment, not intended to please. They were sound and scholarly doggerel, for the most part. The smoke obscured the flame, but now and then a jet rose out of the smoke, and Henry wrote a line or two that shivered its way up the spinal marrow. Sometimes the smoke itself, in a handful of lines, suggested by the Greek Anthology, suddenly turned to incense, and the incense became an Icarian bird, melting its pinions in its upward flight. *Smoke, Mist, Haze* were lyrics not to be forgotten. Nor could one forget *A Winter Scene,* not Greek but Anglo-Saxon,—

> The rabbit leaps,
> The mouse out-creeps,
> The flag out-peeps
> Beside the brook,—

or, for the iron strings, the lines called *Inspiration,*—

> If with light head erect I sing,—

to the end of the third stanza, or, if one insisted, to the end of the seventh, but not a syllable further. There spoke the poet who, for the rest, wrote his poetry in his prose journal, in blank-books bought on those rare occasions when he could find a book with clean white pages, not ruled, as most of them were, for records of dollars and cents. If his poems were often disjointed, like his prose, it was because of this habit of journalizing. He jotted down his paragraphs and verses, a thought or a stanza at a time, and waited for a cooler moment to patch them together,—a good way for epigrams, a good way for the gnomic style, but fatal for the poetry of feeling, and none too good for prose. He was a methodical journalizer, much more so than Emerson. He kept his notes as his father and his father's father, the old French merchant from the Channel Islands, had kept their business-ledgers. He had inherited their plodding habits, akin to the sod as he also was, partaking largely of its dull patience. He sometimes felt that he was in danger of living for his journal, instead of living in it for the gods, his regular correspondents, to whom he sent off

daily bulletins. His journal was a calendar of the ebbs
and flows of the soul. It was a beach on which the waves
might cast their pearls and seaweed.

These were happy months for the seekers of Brahma,
not to be repeated. From Emerson's house, in 1843,
Henry Thoreau went to Staten Island. Later, in 1848,
when Emerson went abroad again, Henry installed himself for a second visit, as counsellor and helper of the
household, in the little room at the head of the stairs.
But, later still, a shadow fell on the glowing intercourse
of the two crusaders. Through whose fault but Henry's?
His journal teemed with innuendoes against the friend
who "patronized" him. Emerson was too "grand" for
him. Emerson belonged to the upper classes and wore
their cloak and manners. He was attracted to Plato, but
he would not have cared for Socrates, whose life and associations were too humble. Emerson would never have
been seen trundling a wheelbarrow through the streets.
He would have thought it out of character. Henry was a
commoner, as he liked to say. He thought there was
something devilish in manners,—and Emerson had had
no right to praise him.[1] "One man lies in his words,"
Henry wrote, "and gets a bad reputation; another in
his manners, and enjoys a good one." But what about
Alcott's manners, so gracious and courtly, consisting with
such artlessness of soul, such frank, open, unaffected
goodness? Alcott had no reputation, surely. Was there
nothing in beautiful manners but foppery, prudery,
starch and affectation, with false pride overtopping all?
Was the noble merely the genteel? Henry's notion of the
art of living was not too comprehensive. Nor his notion
of friendship, either, exacting all and giving back so little.

[1] "Praise begins when things are seen partially. We begin to
praise when we begin to see that a thing needs our assistance."—
Thoreau's *Journal*.

What he gave was solid. As for the rest, the less cared he. When people spoke of the social virtues, he asked about the virtues of pigs in a litter, lying close together to keep one another warm. As for friends, what were they, for the most part? Bubbles on the water, flowing together. Very few were ever as instructive as the silence which they shattered with their talk. When it came to sharing his walks, Henry was rather particular. Alcott served for a stroll, but the real art of walking was beyond him. He always wished to perch on the nearest stump. Hawthorne was even more annoying. One led him to one's loveliest swamp, and Hawthorne stood on the brink, disconsolate. "Let us get out of this dreadful hole," he said. He never even noticed the naked viburnum rising above the dwarf andromeda. Besides, he said that company was a "damnable bore." After all deductions, Emerson was still one's best companion, best but one, Henry's only crony, the moody, witty, generous Ellery Channing, riding his whims like broomsticks, as naturally capricious as a cow is brindled, tender and rough by turns, another social antinomian, even a social outlaw, by his own desire. He was always teasing Henry about his legs, double legs, not cork but steel, which ought to be shown at the World's Fair, he said; and he had a Rabelaisian streak and took pains to shock the sober Henry. There were strange, cold pockets in the air of his mind into which one swam unwittingly. One never knew where one stood with him. But he was crammed with poetry that glittered through the darkness of his reserve like gems in a mine revealed by the gleams of a lantern, or flashed, in his happier moods, like gems in the sunlight. Some of his moods, moreover, were much like Henry's. He wished to be let alone. "If you go to the post-office once," he said, "you are damned."—"No," said Henry, "you are only damned if you get a letter." For Ellery loved solitude. He would sit on the Cliffs by the hour, among the lichens. Then, in the dusk of evening, one saw him flitting past on noiseless pinion, like the barred owl, as wise as unobserved.

Henry, to be sure, had other friends, with whom he exchanged a few words, perhaps on his way to look for mud-turtles in Heywood's luxuriant meadow. There was old Haines, the fisherman, for one, wearing his patched coat of many colours, who represented the Indian still, "Polyphemus" Goodwin, of dubious fame, the one-eyed sportsman of the Concord river, and the crooked old curmudgeon Ebby Hubbard, dressed in his blue frock. There were the musquash-hunters, poets of the wild, up and out early in the wet and cold, ready for any risk at the call of their muse. They were gods of the river and woods, with sparkling faces,—late from the House of Correction, as often as not,—with mystic bottles under their oilskin jackets. How good of George Melvin to follow his bent and not spend all his days in Sunday School! Henry thanked his stars for George Melvin and thought of him with gratitude as he fell asleep. The gawky, loose-hung Melvin, dragging his feet as he walked, who was such a trial to his mother, pleased Henry like an oak-tree on the hill-side. He was one tribe, and Henry was another; and they were not at war. Henry could not deny that hunting and fishing, in spite of his brahminic preferences, were as ancient and honourable trades as the sun and the winds pursue, coeval with the faculties of man. As for his friends, he had some who were wilder than Melvin, the breams, who nibbled from his fingers, while he stroked them gently and lifted them out of the river, the muskrat that emerged from the hole in the ice. The muskrat looked at Henry, and Henry looked at the muskrat, wondering what the muskrat thought of him,—safe, low, moderate thoughts, of course. Muskrats never got on stilts, like some of the Transcendentalists. Once he conversed with a woodchuck, three feet away, over a fence. They sat for half an hour, looking into each other's eyes, until they felt mesmeric influences at work over them both. Then Henry moved closer and spoke to the woodchuck, in a quasi-forest lingo, a sort of sylvan baby-talk. The woodchuck ceased to grit his teeth. Henry, with a little stick, lifted up his paw and examined it; then he turned the woodchuck over and studied him underneath. He had a rather mild look. Henry spoke kindly to him and offered him some checkerberry-leaves. The woodchuck was one of the natives. His family had certainly lived in Concord longer than the Emersons or even the Hoars.

For the sort of friends who never hurt one's feelings, one did not have to look far. Sometimes, in the midst of a gentle rain, Henry felt an influence about him that was suddenly sweet and beneficent. Every sight and sound, the very pattering of the drops, was filled with an unaccountable friendliness. It was to seek this, and all it meant, that he went for his daily walk, with note-book and spyglass in his pocket, and the hat with its lining gathered in the middle to make a little shelf, a botany-box. He was another Linnæus, setting out for Lapland, though he did not wish to be a "naturalist." Looking at nature straight in the eye was as fatal as to look at the head of Medusa. The man of science always turned to stone. Henry wished to look at nature sidewise, or to look through nature and beyond it. Too many observations were dissipating. One had to be the magnet, in the midst of all this dust and all these filings. Sometimes he rose at two o'clock, for a walk to the Cliffs, to wait there till sunrise, or to watch the fog on the river. He loved those valleys in the fog in which the trees appeared as if at the bottom of the sea. Sometimes he spent the whole of a moonlight night roaming the lonely pastures, where the cattle were silently feeding, to the croaking of the frogs, the intenser dream of the crickets, the half-throttled note of a cuckoo flying over. The bushes loomed, the potato-vines stood upright, the corn grew apace. One's eyes were partially closed then; the other senses took the lead. Every plant emitted its odour, the swamp-pink in the meadow, the tansy in the road. One caught the peculiar dry scent of the corn, which was just beginning to show its tassels. One heard the tinkling of rills one had never detected before. The moonlight over the village, as one stole into the street, seemed to bring antiquity back again. The church, with its fluted columns, reminded one of the Parthenon. The houses had a classical elegance.

Sometimes, even in the morning, usually sacred to reading and writing, the wind fairly blew him out of doors. The elements were so lively and active, and he felt so sympathetic with them, that he could not sit while the wind went by. His regular time was the afternoon, from two-thirty to five-thirty, the hour for a voyage to the Leaning Hemlocks, along the Assabet river, or perhaps to examine an ant-hill, nearer home. He had observed it the day before, with its little galleries, wide as a match, covered with the sluggish, crawling ants. In the early spring, the stalks and grasses, left from last year, were steeped in rain and snow, and all the brooks flowed with meadow-tea. Then came the May-days of the warm west wind, the dream-frog, leaping, willowy haze-days, when anything might happen and one thought that next year, perhaps, one might be a postman in Peru, or a South African planter, or a Greenland whaler, or a Canton merchant. Better still, a Robinson Crusoe on some far-off isle of the Pacific. Henry sometimes stood under a tree half a day at a time, in a drenching rain, prying with microscopic eyes into the swarming crevices of the bark, or studying the leaves at his feet, or the spreading fungi. He would watch for an hour a battle of ants, struggling on a chip, a black ant with two red adversaries, till the black ant severed the heads of the others, losing its own feelers and most of its legs,—a second Concord fight, no doubt with as just a cause. Or, catching sight of a fox, in some woodland clearing, he yielded to the instinct of the chase, tossed his head aloft and bounded away, snuffing the air like a fox-hound, spurning the humanitarians and the Brahmins. For he felt as wild, at times,—he who preferred a vegetarian diet,—as if he lived on antelope-marrow, devoured without benefit of fire.

The midsummer days came, when the yellow lilies reigned in the river. The painted tortoises dropped from the willow-stumps as he walked over the bridge. The pickerel-weed sent up its blue and the vireo sang incessantly; the poison-sumac showed its green berries, all unconscious of guilt, the breeze displayed the white sides of the oak-leaves and gave the woods a fresh and flowing look, the rush-sparrow jingled her silver change on the broad counter of the pasture. Henry sometimes felt, on days like this, as if he were nature itself, looking into nature, as the blue-eyed grass in the meadow looks in the face of the sky. He would stand for hours, up to his chin, in some retired swamp, scenting the wild honeysuckle, lulled by the minstrel mosquitoes: for he liked to subject his body to rougher usage than a grenadier could endure, and he dreamed of still remoter retirements and still more rugged paths. He walked to Second Division Brook and watched the yellow pebbles gleaming under the watercress,—the whole brook as busy as a loom, a woof and warp of ripples, with fairy fingers throwing the shuttle, and the long, waving stream as the fine result. Just the place for a hut, with a footpath to the water. Or he strolled over to Boon's Pond in Stow, when the haze seemed to concentrate the sunlight, and he walked as if in a halo, while the song-sparrow set the day to music, as if the sparrow were itself the music of the mossy rail or fence-post. Or perhaps along the Price Farm Road, with its endless green-grass borders, with room on each

side for the berries and birches, where the walls indulged
in freaks, not bothering to run parallel with the ruts, and
goldenrod yellowed the path. On these old, meandering,
uninhabited roads, leading away from towns, these everlasting roads where the sun played truant, one forgot
what country one was in. One waved adieu to the village
and travelled like a pilgrim, going whither? Whither, indeed? On the promenade deck of the world.

Days to sit in one's boat, looking over the side, when
the river-bottom was covered with plants, springing up
in the yellowish water, and little sparkling silvery beads
of air clung to the axils of the submerged leaves. Days
to watch the pout in his flurry struggling to escape from
the turtle that held him. In these few inches of mud
and water, what ironics, what tragedies, what growth and
beauty! In one's ears sounded the roll-call of the harvest-
fly, just as it sounded in Greece, in Anacreon's ode.
Henry was amphibious, he felt. He could see himself
swimming in the brooks and pools, with perch and bream
and pout, and dozing with the stately pickerel, under the
pads of the river, amid the winding aisles and corridors
that were formed by the stems of the plants. And what a
luxury, in a warm September, to muse by a wall-side in
the sunshine, cuddling under a grey stone, to the siren-
song of the cricket. He could always hear in the atmosphere a fine Æolian harp-music, like the mellow sound
of distant horns in the hollow mansions of the upper air.
The critics seemed to think that music was intermittent.
They had to wait for a Mozart or a Paganini. Music was
perpetual for Henry. He heard it in the softened air,
the wind, the rain, the running water. To his expanded
ear what a harp the world was!—even if another sound
reached his unwilling sense in the midday stillness, a tin-
tinnabulation from afar, the rumour of his contemporaries. It was of little moment, in these autumn days, when
a young man's limbs were full of vigour, when his

thoughts were like a flowing morning light, and the stream of his life stretched out before him, with long reaches of serene ripples. Thoughts like wild apples, food for walkers.

CHAPTER XVI

CAMBRIDGE: LONGFELLOW,
DANA AND LOWELL

DICKENS had come and gone, with two red roses in his buttonhole. Half the households of Beacon Hill had asked him to call on Sunday, after tea, on the day of his arrival, and share their pews at the evening service. They took him in their carriages to Mount Auburn Cemetery, the favourite Boston drive; and the great Boz dinner at Papanti's Hall, presided over by President Quincy of Harvard,—for Quincy had succeeded Dr. Kirkland,—was the greatest event of the kind the town had seen.

Longfellow had returned Dickens's visit. The admiring Charles Sumner had scattered in London handfuls of *Voices of the Night,* and Longfellow found that he was an English poet, almost as renowned as Tennyson. He found that he was a German poet, too, after another summer on the Rhine, largely spent with Freiligrath, who had translated his poems, and with whom he read the *Kalevala,* the Finnish folk-epic. The Boston and Cambridge authors were multiplying their ties with the world beyond the Atlantic. They visited Maria Edgeworth in her home in Ireland, and the Nortons imported a gardener from the Edgeworth place. They had memories of moonlight evenings with Mrs. Hemans in the ruins of Melrose Abbey. They brought back roots and ivy from Miss Mitford's garden and sent her little boxes of American plants, the fringed gentian and the scarlet lily. Letters sped back and forth between Beacon Hill and Brattle Street and Edinburgh, Geneva, Bonn and Paris.

Fostered by these reciprocities, a mild haze of Europe spread over Cambridge that gradually deepened as the years went on. The customs of Brattle Street grew softer and warmer. At sewing-bees at the president's house, they still preserved the good old rustic ways, the baskets of cake, the flowing pitchers of milk that foamed as cheerfully in the Spartan air as the punch-bowls on the worldly lawns of Brookline. Cambridge was not likely to forget the Washington Elm or the blacksmith's spreading chestnut, about which Longfellow had written a poem; and good Cantabrigians liked to remember that, in the storm of 1815, the last year of the war with England, the English elms had been battered and broken, while the American elms outrode the tempest, proud and free as Commodore Perry's ships. Cambridge was a Yankee village, dyed as deeply in its proper essence as ever the indigo-bird in its native blue. But foreign streaks appeared upon its surface, blending and melting into one another. One heard Spanish songs to the guitar. There were concerts by the "Germania," fifteen young Germans; there were musical parties, with Chopin, Liszt and Schubert, balls with lamps in the trees, flowers and ices. On June evenings, scented with the new-mown hay, one caught under the moon the strains of Pergolesi's Stabat Mater. Hampers of game arrived from England, grouse and venison from the Scottish moors; and many a capacious Cambridge cellar nursed its racks of cool Johannisberger, spread the protecting cobweb over the hock and the wine that might perhaps have been Horace's Massic. Longfellow represented the changing order that blurred the lines of Norton's checker-board.

Longfellow, too, had married a merchant's daughter, fair as a Portland figurehead; and the Craigie house, bought for the youthful couple, soon became the rival of Shady Hill. There was something Goethean in its air of elegant simplicity and space. Never was a poet more calmly happy. He laid out a garden behind the house, shaped like the seven-chorded lyre. Rising early, brewing his own Mocha, standing at his desk by the southern window, he opened the day by translating some lines of Dante. It was like running a ploughshare through the soil of his mind: a thousand germs of thought started up that otherwise might have lain and rotted there. Then came the lectures and the college work. In the afternoon, a horseback ride or a stroll through Cambridgeport, to the mouth of the river, where the tide-waters spread like the sea, flashing and freshening the air; or perhaps, to slake his thirst for foreign travel, he took the stage to Boston, to the markets, where the colours and scents of the vegetables in the carts carried him to Italy and France. Or, walking to town for exercise, he dined with Sumner and Hillard at the Parker House, a chance for a talk about Goethe and the subdued tone that he recommended, the best for artists in song as for artists in painting. Sometimes he went to Newport, where the sea spoke Italian; often he went back to Portland. There the sea spoke Norse on tempestuous days. The tide gurgled under the wooden piers and softly spread its fans upon the shore, and the sails of the ships gleamed in the vapoury distance. There he recovered his youth, in the beautiful harbour. For, behind the tapestried mind of the Cambridge professor, filled with European shapes and figures, lurked the Portland boy whose longest thoughts were filled with the Atlantic, the driftwood and the seaweed, the lighthouse on its rocky ledge, the wings of the gulls and the whitecaps, the clattering hammers in the busy shipyards, piled with timbers of the lordly pine from the deer-haunted forests of Maine.

Now and then, at almost any moment, after a morning's work on his Dante lectures, under his apple-tree, in the rustic seat, or as he rode on the beach at Newport, where *The Skeleton in Armour* had come to him, or stood with his back to the autumn fire, a poem rose in his mind, stanza by stanza, and whipped itself on paper with arrowy speed,—a song or a sonnet, a ballad of the sea-coast, suggested by some event in the morning paper. He had written his *Poems on Slavery* on shipboard, mainly to please Sumner, who had joined the Abolitionists, and much to the displeasure of most of his friends, who wished to let sleeping dogs lie; but *The Slave's Dream* and *The Slave in the Dismal Swamp* were picture-poems with a child's feeling, for indignation was not one of the chords of Longfellow's garden-lyre. Everything that passed into his mind turned into music and pictures. This was the weakness of *The Spanish Student,* the first of several poems in dramatic form without a dramatic moment; but this was the charm of the poems of cities and legends, *Nuremberg, The Belfry of Bruges,* in a generation for which "Europe," even to itself, was only a half-told tale. "Filled was the air with a dreamy and magical light," as of golden leaves and autumn afternoons, for those who, holding the book in their hands, mused over the scenes of ancient splendour that came to life again in the poet's rhymes. *Evangeline,* too, was a picture-poem. No one could forget the Acadian village, the murmuring pines and the hemlocks bearded with moss, the forest scenes, the lagoons of the Mississippi, the haunts of trappers and hunters and *coureurs de bois,* the far-away Indian lodges in sunny clearings, the swaying branches and the rushing torrents. But *Evangeline* was also a story-poem, the roundest and the ripest that Longfellow wrote. The first King Leopold of Belgium caused to be cut on a seal the word Atchafalaya,—the name of the lake where the lovers passed each other, each unaware of the other's presence,—because "life is like that," he said. Longfellow felt this and conveyed the feeling. It was a feeling that will preserve a poem which has so much simplicity and grace.

Longfellow's mind was never far from the sea. Even on the hills above the valley of Grand Pré, the "sea-fogs pitched their tents." No Massachusetts mind was far from the sea. At one of Margaret Fuller's Conversations, James Freeman Clarke had spoken of the beauty of American ships. Essays, he said, should be written about them, as people wrote of the art of the Greeks, for the ship was the loveliest object in the modern world. The proof of the American search for beauty was the graceful prow and swelling hull, the tall, tapering mast, the shrouds of shredded jet, the bellying canvas and the patron saint who watched the waves from the bow. Shipbuilding followed the laws of fitness: to bring the form of the ship into the right relation with wind and wave was to find perfect harmony and beauty. Emerson had agreed with Clarke. What New England writer would not have agreed? [1] Horatio Greenough, the sculptor, when he returned from Italy a little later, exclaimed, as he looked at a clipper-ship, "There is something I should not be ashamed to show Phidias!" The group of Boston men with whom he was talking had never thought of a ship as a work of art. But Emerson and Clarke would have understood him; and so would Rufus Choate. As Choate lay dying at Halifax, looking over the harbour, he said, "If a schooner or sloop goes by, don't disturb me; but

[1] Most of the New England authors wrote well about ships and shipping. See the fine passage on ships in Harriet Beecher Stowe's *The Pearl of Orr's Island* (Chapter XXX): "Who that has seen one bound onward, with her white breasts swelling and heaving, as if with a reaching expectancy, does not feel his own heart swell with a longing impulse to go with her to the far-off shores? . . . On these romantic shores of Maine, where all is so wild and still, and the blue sea lies embraced in the arms of dark, solitary forests, the sudden incoming of a ship from a distant voyage is a sort of romance. . . . What a wonder! There comes a ship from China, drifting in like a white cloud,—the gallant creature! How the waters hiss and foam before her! With what a great, free, generous plash she throws out her anchor, as if she said a cheerful 'Well done!' to some glorious work accomplished."

if there is a square-rigged ship, wake me up." Longfellow shared these feelings, no one more so,—the author of *The Building of the Ship*,—except, perhaps, Richard Henry Dana, who was also living in Cambridge. Dana's *Two Years Before the Mast*, an Odyssey of the days of the brigs and the clippers, when half the American merchant-marine was manned by young New Englanders, was a poem about the beauty of ships. It had opened a new world for story-tellers.

This younger and bolder Dana, the son of the poet, was the boy who had almost lost an ear at school and who had so much to say on the subject of flogging. He was one of the Cambridge boys for whom the old sloop "Harvard," moored in the river, had seemed like a Viking ship. He had practised navigation on the Winthrop duck-pond and sailed away, as a Harvard junior, whose studies were interrupted by failing eye-sight, on the voyage to California that had made the brig "Pilgrim" famous. With all the positive traits that his father lacked, robust and self-reliant,—he had been one of Emerson's pupils,—he was a day-dreamer, like his father, and capable of mystical ecstasies. Returning from the voyage to finish his studies, he had assisted Professor Edward Tyrrel Channing, whose lectures he edited later, and he opened a law-office in 1840, the year of the publication of his book. He was already known as the sailors' lawyer, and his office smelled like a forecastle, crowded as it was with men from the ships. He battled like an avenging angel for the seamen's rights and alienated all his paying clients, for the lords of the sea, like the "lords of the loom and the lash," as Charles Sumner called them, did not like a man who called attention to the wrongs of sailors and slaves. Dana, an aristocrat in every sense, fastidious in all his tastes, excelled in the fastidiousness of conscience. He had compiled a seaman's manual to help the sailors in their fight for justice.

He had kept a journal on the voyage and written out his notes at the Law School, and he had read the manuscript aloud to his father and his uncle, Washington Allston. Horace Mann, who had also read it, offered to have it published as a tract if Dana would only add a few statistics, talk a little more about imports and exports, cut the descriptions out, make the book useful, with tables of facts, and draw a moral lesson on every page. Horace Mann preferred the "Rollo" style; but in Liverpool two thousand British sailors bought the book in a single day, and the old connoisseur, Samuel Rogers, said that it had more poetry in it than almost any modern verse. It was the real thing, as the sailors knew, the first book written about the sea, not from the bridge or the cabin, but by one of the hands, one who had shared in the humblest form of sailing. To sail for furs to the Northwest coast was a gentleman's occupation, but it was ignoble to go for hides. This was the current opinion. To say that one saw the horns sticking out of his cargo was the sharpest taunt one skipper could give another.

But a reader did not have to be a sailor to be swept along by the book. One did not even have to know the meaning of a jigger, a bunt or a knight-head, a larboard or a starboard watch, a cross-jack yard or a mizzen topsail. To small-pull a main top-gallant yard, to well it, to twig the fore might mean no more to one's etymological sense than if one were engaged in hunting the snark. The "heave ho" and the "heave and pawl," the "heave hearty ho" and the "heave with a will," the "cheerily, men," while all hands joined in the chorus, blew one's mind awake. The book, like the vessel, leaped over the seas, trembling to the keel, while the spars and masts snapped and creaked; and one felt oneself in a wholesome and bracing climate, with spray and the smell of tar and salt, scrubbed wood, glistening brass, the sunlight glancing on the bright blue waves. It was as taut as a

rope from end to end, with sheer high spirits and masculine vigour, with studding-sails alow and aloft, sharp on
the wind, and manned by a genius "going strong" and
decidedly going somewhere. No one could fail to perceive that the ship was a symbol of life, since the first part
of the voyage was spent in getting it ready for sea and the
second part in getting it ready for port. The book was
full of overtones and symbols, and all the details of the
sailor's life were noted with the bold veracity that springs
from a heightened state of consciousness, a tension, well
controlled and even calm, that passed at moments into
exaltation. Such were the moments when Dana, at the
helm, witnessed the breaking of day over the ocean, the
sighting of the iceberg, near Cape Horn,—the enormous
mountain-island, with its dark cavities and valleys, its
pinnacles glittering in the sun, rising and sinking at the
base while its points nodded against the sky, crumbling,
tumbling, thundering in the sea,—or the still, foggy
night, near the Falkland Islands, when the dark silence
was broken by the slow, long-drawn breathing of invisible whales, drifting to the surface or lying at full length,
unseen, beside the ship.

For thirty years and more, in Harvard Square,
promptly at eight o'clock every morning, one saw Dana,
green bag in hand, waiting for the Boston omnibus. He
was always telling tales of the sea; and everyone knew
that his book had done as much for the sailors as Dickens
had done for the debtors and orphans of England and
Uncle Tom's Cabin for the slaves. The dream of his life
was to make some contribution to international law. He
had left far behind him the episode of his youth, with
the pumps and white stockings and the white duck trousers, the blue jacket and the varnished hat and the silk
handkerchief flying from the outside pocket. Once again
only he wrote about the sea, in a little book, *To Cuba
and Back,* which was read by tourists in Havana. But

he never forgot the tropical nights, the soft trade-wind clouds under the stars, "the seas and floods in wavering morrice moving." He said that he was made for the sea and that all his life on shore was a mistake, that he should have been a traveller, with no profession or home, roaming over the world like a gypsy.

Meanwhile, the son of another Cambridge worthy, James Russell Lowell, who lived at Elmwood,—his father's house, the last in Tory Row,—had also appeared as a man of letters. A little younger than Dana, he had similar traits, although he was tethered to Cambridge not by conscience but by an affection for the *genius loci*. With the same animal spirits and boyish charm, he loved the soil as Dana loved the sea. He felt the thrill of the earth under his feet as he absorbed the sunshine like a melon. Short, muscular, stocky, shaggy,—his friend William Page had painted him with long blond curls and a pointed beard, a black jacket and a lace collar, as if he were something more than a reader of Shakespeare,—he liked to think that his ear suggested a faun's. He had an air of the world, although he was rather self-conscious, even a little jaunty. He seemed to be pleased with himself and his early success, mercurial, impressionable, plastic; but under the romantic, susceptible surface there was something timid, hard and wooden that was to show in the grain at certain moments. There was a streak of jealousy in him, an irreducible *amour-propre*, an over-hasty zeal for "the niche and the laurel." He was much at ease in all the Zions, and there were those who even thought him shallow and found his self-confident air very provoking. In fact, he was exuberant and impulsive, and, if there was something wooden in him, there was also something rich and buoyant. His fancy was luxuriant. He was the cleverest young man in Cambridge, and even the most intelligent. He had the makings of a first-rate scholar. But his leading trait was a gift of pure enjoyment, whether of books or garden-flowers, walking, talking, smoking, drinking, reading, a gusto that was new in Brattle Street. He was a capital idler. He could lie on his back for days on end, dreaming in the fragrant air or conning some Elizabethan poet. Moreover, he, like Dana, had his trances, every year, when June, from its southern ambush, "with one great gush of blossom stormed the world."

Elmwood was the hub of Lowell's Cambridge, the large, square Georgian house with the tall pilasters, the old-fashioned garden, the meadows at the rear, where he liked to pitch hay on summer mornings. There, as a little boy, he had fallen asleep to the rhythms of Shakespeare and Spenser, read to him by an aunt who had brought him up, Miss Mary Lowell, one of those Cambridge women who knew a dozen languages and who had learned Hungarian and Polish. He had had hallucinations as a child. Mediæval figures from *The Faerie Queene* had walked beside him on his way to school. He had burrowed among his father's books and rescued from the attic the old prints of Socrates, Plato and Seneca that had adorned his great-grandfather's study. His Latin was as fluent as his English.[2] To the *Natural History of Selborne*, for which his father had an old affection, he felt especially drawn; and he liked to record the events of the garden, the visits of the cross-bills, the battles of crows and robins. His father had led him out to the barn to watch the swallows on the roof, taking counsel together before their yearly migration, as Gilbert White had noted years before; and he had counted seven orioles flashing about the lawn all at once. He had studied the cedar-birds in the hawthorn-bushes and learned where to look for the king-birds, building their nests in the orchard. He had seen a cherry in full blossom, beside his study-window, covered with humming-birds that had

[2] See the macaronic Latin verses in *The Biglow Papers*.

been benumbed by a fall of rain and snow. He knew the plaintive may-be of the goldfinch when it was stealing his lettuce-seeds. He had listened to a pair of indigo-birds singing all day long to one another. He had heard the cuckoo strike the hour, like a Swiss clock, through the night.

Along with the birds, in much the same fashion, he had studied the English poets, observing their notes and their plumage. He could remember the time and the place when each of them had flashed into his mind, Landor, for instance, whom he had read in the old arched alcoves in Harvard Hall. He had made a collection of fragments from Rogers and Campbell, who had written of home as if they had lived at Elmwood. He had been the member of the "band" who had copied out Tennyson's early poems and shown the manuscript-book to the other members, and he had steeped himself in Shelley and Keats,—of whom he had planned to write a life, in the days when Keats was still a morning star,[3]—till his mind was a music-box of impressions and rhythms. With his philological instinct, a natural Cambridge trait, he liked to trace the origins of words, the earliest use of phrases, the history of archaisms and colloquialisms; and this had led him to study the Yankee speech, which he knew as Tennyson knew the "northern farmer's." He felt that "the tongue of the people in the mouth of the scholar" was the right motto for poets, and the Yankee tongue was in his blood. He had heard it all about him in his boyhood, on muster-fields, at cattle-shows, at noonings in the hay-fields at Elmwood, when he had sat with the hired men over their jugs of blackstrap, talking in the shadow of the ash-tree. Yankee was his mother-tongue, the tongue that some of his forbears had brought from England, while others had brought the scholar-

[3] Eighty-five years later, this project was carried out by Amy Lowell, the grand-daughter of Lowell's first cousin.

dialect. He had revelled in the Yankee speech at Concord when, as a senior in college, he had been rusticated and packed off thither, to study with the Reverend Barzillai Frost. The people were forgetting it in Cambridge, but it throve on the Concord farms. For Emerson, who took him on strolls to the Cliffs, he had acquired a feeling later. In fact, he was one of the neophytes who walked to Boston to hear Emerson lecture and who caught the sound of the trumpet in his silvery voice. He was thrilled by one of Emerson's phrases, "The walls of the mind's chamber are covered with scribblings, which need but the bringing of a candle to render them legible." That one should sit alone and meditate was almost a new idea to a college boy whose mind was running over with animal spirits. Emerson appealed to the *exalté* in him. But it was Mr. Frost, the minister, who excited his fancy in Concord. Mr. Frost, the rustic Harvard scholar, was reappearing in *The Biglow Papers,* which Lowell was dashing off in his usual way, with lucky hits up and down the pages. The minister was Parson Wilbur, and Concord was reproduced in some of the idyllic scenes as well as in the Yankee dialect. This was Lowell's happiest tongue in verse.

With his boyish air and his worldly air, his radical sympathies and his Tory habits, his antiquarian tastes and his love of nature, his sudden enthusiasms and his constant affections, his volatility and his love of puns,—similes made of Semele,—together with his industry and patience, his high romantic poses and his zest for old garrets, desks, pipes and friends, Lowell was a complicated soul who left on the mind not one but a hundred impressions. He was compact of incongruities, like many another humorous Yankee, and some of the readers of his earnest poems were shocked by his inconsequence when they met him; for, while he had a streak of the mystic in him, he also had a pantagruelian streak. He was warm-hearted and cold by turns, as many other men in Cambridge were. He would rejoice in a friend and snub him in the next breath. He had a way of setting one gently right.[4] Even his spontaneity had a method, for, while he was really spontaneous, he wished to be more spontaneous than he was. He would stop, in the Yard, in the midst of some grave discussion, vault over one of the great stone columns, clap his hands and crow like a cock, and then resume the argument. If, as occasionally happened, he failed to leap the column, he was annoyed. He would keep on trying until he succeeded, saying, with a wry smile, "I commonly do that the first time." One had to be gay, or appear so, in spite of one's forbears. This note of the *voulu*, the factitious, which was marked in his personality, appeared in his poems also. His liveliest effects were often forced, and some of his sublimities as well.[5] The mixed impression that his poems left, the inconclusiveness of his critical thinking suggested that he had never thought anything out, and that he even felt with reservations. Had he ever found his own "average point," [6] or made up his mind in regard to any question? There was much of the chameleon in his nature, but there was also much that was firm and strong. For the solid and even chunky physical frame housed a substantial Yankee, shrewd, enquiring and tenacious, with a mind which, however inconclusive, liked to coil about its acquisitions. Lowell had what the phren-

[4] Said Howells, "Who in the world ever heard of the Claudian Emissary?" Said Lowell, "You are in Cambridge, Mr. Howells."— Howells, *Literary Friends and Acquaintance.*

[5] This was what Emerson had in mind when he refused to review Lowell's *Cathedral.* "I like Lowell," he said, "but I think he had to pump."

[6] Lowell described himself when he said, in his *Moosehead Journal:* "It is as hard for most characters to stay at their own average point in all companies, as for a thermometer to say 65° for twenty-four hours together. I like this in our friend Johannes Taurus, that he carries everywhere and maintains his insular temperature, and will have everything accommodate itself to that."

ologists called inhabitiveness and adhesiveness. He inhabited Cambridge, he adhered to books. No one "stayed put" better than he. He had a rare feeling for style, though his taste was less perceptive than gustatory. Where others only read, he read with passion. He had a feeling for the romance of letters that only Longfellow shared; and, if one knew his open-sesame, one found within something warm and winning. If one could rise to the charms of Mount Auburn or cap Fresh Pond with a good quotation, if one had something to say for the elms and the willows, or knew how to look at a peewee pursuing a fly, or an oriole building its nest, if one could speak with discretion of Chaucer or Dante and open an Elzevir with affectionate fingers, if one loved black-letter as one loved a meerschaum, or even understood how to be idle, one found oneself at home in Lowell's heart.

Longfellow and he had never met until, one day in 1846, they found themselves together in Lowell's study, the upstairs study at Elmwood, discussing the anti-slavery question. Lowell was an Abolitionist. This was one of his many tinges, for he was a polychromic nature; but there were various reasons for it. His father and his grandfather had had the Boston Negroes on their conscience, and Lowell's young wife, Maria White, a poet like himself,—one of the Watertown girls, a pupil of Margaret Fuller, who had belonged to the "band,"—was deep in all the democratic movements. The two young people had written for the Pennsylvania *Freeman,* and Lowell was contributing a weekly paper to the *Anti-Slavery Standard* in New York. He was full of the zeal of the convert, for all his instincts were conservative. He had ridiculed and satirized in college, like any clever boy, the uncouth ways of the reformers and the causes he was defending now, woman's rights and total abstinence, Abolition, Transcendentalism; and, if he was attacking the Mexican War, respectable Whigs like Prescott also at-

tacked it. But he was in a state of exaltation and found
it exhilarating to have an object that was outside and
beyond his art. Behind his work was all the moral fervour
that characterized the typical New England boy. His literary facility was surprising. *The Biglow Papers, A Fable
for Critics,* scores of shorter pieces in verse and prose were
pouring from his mind at once. Four volumes of his work
appeared together, in the "year of revolutions," '48. He
could hardly write slowly enough to develop his thought;
he could hardly write fast enough to record his impressions. Moreover, he was a lion at twenty-nine. He was
the "best launched man of his time," as N. P. Willis said.
The word had gone round among the reviewers that
Lowell was the poet of the future.

Of all the younger writers, he was the most adroit and
the most accomplished. He seemed to be a master of all
the poetic forms, ode, song, epigram and sonnet, the
narrative poem, the elegy, the idyll. Everyone knew *To
Perdita, Singing, The Rose* and *Rosaline,* as presently
Prometheus and *Rhœcus, The Shepherd of King Admetus* and the *Ode to France, An Indian-Summer Reverie,*
with its charming scenes of Cambridge, especially *The
Vision of Sir Launfal.* Longfellow and Poe alone, among
the American poets, wrote with the colour and music, the
skill and taste that Lowell exhibited in all these verses.
His artistry was highly conscious. He had studied all the
current models. He was almost as good as Keats and
Shelley, as Tennyson, Landor and Hood. The question
was, when Tennyson and Landor, when Keats, Shelley
and Hood were better known, how much would be left
to make a Lowell?—for his poetry, undoubtedly good,
seemed to be largely at second hand. His titles, like his
poems themselves, savoured of other poets,—so much
so that one asked if Lowell's writing was not wholly
prompted by his reading. Comparing him with Longfellow, Emerson, Poe, one saw that Poe, like Emerson, was

unique, while Longfellow claimed little and pretended little. Longfellow's tone was humble, unlike Lowell's. He seemed to write for the joy of sharing his treasures, as if he were glad to be thought a mere translator, a simple story-teller, a nursery minstrel. This was both disarming and deceptive, for Longfellow had an original mind. He was an innovator in metres and rhythms; he introduced new modes of feeling; he touched his world with a magic that was mild but unmistakable. He had a poetic personality, an individual temperament, tame and even flat as it was at moments, scarcely ever intense. He had his own colour-box and varnish, and all the Longfellow pictures, large and small, bore the signature of the Cambridge artist.[7] Longfellow asked for less than his due, while it appeared that Lowell asked for more; for, with his greater energy and depth of thought, his air of accomplished maturity, one looked in his work for the signature almost in vain. Lowell took the colour of his subjects, or, rather, of the poets he had absorbed, and only a phrase here and there,—some outburst of New England moral feeling, some reference to American birds and flowers,—broke one's impression that his work was a medley of English poetry. For each and all of his poems, except *The Biglow Papers,* one found a model somewhere in England's Parnassus, in *Locksley Hall,* in *Don Juan,* in *English Bards and Scotch Reviewers,* Browning's dramatic monologues, *The Faerie Queene,* Shelley's *Prometheus,* Coleridge's *France: an Ode,* Keats's *Endymion,* Shakespeare, Gray or Spenser. In fact, to the end of his life, in Lowell's verses, lines cropped out and passages appeared that obviously belonged, in style and feeling, to Tennyson, Wordsworth or Keats.

That Lowell was a sort of shadow-poet, in spite of all his taste and cultivation, became too evident as the years

---

[7] To feel the originality of Longfellow's style, one has only to see it reflected in Lowell's *The Changeling.*

went on. Even at his best, in *The Present Crisis,* that classic of radical orators, he was rewriting *Locksley Hall;* and would he have written *A Fable for Critics* if Byron had not suggested the form? Tennyson gave him the model for *Sir Launfal,* a touching and popular poem, even deservedly popular, for all its jerkiness and air of haste, as a genuine expression of its time and place, the humanitarian Cambridge of the eighteen-forties. As American poets multiplied, and English poetry grew more familiar, Lowell's reputation slowly sank. Of the splendid mass of Victorian verse, the most bewildering since the age of Shakespeare, could anything be expected to survive that was not entirely fresh? "Desiring this man's art and that man's scope" seemed all too plainly Lowell's state of mind; and that his verse was good, and more than good, with its charming air of literary breeding, that his technical agility was surprising,[8] that his tone was often noble, all this had to face the final question, What did it add to the sum of things poetic? That it added much to other sums, local, moral, political, hardly affected the question. That the drop of Lowell's reputation implied a holocaust of lesser poets was to be taken for granted. The fact remained that one forgot his poems. One read them five times over and still forgot them, as if this excellent verse had been written in water.

Lowell was scarcely the "maker" he longed to be. He was even a little presumptuous, saying of his "kind of wingéd prose" that it "could fly if it would," when obviously the case was otherwise, since poets always fly when they can. That he was a rhetorician, according to the definition of the poet Yeats,[9] was closer to the truth. He deceived himself, and his contemporaries were deceived about him. In taking him for a first-rate poet, however,

[8] E.g., *An Oriental Apologue.*
[9] "Rhetoric is the will trying to do the work of the imagination." —*Ideas of Good and Evil.*

his contemporaries were unjust to what he was. They were no less unjust in taking him for a "radical" poet. It was observed, after his wife's death, that his radical phase rapidly passed; and those who preferred him in this aspect thought of him as a renegade. Three generations later, this view persisted. It was unfair from the first, for the shift in Lowell's point of view might have been taken for granted. Leopards do not change their spots, and Cambridge boys are Cambridge boys even when they marry Maria Whites. The radical note in Lowell's work was a kind of inverse ventriloquism, in which the voice appeared to come from the poet, while actually the speaker was his wife. It was her influence that induced his fervour, for Lowell was highly suggestible, and the influence and the fervour passed together. His radicalism was only a phase that little in his nature sustained or encouraged. It was true that this phase represented his solidest writing. Witness the poem on Garrison and *The Present Crisis*, for all its form was borrowed: witness, especially, *The Biglow Papers*. It was the glory of *The Biglow Papers*,—which made the book almost a folk-creation,—that Parson Wilbur and Hosea Biglow were brothers under their skins. That literate and illiterate in New England met on a common ground of feeling, that they were at one in essential matters, religious and political alike, that their regard for human rights, their hatred of war and false ideas of empire, sprang from their common principle,—this was the burden of *The Biglow Papers*. It was the most profound of Lowell's works because of its instinctive presentation of the folk point of view from which it sprang, for Lowell's moment of radical fervour carried him to the depths of the popular mind.

The Biglow Papers remained as a permanent landmark. No other work compared with it, either then or later, for showing the homogeneity of New England, its common stock, its common faith. But works like *The Biglow Papers* can spring from a divided mind. A heated imagination can produce them, a sudden and momentary dramatic impulse, while part of the man remains in reserve; and a large part of the man remained in reserve in all of Lowell's poetry. For Lowell as a secondary poet, much, however, surely remained to be said. His brooding love of country was a noble trait. If the patriotic odes of his later years, the *Ode for the Fourth of July*, the *Ode Read at Concord*, the better-known *Commemoration Ode*, seemed, in after times, too much like Websterian speeches rewritten in verse,—one felt in them, too much, the lapsed occasion, the rhetoric that required the proper moment,—passages remained that touched one still and longer passages that convinced the mind how Lowell must have touched those who heard him. *A Fable for Critics*,—at its lowest value, the classic illustration of "college humour,"—was something new under the Yankee sun. No one could know how good it was, how frank, fresh, perceptive, who had not read the critics of the eighteen-forties. Beside the New York and Boston reviewers of the "Independent Press," which Lowell satirized in *The Biglow Papers*, in the series of burlesque notices, *A Fable for Critics* had the virtue that Longfellow's poems possessed in the previous decade. Whatever Lowell promised as a critic, no one could deny that he, with Poe, had opened a new era in critical practice: he and Poe were the first American critics to exercise their judgment freely. If, among Lowell's qualities, judgment was the one that developed least, if he was prejudiced and hasty, still *A Fable for Critics* marked an epoch. It formed reputations,—Lowell did not wait till they were formed. It dealt with American letters directly,—Lowell did not wait for English opinions. Aside from this, and *The Big-*

low Papers, his descriptive poems were the best. A book of American verse could scarcely omit *An Indian-Summer Reverie,*—

> What visionary tints the year puts on,
> When falling leaves falter through motionless air
>   Or numbly cling and shiver to be gone!
> How shimmer the low flats and pastures bare,
>   As with her nectar Hebe Autumn fills
>   The bowl between me and those distant hills,
> And smiles and shakes abroad her misty, tremulous hair!

And what could be more veracious than these lines from *Pictures from Appledore,* for another example?—

>   the blind old ocean maundering,
>   Raking the shingle to and fro,
>   Aimlessly clutching and letting go
>   The kelp-haired sedges of Appledore,
>   Slipping down with a sleepy forgetting,
>   And anon his ponderous shoulder setting,
>   With a deep, hoarse pant, against Appledore.

Everything that was rich and sunny, all that was loving, strong and true, in Lowell's heart and talent, spoke through his *Under the Willows* and *The Fountain of Youth, Sunthin' in the Pastoral Line,* the "June" of *The Vision of Sir Launfal,*—with every leaf and blade "some happy creature's palace." The Lowell of May and June was the joyous Lowell, the poet and the lover, off-guard for once and all the time, transfigured with the coming of spring and summer.

CHAPTER XVII

THE BOSTON HISTORIANS: MOTLEY

THE LAST traces of the Doric age were passing away in Boston. The antique severities were gone, along with the floridities of Gilbert Stuart, and a bland and learned elegance had taken the place of the harsh, austere or stately ways of old. The worthies who remembered the Revolution, the open-handed merchants of Stuart's portraits, who had laid down their annual pipe of Madeira, the frugal Romans who, at public dinners, perhaps to celebrate some splendid gift which they had offered to the city, departed so far from their usual rule, when the dessert was passed, as to take three almonds or a fig, the hearty old souls who, at church, sang with might and main, blowing their noses till the rafters rang,—all these types were vanishing one by one. In the old Puritan town, swept by the air of the world, one heard less of Cicero and Plutarch, more of modern Rome than of ancient Rome and much more of London than of Athens.

One by one, the faces that Stuart had painted disappeared from the Boston streets. Judge Joseph Story was dead. So was John Pickering, who had known Chinese and Cochin-Chinese, once so useful in Salem, who had studied the Polynesian dialects and collected the Yankee words and phrases that Lowell had taken up in turn. Dr. Channing had gone before them, in a country inn at Bennington. The frail little invalid's body had been placed in Mount Auburn, while the bell of the Roman Catholic cathedral tolled, as for the passing of a saint; and every good Bostonian wrote in his journal that a generation had been buried with it. For Channing had been the father and bishop of Boston, with a truly paternal love for all that was human. The tomb of the apostle of self-culture, the friend of the slaves and the workers, the scourge of the selfish, whose name had headed all the petitions and who had fought for liberty and grace, was designed by Washington Allston; and Allston, his friend and kinsman, was the next to go. Six hours before his death, he had been working on "Belshazzar's Feast," the unfinished and unfinishable masterpiece. He was carried in the evening to the churchyard, on the edge of Harvard Square, in the flaring light of the torches borne by a crowd of students.

Of the senatorial ancients a few remained, survivors of the old three-bottle days when young men grew up on Pope's Homer, followed the Ciceronian injunctions and fell in love, by candle-light, with damsels who were singing the songs of Burns. Harvard stood firm with President Quincy, that Pharos on a rock; but John Quincy Adams, his noble kinsman, the aged statesman, the aspiring poet, had but a few more lines to write. He still rose at five on winter mornings, groped for his old-fashioned tinder-box,—for he despised the new Lucifer matches,—lighted his candle and fire and took his cold sponge, as once, in the days of his presidency, twenty years before, when he was almost sixty, he had swum across the Potomac and back and walked home under the winter moon. He still toiled over his rhymes and orations, fighting the slave-power, arousing interest in canals and roads, prompting scientific expeditions and founding institutions of research. He had laboured for weeks on a speech on astronomy; he had journeyed to Cincinnati, at seventy-seven, sleeping on the floor of a canal-boat, to lay the cornerstone of an observatory. His hope was to kindle an interest in science in the West. He rejoiced in the spread of German studies, even in Richter and Tieck, who had addled the brains of the young. During the Congressional recesses, one found him at the old house at Quincy, pruning his garden or among his books. Every day, twice a day, one saw him standing in the portico, holding his watch in his hand, timing the rising or the setting sun. And every night, kneeling beside his bed, he repeated, "Now I lay me down to sleep," which he had learned from the lips of Abigail Adams. He had said it every night of his life, in Holland, Prussia, Russia, France and England, in Washington, Boston and Quincy. "I say it out loud always," he remarked, "and I don't mumble it either."

Oratory and history were still the central interests of the Boston mind. The Bostonians had been trained to distinguish the fine points of eloquence; and, as this was still a political Age of Faith, the orators were their tribunes and standard-bearers. The commentators delighted in analyzing the styles of the various speakers,—Webster, whose vocabulary was more Teutonic than Macaulay's and far less Latinized than Burke's, Edward Everett, Webster's under-study, and Rufus Choate, who shared Webster's gift for making his clients feel like heroes and martyrs, so that they wept when he described their actions and saw themselves as Sophoclean figures. Choate was a fiery speaker, witty, weighty, plain and grand by turns, an orator for the thinking few, unlike the mellifluous Everett and the popular Webster. His wit was more than legal. Everyone had heard his phrase about Chief Justice Shaw:[1] "I always approach Judge Shaw as a savage approaches his fetish, knowing that he is ugly, but feeling that he is great." Thus Choate, when his learned sock was on; and, when he wore the buskin, then from his lips came noble words. Everett was the figurehead of Boston. In the years that had passed since he exclaimed, "Welcome, Lafayette!" and greeted Presi-

[1] The father-in-law of Herman Melville.

dent Jackson at Bunker Hill,—placing two cannon-balls in the President's hands, as if this happy thought had dropped from heaven,—he had become the bust on the prow of the ship that beamed upon every passing sail. Who could present the keys of the city, or eulogize a hero or a guest, with more resplendent grace than Everett? No one, facing a crowd of mechanics or farmers, could picture the charms of their lot and their occupations with an air that was more engaging or reassuring. He made one feel that all was going well. But Webster was still the unrivalled leader. His eyes were "catacombs of ancient wisdom," as his admirers said, even though his virtue, like stern Cato's, often warmed with wine, was also, and more often, warmed with brandy. Webster had grown sluggish with adulation, and the Fugitive Slave Bill was to drain away much of his local glory. It was not wisdom, it was prudence that dwelt in the catacombs of Webster's eyes; but prudence, after all, was a statesman's business, and Webster had done much to preserve the Union. Moreover, the second Bunker Hill oration had shown that he was still the master-speaker.

The dignity of history and its importance were constant themes of Everett and Webster. History was the passion of Rufus Choate, when it was not law or Massachusetts, and in his fine speech, *The Age of the Pilgrims,* he expressed the feeling about the past, the origins and greatness of New England, that filled the minds of the younger writers.[2] The stream of historical interest

[2] Another of Choate's speeches, *The Power of a State Developed by Mental Culture,* expressed the feeling of renascent Boston. Choate liked to think of the boast of Themistocles, that he knew how to make a small State a great one,—by making the State wise. How was Massachusetts to maintain its lustre, with its young men drifting westward? Was it destined to fade as the nation grew? Massachusetts had it in its power to retain its intellectual leadership. People had thought too much of banks and cotton, and far too little of the culture that made Athens paramount in Greece, moulding the taste and opinion of Greece and Rome, then of the modern

spread wider and wider. Everett's most attractive trait was an eagerness to help his fellow-scholars, even political enemies like Bancroft. On his journeys abroad, he collected notes for Prescott, examining the libraries of Paris and Florence, the Guicciardini and Medici family archives, the reports of the ambassadors of Venice, the archives of Vienna, and interested Metternich and the Marquis Capponi in the efforts of his Boston friend, learning much that served himself, no doubt, in his own diplomatic career. He exerted his influence to obtain for Bancroft, whose history was advancing from volume to volume, the use of collections of letters and papers in England, although he had broken with Bancroft and sent back the letters he had received from him, as if to put an end to their relations. With a spirit like this prevailing in Boston, all the historical writers advanced together. Before the end of the forties, Sparks, Bancroft, Prescott and Ticknor had published a dozen new volumes, Richard Hildreth had written his *History of the United States,* John Lothrop Motley, a younger student, had set to work on *The Rise of the Dutch Republic* and Francis Parkman had written *The Oregon Trail.* Hildreth, a prolific journalist, had shown imagination in a novel, *The Slave, or Memoirs of Archy Moore,* which he had written in Florida, a book that thrilled the younger generation. He was the spectre of the Athenæum, the tall, grey, silent man who had been seen for years haunting his alcove, but who, in truth, was very far from spectral. He was a blunt, hard-headed hater of shams. He detested the "patriotic rouge" of Sparks along with Bancroft's pyrotechnics. His history, soberly good, was rather tame, a colourless work in six large volumes, written in a plain business style. It carried the story down to 1820 and pleased the conservative and the mat-

world. This was all that Massachusetts needed to hold its place, and more, in the future.

ter-of-fact. Entirely free from Bancroft's nonsense, it also lacked Bancroft's picturesqueness, as well as the charm of Prescott; and it lacked the original documentation that made these other historians important.

In Beacon Street, lovely in October, overhung with golden elms, with crimson creepers on the balconies, Prescott had built a new house, facing the Frog Pond and the fountain. Over the drawing-room, he arranged his study, a lofty apartment reached by a winding stairway through a secret door behind a book-case. There he kept, over the mantel, crossed, the swords of his father's father and his mother's father, who had fought on opposite sides in the Revolution, the swords that Thackeray saw, when he visited Boston. These swords suggested to Thackeray the idea of *The Virginians,* the story of the brother who fought for the king and the brother who fought for Washington. Prescott spent his days there, under the portrait of Cortez, the busts of Washington Irving and other friends, turning over his manuscripts, the twenty thousand folio pages, gathered from every corner of Europe, the books that had come by ship from Cadiz. He had been idle for a while, after his first great effort. He had earned an interlude for loafing. He played blind-man's buff with his guests and children. He amused himself with his cats, for he often had a cat in his lap. He visited Niagara Falls, the wonder of the world in the eighteen-forties, where every traveller was baptized again with a touch of Byronic emotion. In summer, he went to Nahant and Pepperell, where he kept up the old family farm. As much as his eyes permitted, he read Cooper and Dumas, who refreshed his mind. He thought for a time of writing a life of Molière.

Then plans had risen in his mind, shoots from the stock of his Spanish studies. Why should not he, like the Spaniards, gather gold in Mexico and the Andes? Everything combined to push him forward. His blindness, his cheerfulness, his frankness, his youthful high spirits, his engaging mind had caught the imagination of other scholars. Guizot, Mignet, Thierry, Lord Holland and Milman, Humboldt in Germany, Navarrete in Spain plied him with offers of assistance. Irving, hearing that he was at work on the exploits of Cortez in Mexico, his own cherished theme for many years, on which he counted for his bread and butter, gladly gave him the right of way. With all these well-wishers working for him, there was nothing for Prescott to do but to go ahead. Much as he loved Dumas, Marcus Aurelius was his favourite author; and Alfieri's example roused the spark. No need to look for the drama in his subject. The drama of *The Conquest of Mexico* shaped itself; and to use, in building the story, he had eight thousand sheets of manuscript, beautifully copied from the Spanish archives, all the original documents, diaries, letters, never yet published, never even seen, except by a few chroniclers and amanuenses. He had Navarrete's manuscript collection, dealing with Peru and Mexico. The Spanish Academy helped him. The old Spanish families opened their chests of papers, which no other writer had asked to see. Thierry sent him books. The Spanish minister in Mexico City sent him information about the Aztecs. Four copyists in Madrid gathered materials for him. Another friend delved in the British Museum. To study the trees and the birds, the landscape and the customs of the country, which had not greatly changed since the days of Cortez, he did not have to go to Mexico. Madame Calderon de la Barca, who had lived as a governess in Concord and for whose *Life in Mexico* Prescott wrote a preface, filled the lively letters that she sent him with sketches of Mexican scenes and manners, enough to convince Humboldt, who knew the country, that the half-blind Prescott had also seen it. There was enough diplomacy involved in gathering the materials for his work to have founded a small republic.

No need to rope himself to his chair, as Alfieri was obliged to do. He found it easy, in the zest of work, even to master mathematics, which had always baffled him before and which he had to know to characterize the astronomy of the Aztecs. He read various books of martial exploits, Voltaire's *Charles XII* and lives of Columbus and Hannibal. Then he set the stage with a panorama of Montezuma's empire. From the moment when Cortez, burning his boats and landing at Vera Cruz, began his march to the capital, the story moved on to its final result with the frightful inevitability of some drama of nature. The Aztecs, like the Incas, in *The Conquest of Peru,* the work that rapidly followed, were painted as the chroniclers had seen them. Their "feather-cinctured chiefs and dusky loves" were a little operatic, for no archæologist had as yet revealed the reality of these builders of civilizations that crumbled under the terrible feet of the Spaniards. But generations passed before anyone challenged the truth of the picture that Prescott drew of the conquest, grandly in the Mexican book, only less grandly in the tale of Peru,—shorter, slighter, much less unified, as the little black ruffian Pizarro was a lesser man than Cortez. Pizarro's conquest was achieved at once, and the rest of the story was an anti-climax: Prescott had to create his drama out of the sordid squabbles of the seekers of gold, who were little better than bandits. *The Conquest of Mexico* was a natural epic, while all that gave unity to the other work was that the characters were few. But everything that Prescott wrote had the same solidity, and he told these two great stories with an air of effortless ease. Massive but alive in all their parts, they were full of colour and vigorous movement. They were partly composed on horseback. Prescott mentally wrote the final chapter in a gallop through the woods at Pepperell.

While these two books were under way, Prescott and George Ticknor were always together. Ticknor was also at work on his *History of Spanish Literature*, lingering over it with such affection that he could hardly bear to part with it. Ticknor had grown more and more important, with his imposing house and his great position, of which he was by no means unaware. It was he who occasioned Longfellow's remark that "every Bostonian speaks as if he were the Pope." His large head was "full of cold brains," to quote his own phrase about William Godwin; and the more he advanced in life, the more his voice became an affront to strangers. He was a useful citizen, however, the builder of the great collection of books in the Boston Public Library, Prescott's friend and confidant, indeed the willing friend of every scholar. On his second visit to Europe, after resigning his professorship, he had been received in every quarter with the éclat of an ambassador. Humboldt had greeted him as an old acquaintance. He had visited Lamartine and Guizot, spent a happy evening with Sainte-Beuve, discussed philological questions with the blind Thierry, passed two days with Wordsworth, and met the youthful Ruskin, who had shown him the beautiful drawings he had made from nature. With his history constantly in mind, he had consulted countless men of letters and formed a lasting friendship with the model scholar, the Crown Prince John of Saxony, who was translating Dante into German. In Dresden, the prince had invited him to hear Tieck read aloud from his translation. The listeners followed, with the original text, and, at the end of every canto, gave their candid comments on the version. This incident was to have its consequences, for when, years later, in Cambridge, at Longfellow's instigation, the Dante Club was formed, the members, who were all

friends of Ticknor and had undoubtedly heard him tell
the story, followed the same procedure. Ticknor had
travelled through Europe with his own coach and foot-
man and four post-horses, very much *en prince;* and at
Rome, at the Princess Borghese's, he might have joined
six cardinals at whist, if a Boston man could have played
on a Sunday evening.

With many of these scholars and men of letters, he
kept up a regular correspondence. Milman, Hallam, Pasqual de Gayangos were always on the watch for information that might serve him in his great work. Everyone
knew that he was writing it, and he could taste his glory
in advance; for the universal success of Prescott's writings indicated what his own might be. But might it not
be with him as it was with Gibbon, after his task was accomplished,—would he not find the days long and empty
and life short and precarious? He had laboured on the
work for twenty years, removing all the traces of his lectures, growing more fastidious all the time, verifying his
facts again and again, weighing every authority, more
and more indifferent to publication. Great was his reward when it appeared, in three handsome volumes. It
was the literary event of 1849, the one book of the year
that Macaulay recommended to the Queen. There were
not six men living who were competent to review it, as
one of the possible five remarked, and Hallam, who was
another, said that it could never be superseded by any
writer who was not a Spaniard, or even by any Spaniard,
unless there was a radical change in Spain. Its erudition
was impeccable. It was firm and clear in composition.
Everything that knowledge and will could give the work
possessed in overflowing measure, and edition followed
edition, and translation translation, long beyond the day
of Ticknor's death; for it always lay open on his study-
table, ready for new revisions. He liked to remember
what was said of Plato, that, even when he had passed

the age of eighty, he combed and curled and braided the
locks of his writings. The limitations of the work were
the limitations of Ticknor himself, a lack of the spontaneity and imagination that Prescott had so amply. It
was cold and hard in tone and treatment, the fruit of a
carefully trained intelligence that never knew the madness of the poet.

Years later, Francis Parkman, the strenuous man of
genius, a half-blind semi-invalid like Prescott, but with
an explorer's or soldier's instincts, deplored the lifeless
scholarship of New England,—"void of blood, bone,
sinew, nerves and muscle." [3] It was not Prescott that he
had in mind; scarcely even Ticknor. He was referring to
Everett, whom he described as the most finished example
of this devitalized scholarship, "with many graceful addi-
tions." He might have chosen John Gorham Palfrey, that
other *North American* writer, the author of the *History
of New England,* which appeared a few years later
than Ticknor's work,—a man of multitudinous occupations, Everett's successor at the Brattle Square church,
Andrews Norton's successor at Harvard, editor of the
great review, postmaster of Boston, member of Congress,
a "Christian lawyer" in his theology, a theologian in his
literature. A Puritan of an earlier day, in type, without
the fire that burned in the ancient settlers, unimagina-
tive and unmagnetic, a kindly, modest, conscientious
man,—recalled by Henry Adams, in his *Education,* with
various pleasant phrases, as one of the members of his
father's circle,—he was an active Abolitionist. Along with
Dana and Sumner, he endured the sneers and snubs of
Ticknor and his State Street associates and friends. He

[3] According to Parkman, this was the result of an old New
England custom. In households of small means, the privilege of
going to college usually fell on the son whose feeble health unfitted
him for ruder labours. The "narrow-chested hectic Benjamin" was
chosen for the sedentary life, with sad results in the world of books
and thought.

was a thorough and trustworthy scholar, and he spent more than thirty years writing the well-known history, which long remained the authority in its field. It was a monumental work, in five large volumes. If it was almost wholly political, this was the author's intention; it was not too provincial in its point of view, and it was written in the firm historical style which all the Boston writers had developed in common. And yet the vitality of the work was low. Students were obliged to consult it, but few could have relished the adventure.

Boston, however, which had produced a Prescott, brought forth another writer in the eighteen-fifties whom readers were to enjoy for generations. John Lothrop Motley, the son of a merchant,—the author of some of the *Jack Downing* letters, those of the second series, —had much in common with his predecessor. Born in similar surroundings, a few years later, in one of those households where Scott was the staple of reading and Irving and Channing were read as American classics, Motley was a high-spirited boy of whom the last thing to be expected was the drudgery of a scholar's life. Tall and graceful, with hyacinthine hair,—so handsome that Lady Byron, when she saw him, said that Motley looked more like her husband than any other man she had seen,— impetuous, wilful, rather vain, decidedly supercilious, he had an air that suggested a thoroughbred horse when he flung back his head and a wild look flashed in his eye. He was plastic and fickle, or appeared to be so, too clever to be industrious, his friends supposed, and too fastidious for a dull routine. He had learned to read French easily at eleven, and had studied German with Bancroft at the Round Hill school; then, at thirteen, he had entered Harvard. Wendell Phillips and T. G. Appleton, better known in later years, had been his best friends as a boy. Every Saturday afternoon, in the garret of Motley's house, the three friends, dressed in cloaks and dou-

blets, had acted impromptu melodramas. Pretending that
they were bandits and heroes of Byron, they spouted
scraps of poetry to one another.

All these three boys played later parts that had associations with the Motleys' attic. There was a strain of the
actor in Wendell Phillips, T. G. Appleton was always
Byronic, and Motley's love of costume and dramatic effect,—he had made and played with miniature theatres
also,—appeared in his writings from first to last. Prescott, at the same age, dressed in a helmet and breast-
plate at the Athenæum, had shown the same romantic
tendency, common enough in boys but not so common
in historians. Motley had gone to Germany to study, like
Ticknor, Longfellow, Bancroft and so many others. At
Göttingen, where he made a translation of *Faust,* he
had lived in the closest intimacy with Bismarck, whose
"dear Jack" he remained for two generations, perhaps
the closest of all Bismarck's friends, the one to whom he
wrote with least constraint and whom he always welcomed with the warmest affection. They took their meals
and exercise together. Bismarck rejoiced when Motley
sat with his red slippers thrust out of the window; and
Motley, in *Morton's Hope,* his first novel, left a picture
of Bismarck,—peppered all over with freckles, scarred,
with an eyebrow shaved, in his chaotic coat, without collar or buttons, and with his iron heels and portentous
spurs,—that showed his early skill in descriptive writing.
Later, in Motley's diplomatic years, when Bismarck still
sang the American songs he had learned from his friend
at Göttingen, the two saw much of one another, and Bismarck recalled that Motley had "never entered a drawing-room without exciting the curiosity and sympathy of
the ladies." By the time he was twenty-seven, when he
went to St. Petersburg as an attaché, he had met Prince
John of Saxony, Ticknor's friend, the Goethe family at
Weimar, Tieck, who was translating Shakespeare, and

Guizot, who wrote an introduction to his *Dutch Republic,* in the French translation which he supervised. Years before, Cogswell had sent to Goethe's daughter-in-law an essay that Motley had written on Goethe while he was still in college. She had replied, "I wish to see the first book that young man will write." On Motley's second visit to Weimar, Ottilie von Goethe had heard of his novel, but he refused to tell her the name of the book.

No one else expected much of Motley. He had studied law, which he never practised; he had interested himself in politics and even served a term in the Legislature. But this had led to nothing, and *Morton's Hope,* the novel he had published, showed little promise. It was a childish fantasy, carelessly written, with no regard for probabilities. The scene was laid half in Boston, before the Revolution, and half in the Göttingen of Motley's time, between which the hero spent his youth. The pictures of German student-life had a certain air of reality,—the aesthetic tea-party, for one. They were merry enough in tone, with happy strokes here and there; but the author did not seem to be in earnest. In the garden of Morton's Hope, a Brookline house, built by an old China merchant, the lizards "shot to and fro in the patches of sunlight." Young Morton, however, was Motley himself. He, too, burned with dreams of glory. His inflammable nature was filled with a boundless ambition. If he had not breakfasted with a pen behind his ear, or dined with a folio as big as the table, he had longed to write history, also like Morton. He, too, had devoured the English poets, from Chaucer and Gower downward, immersed himself in Latin chronicles, read every historical work that he could find, in German, French and Spanish, and all the books to which the notes referred; and, whatever the book was, on whatever subject, he had planned to write a better one himself.

Motley's second novel, *Merry Mount,* was a very different affair, although no one seemed to know it, then or later. It was a charming picture of early New England, in its more Arcadian aspects, a fantasy of the greenwood, the story of Morton's crew at Wollaston. Hawthorne had sketched the theme in his *Twice-Told Tales,* which Motley had refrained from reading, in order not to confuse his own impressions; and *Merry Mount,* in some of its scenes, might have been written by Hawthorne. It pictured the dim, unsettled time, at the dawn of Massachusetts history, when various men who seemed like apparitions, as they flitted through the early chronicles, played parts that later historians had forgotten. Who were those pale and misty figures, Blaxton, the first settler on the site of Boston, Morton and his comrades of the may-pole, wanderers from Elizabethan England whom the colony harboured in its sylvan depths? The forest scenes, the hawking scenes, the scenes in the woodland fortress, the portrait of the hermit of Beacon Hill, of Miles Standish and the giant blacksmith, of the mysterious knight, Sir Christopher Gardiner, were Motley's reply to the question. There was an element of historic fact behind every detail of the vivid picture, and it was all suffused with a glow and feeling that brought back the Shakespeare of *As You Like It.*

Meanwhile, in the middle eighteen-forties, Motley wrote a number of essays for the *North American Review.* One of these papers, on Balzac, who had begun to be widely read,—Hawthorne, for instance, had read him,—made a great stir. It was a lively defense of the artist as man of letters, the sort of defense that Poe was making and that Hawthorne might have made, but that, in fact, had not been made by any other writer in New England. Motley envied the French their freedom of speech, praising Balzac for his disregard of ordinary notions of the "nasty" in his passion for detached observation. In this he agreed with Fanny Kemble, who constantly protested, when she lived in Lenox, against the silly prudery of American women, which took the life out of novel-writing. This prudery, a recent thing, at least in circles that knew the world,—for the Boston folk of old, like other Americans of an earlier day, rejoiced in Fielding and Smollett, who spoke their own language, —was to spread like a film for generations over the work of the novelists, to break in the end with a vengeance that might have been foreseen. Motley had registered his protest, and he had carried it further. He praised the detachment of Balzac as the proper attitude of the artist in letters, and he uttered a phrase that resounded through New England, "Certainly the world should be reformed, but not by novel-writing." Few readers thought of novelists as artists, in spite of Hawthorne's presence and example; and Motley, following Prescott, was soon to show that history also was a form of art. For Motley, whose early motives had been confused, had embarked on historical writing. His essay on Peter the Great, perhaps suggested by his year in Russia, first revealed his gifts in this direction.

The essay appeared in 1845, when the rage for Carlyle was at its height, and Peter the Great was a typical Carlyle hero. This "strong, silent man," who had carved a nation out of a Scythian wilderness, who had tried to Europeanize Russia and turn it into a modern civilization, who "preferred to go to the ocean rather than wait for the ocean to come to him" and who raised his capital in the northern marshes, was another Oliver Cromwell, in his way. Better still, he was an empire-builder, one of the men who "do" things and who were doing them for the Anglo-Saxons in all the four quarters of the globe. He was even, one might have thought, a Russian Yankee, an Abbott Lawrence on a larger scale, this prince who worked as a carpenter, in his apron, in a shipbuilder's yard at Amsterdam, learned his trade from the bottom and laid down and built, from his own draught and model, a sixty-gun ship. Peter was a Portland or Salem hero, the kind they understood in the Yankee seaports, the self-made man *nulli secundus,* the sort that makes things hum, who had made Russia hum like another New Hampshire, multiplied by two or three dozen Maines. Motley, like Carlyle, admired the type, much as he disliked its brutal aspects, those that Carlyle came to admire the most. It represented what the age called Progress. Motley did not labour the point. Perhaps he was scarcely aware of it. But, shorn of its barbarian elements, this was the type that had built his own republic.

What was the history of this type? Where had it first emerged? How had it emerged from the mediæval world that held it back? At what point in the history of Europe had the enterprising man declared himself, demanded the free institutions that gave him scope, cast off the burden of privilege? Where had the merchant, the burgher, the craftsman, the sailor, the builder of civilization in its modern form, the man who believed in freedom of thought and action, first come to grips with the old regime? In Holland, where Peter the Great had learned his trade and the Pilgrim Fathers from England had found a refuge before they sailed for America. Just why Motley chose the history of Holland none of his friends knew. When his essay on Peter the Great appeared, they felt that history was his real vocation, and one of them found him at work, soon afterward, with a huge Dutch folio and a dictionary. He had turned to another use than novel-writing his art of painting scenes and characters, though few could have seen the connection between the history of Holland and the history of the American republic. But for Motley, the United Provinces, in their struggle to liberate themselves from Spain, suggested the struggle of the United States. William the Silent, for him, was a prototype of Washington, and behind this political aspect there was another. In celebrating the rise of the Dutch Republic, Motley was celebrating the modern man, the American type in its first historic appearance.

This was the larger meaning of Motley's work, the motive, scarcely expressed, that gave him his vast popularity. It might have been called the tendency of all his writing. American readers felt that he was defending their kind of man, almost as much as Bancroft. For the rest, they were interested in Holland. It was a camp of the Pilgrims, it was the battle-ground of Protestantism, it was the home of many of their forbears; and Holland had been the laughing-stock of Europe long before America became so. Motley had not chosen the theme, which had become his life-study. He felt that the theme had chosen him, before he knew that Prescott was planning to cover almost the same ground. Prescott, to whom he described his design, treated him as kindly as Washington Irving had treated himself in a similar situation; he welcomed Motley's rivalry and even thought of giving him the manuscripts he had gathered for himself. Motley had hoped to write his book at home. In fact, he had begun it at Nahant, in an old house in the village street, overhung by two great willows, where Longfellow later spent a summer. Prescott's presence gave Nahant an atmosphere for historical writing. Motley did not know, when he undertook *The Rise of the Dutch Republic*, what hours of dusty labour lay before him.

It was ten years before the book appeared, years that were largely spent in Dresden, Berlin, the Hague and Brussels, where Motley worked obscurely in the archives, turning up almost as many unpublished papers as Prescott had read for his Spanish histories. These were the original documents, in all their native crabbedness, not neatly copied as Prescott's were. Thousands of them had never been read by any Dutch historian, and sometimes they were indecipherable.[4] Motley felt, at times, as he toiled in the subterranean depths of black-letter folios in Latin and German, as if he were working in a coal-pit, grimy, dark and cheerless. His life reminded him of a Dutch canal, slow, silent, stagnant. But the novelist in him never slumbered. At night, as he walked the streets of Leyden and Brussels, he lived over the scenes of the day's reading and seemed to see Egmont and Horn, Granvelle, the Duke of Alva and William of Orange in the ghosts that flitted over the moonlit squares. In one of his letters, writing of Rubens, who did not appear in the *Dutch Republic,*—one of the weaknesses of the book, in fact, was that it omitted all mention of the flowering of Dutch and Flemish art,—he showed his delight in the glowing colour that appeared in his own writing. His friendship with Bismarck, meanwhile, whose career he watched with a natural interest and rather more benevolence than the case required, sharpened his understanding of the European statecraft that formed the principal theme of all his volumes.

In later life, as minister to Austria and England, Motley was immersed in politics. *The History of the United Netherlands* and *The Life and Death of John of Barneveld,* in which he continued his unfinished series,—for he planned to tell the story of the Thirty Years' War,— were all too much concerned with statesmanship. At least, they were little concerned with anything else. They were largely compilations of documents, like Bancroft's later volumes. Where was Dutch life, one might have asked, the life of the people, their art, their thought, their customs, in the history of the United Netherlands? Even in *The Rise of the Dutch Republic,* one found too little of the common scene, in its multifarious aspects, for

[4] Motley's work was instrumental in stirring the Dutch historians to publish these original documents.

which the battles were fought and the statesmen existed. Only the great individual interested Motley, and, generally speaking, only the man of action, although the escape of Grotius, in *Barneveld,* was one of his liveliest episodes; and his psychology was so simplified that his great men were supermen or devils. His William of Orange was a boy's hero, his Philip was a nightmare. The characters he understood the best were those whom he might have met in Boston; for the lawyers, manufacturers and bankers who founded the Dutch Republic were such as he had known in his father's circle. John of Barneveld would have felt at home with Amos and Abbott Lawrence, Webster and Choate. These were types that Motley knew, and his imagination scarcely moved outside their burgher atmosphere. His sympathies were all with oligarchies, such as the Essex Junto had represented,—the leaders of a legal and commercial world. He had little feeling for the people, and less for saints, poets, artists and thinkers. But Motley was a preëminent story-teller. For sheer narrative power, the dense, moving mass of the *Dutch Republic* stood with the greatest of its kind; and some of Motley's scenes and incidents,—the executions of Egmont and Horn, the defeat of the Spanish Armada,—were destined to live with the best of Prescott and Parkman.

CHAPTER XVIII

DR. HOLMES

MEANWHILE, the son of another historian, Dr. Abiel Holmes, had made his appearance as a poet. As far back as 1830, Oliver Wendell Holmes, a young student of the Harvard Law School, who was soon to abandon law for medicine, had written a poem called *Old Ironsides*. He had composed it with a pencil, standing on one foot in the attic of his old house in Cambridge. The battle of Bunker Hill had been planned in this house, and one saw the dents of the muskets on the floor. The frigate "Constitution," in the Boston navy-yard, was about to be dismantled and abandoned. The poem, reprinted on handbills from a newspaper in Boston and scattered about the streets of Washington, saved the ship and made the poet famous.

He had "sneaked in," as he later said, in the same year with Tennyson and Darwin, the man of science and the man of rhymes whose natures he was to share in equal parts. His father, a moderate Calvinist, had still defended the faith of Jonathan Edwards, who said that little boys were more hateful than vipers. Against this faith the son was to fight with the diligent wit of a doctor who knew that such ideas were very harmful. But the father, kinder than his creed, a lover of books and the art of living, was also a poet in his fashion. One evening, when the children were in the parlour, he had stepped to the frost-covered window and sketched on the pane with his knife-blade a cluster of branches and stars. Above, he had written, *Per aspera ad astra*. The family had come from Connecticut, but they had Boston connections, and among their portraits was one of Dorothy Quincy, about whom Holmes was to write a poem. Another of his forbears was Anne Bradstreet, the old New England poetess whose blood ran in the veins of so many writers. Wendell Phillips was one of his cousins. Others were the Channings and the Danas.

To the end of his life, the rhythms of Moore and of Pope, softened and sweetened in Goldsmith, were to ring through Holmes's poems, together with those of Byron, Hood and Campbell. These were the favourite poets of the Cambridge household. He had gone to the little school in Cambridgeport, where his younger cousin, Richard Henry Dana, had had so much trouble with the master. One of his fellow-pupils was Margaret Fuller, who was always reading "naw-vells," as she called them, and whose long and flexible neck looked like a swan's, —that is to say, if one liked her, for it looked like a snake if one didn't. But he had learned something from Margaret Fuller. He happened to see one of her themes, which began with the phrase, "It is a trite remark." Having learned that trite remarks existed,—for the word was entirely new to him,—he was better prepared never to make one. He found it easy to elope from school to see Revenge and Prospect on the race-course; for, although he loved learning as he loved his country, he also loved horses, observing that, wherever a trotter went, he carried in his train brisk omnibuses, lively bakers' carts, and therefore hot rolls, the jolly butcher's wagon and the cheerful gig. Every New England deacon, Holmes reflected,—the more he had occasion to study the species, —ought to see at least one Derby day to learn what sort of a world it was he lived in.

After he had won his degree at Harvard, in the class of 1829, and having dropped the law for medicine, he found his father eager to send him abroad,—equipped with a good Dutch liquor-case, filled with six kinds of strong waters,—to study for a year in Edinburgh, the favourite training-school for American doctors, and two years in Paris. The class of 1829 included the author of "My Country, 'Tis of Thee." Holmes had his own ideas about this poem,[1] but he thought the class worthy of endless odes, to warm and hearten its members,—other people were not obliged to read them,—odes and odes, stretching from decade to decade, till the poet himself had reached three score and twenty and the first line had to begin, " 'Tis sixty years since." As for the years in Paris, aside from all they meant for a medical student, they sharpened the wit of this ingenious Yankee, confirming the natural bent of his mind as the softly romantic sentiment of the Rhineland confirmed Longfellow's natural bent. For the rest, the evenings at the Trois Frères, when the Chambertin or the Clos Vougeot came in and the Scotch-plaided snuff-box went round the table, had their effect on a mind that loved gracious living and was to claim the rights of gracious living on behalf of his somewhat frost-bound countrymen.

Certainly, a good slice of Paris sandwiched between two slices of New England created a sense of contrast that enlivened his critical spirit. With other scenes in mind, the returning pilgrim observed the well-known vista in the high relief that is always the fruit of comparison. He observed its lovelier aspects and other aspects that were not so lovely,—for instance, the acidulous Yankee voice, acidulous and stridulous, bred by commercial habits, east winds, a lean soil and too much enterprise. The young medical student never forgot the soft and liq-

---

[1] "Sam Smith will live when Longfellow, Whittier and all the rest of us have gone into oblivion. And yet what is there in those verses to make them live? Do you remember the line 'Like *that* above'? I asked Sam what 'that' referred to. He said 'that rapture'!" And Holmes made one of his wry little faces.—See M. A. DeW. Howe, *Memories of a Hostess.*

uid inflections he had heard in France, so winning, so delicious, with so much woman in them. The voices of the brave Yankee girls,—too often at least, he thought,— would not be among the allurements the Enemy would put in requisition were he planning another assault on Saint Anthony's virtue. But most of his impressions were happy enough. He had said to himself, with joyous confidence, in Florence and Pisa, as in the streets of Paris, "I am a Cambridge boy!"; and he was to remain a Cambridge poet. His lays were

> of one whose natal star
> Still seemed the brightest when it shone afar.

They dealt with the homeliest facts of the Yankee world, washing-day, the spinning-top, the katydid, the gale, the dinner-bell, the oysterman, the churchyard, the family portrait, the unmarried aunt, scenes and subjects touched by a fresh and original mind, however composed in forms that English and Scottish poets had made familiar. Well he knew how to dress the fable

> in which genius poured
> And warmed the shapes that later times adored.

However this genius seemed in times still later, it was a revelation in a day when foreign writers ruled the imagination. It evoked, for the Yankee ear and eye, the train of associations that made it classic.

The medical student soon became a doctor, established in a modest street in Boston. He also became a professor at the Harvard Medical School; and, as if to enlarge his field for the study of human nature, he gave Lyceum lectures in the country towns on some of the English poets, among them Wordsworth, Keats, Shelley, Moore. For his animal spirits superabounded,—his curiosity likewise. He kept a rattlesnake in a cage to study its manners and habits. He kept a little gold in his house, to handle now and then, in order to analyze a miser's feelings. He was known to have inhaled a dose of ether, to record his sensations and thoughts. In Springfield and Pittsfield, where he spent his summers, they liked to see the lions and hear them roar; and the doctor, who belonged to the lion family, as one of its younger members, was willing to be seen on all occasions. He was a poet laureate by avocation, always prepared to present his bouquet at a banquet or an ode at a county fair. He knew the vexations of lecturing all too well, the cold parlours, the cold apples and water, the cold beds in the cold hotel bedrooms, the cold congratulations of the committees, to whom his remarks had given "satisfaction." He was placarded and announced as a public performer and saw his name stuck up in letters so large that he scarcely dared to appear in the town by daylight. Well he knew the dangers of lecturing, too,—for he was aware of everything: one would have had to get up very early to take the doctor in,—the danger of talking down to muddier wits, the danger of shaping one's thoughts in a popular mould. How often the lecture-platform was a slippery slide down to the Avernus of the windy bores. But, if you knew yourself as your maker knew you, knew even that you had your vanities, and if you knew where to draw the line and picked out the most intelligent faces, and talked only to them, lecturing had its rewards for a student of human nature. One learned, for instance, the law of averages. Two Lyceum assemblies of five hundred each were much the same in Springfield as in Boston, and perhaps the doctor would have added Paris. And one learned to know the tribe of the Pooh-Poohs, so called from their leading expression. No doubt this tribe served a useful purpose in keeping down the noxious animals, the thinking, or rather talking and writing ones. Beyond this, they were of small value; and they were always retreating before the advance of knowledge, facing it and moving backwards, with their inextinguishable war-cry, Pooh-Pooh!

A good corrective, lecturing, for a mind a little too ready to think a little too much of its own time and place. Nor was this the only egg that was dropped into the doctor's intellect by the solemn fowl Experience, fed by so many crumbs from the lecture-platform, a fowl which, amid its idle cacklings, sometimes cackled in earnest. One of the doctor's whims was to think of all New England, and even all America, as a large and friendly boarding-house, a house with an ample breakfast-table, at which, for a number of years, he found himself appointed to preside. The role of an autocrat had been thrust upon him, for had not fate endowed him with a luminous mind, the same fate that had endowed New England with a hunger and thirst for knowledge? Well, what an opportunity these lectures gave him to study his fellow-boarders, the schoolmistress, just below the platform, whom he always found so sympathetic, the divinity student, whom he could tease a little about the One-Hoss Shay of Calvinism,—which had long since dropped to pieces, "all at once, and nothing first," in Boston, but was still a handsome carriage in these country districts, —the old gentleman opposite, who brought him down with a joke or a volley of facts if he became a little highfalutin, the landlady's daughter, lockets and ringlets and all, and Benjamin Franklin in the back row. This Benjamin Franklin, Junior, was the symbol of the rising generation, still up and coming, unversed in the *suaviter in modo* but bent on acquiring his French and science and prepared for the words of Erasmus on religion and morals. Was not the doctor himself an Erasmus or Franklin, who was planning a new *Poor Richard's Almanac* for more advanced students? There they all were, all the boarders, even the lady in black bombazine with the soul-subduing decorum, and the sad-eyed gentleman in the

Spanish cloak, he of the fluted cheeks, worn by the passions of the melodrama, the symbol of the poor old Yankee theatre. What an opportunity for the doctor to take them into his confidence and plant in their minds a few well-chosen seeds,—seeds of moral etiquette, for instance, and even etiquette without the morals, Erasmian seeds, Confucian seeds, seeds of a worldly wisdom that was based on all the Commandments, and even some that Moses knew not of. When a doctor, thanks to his Creator, possesses such a store of sense and wit, and tempers it to the lambs that know not Boston, when he has learned how to approach his patients so that they swallow his pills with high good humour, when they feel better for his doses, why should not a spade be called a spade? Why should he not be called an Autocrat?

The doctor did not possess the gift of silence, and, possessing the gift of wit, he meant to use it. What would be the state of the highways of life, he said on one occasion, if we did not drive our thought-sprinklers through them, with the valves open? He enjoyed his journeys through the rural districts, where, pursuing his mission, spreading the light of the metropolis, he learned so much about his countrymen. Whether in man or tree, as he soon discovered, the provinces did not know a first-rate thing, even when they possessed it, and constantly took the second- and third-rate for nature's very best, for they had no standards of comparison; and, filled with the love of excellence as he was, he was always looking for it, and always making notes of it "when found." He carried in his pocket a measuring-tape, as Emerson carried a compass. This tape, thirty feet long, was long enough to encircle the largest brain, even Daniel Webster's; but the doctor commonly used it to measure trees. In his younger days, when he was much devoted to the young-lady population of Rhode Island, he had measured the great Johnston elm on the Providence Plantations, and with time he had formed the acquaintance of every considerable tree in New England. He knew the grand willows down in Maine, and the grand elms up the other way, the West Springfield elm, the noble Hatfield elm, the Sheffield elm, the great tree on the Colman farm at Deerfield that was living on its past reputation, the poor old Pittsfield elm, the horse-chestnut tree near the Rockport station, as well as all the elms on the Boston Common. Some of these great trees looked very meek when they saw the fatal measure begin to unreel,—like one of those politicians in the country towns who had puffed themselves up to look like Webster. They had never been measured before by a metropolitan eye when the little doctor approached them. The American elm, he observed, was tall and slender, and drooped as if from languor, while the English elm was more robust, and held its branches up, and carried its leaves longer than the native tree. Was this symbolic of the creative force on the two sides of the ocean? Did it indicate that Dr. Knox was right in thinking that Anglo-Saxons could not survive, outside the mother-country, that they were destined to die out unless they were kept up by fresh supplies? The doctor did not wish to decide a point that filled him with misgivings, although he argued stoutly the other way.

As for the "great tree" on the Boston Common, it belonged in the second rank, like the tree at Cohasset. The doctor admitted this without hesitation, for where Boston was concerned he was always candid. He had, of course, a modest pride in Boston, and, when some impertinent New Yorker asked one of his friends how he could endure the fulsome things that were constantly said of the town, he was rather inclined to agree with his friend's reply, "Because we feel that they are *true*." Boston was the hub of the solar system: you could not pry this out of a Boston man if you had the tire of all creation straightened out for a crowbar. But how did the New

Yorkers feel about New York? Did not the axis of the
earth stick visibly out through the centre of every city?
Did not the smallest village of Massachusetts read, to its
own advantage, Pope's well-known line, "All are but
parts of one stupendous HULL"? In his weaker moments, the doctor admitted that Boston men ran a certain danger of taking their local scale for the absolute
scale, an error that was natural enough, since Boston was
so bright and wide-awake. But when he was his own
cheerful self, he forgot these doubts and compunctions.
Why not regard the Common as the unit of space, and
the State House as the standard of architecture? Boston,
of course, was just like other towns, except for its excellent fish-market; but one had to remember its fire-
department, its admirable monthly publications, which
everyone acknowledged, together with its use of the English language, which everyone ought to acknowledge.
What was the real offence of Boston? One had to say this
without fear or favour. It drained a water-shed of intellect with which no other could be compared, and it
would not let itself be drained in turn.

This was the open secret that gave the doctor's face its
honest glow. This, and another secret, if it was one: the
doctor loved his Boston with an affection that deepened
as the wonder of it grew. Had he not, in his daily travels,
bored this ancient city through and through? He knew
it as an old inhabitant of a Cheshire knows his cheese;
and when, with his mounting fortunes, a few years later,
he moved into Beacon Street,—the last of his "justifiable
domicides,"—whence he could see Bunker Hill, from his
window facing the bay, and Cambridge across the water,
his cup ran over. There he could indulge his whims at
last. At the Medical School, he continued to give his lectures, darting about the laboratory as nimbly as a cat,
while his pupils laughed and cried as he told his stories,
as often pathetic as witty, running out of the room when

a rabbit had to be chloroformed, beseeching his assistant not to let it squeak. He was always tinkering at something, developing photographs or "mending things," breaking a chair or table to put it together better. He invented the best of stethoscopes and wrote a medical classic on puerperal fever, an essay that saved as many lives as Bowditch's *Practical Navigator*. He shut himself up with his violin and fiddled away industriously until he could play "Auld Lang Syne" so that anyone could recognize the tune. He never missed a horse-race and knew all the points of the favourites and winners,[2] as he knew the virtues of a sportsman,—to pay up, own up and shut up, that is, if you were beaten. He liked to go to the circus and the sideshows and chat with the freaks and the giants and measure their chests with his tape; for, being small himself, he had a relish for size, whether in trees or men. He knew the deeds of the prize-ring. Charles Freeman, who fought the "Tipton Slasher,"—a very superior type of American giant,—granted him confidential interviews; and the double-headed daughter of Africa allowed him to question her on the delicate subject of avoirdupois equivalents. Prudence and propriety and all the other pious P's had very little interest for the doctor; and, as only a good anatomist can, he loved to see a man prepare for boxing. Where could one find a handsomer spectacle than a fine Boston citizen resolving himself into the primitive elements of his humanity? If only the manly art of self-defense had been introduced among the reverend clergy, humankind would have had better sermons.

For the doctor never forgot that he was a doctor, even when he felt most the poet. And he never forgot that he was a poet. Sometimes, in the early morning, before the

[2] Emerson, who admired skill, whether in men or horses, as much as Holmes, once corrected the doctor in a matter of horse-racing. It was a quarter of a second difference in the record of the race-horse Flora Temple at Kalamazoo, 1859. The time was 2.19¾.

sun was up, he put out from shore in his little skiff, his "water-sulky," as he liked to call it, and glided round the bay, up the Charles to Watertown or about the wharves, under the stern of some tall Indiaman, rubbing against the hulls of the old wood-schooners, propelling himself swiftly over the water or drifting with the tide. Only in his poems could he tell the delights of those sweet June mornings, when the bay was as smooth as a sheet of beryl-green silk, as he lay in his shell motionless over the flats, as he watched the crabs crawling in the shallows, the sculpins wavering silently under the boat, as he rustled through the long, harsh grass that led the way up some tranquil creek and paused there, moored unseen, in a loneliness so profound that the columns of Tadmor in the desert could not have seemed more remote from life. A city of idiots Boston seemed to him then, not to have covered this glorious bay with gondolas and wherries,— this bay where a poet might almost find a chambered nautilus, or at any rate might be reminded of one, brought back perhaps in that tall Indiaman, to write a poem about, one poem, at least, to make his name immortal.

For the doctor was a poet, for all he could "write so funny," a solid poet whose fruit was never green. He had observed that American poets did not commonly ripen well. They lacked severe standards; they had no sound thermometers for gauging their talents; and surely, the doctor thought, the United States furnished the greatest market in the world for the green fruit of the intellect. There were certain things, he felt, that were good for nothing until they had been kept a long while, and some that were good for nothing until they had been long kept and *used:* wine, meerschaum pipes and violins. A poem was like a violin, the parts of which were strangers to one another till they had learned to vibrate in harmony. A poem was as porous as a meerschaum,—in order to be

good, it had to absorb the essence of one's own humanity. One had to keep one's poem until its sentiment har-
monized with all the aspects of one's life and nature,
until one had contrived to stain oneself through all its
thoughts and images. That was what made poems, real
poems, so much like buckwheat cakes, as the young fellow said at the breakfast-table, buckwheat being decidedly scarce and high.

So it was with the doctor's poems. Whatever else they
were, they were always ripe. If they were largely occasional, and largely local, what else could be expected of
a harper who could never refuse the appeal "by request
of friends"? He knew his audience,—

> All the gay and young
> Love the light antics of a playful tongue,—

and he cheerfully plied the strings on all occasions, Commencement feasts, meetings of fellow-doctors, birthdays
of eminent citizens. Would he just this once comply? Be
the truth at once confessed; he wavered, yielded, did his
best. And why not, when, from his nimble tongue, as
from no other American tongue or pen, tripped the
phrase, the epithet, on each occasion, that fired in every
mind the appropriate train? These rhymes of an hour
were fresh, adroit, correct. The doctor never said, in
flowery language, that life was full of trials. He never
said that youth was like the dewdrop. Moreover, he often
glowed with intenser feeling. Well he recalled the moments when a "lyric conception" had struck him like a
bullet in the forehead, when the blood dropped from his
cheek and he felt himself turning as white as death.
Once or twice only he had had this feeling,—as when he
wrote *The Chambered Nautilus,*—a creeping as of centi-
pedes running down the spine, a gasp, a jump of the
heart, then a sudden flush, a beating in the vessels of the
head, then a long sigh—and the poem was written. For

the rest, his happiest vein was that which most resembled his conversation, when he felt like a jockey on the race-course, a good Yankee jockey, rejoicing in his own ver-nacular, and confident, old as his horse might be, that he would win the bet.

In this vein, he always won the bet. Had he not, in his *Rhymed Lesson*, that *Essay on Man*, or rather essay on manners, rewritten for another time and country, re-vealed himself as a Yankee Pope, even as he revealed his limitations? Prickly pears are also edible, along with the other varieties, and most of the doctor's prickles were salutary. There were more things, it was true, even in Boston than the doctor's philosophy dreamed of, more in the "bores" and "earnest sages," whom Pope would have disliked as much as he, more in Bronson Alcott,—

> groping vague and dim,
> Whose every angle was a half-starved whim,—

more in Emerson, too, something he never gathered even when he knew the "wingéd Franklin," whom he loved and wished to comprehend and even "explained," years later, in a patient study as good as a clever intellect could make it. Far less could he understand those uncouth he-roes,—

> such as Homer's, who, we read in Pope,
> Dined without forks and never heard of soap . . .
> Such as May to Marlborough Chapel brings,
> Lean, hungry, savage anti-everythings,
> Copies of Luther in the pasteboard style.

The reformers were not for him, any more than the "genuine article," Luther himself, or Luther's disciples, rather, were for his dear Erasmus. But has not history, which Erasmus fills, a case to make also for the doctor, whose "Reformation," though of a mundane kind, also brought its blessings? Was he not also a reformer who, with his ass's jawbone, slew in a thousand households the pestilent lion that masked itself in a Geneva gown? He was a reformer in medical matters, bent upon destroying, root and branch, the nostrums and the notions of human nature that a narrow past had bred in the Yankee mind; and he was even a reformer of the art of living,—was not the lack of any real sense of this the original cause of the nostrums and notions in question? How many lines of reform can a man pursue without losing that fulcrum in common sense which gives his lever purchase? Great is the office of wit, ye deluded reformers, whose reforms are all in the air because your feet have no firm ground to stand on! Great is the office of wit, O optimists, who take so much for granted!—ye who will never know

> Some doubts must darken o'er the world below
> Though all the Platos of the nursery trail
> Their 'clouds of glory' at the go-cart's tail!

Because your forbears saw only the evil, can you see only the good? You must see the black squares on the checkerboard, as well as the white squares, if you wish to play the game to any purpose. And you must learn to write, like men of this world, if you are going to change the world by writing, you Transcendental authors who foist upon your readers

> Mesmeric pamphlets, which to facts appeal,
> Each fact as slippery as a fresh-caught eel . . .
> Poems that shuffle with superfluous legs
> A blindfold minuet over addled eggs . . .
> Essays so dark Champollion might despair
> To guess what mummy of a thought was there,
> Where our poor English, striped with foreign phrase,
> Looks like a zebra in a parson's chaise.

What if, afflicted by these effusions, a wit should

> spread them to the smiling day
> And toss them, fluttering like the new-mown hay,
> To laughter's light, or sorrow's pitying shower?—

would it not be, for you and your readers' good, to send you back to school where *you* might learn how to win the bet?

No doubt, the doctor had his incomprehensions, along with his little vanities. It was his passion to define himself, and those who define themselves too readily are men whose imagination has its limits. He disliked some of the friends of progress because of their muddy brains, or because of their Sunday frowns. Some of them he thought were moral bullies. He also disliked them for their dingy linen, a pardonable distaste, and yet it encroached a little on the comic spirit, or, shall one say, the tragic spirit, of which the imagination is all compact, and which, in minds of a larger calibre, resolves these lesser discords. But the doctor seldom lost his sense of proportion. He never professed to see with the eye of God, and he was well aware of his limitations. The essence of wit, he said, consists of a partial view of whatever it touches. It throws a single ray, separate from the rest,—yellow, red or blue,—upon an object, never the white light: that is the province of wisdom.

There were men wiser than he, and well he knew it; but in all America there was none more witty. No one else could have written *The One-Hoss Shay, The Morning Visit, The Moral Bully,* or *How the Old Horse Won the Bet.* That was the region where the doctor's rhymes were safe from all rivals and invaders, where the rhymes added a relish to the doctor's talk. For talk was his native element and his mission. Who knew, as he,—

> the little arts that please,
> Bright looks, the cheerful language of the eye,
> The neat, crisp question and the gay reply?

Who had such a festive air of finding life interesting and full? Who liked people to speak their minds so fully?

Who opened a conversation with such a look of expecting something good from his next-seat neighbour? He rejoiced in every kind of conversation, the kind that floated safely over the shallows, the kind that floated over a few fathoms, the philosophical parley, better still, that called for a deep-sea line to reach the bottom, and best of all the contact of two minds when they were off soundings in the ocean of thought. The doctor was never a monopolist. Well, hardly ever. It was his rule to talk only of subjects he had long had in his mind, and to listen to what others said of subjects that he had only recently studied, for knowledge, like timber, he felt, should not be used until it was properly seasoned. Who could have censured him if, in later life, he talked about all subjects, and most of the time, considering that he had had them all in mind longer than anyone else? He never made puns, unless the occasion enjoined some very rare pun in Old Italian, the well-known tongue invented by Andrews and Stoddard. He considered conversation one of the arts, from which one ought to refrain—inasmuch as listening also was an art—unless one could match one's glass of wine with an equal glow of light and warmth and colour. He was a master of the art himself. At moments, when conditions favoured him, when the candles shone in the deep mahogany, his spirits rose like mercury under the summer sun and flashed like the Shah's regalia. His talk was the eighth wonder of the Boston world. In later years, on one of these occasions, Henry James the elder said to him, "Holmes, you are intellectually the most alive man I ever knew." And the little doctor replied, and he almost danced as he spoke, "I am, I am! From the crown of my head to the sole of my foot, I'm alive, I'm alive!"

CHAPTER XIX

THOREAU AT WALDEN

HENRY THOREAU had built a hut at Walden. In March, 1845, he had borrowed Alcott's axe,—which he took pains to return with a sharper edge,—and cut down some tall, arrowy pines for the timbers, studs and rafters. For the boards he bought a shanty from one of the Irish labourers on the railroad. The hut was ten feet by fifteen, shingled and plastered, with a garret and closet, a trap-door below, a brick fireplace, windows at the sides and a door facing the cove. The cost, all told, was $28.12½,—less than the annual rent of a student's room in Cambridge. There was a bean-field, close by, with a patch of potatoes, corn, peas and turnips. As a quasi-Pythagorean, Thoreau seldom indulged in beans. He exchanged his crop for rice in the village. Rice was the proper diet for one who loved so well the writings of the Oriental sages.

He had long cherished the notion of a forest-life. Ellery Channing had built himself a hut on the prairie in Illinois, and Henry's college class-mate, Stearns Wheeler, who had just died in Leipzig, had also built a rough woodland cabin, over at Flint's Pond, where he had lived for a year to save money, to buy Greek books and pay his way to Germany to study. Henry had spent six weeks in Wheeler's cabin, sharing one of his bunks of straw. There was nothing new in his own adventure, and he could not understand why his friends thought it was so peculiar. Some of them spoke as if he had gone to the woods in order to starve or freeze. Emerson had bought

land on both sides of the pond, intending to build a summer-house, and Henry had carried out the project. Alcott,
who liked to tinker at rustic architecture, helped him
with his saw and hammer, along with the young Brook
Farmer, George William Curtis of New York, who was
boarding at Edmund Hosmer's in the village and working as a farm-hand. Henry felt at home in his sylvan
dwelling. It made him think of some of those mountain-
houses he had seen on his inland excursions, high-placed,
airy, fragrant, with a fresh, auroral atmosphere about
them. It was quiet, clean and cool, fit to entertain a travelling god. For company, birds flitted through his chamber, red squirrels raced over the roof, chickadees perched
on the armfuls of wood he carried. There were moles
living in the cellar. He had occasional visits from a hare.
As he sat at his door in the evening, he remembered that
he was descended from the Greeks of old. He was a wanderer, too, one of the crew of Ulysses. The shore of the
cove was another Ithaca.

There was nothing about his "experiment," as his
friends liked to call it, to arouse such curiosity and contempt. It was a common-sensible undertaking, and only
a slight departure from Henry's usual mode of living.
His average weekly outlay, for necessaries he could not
supply himself, was twenty-seven cents. A few days at
manual labour, building a boat or a fence, planting,
grafting or surveying,—six weeks of work out of the year,
when he had grown extravagant and had to have a mi-
croscope,—gave him an ample surplus. Why should anyone live by the sweat of his brow and bore his fellowmen
by talking about it? Why should not everyone live with
an ample margin?—as anyone could do, provided he followed the path of simplification, logically and ruthlessly
enough. The mass of men led lives of quiet desperation.
Why, if not to maintain a "standard of living" that every
law of the universe controverted? Did they not know that

the wisest had always lived, with respect to comforts and luxuries, a life more simple and meagre than the poor? Had all the philosophers, Hindu, Greek and Persian, lived and taught in vain? Had anyone measured man's capacities? Was it fair to judge by precedents, when so very little had been attempted? Who could say that if a man advanced, boldly, in the direction of his dreams, endeavouring to live the life he had imagined, he would not meet with a success that he had never expected in common hours? Henry believed, and wished to prove, that the more one simplified one's life the less complex the laws of life would seem. Why all this pother about possessions? He liked to think of the ancient Mexicans, who burned all their goods every fifty years. Hawthorne, in one of his stories, had pictured a similar holocaust; and this was the kind of reform that Henry thought was worth considering. He meant to have his furniture, actual and symbolic, as simple as an Indian's or an Arab's. There were three bits of limestone on his table. They had to be dusted every day, while the furniture of his mind was still undusted. Out of the window with them!

If he had had the wealth of Crœsus, Henry's mode of living would not have been different. Space, air, time, a few tools, a note-book, a pen, a copy of Homer, what could he wish more than these? A bath in the pond at sunrise, a little Spartan sweeping and cleaning, then a bath for the intellect, perhaps in the Bhagavad-Gita, the pure water of Walden mingling in his mind with the sacred water of the Ganges. The day was his, for any wild adventure. Sometimes, on a summer morning, he would sit for hours in his sunny doorway, amid the pines and hickories and sumacs, in undisturbed solitude and stillness. The birds flitted noiselessly about him. He could feel himself growing like the corn. He knew what the Orientals meant by contemplation and the forsaking of works. He was a Yogi, too, a forest-seer, who might have composed the Upanishads. His Reality was also Brahma, not the actualities of the world but its potentialities. What did he care for temporal interests? It was his vocation to discover God. His days were no longer days of the week, bearing the names of pagan deities, nor were they minced into hours or fretted by the ticking of a clock. He felt like a Puri Indian or a Mexican. If you had put a watch in his hand and asked him what the hour was, he might have looked at the dial and said, "Quien sabe?" The sounds of the railway rose and died in his ears like the distant drumming of a partridge.

His life here seemed to flow in its proper channels. It followed its own fresh currents, and he felt himself lurking in crystalline thought as the trout lurked under the verdurous banks. Not so much as a bubble rose to the surface. At sunset, he jumped into his boat and paddled to the middle of the pond. There he played on his flute, while the charmed perch hovered about the stern, and the moon travelled over the floor of the pond, strewn with the wrecks of the forest. The wildest imagination could not conceive the manner of life he was living, for the Concord nights were as strange as Arabian nights. He struck the side of the boat with his paddle, filling the woods with a circle of sound. What a pleasant mission it would be to go about the country in search of echoes! He knew where to find the prophetic places, the vocal, resounding, sonorous, hollow places, where oracles might be established, sites for oracles, sacred ears of Nature.

What could he say to a man who feared the woods, who shuddered at their solitude and darkness? What salvation was there for such a man? Did he not know that God was mysterious and silent? Henry could never have wearied of the woods, as long as he could visit a nighthawk on her nest. He could hardly believe his eyes when he stood within seven feet of her. There she was, sitting on her eggs, so sphinx-like, so Saturnian, so one with the earth, a relic of the reign of Saturn that Jupiter had failed to destroy, a riddle that might cause a man to go and dash his head against a stone. No living creature, surely, far less a wingéd creature of the air,—a figure in stone or bronze, like a gryphon or a phœnix. With its flat, greyish, weather-beaten crown, its eyes were all but closed with stony cunning; and yet all the time this sculptured image, motionless as the earth, was watching with intense anxiety, through those narrow slits in its eyelids. Wonderful creature, sitting on its eggs, on the bare, exposed hill, through pelting storms of rain or hail, as if it were a part of the earth itself, the outside of the globe, with its eyes shut and its wings folded. It was enough to fill a man with awe. Henry thought for a moment that he had strayed into the Caucasus, and that around the hill, on the other slope, he would find Prometheus chained to the rock.

Round and round the pond, Henry followed the footpath worn by the feet of Indian hunters, old as the race of men in Massachusetts. The critics and poets were always complaining that there were no American antiquities, no ruins to remind one of the past, yet the wind could hardly blow away the surface anywhere, exposing the spotless sand, but one found the fragments of some Indian pot or the little chips of flint left by some aboriginal arrow-maker. When winter came, and the scent of the gale wafted over the naked ground, Henry tramped through the snow a dozen miles to keep an appointment with a beech-tree, or a yellow birch perhaps, or some old acquaintance among the pines. He ranged like a grey moose, winding his way through the scrub-oak patches, bending the twigs aside, guiding himself by the sun, over hills and plains and valleys, resting in the clear grassy spaces. He liked the wholesome colour of the scrub-oak leaves, well-tanned, seasoned by the sun, the colour of the cow and the deer, silvery-downy underneath, over the bleached and russet fields. He loved the scrub-oak, with its scanty raiment, rising above the snow, lowly whispering to him, akin to winter, the covert which the hare and the partridge sought. It was one of his own cousins, rigid as iron, clean as the atmosphere, hardy as all virtue, tenacious of its leaves, leaves that did not shrivel but kept their wintry life, firm shields, painted in fast colours. It loved the earth, which it over-spread, tough to support the snow, indigenous, robust. The squirrel and the rabbit knew it well, and Henry could understand why the deer-mouse had its hole in the snow by the scrub-oak's stem. Winter was his own chosen season. When, for all variety in his walks, he had only a rustling oak-leaf or the faint metallic cheep of a tree-sparrow, his life felt continent and sweet as the kernel of a nut. Alone in the distant woods or fields, in the unpretending sprout-lands or pastures tracked by rabbits, on a bleak and, to most, a cheerless day, when a villager would be thinking of his fire, he came to himself and felt himself grandly related. Cold and solitude were his dearest friends. Better a single scrub-oak leaf at the end of a wintry glade, rustling a welcome at his approach, than a ship-load of stars and garters from the kings of the earth. By poverty, if one chose to use the word, monotony, simplicity, he felt solidified and crystallized, as water and vapour are crystallized by cold.

All praise to winter, then, was Henry's feeling. Let others have their sultry luxuries. How full of creative genius was the air in which these snow-crystals were generated. He could hardly have marvelled more if real stars had fallen and lodged on his coat. What a world to live in, where myriads of these little discs, so beautiful to the most prying eye, were whirled down on every traveller's coat, on the restless squirrel's fur and on the far-stretching fields and forests, the wooded dells and mountain-tops,—these glorious spangles, the sweepings of heaven's floor. He watched the men cutting the ice on the pond. Some of this ice, stowed in the holds of ships, was going over to India; and many a seeker of Brahma in Calcutta was destined to drink from his own Walden well. If winter drove one in-doors, all the better. It compelled one to try new fields and resources. Days of merry snow-storms and cheerful winter evenings by the fire. Evenings for books of natural history, Audubon, for one. It was pleasant to read about the Florida Keys, the flowering magnolia, the warm spice-breezes, while the wind beat the snow against one's window. Days to sit at home over one's journal, in one's own nest, perhaps on a single egg, though it might prove to be an egg of chalk.

These were the days for writing, days to speak like a man in a waking moment to others in their waking moments. For Henry was hard at work. He was writing articles, which Horace Greeley placed for him. He had begun to write a book, and he wished to pay his tribute to Carlyle, who had liberated the English language, cutting away the fetters imposed upon it by the pedantic writers of the British reviews. The frigid *North American* was even worse, a venerable cobweb that had escaped the broom. He liked to think of Carlyle, on his vacations, riding on his horse "Yankee," bought from the American sale of his books. His own book, rewritten from his journal, was the *Week on the Concord and Merrimac Rivers*, the story of the journey with his brother, never to be forgotten, when they had doubled so many capes and run before the wind and brought back news of far-away men. He did not propose to crowd his day with work, even if the book had to be written. A writer, he thought, should saunter to his task surrounded by a halo of ease and leisure, and the labour of his hands should remove from his style all trace of sentimentality and palaver. One did not dance idly at one's writing when one had wood to cut and cord, and as the strokes rang cheerily through the wood, so the stroke of the pen should ring on the reader's ear. Was the voyage an old story, eight or nine years old, and only a week at that? It represented a lifetime's memories. No boy who had grown up on the Mississippi recalled those floating enchantments, the river-boats, and the fabulous river-men, with more of a thrill than Henry felt, remembering the canal-boats of his childhood. The news had spread through Concord that one of these boats was stealing through the meadows, silent as a cloud, with its crew of "foreigners" from New Hampshire, and all the village boys had flocked to see it. Henry wished to write a book that would be saturated with his thought and reading, yet one that would not smell so much of the study, even the poet's cabin, as of the fields and woods. He dreamed of an unroofed book, lying open under the ether, a book that could hardly be forced to lie on a shelf.

He was not by nature a hermit. He might have frequented the bar-rooms, he thought, if he had had any business that called him thither. Almost every day he walked to the village, to trade his beans for rice, to get a boot repaired, to collect the news of the family. Sometimes he returned late at night, with a bag of rye or Indian meal, sailing back under the moon to his harbour in the woods. But he was wary of gossip. He did not wish to lumber his mind with the rubbish that most men seemed to rejoice in, the details, for example, of some case in court. One day he was arrested in the village for refusing to pay his poll-tax. He felt as Alcott felt. The government supported slavery, the government was backing the Mexican War; well, he would not support the government. He did not wish to trace the course of his dollar until it bought a man, or bought a gun to shoot a Mexican. He spent the night in jail,—a fruitful night. It inspired his essay on *Civil Disobedience*. He wished to establish a principle, that one man locked up in jail for

refusing to countenance slavery would be the end of
slavery, or, to express it on a broader basis, "If the alter-
native is to keep all just men in prison, or give up war
and slavery, the State will not hesitate which to choose."
A foolish notion, many people thought, but some of
them changed their minds, in later years, when one of
Henry's Hindu readers, Gandhi, acting on the principle,
disturbed the British Empire for several months. The
next morning, Henry, released from jail, gathered some
of the boys and girls for a huckleberry party, on a hill,
whence the State was nowhere to be seen. He never fastened his door at Walden, though sometimes, in his absence, he had unwelcome visitors. How did Mrs. So-and-so
discover that the sheets in his hut were not as clean as
hers? But nothing was ever stolen, except his copy of
Homer. One had to keep one's eye on bookish people.

He had other guests, especially in April, when all the
world seemed to be on the move. A runaway slave appeared, then Alek Therien, the French-Canadian wood-
chopper, a true Homeric peasant who had learned a
little Greek from his priest in the north, then Hugh
Quoil, an Irish soldier, who had fought at the Battle of
Waterloo. Old Quoil, with his wife and his jug, was pa-
tiently waiting for death in a cabin in the woods. The
shanty-Irish folk along the railroad sometimes came to
see him. Henry thought them shiftless enough, with their
women washing under the trees and the pigs poking
about among the tubs. He eyed them with a vague hostility, as the red men had eyed the first settlers, and with as
much reason; for were they not the first wave of the sea
that was to sweep away so many landmarks? Among the
little ragamuffins that swarmed about these cabins, there
were some in whom the prophetic eye might have seen
the masters of the future, the lords of Greater Boston,
mayors, governors, captains of police, even, perhaps, a
cardinal. Henry had one good friend among them, little

Johnny Riordan, with his quaint "old worthy" face, behind the sober visor of his cap, plodding to school through the snow in his next-to-nothing, facing and routing it like a Persian army. A great sight, Johnny, in his rags, beside the well-fed villagers, waddling about in their furs and finery. Emerson also came, of course. Henry read aloud to him some pages from his book, while they sat under an oak beside the pond. Alcott arrived one night, struggling through the snow. Ellery Channing spent a fortnight with him. When the poets and sages came, he was glad that his dwelling was so spacious. As the conversation assumed a grander and loftier tone, they shoved their chairs further and further apart, until they touched the walls in opposite corners. This left plenty of neutral ground for their sentences to deploy in martial order.

Once Henry left his house for a fortnight's excursion. He had cousins in Bangor, Maine, one of them in the lumber-trade, a good excuse to visit the northern woods. He wished to study the Indians in their forest wilderness, and he wished to climb Mount Ktaadn. He never travelled without prayer and fasting, for he did not wish to dissipate his mind. With all the industry of a busy life, how could one hope to know, really know, an area more than six miles square? Isaac Hecker had asked him to go to Rome, the two of them together, Hecker to pay the expenses, for Hecker, who had tried Brook Farm and Fruitlands, was boarding with Mrs. Thoreau for a taste of Concord. He hoped to carry Henry over to Rome, in more than one fashion. Later, another friend, an Englishman, invited him for a visit in England. In both cases, Henry said, No. If Europe was much in his mind, and became more and more to him, Concord might become less and less; and what sort of bargain would that be? He did not wish his life to lose its homely savour. If the fields and streams and woods that he loved so well,

and the simple occupations of his townsmen, ever ceased
to interest and surprise him, what culture or wealth
could ever atone for the loss? He did not wish to go to
Europe, nor did he wish to go—like the farmers—west.
What could he think of this foolish American habit, going east or west to a "better land," without lifting an
honest finger to till and redeem one's own New England
soil? As for the rush to California, it was a disgrace to
humankind,—digging gold, the merest lottery, a kind of
toil, if it deserved the name, in no sense beneficial to the
world. A startling development, this, of the ethics of
trade and all the modes of getting a living. It filled
Henry with a cold scorn. For the rest, he had his own
western horizon, towards which he was always moving,
pitching his tent each day nearer the Golden Gate. But
the really fertile soils and luxuriant prairies lay on one's
own side of the Alleghanies, wherever a man minded his
own business. Were not all the essentials of life to be
found in Concord, ten times found if one properly valued them?—which a man could only do if he stood his
ground. Henry had a word for the men in the covered
wagons, who were running away from something besides
the rocks. If the men in the covered wagons had no ears
for Henry, he would be glad to wait for a few generations. The great-great-grandsons of the covered wagons
would be ready to listen to him.

Nobody knew the riches of Concord. As for natural
history, he had found some of the Arctic phenomena
there, red snow and one or two Labrador plants. Still, a
little travel now and then was not so bad to give one's
mind an airing, especially if it offered him a chance to
observe the ways of the Indians. For the Indians had a
special charm for Henry; they suggested a simpler mode
of life and a greater nearness to the earth. Were there
not two eternities, one behind him, which the Indians
represented, as well as one before? Wherever he went, he

trod in their tracks, yet only a few poets remembered them. Here and there, one saw their lonely wigwams, on the banks of some quiet stream, like the cabins of the muskrats in the meadows,—an old squaw, perhaps, living in her solitary hut, with her dog, her only companion, making baskets and picking berries, insulted by the village boys and girls. Henry dreamed of writing a book about them;[1] for their memory seemed to him to harmonize with the russet hue of autumn that he loved. A race that had exhausted the secrets of nature, a race tanned with age, while the young, fair Anglo-Saxon slip, on whom the sun had shone for so short a time, was only just beginning its career. As sportsmen went in pursuit of ducks, and scholars of rare books, and all men went in pursuit of money, Henry went in search of arrowheads, when the proper season came round again. He often spent whole afternoons, especially in the spring, when the rains had washed the ground bare, pacing back and forth over a sandy field, looking for these relics. It might have rained arrowheads. They lay all over the surface of the country, sometimes mingled with arrowheadiferous soil, ash-coloured, left by Indian fires. They were like so many fossil thoughts to Henry, forever recalling the far-away mind that shaped them.

To Maine, then!—where the Indians grew with the moose. A fortnight in the forest, the home of the bear and the caribou, the wolf, the beaver and the Penobscot redskins, where the wild fir flourished and the sprucetops, seen from an elevation, were like the odour of cake in a schoolboy's nostrils. Hemlocks and cedars, silver and yellow birches, watery maples, damp and moss-grown rocks, real woods, these, wild and bearded. One caught the whistle of ducks on solitary streams, the flicker of the darting chickadee, the loon's deso-

---

[1] Thoreau left eleven manuscript volumes, about 3000 pages, filled with notes about the Indians for the book he had hoped to write.

late laugh. Sometimes, through the moss-clad aisles, one heard a dull, dry, rustling sound, as if smothered under the fungus-covered forest, the falling of a tree, like the shutting of a door in some distant entry of the dark and shaggy wilderness. There one could feel at home, shooting the rapids in one's birch canoe, like a bait bobbing for some river monster, darting from side to side of the stream, then gliding swift and smoothly. This was the place to sing the "Canadian boat-song," or to play on one's flute, at night, under the stars, while the wolves howled about, in the darkness of the continent. Henry watched Joe Polis, the Indian guide, glued to the bank on his stomach, talking to the muskrats in their sylvan language. Sometimes, by the fireside, Joe Polis also sang, a mild and simple nasal chant, like the dawn of civilization over the woods. The white man's brow was clear and distinct, but over the brow of the Indian lingered a haze of mist. For the Indian, the white man's noon was four o'clock in the morning.

A journey like this was only a foretaste, too rewarding not to be repeated. Henry was writing about his travels, and one of the magazines was glad to print his essay on Ktaadn. Later, on two occasions, he went to Maine again. He wished to visit Chesuncook, the Allegash and the East Branch. He was in his element in the woods, as Richard Henry Dana on the sea, as an old French-Canadian *coureur de bois*. Was he not a Frenchman as well as a Yankee, who might have run wild with Du Lhut and harried the woods for beavers? In the meantime, he had left his Walden cabin. Why? For as good a reason as he had gone there. He had other lives to live, and he had no more time to spare for this one. He wanted a change, he did not wish to stagnate. About two o'clock in the afternoon, he had felt the world's axle creaking a little, as if it needed greasing, as if the oxen laboured with the wain and could hardly get their load over the ridge of

the day. Who would accept heaven on terms like this?—
and a ticket for heaven had to include, for Henry, tickets
for hell and purgatory also. Walden was only a bivouac
in his campaign. He had other journeys in mind, to
Cape Cod, for instance, with Ellery Channing, and later
a jaunt to Canada, Quebec and Montreal. (Total expense, two guide-books included, $12.75.) Ellery was not
a man for camping out,—that was an art one had to ac-
quire slowly; but he shared Henry's taste for a simple
equipment. And Henry would no more have thought of
dressing,—dressing for a journey!—than he would have
blacked his boots for fishing. Honest travelling was dirty
work. A pair of overalls was the proper costume, a grey
sack, corduroys perhaps; and as for this blacking of
boots, he despised it on all occasions. In this, he was like
some of the Harvard professors, who, as Mrs. Story was
shocked to note, on one of her visits from Italy, did
not have their boots blacked even for Commencement.
Henry, who always carried a piece of tallow, in order to
keep the water out of the leather, looked like a woodchuck or a musquash. This was his desire, at least,—the
more like a quadruped the better, tawny, russet, yellow-
brown, the colour of the sands. Vermont grey was not so
bad; and once he had had the perfect suit, a skilful mix-
ture of browns, with light and dark cleverly proportioned, and a few threads of green. He had looked like
a corner of a pasture, with patches of sweet-fern and
lechea. He had been able to glide over the fields, as un-
perceived from the farmer's windows as a painted cruiser
through a spyglass. The wild animals thought he was one
of them. Ellery, who was not so systematic, shared Henry's feeling in the matter of hats. His own hat was old
and weather-beaten and had plenty of holes around the
brim. It was as rare and high as a good Stilton cheese.
As for the rest of Henry's outfit, a handkerchief served
for a bag, or a firm, stout sheet of brown paper, well tied

up. What else? An umbrella, of course, a knapsack, with partitions for books and papers, a music-book for pressing flowers, a field-glass and a measuring-tape. A fish-line, spoon and dipper, a little salt and sugar, tea, Indian meal and a slice of fruit-cake. If anyone asked him along the way to do a little tinkering, that was a tribute to his common sense.

So Henry tramped to Provincetown. Having seen the woods, he wished to see the ocean, and Cape Cod was surely the place to see it. There, on the stretches of sand blown clean by the wind, he could forget the towns, where he felt so unspeakably mean and disgraced. He could forget the bar-rooms of Massachusetts, where the full-grown were not weaned from their savage and filthy habits, sucking cigars and guzzling whiskey-punch. On the Cape, one saw wholesome faces, well preserved by the salty air, faces bleached like old sails, hanging cliffs of weather-beaten flesh. The Cape Cod boys leaped from their leading-strings into the shrouds; it was only a bound from their mother's laps to the masthead. They boxed the compass in their infant day-dreams. They could hand, reef and steer by the time they flew a kite. This was a country almost as thrilling as Maine. Henry had three books more or less on the stocks: *The Maine Woods,* full of the scents of the forest, *Cape Cod,* redolent of the sea, even *A Yankee in Canada.* The well-known publishers, Time & Co., could be trusted to see that they were safely printed. One of his neighbours wrote about Human Culture. Why should he not write about Cape Cod, another name for the same thing, and hardly a sandier phase of it? Or Canada, for that matter? He wrote an opening paragraph, with both hands clenched: "Read my book if you dare!"

CHAPTER XX

WEST OF BOSTON

AFTER EIGHT years of ups and downs, Brook Farm
had come to an end, not without important consequences. There were not wanting well-informed observ-
ers who were to assert, in later years, that from the farm
had sprung the movement of organized labour in New
England and even throughout the nation. It had other
results of a personal kind. Two well-known journalists
of the future, Charles A. Dana of the New York *Sun* and
John Sullivan Dwight of the *Journal of Music,* received
their first training as editors of *The Harbinger,* the
magazine published at the farm. *The Harbinger* had
opened with a translation of George Sand's *Consuelo,*
and almost every writer in New England contributed an
essay or a poem. But the farm had not long survived the
coming of the Fourierists, Owen, Horace Greeley and
Albert Brisbane, who had translated Fourier's writings.
Brisbane wished to turn it into a phalanstery, where all
the ideas of the master were to be applied. With certain
modifications, the plan was adopted, and the members
were divided into "groups" and "series." But something
went out of the life of the farm. Ceasing to be voluntary,
it ceased to be poetic; and when disaster fell, the farm
fell with it.

Dwight, the chief of the "Festal Series," was all but
broken-hearted. The music-master had been a pretty
sight, surrounded by his class of singing children. He was
happy to hoe the corn on Sundays, paying his regards to
the Puritan sabbath by breaking it in every way he could;

and, although he did not like to hoe on week-days, he had contrived to put up with the new routine. He did not know what to do when the sad news broke. He struggled on for a time in Boston, trying to maintain a "combined household" for some of the Brook Farmers. He never lost his faith in association; he felt that a communal life was the only life for humanity and that society must be set in order before the individual could be himself. The organization of labour, the abolition of competition, this was the road to the future, as Dwight conceived it. It was not until 1852 that he was able to start the *Journal of Music,* which he was to conduct for thirty years. This was the journal that set the musical standard of Boston. It published the musical news of Italy, Paris, Germany, England, Liszt's *Life of Chopin,* a serial life of Mozart, hundreds of original compositions. It even led the musical thought of the country, till the editor's dislike of Brahms and Wagner gradually destroyed its influence. This was in the far future, when Dwight was the dictator of music. He had made his way by lecturing and writing, carrying on, in Boston and elsewhere in New England, the "mass clubs" he had started at the farm.

"Archon" Ripley went to New York, with Dana, to work on Greeley's *Tribune.* It was a sad descent, sitting all day long in a little office, on the fourth floor of a huge, dirty building, reached by winding, narrow, littered stairs, with machines whizzing and clanking about him, paragraphing and clipping for *The Tribune.* One never heard the vireo there, and Utopia seemed very far away. Every night he plodded home to Brooklyn. He shared a single room with his wife in a shabby boarding-house in a dingy street. In this room his wife died of cancer, while, Ripley, at his table in the corner, worked away for dear life,—the modest, laborious Ripley, too humble to collect in volume-form the clear and scholarly essays he wrote for his paper on Lessing, Voltaire, Rousseau, Hartmann, Spencer. These essays, like Dwight's,—never collected either,—deserved a place of honour in the literature of criticism. Two decades were to pass, in this Grub Street twilight, while he composed, with Dana, the *New American Encyclopædia,* before the sun rose again for Ripley. He had a brief, happy second youth, with means, a little travel, a brougham to drive about in Central Park. For even Brook Farmers came to gigs at last.

Two notable women, members of Ripley's circle, had gone to New York, at least for a while, before him. Lydia Maria Child, the novelist, had written thence her *Letters from New York, 1841–1844,* an unpretentious picture of the city that was to have its interest in later years. Mrs. Child was at home in the rural outskirts, the charming villages on the New Jersey shore, the woody banks of Weehawken, a wild garden of early flowers. In the Hoboken meadows, she found violets nestling in moss-grown stumps. New York itself was too much in a hurry-scurry, and there was something brutal in its life. The dog-catchers trooped down the streets, their clothes bespattered with blood; they had clubs over their shoulders to beat to death every dog they found without a master. She had never seen such sights as this in humanitarian Boston. She studied the prisons, the care of the poor, the Swedenborgian meetings, the meetings for the discussion of mesmerism, the popular acclaim of Ole Bull, who had just arrived from Norway. New York was not like Boston. It never entered the head of a Wall Street merchant that he was himself responsible for the evils of the town; and, although she found "Transcendental muslins" advertised in the Bowery, she never met with the well-known cult in any other form. Was she herself a Transcendentalist? She had certainly used the phrase "highly gifted"; and yet she had been mystified in some of the Boston circles, where she had had to bite her finger to be sure that she herself was really solid. She felt a good deal of sympathy with the plain man of business, and she drew a kindly, generous, motherly picture of the town that he had built for his habitation. But, as for his toleration of slavery and a thousand other abuses, she did not abate a word of her honest abhorrence.

Margaret Fuller, with her intenser mind, had also surveyed the metropolis. She had gone there in 1844 to join the staff of *The Tribune*. She lived in Horace Greeley's house and carried on raids of observation into the territories of the prince of darkness, Sing Sing, Blackwell's Island, the Five Points, even the salons of the literati. Greeley had been attracted by her books, which had appeared in *The Dial*,—the well-known feminist treatise, *Woman in the Nineteenth Century,* and the notes on Western travel, *Summer on the Lakes.* He felt that hers was the sort of pen to make his own paper a living force; for this female Montesquieu, as her followers thought her, who had given her own sex its title-deeds, seemed ready to forward every enlightened cause. She had written well of the West. With James Freeman Clarke's art-ist-sister, she had spent the summer of 1843 in Cleveland, Chicago and Wisconsin. She had mingled with the New England pioneers, bent on seeking their fortunes, the fathers and mothers of a race to come. What had been their one preoccupation? Alas, from the oldest man to the youngest child, they talked not of what they were going to do but of what they were going to get, ease and money. Could anything more be hoped of the Germans and Swedes, who were flocking into these beautiful wildernesses, amid the prairie flowers and the lowing cattle? The scene, she knew, had a mighty meaning, and she hoped to divine the law by which a new poetry and order might be evoked from this chaos. She liked the outdoor festivals of the pioneers, the huskings and the hop-gath-erings, as merry as the Scottish harvest-home or the

Italian vintage, the groups of men and girls filling their baskets with the gay festoons. But everywhere she saw, in germ, the fatal spirit of imitation, a reference to European ways. She noted the fine taste the Indians showed in the sites of their clustered lodges on the lakes and streams. Let the white men blacken the Indians as they might, talk of their filth and brutality: she could well believe that an Indian brave, rambling on these paths, in the beams of the sun, might be mistaken for Apollo. The Indians had loved the French. How could they love the Protestant missionary, with his niggardly conceptions, his unfeeling stare? As for the general prospects of these regions, whatever the future might bring she was bound to say, "There is nothing real in the freedom of thought at the West. It is from the position of men's lives, not the state of their minds."

Now, in New York, on *The Tribune,* she was writing on current literature. She hoped to clarify American thought, in its dim and struggling state, and introduce the new European writers. She paid no attention to the magazine-stories, "written for the press, in a spirit of imitation and vanity, the paltriest offspring of the human brain." What was her criterion? "Most men, in judging another man, ask, Did he live up to our standard? To me it seems desirable to ask, Did he live up to his own?" She added that Goethe's faults fitted him all the better for the part he had to play. She interpreted the more significant writers, looking to the day "when our population shall have settled into a homogeneous national life, and we have attained vigour to walk in our own way, make our own world and leave off copying Europe." Her judgments were remarkably just,[1] and some of her general

---

[1] E.g., in regard to Longfellow, that "the ethical part of his writing has a hollow, second-hand sound," as also in regard to Emerson, that "he raised himself too early to the perpendicular and did not lie along the ground long enough."

intuitions gave her work a measure of permanent interest. She contrasted the boyish crudity that marked so many American writers, timid and boastful at once, with the tempered, manly equipoise of the thoroughbred European; and, regarding the larger aspects of civilization, she spoke for the longer time as well as the shorter. "Since the Revolution," she observed, "there has been little, in the circumstances of this country, to call out the higher sentiments. The effect of continued prosperity is the same on nations as on individuals,—it leaves the nobler faculties undeveloped. The superficial diffusion of knowledge, unless attended by a corresponding deepening of its sources, is likely to vulgarize rather than raise the thought of a nation, depriving it of another sort of education through sentiments of reverence, and leading the multitude to believe themselves capable of judging what they but dimly discern. . . . In a word, the tendency of circumstances has been to make our people superficial, irreverent and more anxious to get a living than to live mentally and morally." A statement that could hardly have been challenged a century later.

In 1846, Margaret Fuller set out for Europe. She had read the invisible ink in many minds and lives, in Hawthorne's, for one, the American writer whom, after Emerson, she most admired. Hawthorne had returned for three years to Salem. His friends, Horatio Bridge and Franklin Pierce had gone to Concord, to the Manse, to see him. They found him chopping wood in the shed, dressed in his old blue frock and troubled over the problem of earning a living; and they promised to use their influence with Bancroft, who had risen in the political world and was Secretary of the Navy, to find a post for him that would give him an income. Horatio Bridge himself was in the navy, and he had written a book, with Hawthorne's help, the *Journal of an African Cruiser,* a collection of lively impressions of the African Gold Coast,

Liberia, Sierra Leone, the Canaries. Hawthorne went back to Salem with a heavy heart, as the new surveyor of the custom-house. A botanist who lived in the town had recently noted that the English white-thorn, the hawthorn of the poets, had slowly naturalized itself in Salem. It was otherwise with the flower of Hawthorne's mind. The mud, the dust, the east wind, the petty trickeries of the politicians, the chilliness of the social atmosphere— "Who ever heard of the Hawthornes?" one of the ladies of Chestnut Street remarked—benumbed and befogged his senses. He went about his work with the dogged and silent practicality that always characterized his mundane life, testing the rum that was sent to the Guinea Coast,— for he meant to see that the Negroes had good, strong rum,—while the poet slept within him. Three years of an outward stupefaction, years in which the shipmaster's son, who might have quelled a mutiny, obliged his incompetent staff to toe the mark. In the evenings, he read De Quincey with his wife. What music, what perfection of style in the less laborious passages! How could Hawthorne talk to the Salem people? Why should he talk, indeed, when the presence of an uncongenial person caused an almost physical contraction of his great masculine frame?

At the end of the three years, he moved to Lenox. He had written *The Scarlet Letter* in Salem, the book that had won his freedom; for under his mask of insensibility the poet had been alive and brooding there. In this winter of his discontent, he had also written a few fables and sketches, worthy of one whose first American forbear had brought from England with him a copy of Sidney's *Arcadia*. The tone of *Main Street* and *The Great Stone Face*, like that of *The Snow-Image*, was of a dove-like innocence that often cloaked the wisdom of the serpent. No one else in New England had written such stories, or only one man, William Austin, the Boston lawyer, Dr. Channing's class-mate. This well-known Harvard scholar and legislator, who had studied law in London, where he had known Washington Allston and written the *Letters from London,* which all the American lawyers read because they contained such good descriptions of the British lawyers and statesmen, had published a handful of tales in the eighteen-twenties that were almost prophetic of Hawthorne. In *Martha Gardner,* Austin, a Democrat and a radical, castigated the modern corporations that fed on the miseries of the poor. Better than this was *The Man with the Cloaks,* based on a German fairy-tale. The best was *Peter Rugg, the Missing Man.* Austin had a robust, Rabelaisian humour that ran to the gigantesque, as in the story of the hungry teacher who wandered about the country drinking all the cows dry and cutting steaks out of the living oxen. *Peter Rugg* was a great invention, or one of those bold formulations of ancient inventions, whether the Flying Dutchman or the Wandering Jew, which, like *Rip Van Winkle* and *Peter Schlemihl,* come to the same thing. This tale of the man who disappeared from Boston and was constantly seen on the roads for fifty years, desperately whipping his horse, trying to find his way back, had all the overtones of the true folk-legend, the haunting suggestions of a symbolism that is always lending itself to some new turn of affairs. There were many Peter Ruggs, in days to come, trying to find their way back to Boston, the good old Boston of 1820; and the story was retold by later writers as if it had been a popular myth.[2] The ambiguous atmosphere of the tale, the mingling of the dubious and the real, the play of light and shadow suggested Hawthorne. So did the old New England setting and costumes. Hawthorne was familiar with it. Peter Rugg appeared in one of his own tales. He was the door-keeper in *A Virtuoso's Collection.*

[2] Peter Rugg was the subject of a ballad by Louise Imogen Guiney and a prose-poem by Amy Lowell.

At Lenox, the air was scented with sweet-grass and clover; and there, in the little red cottage on the lonely farm, Hawthorne had his year of wonders. There he wrote *The House of the Seven Gables* and planned *The Blithedale Romance;* and, while his wife made tracings of Flaxman's outlines on the dull-yellow painted chairs and tables, he told the children stories that explained the drawings, *The Wonder Book* and *The Tanglewood Tales.* Tanglewood, as the children called it, was a wild spot in the woods close by where they all went for picnics in the summer and autumn. Hawthorne played the magician there. He was a great tree-climber, up in a flash to the topmost bough, showering nuts all over the floor of the forest. From old door-knobs and strips of shingle, he carved little yachts and figures, a pugilist who swung his arms in the wind. In winter, he made images of snow. The image in the tale he wrote was singularly like a man of genius, a moral that he neglected, however, to point. The father of the children who made the image, a man of common sense and kind intentions, wished to make the image comfortable, even in spite of itself. He carried it into the warm room, where it rapidly melted away beside the fire. Alas, for the poor snow-image that loved the cold, the frosty air, the north wind! The children had known very well it could only live under the stars that glimmered in the arctic night.

Hawthorne had become a father-confessor. Letters poured in upon him from unhappy souls who had been touched by his books. Secret criminals sought him out and came to him for counsel and relief. Most of his Berkshire neighbours were less exacting. Miss Sedgwick, the aging novelist, lived at Lenox. At Mrs. Sedgwick's school, Harriet Hosmer, the merry little gnome, the sculptor of the future, was one of the pupils. Hawthorne was to meet her again in Rome; still later, he described her in *The Marble Faun*. The Sedgwicks pervaded the Berkshires.

Even the grasshoppers chirped, "Sedgwick, Sedgwick!"
as one of their friends remarked; and Mrs. Sedgwick said,
with a measure of truth, "En France tout arrive." Everything happened at Lenox, and everyone came there.
Close by lived the lovely Fanny Kemble, whose Shakespeare readings in Boston were events of the forties and
who also appeared in one of Hawthorne's novels.[3] Samuel Gray Ward had another villa. This dearest of Emerson's friends, not to be confused with Longfellow's
friend, Samuel Ward of New York,—Julia Ward Howe's
brother, who was later known as the "King of the
Lobby,"—was a Boston banker and patron of art. His
youth, before he entered business, had been devoted to
painting, literature and German studies. He had translated a volume of Goethe's essays and had written a
paper on Boccaccio that was one of the best in *The Dial*.
His admirable essay on criticism, in Elizabeth Peabody's
Æsthetic Papers,[4] contained two phrases, "creative criticism" and "significant form," that other men in later
generations were to render more than familiar. Ward had
bought Lafayette's library at La Grange and had paid for
the publication of the poems of his old friend and school-
mate, Ellery Channing.[5] At Pittsfield, which had once

[3] In the character of Zenobia, in *The Blithedale Romance*, also
drawn partially from Margaret Fuller.

[4] A projected magazine, 1849, discontinued after the first number.
In addition to Ward's essay, it contained papers by Dwight, Miss
Peabody, Emerson, Thoreau and Hawthorne. In Emerson's contribution, the essay on War, one finds the following observation: "The
manhood that has been in war must be transferred to the cause of
peace, before war can lose its charm, and peace be venerable to
men." This was perhaps the germ of William James's later essay,
The Moral Equivalent of War.

[5] Samuel G. Ward was the "friend" of Emerson's *Letters to a
Friend*, edited by Charles Eliot Norton. His essay on criticism contained the following observations: "Our first misfortune is, that
there is a reference to a standard from without, viz., England. As
the spirit that dictates it is, from many causes, unfair and depreciat-
ing, a natural consequence has been to cause all our own criticism to
take the opposite ground, to over-praise that which is felt to be un-

been Wendellboro, named after his forbears, Oliver Wendell Holmes spent his summers. There he planted seven hundred trees and built himself a snug little villa on a knoll on the old Wendell farm; and there he wrote his best bucolic poems, *The Ploughman,* for one, for he liked to play his part at the Berkshire agricultural fairs. At Broadhall, the old Melville house, where Major Thomas Melville had lived,—Holmes's "Last Leaf,"— Longfellow spent a summer, with Ex-President Tyler and Charles Sumner, for it was now a boarding-house. Major Melville's grandson, Herman Melville, was living at "Arrowhead," on the outskirts of Pittsfield. Melville was composing *Moby-Dick,* and the great white whale was in his flurry. He was attracted to Hawthorne and wrote an essay on his books, and he often drove up to the little red cottage, with his big Newfoundland dog in the buckboard beside him. He and Hawthorne liked to lie in the barn, on piles of new-mown hay, discussing time and eternity.

Not far away, at Northampton, where Bancroft, at the Round Hill school, had taught Ward, Motley and Ellery Channing, still another writer had spent his childhood, the Hawthornesque novelist, Sylvester Judd. This hypersensitive, humble, shrinking soul, a Unitarian minister at Augusta, Maine, bred in the rigours of Calvinism, had passed through the Transcendental movement. His doubts and ecstasies had deranged his nerves.[6] As a

---

dervalued or invidiously regarded .... Although all original literature comes from and refers to the heart of the people, it cannot, except in a rude age, address itself to that people except through a class capable of receiving it. If great works do not find such a class in their own age, they wait till time and their own influence create it .... We believe a conscious greatness inseparable from critical literature, and such, therefore, we look for in this country;—a literature and art based on thorough criticism, and thorough knowledge of what already exists in the world."

[6] It was of Judd that Emerson wrote: "I once asked a clergyman in a retired town who were his companions? What men of ability

student of theology in Cambridge, he had been stirred by Goethe and Carlyle. He wished to destroy the barriers of the sects, and exhibit the errors of false theology, war, capital punishment, the prison system. His *Margaret* was a Utopian romance, the story of the daughter of a German musician, brought up in an old New England village, who ends by transforming the village into a Mons Christi, with fountains like those of the Tuileries, belvederes and gardens, music-rooms, observatories, halls of art and barren lands blooming with rye and corn, where statues of Peace and Truth and marble muses line the Delectable Way, where industry, economy and love, simple fare and attractive toil create an earthly paradise and men of all nations meet as brothers. This Fourieristic fantasy, more than a little drawn from *Wilhelm Meister*, with a heroine often suggestive of Mignon, was quite in the Brook Farm spirit. It symbolized the feeling for art that was dawning in New England, the messianic socialism, the inspiration of German studies; and Judd's poem, *Philo*, a metaphysical epic, found readers who believed it would convert the world. *Margaret* was obscure and confused, but many pages and even chapters were vividly picturesque and charmingly written. Judd had studied New England. He had filled his note-books with observations of old houses, costumes and village ways, the talk of the farmers, the husking-bees, Thanksgiving, the pedlars and hawkers of ballads at country fairs. His best scenes were almost as good as Hawthorne's. There was a touch of ecstasy in some of his descriptions, the thunder-storm, the winter scenes, the snow-storm, the sunny clearing in the summer forest, the

he saw? He replied that he spent his time with the sick and dying. I said, he seemed to me to need quite other company, and all the more that he had this; for if people were sick and dying to any purpose, we should leave all and go to them, but, as far as I had observed, they were as frivolous as the rest, and sometimes much more frivolous."—*The Conduct of Life*.

coming of the flowers in spring, the horse-tails with their storied ruffs, the fleecy mouse-ear buds, the straw-coloured blossoms of the bell-wort, the little polypods with their feathery fronds and the young mulleins, velvety, white and tender.

These were the scenes that Hawthorne knew at Lenox. Never quite at home away from the sea-shore, he still had hours there, on summer evenings, when he felt as if he could climb the sky and run a race along the Milky Way. Free at last after the leaden years he had spent at the Salem custom-house, his mind was at its fullest flood. His bones were astir, even to the marrow. Salem, the ancient seaport of his boyhood, never loved by him, shunned indeed, and yet his own so deeply, seen afresh after his life at the Manse, which had given him a standard and a measure, Salem, dust of his own dust, and with it the Boston of Puritan times, pressed against and filled his consciousness. The scarlet letter A that had haunted his mind ever since he had written the *Twice-Told Tales*, the witch, whisked up the chimney on a broomstick and flying away to a devil's communion far in the depths of the dark, still forest, the old colonial governors, the ruffed physicians, the ministers godly and of ungodly fame, the women not to be repressed, the inquisitorial deacons, the elfin children of that Gothic world, prolonged from the Middle Ages, the Boston he had imagined and the Salem he had known, the queer gabled houses and the queerer people, the cobwebs visible and invisible, cobwebs of family pride and secret fraud, bloodstains telling tales and beams of innocent sunlight piercing through: all this had waited for the dam to break, for the moment of leisure and freedom, for his dismissal from the custom-house,—another of those politicians' tricks, and a score that he could repay by picturing his enemy in Judge Pyncheon,—to be written out at his desk with the secret drawers, the haunted writing-desk with the tiny panels. He had painted these little panels with impish faces, staring and smiling, while he sat in his purple writing-gown, covered with golden palm-leaves. The dam had burst, in Salem, with *The Scarlet Letter*. The overflow was *The House of the Seven Gables*.

Years before, in Hawthorne's youth, in Salem, when he had written his tales in the little chamber, there had always seemed to be a driving snow-storm on the other side of the casement, or a cloud of dust in summer, a film, a veil. When he had stood at the window, on Sunday mornings, studying the church across the way, watching the sunlight stealing down the steeple, he had always stood behind the curtain. To see the world with a side-long glance, by a certain indirection, was second nature with him; and this was the mood his romances conveyed, as if, in spite of all their air of daylight, he had never looked straight at Boston or Salem, as if he had always seen them over his shoulder. It was this that gave him his effect of magic and made these beautiful books, with their antique diction, something other than novels and, if not greater, more intimate in their spell than novels can be. They clung to the mind like music, like Gluck's mournful strains of the land of shades or the solemn joy of Mozart. Or, better still, like masques written for music in the far-off days in England of which one caught the dim reverberations in the scene of *The Scarlet Letter*. Round about the players in the greenwood, one felt and saw the encircling darkness gather. The deepest shade covered *The Scarlet Letter*. But the flickering play of the sun and the leaves set the note of *The House of the Seven Gables*. The story moved in a soft September light, melting like a happy dream of Shakespeare.

CHAPTER XXI

THE ANTI-SLAVERY WRITERS

OUT OF the depths of the country, far from Beacon Hill
and Brattle Street, one "heard as if an army muttered."

> And the muttering grew to a grumbling,
> And the grumbling grew to a mighty rumbling.

The Anti-Slavery movement was on its way. Not from
the churches, not from the men of property or culture
—or from them only on second thought—came the call
to reform. It was the village centres that grumbled and
rumbled, the back streets of the manufacturing towns,
the tailors' shops and rural printing-presses, the Quaker
farms and solitary homesteads. Thence came those that
troubled Israel. There *The Pilgrim's Progress* and the
Book of Martyrs were much more living facts than all
the culture of the later epochs. There dwelt, unchanged,
the spirit of the Puritans and the Friends, the stiff-necked
sectaries of Cromwell's army who had been glad to stand
in pillories and suffer their ears to be cropped rather
than put bread in the mouths of priests, men who had
fought for the right to wear their hats where others stood
uncovered, fought for a beard as they fought for a principle and chosen the *peine forte et dure* if they were
asked to surrender their opinion regarding some phrase
in the Scriptures. Such were the readers of *The Liberator*.
In their bones, as Garrison spoke, stirred the fires of the
days of Pym and Hampden. "I am in earnest, and I will
be heard!"

This was very far from the tone of Boston, far from

the tone of Cambridge. It was the voice of the ploughman, the mechanic, the humble cottagers of the homespun class whose minds were steeped in Bible and
Quaker tracts. Out of these circles Garrison had come.
In them he remained, in his little room with the dingy
walls, bespattered with printer's ink, living on snatches
of bread, fruit and milk, sleeping on his table for a bed,
with his printing-press beside him. Thence had come, in
minds of a similar stock, the dream of the pedlar Bronson Alcott, the vision of the Concord pencil-maker, who
had built his hut at Walden. Thence came N. P. Rogers
of New Hampshire, tenth in descent from the Reverend
John Rogers, the first martyr of Bloody Mary's reign,
and the "acts of the anti-slavery apostles," those whom
neither courtesy nor money, nor hard words, eggs, blows
or brickbats ever deterred from prophesying. The age of
Queen Elizabeth had reawakened in the scholarly Cambridge mind. The age of Laud and Charles the First
had reappeared in the minds of harness-makers, village
barbers, farmers, tavern-keepers. They drove about the
country in borrowed buggies, speaking at the Lyceums
and meeting-houses, faring on a few cents a day, a handful of biscuits and raisins, courting the lampblack and
the tar and feathers. They lived among revelations and
ghostly voices. An old Sandwich Quaker on Cape Cod
wrote down a vision that befell him as he stood in his
field at noonday. Darkness fell upon his sight and covered the whole earth. He saw the nation divided in civil
war.

Under the Boston mind worked the same leaven, but
much more complicated thoughts restrained it. The
fears of the "cotton interest" inhibited many; so did the
social ties of the merchant families, which bound them to
the families of the planters. The Whigs, who had taken
Webster for their leader, followed him in all his com-
promises. They followed Everett, who followed Webster,

and who, with his eye for the "good in everything," found something good in slavery: he had visited a plantation in Louisiana, and he was happy to report that the quarters of the slaves were neat and clean and the beds were furnished with mosquito-nets. This was reassuring to Christian souls who counted on the slaves for their bread and butter. Beside these bread-and-butter fears, moreover, there was a motive that deserved respect, the fear of the disruption of the Union, which had been established against such odds. Dr. Channing had expressed this fear, and no one suspected Channing of partisan interests. He had shown how the Union preserved the States from wasting and destroying one another, how the country would be broken by disunion into restless, grasping sections, all the more hostile to one another because, as one saw in South America, a common language multiplied jealousies; and Europe would make use of this dissension to break the nation further for its own advantage. This was enough to sober Boston minds that had not forgotten the Revolution.

Even in Boston, however, as in the inland regions, the question worked like madness in the brain. Channing's little treatise on slavery had made a measure of opposition to it almost a condition of self-respect. This book was embarrassing to the prosperous classes, who for a generation had nursed the illusion that, having won their independence, they had solved the problems of the world. The educated mind could not ignore a calm analytical essay that set the theme in a philosophical light. It showed, as no writer had shown before, the disastrous effects of slavery, both on the slaves and on the masters, and thenceforth no one who professed to think defended the "peculiar institution" without reservations or misgivings; and the more the South advanced its claims, in the new States of the West, terrorizing the central government, and forcing the Fugitive Slave Law on the North, the more the New England mind rose against it. Officially both Church and press took sides with the merchants and the lawyers; but the Abolitionist cause made rapid progress even among those whose tastes and feelings Garrison most offended. The converts ran unpleasant risks. One might be a popular author, like Mrs. Child, but, if one published a plea for the slaves, one's fame went out like a candle. Nobody bought one's next book, one could not get a ticket for the Athenæum and a well-known lawyer might pick one's pamphlet up with a pair of tongs and fling it out of the window. One might have sixteen Boston quarterings and a gallery of Copleys and Stuarts, but, if one uttered a phrase with "colour" in it, one's cousins would cut one dead in Beacon Street. One appeared in the press as an "aristocrat," but also as a "hyena" and a "squash." In the morning mail one might receive a bulky anonymous letter from the South, containing a withered ear and a piece of rope. The ear had been cut from a slave who had tried to escape. The rope was for the Boston gentleman, in case he crossed Mason and Dixon's line.

But this was the sort of embarrassment that animated generous minds. While the bankers and politicians grew colder and colder, the poets and the literary men, always in search of a cause, a just and proper focus for their feelings, could say Ha! Ha! once more to the sound of a trumpet. Some of the lawyers joined them. Not all, as Charles Francis Adams said, were "broken in to the cotton interest." Richard Henry Dana, the sailors' lawyer, whose natural instincts and interests were all on the conservative side, threw prudence to the winds. In the name of the old Northern gentry, who had always stood for freedom, and to show how he despised the Boston cringing to the Southern oligarchy, he never lost an opportunity to act as counsel for the runaway slaves. Rockwood Hoar, the judge of later times, who had twice swum the

Tiber, like Horatius, made a famous speech in the Legislature, saying that the conscience of Massachusetts had a right to be represented as well as its cotton.[1] Thenceforward there were two kinds of Whigs, the "cotton Whigs" and the "conscience Whigs," and most of the writers belonged to the second group. It was true that George Ticknor and his circle,—all but the tolerant Prescott,—"Hunkers" of the darkest hue, to whom all agitation was abhorrent, closed their doors to Dana and Charles Sumner, snubbed them on all occasions and cut them on the street. Ticknor grew bitter and vindictive. Sumner, he said, was outside the pale, and he even snubbed the charming Edmund Quincy, the son of the Cambridge Cato, who had betrayed his caste. But Quincy was of bluer blood than Ticknor's. He represented the oldest Boston strain, not only in its love of liberty. He had a cavalier's disregard of the interests of money and property. He scorned the cold respectabilities of the upper-bourgeoisie of Beacon Street. A man of the utmost elegance, with the easy grace of a *grand seigneur,* a lover of ancient customs, with little taste for a mercantile world, he had a paternal affection for the Negroes, like that of the old Virginians of the days when they wished to free their slaves. His mind was filled with the lore of colonial times, which he had heard as a child at his father's table, stories of Boston drawing-rooms of old, tales of the Massachusetts Negroes; and although, as an active Abolitionist, he wrote to further the cause, his sketches, *Lewis Herbert, Dinah Rollins, Two Nights in San Domingo* and several others, *Mount Verney, Old Houses,* were admirable from any point of view. His short novel, *Wensley,* better known, a Thackerayan picture of New England life, with touches from *Don Quixote,* excellent in character and setting, missed its mark in a common-

---

[1] It was Rockwood Hoar who described the three stages of the too-enterprising Yankee,—"to get on, to get honour, to get honest."

place plot; but *The Haunted Adjutant* was a first-rate
story. Quincy, a brilliant amateur, with a humorous eye
for human traits, wrote with a dash and colour, an ease
and freshness that were later to be known as "modern."

In this Abolitionist campaign, which was dividing
households, as the Unitarian movement had formerly
done, the orators especially had found a cause. They
were in need of a cause, for the tale of the Revolution
and the patriot fathers had grown rather stale, flat and
thin. Eulogies of Washington and Adams, profitable to
Edward Everett, rang hollow in the ears of the new generation. What was the meaning of these declamations,
this cant about the inalienable rights of men in a country
where it was known that Jefferson's nephew had chopped
a slave to pieces with an axe, where beating, brand-
ing, mutilating slaves, selling them, kicking them, killing
them was all in the nature of the situation? [2] The ancient
art of oratory, the pride of ancestral Boston, had become
an abuse. It was breathing out its vacant life in words,
empty as a cloud, cold as the frozen Frog Pond; and suddenly, as if by a blood-transfusion, its slow pulse began
to beat again. Oratory once more possessed a function.
It touched the springs of action, for the voices of Charles
Sumner and Wendell Phillips were voices to which Boston was obliged to listen. Their doctrines, their ideas
were scarcely new. What was new was their personal
style, their passion, their conviction, their sense of fact.
They were members of a family of minds that had appeared in all the Western countries, in Italy, in Germany,
in France, to defend the religion of liberty, poets mili-
tant, intellectual men who were glad to fight and die
for their beliefs, figures that were appearing in flesh
and blood on battlefields and barricades in Europe.

[2] See Mrs. Stowe's incontrovertible evidence in the *Key to Uncle
Tom's Cabin;* also Mrs. Child's *Plea for that Class of Americans
Called Africans.*

Brothers of Mazzini, heirs of William Tell, men of the world themselves and men of culture, they roused the indifferent minds of the thinking masses and made the American anti-slavery movement a part of the great world-struggle of darkness and light.

A century later, reading Phillips's speeches, one could still feel the moral passion that seemed to rekindle the eyes of the watching portraits when he invoked the fathers in Faneuil Hall. One could still feel the electric excitement that played about the speaker's head. It was known that the careless, courtly Phillips, so buoyant, so disdainful of the mob, the son of the first mayor of the city of Boston, was a convert to the cause. As the college friend and champion of the Southern students, with a touch of the actor in his make-up, as a brilliant and promising lawyer, he had not suggested the reformer. It was not known that at college he had made a profound study of English history at the time of the Civil War, and had read every document connected with it, every novel, play, speech and memoir, from Clarendon to the days of William Godwin. This was the arsenal of learning from which he drew when he had found his cause. With his patrician air and his flashing wit, his volleys of historical allusions, he magnetized the crowd, although he carried his life in his hands when he walked home after a stormy meeting. He seemed to say that threats were beneath contempt. There was no room for rhetoric in his fiery style. Phillips's mind was like a gatling-gun. Sumner was a siege-gun beside him, less effective in direct attack, although Sumner, his fellow-lawyer, born in the same year, had gifts that a legal world was bound to respect. Phillips, with his colloquial manner, something new in Boston that killed the Edward Everett style forever, raked the audience with his sudden sallies. Sumner obliged them to reason. Rather a lecturer than an orator, he piled his legal precedents mountain-high. His

speeches were vast oral essays, bristling with quotations
and citations. A little grandiloquent, compared with Phillips, but solid where Everett was hollow, he had appealed
to thinking men by his speech on *The True Grandeur
of Nations.* This was an attack on war, and he had
shown that every warship cost as much as a college to
build and keep. Each port-hole cost as much as one professor,—an argument that greatly impressed New England. Sumner had suggested a world-court and a League
of Nations.

Many a New England schoolboy knew by heart Webster's philippic against the slave-trade, delivered in the
far-off days before the great question had threatened the
Union. But Phillips and Sumner had kept the "prejudices" that Webster was begging men to conquer. As they
advanced, with Garrison,—Phillips as a free-lance, Sumner as leader of the "conscience Whigs,"—the movement
rent society more and more, leaving wealth and power
on the Southern side. One by one, however, the men of
letters, the poets first of all, joined in the crusade, even
those for whom "emancipation" was not a simple matter
of blacks and whites, those who had other slaves to liberate, the "white slaves" of the North,[3] and other forms
of slavery to contend with, not to be abolished by Acts
of Congress, the slavery of popular indifference, timidity,
sloth, stupidity, the slavery of shabby-mindedness and
callous dollar-worship. What could emancipation ever
mean unless there was a world worth living in? And
what was a world that lacked the imagination without
which freedom and slavery were empty words? Emerson
was not the only writer who, when he deserted his proper
studies, found that the Muse, not to be trifled with, put
chaos and confusion in his brain. He had his work to do,

---

[3] "Northern gentlemen think to govern us by our black slaves;
but, let me tell them, we intend to govern them by their white
slaves."—John Randolph.

like Prescott and Hawthorne, although for him, too, the hour came,—when the Southerners seized and enslaved free-Negro citizens of Massachusetts. Meanwhile, for simpler and more emotional minds, the cause was a kind of benefaction; and when volunteers from Germany, Italy, France, exiles and revolutionists, joined in the guerrilla war in Kansas, when Walter Savage Landor wrote an ode and eloquent voices rose all over the world to hearten the Abolitionists, they felt that great days had come again, like the days of '76, that America had once more become the focus of the world-old struggle for liberty. "One learns in a single day," wrote one of the New England men who were taking part in the Free-soil drama, "more about Greeks and Romans and English Puritans and Scottish Jacobites and Hungarians and all heroic peoples, than any course of history can teach. The same process is producing the same results before your eyes, and, what is most striking, the same persons whom you saw a year ago in Boston, indolent and timid, are here transformed to heroes." [4]

Whatever in the way of stimulus the movement afforded the poets, the poets repaid ten-fold. Even the angular Garrison wrote sonnets, in the gravest style of Milton, composing them in his midnight walks across the bridge to Cambridge; and John Greenleaf Whittier, his lieutenant, had long had cause to know that words, in times like these, had consequences. One of Whittier's anti-slavery pamphlets, *Justice and Expediency*, had caused the death of a friend. Merely for lending it to a brother-physician, Dr. Crandall of Washington had been put in prison, where his health had given way in the dampness and darkness. In fact, in the Whittier of these feverish years, there was more "deed" than "word," strangely in a Quaker non-resistant who clung to the old Quaker ways that enabled him to get "into the quiet."

[4] Thomas Wentworth Higginson.

But the lithe, quick Whittier, tall and eager, with his black hair and burning eyes, was anything but passive. As a child, in the "snow-bound" Haverhill farmhouse, he had seen or heard of a neighbour melting a minister's image in wax to send his soul to hell; and he himself had not read for nothing the journals of the old fighting Quakers who had wrestled with men and angels in Cromwell's day. He liked to face a mob. His black Quaker coat had been pelted with eggs, and he had seen his newspaper-office, the office of the *Pennsylvania Freeman*, burned over his head. Garibaldi was one of his heroes. Moreover, he was a skilful politician. It was Whittier who had induced Charles Sumner to stand for election to the Senate. There was no lobbyist like him at the State House, when it came to pulling wires "for righteousness' sake," in behalf of the Indians or woman's suffrage, the blind, felons, animals. This befitted the only man of his time who had read all the Utopias. Whittier had had no connection with the Brook Farm movement, but no one in America more than he longed to realize Milton's "true commonwealth."

Whittier was a shoot of the oldest New England. His family had lived in the Haverhill farmhouse since 1688, and no one had known, or was ever to know, the lore of the Merrimac Valley better than he, the legends of Essex and Middlesex and the woods of lower New Hampshire. His forbears had been farmers for six generations and had married the daughters of farmers, and his mind was steeped in local associations, tales of witches, tales of the Indian wars, the gossip of wandering farm-hands and gypsies. A Scottish farmer lived near by who wrote in the manner of Burns for the Haverhill paper. He had often stopped at the Whittier house and sung *Highland Mary* in the kitchen, over his bread and cheese and mug of cider. There were no Yankee pastorals, he had said. The domestic life of New England had not been hallowed by tender associations. Yet how poetic was the farmer's life!—the scent of the hay-mow, the breath of the cattle, the greenery by the brookside, the huskings, berry-pickings and winter sleigh-rides. These were the days when scriptural themes and scenes had occupied the American poetasters and Jared Sparks and Bancroft had just discovered the romance of American history. Whittier had written his first verses in chalk and charcoal on the beam of his mother's loom and had hidden his manuscripts in the farmhouse garret. He longed to escape from farming, for exposure and over-exertion had broken his health. The rigours of the New England winter had left in Whittier's mind impressions that tougher boys would have forgotten. Then Garrison had discovered the "star of genius" who had sent a poem to his paper. He had driven out from Newburyport to find him, and, while Whittier hastened to change his clothes,—he was burrowing under the barn in search of eggs when the great man appeared at the gate,—had begged his father to give him an education. Why make war on a young man's nature?

Whittier's reputation was that of a newspaper-poet. In Cambridge, they had forgotten or scarcely known that his *Legends of New England,* published in 1831, was the first collection of poems of the young New England school. He had versified stories from Mather's *Magnalia,* anticipated Longfellow's *Hiawatha* with ballads of Indian exploits, written tales of the colony times that suggested a metrical Hawthorne. Before these writers had been heard of, Whittier had been widely known. But he had abandoned his early subjects, and there were reasons why he was not remembered outside the obscure and humble public that always cherished him most at the best of times. He had written with a reckless facility, in the well-worn metres of Scott and Campbell, with almost no distinction of language. Aside from a word here and there with a local tang and value,—lug-pole, chimney-lug,—his diction had no nap or freshness: it was a threadbare diction, and it largely remained so. His associations had never been literary. Among the New England poets his only friend had been Mrs. Sigourney of Hartford, where he had lived for a while. His active life had been spent with orators and reformers, editors, propagandists and politicians. He was regarded as an unlettered rhymester, an anti-slavery journalist in verse, and when he asked in one of his poems—

> Wilt thou prize my poor gift less
> For simple air and rustic dress,
> And sign of haste and carelessness?—

what could one say in reply? His senses were defective. He was totally colour-blind and partially deaf. When he looked at an apple-tree, he could not distinguish the leaves from the apples, and once, in a moment of affluence, he bought a carpet that was garishly bright and showy, supposing it was a mild grey and brown, suitable for Quaker feet to walk on. His eye and ear were imperfect. His rhymes were often a scandal. Two hundred years of silence, as he put it, had "taken all the sing" out of the Quakers; and widely as he read, in later years, and carefully as he worked over his poems, he never knew when to cut them short. It was as if, having broken silence, he could not say enough. His technical methods were stereotyped. The simplest and most conventional ballad metres, the sentiments, phrases and rhythms of other poets served him to the last. He had no pride of artistry. When editors revised his manuscripts, Whittier accepted their changes without remark.

In certain aspects, he suggested a lesser Thomas Hood. But Whittier had a verve and flow as notable as Hood's, a force of moral passion, a fund of feeling. Spirited improvisation was his special gift. Moreover, he had some-

thing to say that no one else had said, something that
many others after him, true bards and simple, or bards
who were merely simple, could only repeat and echo.
There was even a touch of grandeur in him, the fiery
zeal of a Puritan prophet, the fruit of a passionate nature that "strove in chains." The girls had led Whittier many a dance. In the days when he had longed for
wealth and glory, before he became a reformer, it was the
worldly girls who attracted him most. They had snubbed
him for his poverty and rustic manners and teased him
to the brink of suicide. No doubt, this increased his love
of money, for Whittier dearly loved to turn a penny,
much as he liked others to think him poor; and one of
his favourite themes was the happy after-life of a high-
born lady who has married a farmer's boy. The girls had
made a mistake, he seemed to say, when they had jilted
Whittier. For the rest, he had had his compensation, for
his virginality fed his poetry. He was a philanderer all
his days and could scarcely hold back the flood of "pilgrims" that threatened to engulf his later years, the lady-
poets who sent him snips of their dresses, begged him for
intimate souvenirs, proposed to marry him on two occasions, built houses near his own, with room for two, and
popped in and almost gobbled him up, till he had to set
a spring-trap at his door to warn him that they were
coming and give him a chance to escape at the rear of
his house. These were the days when he always put on
his hat before he answered the door-bell, so that he might
appear to be going out. He spent whole afternoons roaming the streets, trying to lose the curiosity-seekers. "I had
hard work to lose him, but I have lost him," he would
say to his sister when he reappeared. "But I can never
lose a *her*." But who had encouraged the "pilgrims," the
lady-poets, as if he wished to keep the fires burning? He
kept the fires burning and thriftily banked them up a
single chimney. Poetry was Whittier's vestal altar.

As time went on, he returned to the scenes and subjects that had characterized his early verse; and, while he continued to write for the Abolitionist cause, he became more and more the rural poet. Whittier and Longfellow, whom he scarcely knew, were rivals in popular fame, after he had published the *Lays of My Home*. Longfellow's mind was of a higher cast. Whatever it lacked in intensity, it was poetic in grain. Whittier's mind was sandy and thin beside it, though it had more spontaneity than Lowell's. It glowed with moral feeling, if only here and there with imagination. But Whittier's best work was still to come, in the early eighteen-fifties. Meanwhile, he enlarged the little cottage into which he had moved at Amesbury. He built the garden-room, always filled in season with harebells and laurel, where he liked to read his poems aloud to his friends, while his sister, Elizabeth Whittier, who was also a poet, guarded the vestal flame. In the afternoons, he sat in the village store, perched on a sugar-barrel, joining in the local gossip and putting in a word now and then to turn the vote of the farmers. No other writer had done so much to arouse public feeling for Abolition; and *Ichabod,* the poem on Webster, and *Massachusetts to Virginia* were a part of American history, as everyone felt. But he was only at home in the cause during its prophetic phase. As it entered the violent phase that preceded the war, he grew more and more quietistic and even broke with his old friend Garrison. There were limits beyond which a Quaker poet could not sincerely follow the path of action. This was the period of his prose papers, on Bunyan, Ellwood, Baxter, the notes on the Quakers of Cromwell's time, whom he defended against Carlyle's attacks. Of these the best was the essay on the old New Jersey Quaker, John Woolman, whom Lamb had urged his readers to "get by heart" and who had largely started the anti-slavery movement, —for Garrison was a disciple of one of Woolman's followers. Whittier's longest prose-piece, *Margaret Smith's Journal*, was a picture of the New England settlements in the days of the Salem witches. In a semi-archaic style, composed in tone and only less intense than Hawthorne's pictures, it conveyed the state of mind of the Pilgrim settlers with a haunting particularity. One saw the witchcraft working in the lonely cabins, the irons jumping into the pots, the tools flying about the rooms, the baskets dropping from the chimneys, the goodwives flocking to Boston to see the hangings, while the merry birds carolled in the trees and the white and yellow flowers besprinkled the banks. Through the bedevilled air, one caught the scent of the mayflower, the trailing arbutus, the symbol of a springtime innocence.

This was Whittier's element, and more and more the "wood-thrush of Essex" sang the summer pastorals and the songs of home that had so much of New England in them:

> Along the roadside, like the flowers of gold
> The tawny Incas for their gardens wrought,
> Heavy with sunshine droops the goldenrod,
> And the red pennons of the cardinal-flowers
> Hang motionless upon their upright staves.
> The sky is hot and hazy, and the wind,
> Wing-weary with its long flight from the south,
> Unfelt; yet, closely scanned, yon maple leaf
> With faintest motion, as one stirs in dreams,
> Confesses it. The locust by the wall
> Stabs the noon-silence with his sharp alarm.
> A single hay-cart down the dusty road
> Creaks slowly, with its driver fast asleep
> On the load's top. Against the neighbouring hill,
> Huddled along the stone-wall's shady side,
> The sheep show white, as if a snow-drift still
> Defied the dog-star. Through the open door
> A drowsy smell of flowers—grey heliotrope,
> And white sweet clover, and shy mignonette—
> Comes faintly in, and silent chorus lends
> To the prevailing symphony of peace.

In rudely vigorous ballads, he told the old legends of
the sea-coast, *Skipper Ireson's Ride, The Dead Ship of
Harpswell*. In his *Songs of Labour,* recited at working-
men's meetings for three generations, he glorified the
trades that he knew so well, shoemaking, lumbering, shipbuilding, droving, fishing; and his husking-poems and
corn-songs, his idylls of the village and the farm, *The
Old Burying-Ground, Telling the Bees, In School Days,
The Barefoot Boy, My Playmate,* redolent of sweet-fern
and clover and meadows ripe with corn, brought back
to countless readers the world of their childhood. They
saw once more the old roads winding, the gap in the wall,
the stepping-stones in the brook,—

> Glimpses of chimneys and gabled eaves,
> Through green elm arches and maple leaves.

The night-hawk's sullen plunge in the woods of New
Hampshire, the grey fort's broken wall on the coast of
Maine, the rocky capes, the heavy hay-boats crawling, the
salt sea-scents along the shore, the quilting-parties and
the winter sleigh-rides, the pumpkins and the huckle-
berry-thickets lived again in the songs of the "barefoot
boy."

CHAPTER XXII

NEW ENGLAND AT LARGE

UNDER a tree in front of his house at Marshfield, Daniel Webster lay in his open coffin, dressed in his blue coat with the brass buttons, his right hand over his breast, the sun full in his face. It was 1852, a warm, hazy October day. As far as one could see from the slopes of the hill, a multitude as of grasshoppers covered the land, and the fields were filled with wagons, chaises and sulkies, omnibuses and coaches. Over the silence of the vast assembly, one heard the cattle lowing in their barns.

To the remotest hamlet of the Androscoggin, New England hummed with tales of the fabulous man, how, when he knew that he was dying, he sent his faithful black servant William to hang the lantern at his shallop's mast-head and raise the colours there, saying, "I want to keep my flag flying and my light burning till I die." This was the grand style of a day that was passing, the epoch of the building of the Union, the confident young republic; and even the Abolitionists remembered that Webster, whether "Ichabod" or not, was a great New England worthy, perhaps the greatest, a masterpiece of Yankee blood and sinew whose life had been connected at every point with the interests and hopes of the people. He had thriven with their progress and their success, their farms, their mills, their schools. He symbolized their energy and triumph. Countless boys, like John Fiske, who lived at Middletown, Connecticut, felt that life had grown suddenly small and lonely and wondered how the sun could rise without Daniel Webster.

"I still live"—Webster's last phrase—was engraved on the Sheffield razors that hundreds of farmers used on Sunday mornings. New England was more alive than ever, in the towns, in the manufacturing centres, but farming life had begun to decline. The old farmers were dying out, or so it seemed to those who loved the country,—the men whose hoeing was a sleight-of-hand, who made their own ox-yokes and axe-helves, chopped their three cords of wood a day, knew every medicinal herb that grew in field or stream and knew how to select a piece of timber, chestnut or oak or walnut, that measured a given amount, cut it and score it and load it. These tamers of the wilderness were vanishing from the land. They were hewing their way to the West, along the Great Lakes, while the young men were turning to the cities, learning to pronounce their "ben" as "bin," and sometimes even "bean," and rising with the factories and the railroads.

As wealth advanced and the towns increased, the region grew more self-contemplative. Novelists were appearing here and there, picturing local manners, with an interest in social relations that was aroused by the spread of urban standards. One had to tolerate human nature first, a thing that Calvinism had scarcely encouraged, before one could find it amusing. Landscape-artists appeared in the train of the poets. Thomas Cole, Kensett, Church and others were painting up and down the coast, sketching in the Berkshires, tramping the White Hills and the Green Mountains, looking for the picturesque, catching the scent of Indian legends, following the lead of the landscape-poets; for Whittier, Longfellow, Lowell and Holmes had filled the country with associations. Every waterfall and stream and hilltop, Ossipee, Winnepesaukee, Hampton Beach, Chocorua's horn, the Kennebec, the Saco, every ancient house and rocky ledge was the theme of some ballad or sonnet that called for the

pencil. Summer visitors at Nahant noted in their journals the little scenes that pleased the landscape-painters,
the cows going over the beach at sunset on their way to
the cow-yards at Lynn, their red hides reflected in the
wet sand and lighting up the grey of the sky and the
surge. The influence of Ruskin had begun to spread, and
people spoke of the beauty of rocks and the sacredness
of colour. They compared the effects of changes of air in
the mountains and wondered just how much of the vague
and dreamy, in the matter of mist or spray, a scene had
to possess to be sublime. Intervale was a favourite spot,
where artists and tourists gathered. Connoisseurs of landscape from Boston or Hartford, parties from Worcester
and Burlington drove on the tops of stages or in private
buckboards through the Franconia Notch, observing
Mount Webster and Lafayette as if they were two pictures
in different styles by the hand of the same master. They
scrutinized Wachusett from Monadnock; they looked at
Franconia from the Pemigewasset. They studied the
slopes and the cliffs, the Flume and the Profile, an older
piece of sculpture than the Sphinx, climbed up to the
Nose or the Chin, botanized with Asa Gray in mind and
longed for a little talk with Agassiz. For Agassiz had made
these scenes exciting, even more exciting than Ruskin
made them. Speaking as a geologist, he had said that
New England was the oldest spot on the earth's surface.
They sprang out of their beds at the Mountain House
when the porter, walking through the halls, rang his big
bell and shouted, "Sunrise!"—assembling on the piazza
to see the Franconia Mountains at earliest dawn. They
tried the echo on Echo Lake and quoted Tennyson on
the "horns of Elfland." They noted the yellow fields of rye
and the beautiful cone of Mount Washington, yielding
harvests of colour.

The more the ancient rural life receded into the back-
ground of men's lives, the more it roused their feelings

of romance. The farm, the village ways, harsh enough in actuality, seemed, to the barefoot boys who had gone to New York or were making their fortunes in State Street, merry and jolly or softly sweet as Goldsmith's scenes of Auburn. They liked to remember their school-days, the wadded hoods, the knitted caps and mittens, the snow-bound evenings under the lamp, the games, the slates and pencils, rosy apples in the dish, nutting-time, coasting-time. Sawing wood in the frosty air had surely seemed less dull than adding figures. This was the theme of a hundred poems and stories that multiplied with time, as the farm became a universal symbol,—the farm, the weather-painted house and barn, the well-sweep, the or-chard, the sandy field surrounded by the woods, the small blue lake at the foot of the hill. No New England boy or man could ever forget the country, the cider-making days of old, the heaps of golden apples under the trees, the cider-mill worked by the plodding horse and all agush with autumn juices. The new generation of city-dwellers longed to be reminded of these rural scenes, and the popularity of the "household poets" rose with the exo-dus from the "household" setting, the homestead and the farm. This was the secret of Whittier's fame. He was the emblem of Thanksgiving, when two or three New Eng-landers gathered together, or a houseful of scattered un-cles and aunts and cousins, in far New York or on the Western plains. He brought back the painted autumn woodlands, the pumpkin pies of old, the succotash, the doughnuts and the chowder, the wild grapes, the tubs of maple sugar, the school-house, the old-fashioned winter that seemed so different from the modern winter because of the modern devices that had softened its rigours. The pioneers carried Whittier with them, as emigrant Scots-men carried the poems of Burns. *Snow-Bound* was their image of Pallas, the safeguard of their memories. It was the touchstone of their past.

For New England men were scattering far and wide. They were sowing schools and colleges over the West. In the South Sea Islands, in China, in Burma, they were planting Orthodox churches and mission-centres, writing their versions of the Bible in half the tongues of Asia. Some of the missionaries were learned men, two or three were great men.[1] They remembered Thanksgiving Day in the Himalayas and read their *Snow-Bound* on the Yang-tse River. New England seemed romantic in the distance, as Shanghai and Canton had seemed in their barefoot boyhood. The Rollo Books, to be sure, were not romantic, even to the remotest Yankee, redolent as they were of the barn-yard and pasture, the hired man, the chopping-block, early hours and earnest aspirations, nor were Elijah Kellogg's tales of boys in the good old days in the "State of Maine,"—as Maine men liked to call it, to remind the world that their State was no longer a "District."[2] If the fathers of Jacob Abbott's generation enjoyed the adventures of Rollo as much as their children, it was for a more substantial reason than that which drew them to the household poets; for Rollo was the model boy, in whom the model parent saw himself, the leading manufacturer in his earlier stages. Here the New England passion for self-improvement, as it was understood by the plainer folk, found its completest record. How to be dutiful, how to be conscientious, how to be genteel and well-informed, in order to be right on all occasions and able, especially, to set others right, this was Jacob Abbott's open secret. In Rollo, the reader be-

[1] Of the original writings of these New England missionaries,— Adoniram Judson, Hiram Bingham and others,—an admirable example is *The Middle Kingdom,* a survey of the Chinese Empire. The author, S. Wells Williams, wrote two Chinese dictionaries and was later professor of Chinese at Yale.

[2] Kellogg's *Lion Ben of Elm Island* and other books for boys, lifeless and wooden enough, are filled with authentic details of pioneer life on the coast of Maine.

held in all its phases the shaping of one of Webster's "solid men."

No one could have doubted Rollo's future. He was destined to rise in the world, with the other factory-owners and cotton-brokers who had left their ancestral farms in Vermont and Maine, the farms that seemed idyllic in their fancy as they drowsed in their office-chairs at the end of the day. "Ik Marvel's" books, *Reveries of a Bachelor* and *Dream-Life,* appealed to this nostalgic mood. One went to the city, accepted the ways of the world, made one's pile and married for advantage, while all the while, in one's heart of hearts, one clung to the simple, wholesome dreams of childhood. Such was the burden of these romances, composed in a style that suggested Irving and Lamb. The fields, the trees, the brooks, the sweetheart whose name one had cut on the bark of the birches were much more real than the noisy, ambitious life of the changing, bustling town, the sharp transactions of the business day, all blaze and vanity. Rain in the garret, as one recalled it, school-dreams, first love, fishing, boy-romance and first ambition were the stuff of the bachelor's reveries. That the bachelor who thought of nothing but marriage was the best of advocates of the married state, that all his dreams were "pipe-dreams" added to the charm of the make-believe. That he acquiesced in what he assumed to reject, the reader quickly gathered. These aspirations and visions were only "smoke," a comforting reassurance for the practical man who had left them far behind him. For the rest, Ik Marvel's enormous vogue showed how many people desired in books the opposite of what they desired in life. It was the busiest souls, those that were eager for all the latest inventions, who most rejoiced in this philosopher, this lover of old ways who never used a watch to measure time, preferred a burning taper to a gas-jet and lighted his cigar with coal and tongs.

But Ik Marvel,—Donald G. Mitchell,—was an engaging writer. His charm of style, his gentle bookishness, the slightly archaic flavour of his mind carried these youthful romances round the world; and long after men had ceased to read them, they were to survive as books for boys, who found their vague feelings, doubts and passions reflected in the bachelor's dreams. Mitchell's later books, *My Farm at Edgewood* and *Wet Days at Edgewood,* were of a hardier quality. Written during these years when rural life was falling into decay, when the city was attracting the ambitious and many farmers were moving West, they pictured the art of husbandry, its pleasures and its benefits, as Alcott was picturing it in his Concord essays, but with more system and practical knowledge. Mitchell, a graduate of Yale, a former consul at Venice and a landscape-gardener by avocation, who had laid out the grounds of Princeton College, had retired in poor health to a farm at New Haven, where he lived among his books. His mind was filled with garden associations, the literary farmers of Greece and Rome, Hesiod, Pliny, Virgil, the old British authors and country storytellers, from Piers Plowman to the Ettrick Shepherd; but he was a practical farmer, too, who longed to revive the dying interest in the oldest of New England occupations. He rebuked the shams of the farmer's life, the blinded front-parlour that was only entered once a month or so, to consult some gilt-bound dictionary, while it engrossed the best half of the house; and he made no false claims in regard to farming, its profits and advantages. His observations on bees and the care of cattle, on dairying, on the orchard and the garden, on the treatment of grapes, plums, apples, pears, on the dwarf trees that had to be fondled and humoured, on rural decoration, crops and markets were as shrewd and precise as Evelyn's, or Walton's observations on the angler's art, which, with Jeremy Taylor, Browne and Bunyan, had left their traces in his style. Ik Marvel was at his best in these country essays; and Elihu Burritt, the "learned blacksmith," also wrote eloquent papers on pastoral life. Burritt, who had left his Worcester forge and made a new career for himself as a philanthropic lecturer, had organized congresses of the Friends of Peace at Brussels, Paris, Frankfort and in England, where he served as American consul at Birmingham. With his farm at New Britain, Connecticut, always in mind, he visited farms in every corner of England, making careful notes and observations, in the hope of improving rural conditions at home. His *Walk from London to Land's End*, suggesting Cobbett's *Rural Rides*, was filled with unassuming information. Burritt's account of his visit to the Queen's dairy at Windsor Castle was a more rewarding travel-sketch than most of the current essays on the Coliseum. It was a model dairy, but Burritt thought the milk-pails were too heavy. In exchange for all he had learned, he would have liked to send the Queen some of the light, white-cedar, seamless pails which the farmers used in New England.

Alcott, Burritt, Mitchell, three Connecticut men,—for Burritt was born in New Britain, as Alcott was born at Wolcott, ten miles to the west,—were the three outstanding writers of their time on pastoral life and farming. Frederick Law Olmsted, who had begun to write in the fifties, was also a Connecticut man, the son of a Hartford merchant. This local development was not surprising, for Connecticut was more rural than Massachusetts, where town-life and shipping had occupied so many minds. But even in fertile Vermont, most pastoral of all the States, factories were appearing here and there, at Burlington, especially, on Lake Champlain, where the well-known minister to Turkey, the lawyer-scholar, George Perkins Marsh, who had been offered Sparks's chair at Harvard, carried on his studies and wrote his books. Marsh, a life-long friend of his fellow-Vermonter, the sculptor Hiram

Powers, and a class-mate at Dartmouth of Rufus Choate, a stalwart, inquisitive man and a notable linguist, had published a grammar of Icelandic and was known far and wide as a Scandinavian scholar when Longfellow was studying Swedish and Finnish. The library of Scandinavian books that he kept in his Burlington house was the most complete in the world outside the Scandinavian countries; and he had printed, in 1843, an essay called *The Goths in New England,* suggested by the Northern myths and sagas, that was one of the many forerunners of the modern "Nordic" movement. With none of the animus that later writers, the Houston Stewart Chamberlains and their kind, imported into the Nordic cult, Marsh traced all the virtues of New England to the Gothic element in its forbears. What was the age of the Puritans, which had given birth to New England, but that in which the Gothic strain in England had cast out the Roman element? The Goths were the noblest of races: it was their blood that flowed at Bunker Hill. Whatever the Anglo-Saxons possessed of intellectual power and moral grandeur, they owed to the Gothic mother. Their grasping ambition, their materialism, their spirit of exclusive selfishness were due to the Roman nurse.

This represented one of those germs of feeling, innocent at the outset, like Bronson Alcott's preference for the blond complexion, that sometimes flower in sinister ways. Marsh, who had a scientific mind, would have been horrified if he had foreseen the use that later anthropologists, in the interests of tribal factions, were to make of his Gothic theory. His object was to preach the ancient virtues and simplicities, not to make invidious distinctions. Besides, *The Goths in New England* was only a pamphlet. Marsh wrote several more important works, an entertaining study of *The Camel,* filled with curious and amusing lore gathered in his Oriental travels, two philological books on the English language, based on lec-

tures that he had delivered at Harvard, and the masterly
Man and Nature, better described by its later title, *The
Earth as Modified by Human Action.* This was to remain
a classical work in the field of modern geography, for
Marsh was one of the first to understand the relation between man and his physical setting. He was almost the
first to protest against the wanton way in which man
disturbed the harmonies of nature. It is true that, long
before, a writer who remained anonymous contributed
to Miss Peabody's *Æsthetic Papers* an essay, *Vegetation
about Salem,* describing the reckless fashion in which the
American forests were being destroyed. "Posterity must
feel the consequences" was the moral of this unregarded
paper, a moral that no one drew till the "conservation"
movement of later years. Marsh was the prophet of this
movement. No one had written with such breadth of
knowledge of man as a geological agent, who can up-
build or destroy his home, the earth. No one had shown
before how man had played the destroyer and what he
could do to reëstablish the partnership between himself
and nature.

Marsh, who died in Italy, at Vallombrosa,—he was
the first American minister to the newly-established kingdom,—was the chief contributor of Vermont to the "literature of knowledge." To the "literature of power"
Vermont made a modest contribution, a novel that belonged to the school of Cooper and was destined to be
read almost as long as Cooper. Daniel Pierce Thompson,
the author of *The Green Mountain Boys,* was a lawyer
and judge at Montpelier, where he edited *The Green
Mountain Freeman.* One saw him shuffling through the
streets in his battered carpet-slippers, on his way to the
newspaper-office where he had printed his book; for, although he was a local dignitary and lived in a clapboard
Parthenon, he was a jolly old sloven whose greatest pleasure was to go hunting and fishing with the boys. They all

knew that he had been born in Charlestown, in the
shadow of Bunker Hill; but at the age of five, in 1800, he
had been brought to Vermont, and there was not a worthy in the State who knew as much about it as the judge.
He had grown up on a farm near Montpelier, where he
had watched the building of the State House, and had
seen the youthful commonwealth emerge from its old
border life, which resembled that of Cooper's New York
and the Scotland of some of the Waverley novels, into a
thriving republic. He had gone through Middlebury College and studied law in Virginia, where he had met and
talked with Jefferson on the grounds of the university he
was building. As they stood together, the old President,
who was almost eighty, took a chisel out of the hand of
one of his Italian stone-cutters and showed him how to
turn the volute of a capital; then he leaped on his horse
and galloped away. Thompson was full of these tales of
the men of the Revolution. He had wandered all over
Vermont, with his horse and his fishing-rod and gun,
shooting wolves and catching trout, chatting at farmhouse doors, talking with the pioneer settlers, listening
to yarns about Ethan Allen. A born antiquarian, like
Scott, a lover of ballads and folklore, he kept careful
notes of these conversations. Every client of the country
lawyer gave him an anecdote or a bit of gossip.

In these little towns of Vermont, surrounded by rolling
pastures and groves of maples, far from the bustling sea-
coast, the eighteenth-century mind lived quietly on. The
new-fangled Boston books seldom reached Montpelier,
and country judges and editors read Pope and Fielding as
if the good old world had never changed. Thompson, a
born story-teller, although he never became a professional
author, wrote his first book in the manner of Smollett.
First and last, he wrote many books, all of them, save
one, surpassingly dull, and all, even the best, amateurish;
for he had few relations with other authors and scarcely

knew the meaning of criticism. Like most unprofessional writers, he never knew where his strength lay and constantly tried his hand in directions where he was foredoomed to fail. But he had not read Scott and Cooper for nothing, he had steeped himself in the legends of Vermont and, if he was a man of one book, this book, which he largely wrote on his father's farm, sitting under a pine-tree, was a most engaging performance. *The Green Mountain Boys* was a home-grown product, if ever literature saw one, as unpretentious as a log-cabin, but it was built on such a good model that no faults of style or execution counted in the final result. It was the classic picture of Vermont, in the days of its struggle for independence, first from New York and afterwards from England; and the picture was undoubtedly true in its atmosphere and feeling. One saw the beaver-hatted mountaineers, the bold, high-hearted borderers, handsome and fearless, Seth Warner and Ethan Allen, threading their way through the greenwood, like Robin Hood and his band, bearing the noble buck on their shoulders; one heard their whistle echoing through the sylvan glades. One saw the fond and spirited young ladies, imprisoned in block-houses and woodland cabins, ready for brave escapes and enchanting elopements; and over all one breathed the fragrant air of pine, fir and balsam, a world of sparkling lakes and flashing trout-streams, youth, adventure, freedom and true romance.

This was a Yankee tale as brisk and wholesome as any mountain-ballad. It was a border-song in prose, and these were the days when the Yankee ballads throve as never later. Catch a "real, green, live Yankee," as Father Taylor liked to say, and you always caught a man who could sing a song, especially on the sea-coast. In Maine, among the old fish-houses, where they still used words that one found only in Chaucer, there were men who could sing all night, seven score songs in succession, and count up to two or three hundred. On the Isles of Shoals, near Portsmouth, where "Old Bob," the spectre, one of Captain Kidd's men, haunted the coves and the wharves, and Celia Thaxter, the lighthouse-keeper's daughter, lived at Appledore, one might have heard an old shoaler, who had fought at New Orleans in 1815, singing by the hour, while he sat bent forward with his arms on his knees, or played on a cracked old fiddle, with his wrinkled eyelids screwed tight together. Where had his queer tunes come from? They were like the creaking and groaning of masts or the whistling of the wind in the cordage of a clipper.[3] *Lord Bateman* was a favourite with these singers, who added their own variations, or the deeds of "Brave Wolfe," or

> With sixteen brass nineteens the Lion did growl,
> With sixteen brass twenties the Tiger did howl.

There were minstrels and rural singers all over New England, and often a well-known poem became an anonymous ballad. Such was Walter Mitchell's *Tacking Ship off Shore*. This was adopted by the fishermen, who had never heard of the author. Dr. Holmes's *Ballad of the Oysterman* was sung up and down the coast, with hundreds of alterations and elaborations.

Aside from Thompson's tale of Vermont, few New England novels of the moment could have been described as brisk or wholesome. *The Wide, Wide World* of Susan Warner was a swamp of lachrymosity. It was a malarial book. So was *The Lamplighter,* by Maria Cummins, the story of another Cinderella, which had, however, something vigorous in it that *The Wide, Wide World* totally lacked. One felt and saw the Boston slums,—for slums had appeared in Boston with a vengeance,—the street-lamps and the snow, suggesting Dickens's London. What was real in both these books, as pictures of their time,

---

[3] See Celia Thaxter's *Among the Isles of Shoals.*

was the pervasive presence of religion.[4] Little Ellen was a prig, but when she was dazzled by the array of Bibles, of which her mother had promised her one, "so that her wits were ready to forsake her," and when she spent her evenings singing hymns, and "hymn succeeded hymn, with fresh and varied pleasure," she was behaving as Harriet Beecher Stowe certainly behaved at sixteen; and Mrs. Stowe had never been a prig. Her large, frank, fiery, generous nature had nothing in it of the goody-goody; and hymns, in the passionate world in which she lived, were as much a part of the atmosphere as ballads ever were in time of war. All the New England poets were writing them, following Dwight and Barlow, and the best American hymns that have ever been written appeared when Mrs. Stowe was in her heyday.[5] In the two hundred years that had passed since Governor Winslow refreshed himself "with singing of psalms, making joyful melody," New Englanders had exulted in hymns. Mrs. Stowe, as a child in Litchfield, had listened with ecstasy to the "fuguing tunes," those billowy compositions which they sang in church, when the four parts of the choir took up the song, and went racing round after one another, each singing a different set of words, till at length, by some inexplicable magic, they all came together again, and sailed smoothly out into a sea of harmony. She had looked with wonder from side to side when treble, tenor, counter and bass were thus roaring and foaming, and it verily seemed as if the psalm were about to be wrecked among the

[4] The religious note entirely dominated R. T. S. Lowell's *The New Priest in Conception Bay*, a novel of Newfoundland, with a few good scenes of sea-coast life. The author, an Episcopal clergyman, was a brother of James Russell Lowell.

[5] E.g., Holmes's "Lord of all being, throned afar," Whittier's "Dear Lord and Father of mankind," E. H. Sears's "Calm on the listening air of night" and "It came upon the midnight clear." Samuel Francis Smith, who, at twenty-four, wrote "America" in half an hour, produced almost one hundred and fifty hymns.

breakers. And then, to her delighted sense, every verse emerged whole and uninjured from the storm.

Harriet Beecher Stowe was one of the volcanic souls whom the Abolitionist movement brought to the front. As the daughter of Lyman Beecher, she had lived through the days of her father's "Revival." She had studied at Hartford, at her sister's school, where Catherine Beecher wrote her well-known essay refuting Jonathan Edwards on the Will, and, learning French and Italian there, she had answered with a "yes" her father's question, "Do you feel that, if the universe should be destroyed, you could be happy with God alone?" At twelve, however, hearing of Byron's death, she had wandered off to a lonely hill-side, laid herself down in a field of daisies, looked up at the sky and wondered about Byron's soul. The vehemence and intensity of Byron's feeling fascinated all the Beechers, who felt the Calvinistic inheritance in him, and Harriet, who adored *The Corsair,* had sung "Fare thee well" with the other schoolgirls, who felt that they would never have let Byron go. Many years later, in her *Vindication of Lady Byron,* in which she turned against the poet, she showed how deep these early impressions were. Her father, who did not approve of novels, made an exception of Scott, whom his children had to read; and Harriet found the *Arabian Nights,* in the family garret, in a barrel of sermons. She dreamed of some heroic cause, some mission or crusade, that would call out her powers of devotion.

She had visited in Boston, as a girl, when Lyman Beecher, at the Park Street church, had pelted the Unitarians with his sermons, and had followed him in the rout to Cincinnati. Boston was past redemption by any Connecticut method, but the "capital of the West" received him gladly. He preached revival sermons all the way. It was there that Harriet married Calvin Stowe, a teacher in her father's seminary, "rich in Greek, Arabic and Hebrew" but as poor as other missionaries in everything else. There, during a cholera epidemic that was like the black plague of the Middle Ages,—nine thousand people in the city died in three months, and there were ten thousand cases of smallpox,—she wrote a tract that was widely read, *Earthly Care a Heavenly Discipline*. Of care she had enough herself, but there were compensations in Cincinnati. The town was half made up of New England people, with a literary club and a magazine. She began to write stories and essays, often on the kitchen table, surrounded by pots and pans, with half a dozen children asking questions. These stories, elementary enough, paler than Miss Sedgwick's, pleased a circle of readers for whom the visible world had begun to exist and the simplest observations were all-sufficient. But Dr. Stowe knew that she had a power of which these tales gave little evidence. He told her that she could form the mind of the West.

It happened that her father's seminary was an Abolitionist centre. Runaway slaves who appeared there were kept and passed along to the north, and just across the river, in Kentucky, were large slave-plantations. Mrs. Stowe spent several days on one of these plantations, which she afterwards described as Colonel Shelby's; and, although she had never lived in the South, she heard so much about it, and met so many Southern men and women, that she was prepared to picture it as no Southern writer had ever done. The moment for this came later, when she moved to Brunswick, Maine, where her husband was asked to teach in Bowdoin College. The Stowes lived there in a house where Longfellow had lodged as a student. The Fugitive Slave Law had just been passed, and letters came pouring in upon Mrs. Stowe describing its tragic consequences, the separations of husbands and wives, the scattering of mothers and their children. Her mind became suddenly incandescent. She felt she had an apostolic mission to put an end to slavery once for all; she felt that it was not herself but God who wrote the tale of *Uncle Tom's Cabin*. If this book was not the cause of the Civil War, as Lincoln said later, it was at least one of the major causes, for it blocked the operation of the Fugitive Slave Law. As a literary event, it was the greatest since Prescott's *Ferdinand and Isabella*. It was a world-event, in fact. Macaulay, Heine and George Sand reviewed it. Three Paris newspapers published it at once, and Uncle Tom's Cabins rose all over Europe, as restaurants, creameries and bazaars. It appeared in thirty-seven languages, and three times over in Welsh, into which Scott and Dickens had never been translated; and it sent Heine back to his Bible and made such an impression on Tolstoy in Russia that, when he came to write *What is Art?*, he took it as an example of the highest type, with Dostoievsky's *House of the Dead,* and much of Victor Hugo. In all the history of the printed book, the Bible alone had appeared in so many versions.

Was Tolstoy right in his opinion? On the whole, yes; and this was not only because of the moral force that carried *Uncle Tom* around the world. Everything in Mrs. Stowe was large, her experience, her humour, her feeling for justice, her passion for the realities of human nature. Her mind had the swing and rhythm of the great story-tellers, like Dickens, Cooper, Scott and Victor Hugo, and she showed in her later novels, *The Pearl of Orr's Island* and *The Minister's Wooing,* how little she needed a moral thesis to bring all her gifts into play. "A work is great," the English writer C. E. M. Joad remarks, "when it has ceased to matter that it is bad," and as Dickens was great enough to be "bad," so was Mrs. Stowe, who was also of the technically rough-and-ready. For her characters were not only real, boldly conceived and presented, but they were involved in situations of a crucial and primary kind. She had a panoramic eye and a just and truthful feeling for human relations that carried her out of the sphere of propaganda. There was no touch of cant in her moral feeling, no disposition to blame the South; she made one like the Southerners more than ever, and she chose a native Vermonter, Simon Legree, to symbolize all that was worst in a national evil. Removed from the atmosphere in which it was written, *Uncle Tom's Cabin* remained a great folk-picture of an age and a nation. For one saw the Quaker colonies in Indiana and the far-away farms of Vermont bound up with the slave-planta-tions and the Mississippi, the camp-meetings, the Negro life; and the characters, St. Clare and Miss Ophelia, Uncle Tom, Topsy and Simon Legree, were drawn with a force that made them types and symbols. Mrs. Stowe's New England novels, written with the same rude strength, established a school and a method. It was her New Eng-land, not Hawthorne's, that gave later writers their point of departure. She set the stage for Sarah Orne Jewett. But the final proof of Mrs. Stowe's power was that she created the Southern novel,—as distinguished from the Southern romance,—and that, three generations later, Southern writers still had to reckon with her picture.

CHAPTER XXIII

CONCORD IN THE FIFTIES

EMERSON HAD revisited England in 1847. Carlyle had urged him to lecture there, and he had spent nine months, in London, Manchester and Scotland, talking and taking notes. In his pocket he carried a compass. "I like to hold the god in my hands," he said.

He had reached a solstice in his life, one of those dead points when one requires some foreign force in order to avoid stagnation. He had travelled for a whip for his top, and his top had come home spinning. Never had the "parlour Erebus" encountered so many first-rate thinkers and writers, eupeptic studying-mills, cast-iron men, whose powers of intellectual endurance compared with those of most Americans as a steam-hammer with a music-box. He had always wished to measure his valour by his ability to cope with giants, who aroused one's own central courage of insight. He wished to observe the hygiene, the gymnastic, their experience suggested and approved; and he longed to be challenged and frightened, if anyone could frighten him, to put his own thoughts to the proof. In his depressed hours, when his mind was ebbing,—

> Doomed to long gyration
> In the sea of generation,—

America seemed of a village littleness; and it was hard to go beyond one's public. Carlyle, Macaulay, De Quincey, Faraday, Tyndall, all of whom he had met and who had heard him, had roused in him anew the fire of emulation. Tyndall said that he owed to *Nature* all that he had done in the world, and Emerson found that in Oxford he had stirred and heartened Clough and Matthew Arnold, who had been bewildered by Carlyle. He had visited Wordsworth again at Rydal Mount and had spent a month with Clough in Paris, observing the first movements of the revolution of 1848. He had come home filled with fresh ideas. Better still, the need to express himself so that a foreign audience would understand him, the challenge of so many sceptical hearers had led him to define his thoughts more closely. His style was becoming more and more concrete; the Franklin in his nature was growing more apparent, the wisdom of the man who had dealt with men. He was preparing to write his finest books, *English Traits* and the great *Conduct of Life*. Best of all, much as he liked the English, he felt as never before the hope and faith of America. He had returned with joy to the Concord woods and pastures.

> Caesar of his leafy Rome,
> There the poet was at home.

Henry Thoreau, meanwhile, had gone to live in his father's house, the new yellow house on Concord Main Street. He had his den in the attic. There he kept his collections, the birds' nests, mosses, plants and arrowheads. His books were arranged on shelves he had built himself, using the driftwood on the river-banks. Concord was the old coat he wore, his morning-robe and study-gown, his walking-dress and suit of ceremony. If he had had to spend all his days confined to a corner of this attic, like the big spider on the rafter, he would have felt at home there. The world would have been just as large to him, as long as he had his thoughts.

He cultivated poverty like sage, the best of the garden herbs. What poverty and obscurity meant to him, no one could ever have told,—a more than princely leisure, a poetic leisure, without care, without engagements, fancy-free. How many springs and summers he had lived, how many autumns and winters, with nothing to do but to live them, imbibing the nutriment they had to yield! Two years with the flowers, for instance, observing when they opened. He could afford to spend a whole fall watching the changing tints of the elms and the maples. He could record the drama of the month of March, when the woodchucks' holes were still choked with leaves and he saw the bluebird, the robin and the wild geese arriving.

Poverty had given him all this wealth. The leisure to spend a day, whenever he chose, walking twenty or thirty miles, or voyaging about the river in December, when the drops froze on his oars, pleased with the silvery chime of the icicles against the stems of the button-bushes. Leisure to visit his birches and tap them on an April afternoon, while he sat on a rock in the warm, sunny swamp, waiting for his vessels to be filled, watching the great black butterflies, with their buff-edged wings, dancing and fluttering about him. Leisure for a day in Gowing's swamp, where the hairy huckleberries grew and he paddled like Socrates, barefoot, in the Ilyssus; leisure to note the temperature of the springs and ponds, or look for Indian soapstone pots or mouse-holes in some hollow, or watch the flying squirrels by the hour, skimming their way like hawks between and around the trees; leisure to stop at a grist-mill and observe the cobweb-tapestry, engaging the miller by questions while his eye sought the cobwebs on the miller's hat. Leisure for all his pursuits and contemplations, and more than amply paid for. Did some of his neighbours think that he sat on his father's shoulders? They should have seen him in the family work-shop, taking his turn, and more than his turn, at the pencils. It was he who saved the business when the German pencils threatened to drive their own out of the market. He solved the problem, bought the German clay, contrived machines for cutting the hardened paste and drilling the blocks of wood. He even supplied the Harpers of New York with their plumbago for electrotyping.

Across the way dwelt Ellery Channing. He had moved from Ponkawtassett Hill and bought an old house for himself on Main Street. He was living all alone there, with only his dog for company, to stir up the air of the room when it grew too deadly quiet,—for he experienced awful solitudes. He had fallen out with his family. He continued to write his verses, Wordsworthian meditations, winter wood-scenes, with all his old whimsical zest, and he had published his *Conversations in Rome*. This was a dialogue between an artist, a Catholic and a critic, for Ellery had visited Italy in 1845 and had almost been converted to the Roman church. He had something to say about Italian farming, as well as Salvator Rosa and Montaigne, and he was the Catholic in the "conversations." He had found himself murmuring prayers with the best of them. But for all his frequent petulance with Concord, he said the New England folk were his own flesh and blood; and he and Henry Thoreau were thicker than ever. Ellery was the rustic rhymer who had walked to Walden, after Henry deserted his hut, and hung up the verses on the wall; and Henry had actually seen a man buying a copy of Ellery's poems at Little and Brown's book-shop in Boston. Alcott was living in town, more or less, though he often came out to see his friends. The ever fresh and jubilant Alcott had built a summer-house on Emerson's lawn, rejecting the angular timber that others used, preferring the rustic branch. He had even added a second story, hung with beautiful mosses. It was a philosophic, a Euclidian structure, rather metaphysical than real, designed to exhibit the nature and value of curves. For it seemed, when Alcott walked in the woods, as if nature had looked for his coming and grown all his materials in the brush, along the lines of the fence-rows, where the young pines, bent by the snow or the axe, described, in their efforts to regain their natural rectitude, every graceful form of curve or spiral that he required for his rustic works. They lent themselves to varied combinations. Others might compose their poems and pictures. Alcott composed arbours. None knew better than he the romance of gardens. Why should not Emerson's garden have an additional touch that recalled the Garden of the Hesperides?

Henry, lending Alcott a hand, and sitting on the ridgepole, had felt that he was "nowhere, doing nothing." Henry was a practical man, all for straight lines; he had no use for the "natural curve" in branches, men or women. No matter, Alcott also was a man who knew what nature meant him to do with her, a Virgil, a White of Selborne and a Yankee settler, wrapped in a single frame. He loved sage, too, sovereign sage, excellent for longevity, and often spoke of Pliny's good housewife who went to her herb-garden for her seasonings, instead of spending money at a spice-shop, and thus preserved the health of her family, the while she saved her purse. He had his knock-down answer for anyone who questioned his qualifications, "If Pythagoras came to Concord, whom would he ask to see?" His only fault was a lack of worldly wisdom,—the truthful, candid, always magnanimous man. There were precious goods on his shelves, as Emerson said, but he had no show-window, and whether you were a child or a beggar, a lunatic or a Boston gentleman, you got the same reply from Bronson Alcott.

His chief preoccupations were the same as ever, keeping his journal and holding his Conversations.[1] The journal brimmed over with his thoughts, many of them thin, diffuse, abstract, others nutty and pregnant, phrased

---

[1] Alcott's manuscript journal, fifty volumes or more, is still preserved in Concord. Louisa Alcott had it bound in stout black leather.

in a rare, flowing, antique style, on rural affairs and recreation, friends, books, philosophy, childhood, literary
courtesy, hospitality, with a store of apt quotations. The
habit of journalizing had been for him a lesson in the
art of composition. Alcott no longer wrote in the vague,
inadequate fashion of the "Orphic Sayings." He had
learned to expand and express these tight conceits. He
had slept on his writing and reviewed it on his walks, and
Concord Days and *Tablets* were the fine result. Time had
ripened his life and mellowed its fruits. His Conversations
in Boston were difficult still, for there he rode his hobbies, but Emerson and Thoreau went in from Concord,
and Garrison sometimes came, with Theodore Parker,
Lowell, Elizabeth Peabody, James Freeman Clarke, various travelling foreigners. He spoke on "Self-knowledge"
or "The Times." He began by reading aloud a poem,
George Herbert's *Man,* or some of his own philosophical
verses, selected from the red-covered note-book. Then he
unfolded his favourite doctrines, diet, complexion, race,
the "demonic man." A real demonic man appeared one
evening, with blazing eyes and swarthy face, the kind of
man who lives on beef and brandy, smokes black cigars
and possibly builds a railroad. This somewhat embarrassed the sage; and objectors sometimes came, as if for
the purpose of throwing him off his track. Another
trouble-maker was Theodore Parker, who quoted Scrip-
ture as he walked away, "The multitude separated, and
no man knew wherefore they came together." What
could one do with these dogmatists who took delight in
shooting balloons and who asked a man for proofs when
revelations were his stock-in-trade? Would they catechize
the sybil in her cave? Would they ask the Delphic oracle
for a demonstration? No doubt, if they lived on Beacon
Street or if they preached in a Unitarian pulpit.

　　Alcott was not himself in these urban surroundings.
He was at home in the country, amid the woods and wa-

ters, under the sun and stars, turning about his grounds, sauntering by a brook-side. He was a pagan after Henry's fashion, much as he loved good manners. He was very different from Margaret Fuller, who, after finding her soul in the world of affairs, had just lost her life at the age of forty. Henry had hastened down to Fire Island, on behalf of the Concord circle, to investigate the shipwreck. Margaret had sailed with many misgivings, and the voyage from Italy had been mismanaged. The little boat had broken up at once, for the hold was laden with Italian marble and Hiram Powers's statue of Calhoun. Charles Sumner, who had lost a brother, had already arrived and left, with William Henry Channing. They found Margaret's desk on the beach, with some of her papers in it, a carpet-bag of the Marquis Ossoli's, the body of the child. Nothing else, no trace of the tragic lovers, no trace of the great history of the siege of Rome.

The book was a loss. The Brownings and Landor agreed that no Italian had known Mazzini better, and Ossoli's family connections had given Margaret the other side of the story. No doubt, the substance of the book, however,—*Italy in 1848–'49,*—appeared in Margaret's letters to *The Tribune,* soon to be collected in *At Home and Abroad,* letters that brought the siege before her readers as if they had seen it for themselves. She was a journalist in grain and fibre, none more brilliant, none more sympathetic, but scarcely a historian or a critic; an energetic, perceptive soul, not a great writer, but certainly a great woman writing. This was the fact that her friends wished to proclaim. Carlyle, who had been so kind to her in London, had summed up her qualities. He had small faith in his wife's friend Mazzini. He thought that Italy needed an Oliver Cromwell; he would have been delighted with Mussolini. No matter what happened in the back parlour, provided there was "order" in the front. But he said that Margaret's courage was "high and clear," and that she had "a truly heroic mind, altogether unique, so far as I know, among the writing women of this generation."

The logic of events had sent her home. Mazzini's cause had failed, and thought and speech like hers were contraband in Italy. No matter, she had lived and left her record, in England, France and Rome. She had had her full taste of the "artist life," so long and happily dreamed of. She had found *The Dial* widely read in England; Chopin had played for her; she had met George Sand. She had had her say about the American artists who were flocking to Rome and Florence, their minds filled with American subjects, of whom she had written with understanding. She had described the American tourists, the colonists and foreign residents, the servile types, the braggarts and "booby truants,"—"Jonathan in the sprawling state,"—as well as the thinking Americans whom she admired; and at last she had found the cause for which she had been waiting, to lavish all her powers of devotion, Mazzini's "God and the People." She had met Mazzini in London, where she told him that the best friends a man of ideas could have were necessarily women. How could Carlyle have comprehended him?—Carlyle, with his old Scandinavian berserker mind, following its impulse as a hawk its prey. Mazzini had taken Margaret at her word and put her on her mettle. She had shared in the drama that she had longed to witness, a heroic passage of history, a nation rising up like Milton's eagle, mewing its mighty youth: Italy cured of its hasty boasts and meaner adulation, learning to prize and seek realities. She had thought of her own America, stupid with the lust of gain and the sloth of slavery, the criminal greed of the Mexican War, the aims of its politicians petty and selfish, its literature venal and frivolous. In Europe, a nobler spirit struggled, a spirit that animated and cheered her own. She had heard earnest words of faith and love and seen the deeds of brotherhood, all that made up the America of which she dreamed. She could not distrust her country deeply. America was not dead, it was only sleeping. She had thought of the Abolitionists, whom she had found so tedious, so narrow and so rabid in their tone. They had their lofty motives. There was something eternal in their desire and life; and they, too, understood Mazzini. In the end, she had had her great romance, just as it might have occurred in the novels that once enchanted her,—lived those high, tumultuous hours, married her Count de Rudolstadt, played the part of Countess Emily Platen. It had led to sorrow, anxiety, toil and death.

In Concord, as in Rome, they had understood her; and Emerson made haste to write a memoir that would convey his feeling for her, an ode in prose outrivalling the ode that Landor wrote in verse. She was the Ugly Duckling who had died too soon to counteract the legend of the barnyard; but the poets and the novelists never forgot her. The Boston Aspasia who had corrupted her sex by means of intellectual orgies lived again in Hawthorne's pages and Holmes's *Elsie Venner*.[2] Meanwhile, in Concord, even the farmers were writing books, Minot Pratt, for one, who was carrying on botanical studies for an ambitious work on the local flora. In 1855, another writer settled in the village, the future Boswell of the Concord worthies. Frank B. Sanborn, the schoolmaster, rented a room from Ellery Channing and took his meals at Mrs. Thoreau's, spending an evening every week at the Manse, reading Greek aloud with Mrs. Ripley; and no one could have said, in years to come, that this long, lank

[2] Hawthorne did not admit that he had drawn his Zenobia from Margaret Fuller, with certain touches suggested by Fanny Kemble, but no one ever questioned the fact. That Dr. Holmes had Margaret Fuller in mind is evident from a passage in *Elsie Venner*. It was natural that she left some sort of trace in almost every imaginative mind of the time.

worthy with the rosy cheeks did not know the Concord he
wrote about. He was a born antiquarian; nothing pleased
him more than to pore over old family papers; and Mrs.
Ripley showed him the dusty records preserved in the
"prophets' chamber,"—old Dr. Ripley's memoranda
about half the souls who had lived in the village. Sanborn, with his hero-worshipping instincts, soon knew
more about the Concord people than most of them had
ever known themselves. He was preparing himself for the
many books he wrote in later years. His school became a
Concord institution. He followed, in a measure, the
methods of Alcott, his special friend and master, taking
the children for walks in the woods and fields, with picnics, plays and boating parties, and skating carnivals at
Walden Pond. First or last, he had among his pupils
Emerson's son, Hawthorne's son, two daughters of John
Brown, Horace Mann's sons and two of Henry James's.

It was Sanborn who, a few years later, brought John
Brown to Concord, where the anti-slavery cause had
many friends. Sanborn, moreover, was a member of the
Walden Pond Association, for so the "Sunday walkers"
were called in the village,—Emerson, Alcott, Thoreau
and one or two others who never sat in pews. One had to
pass a stringent test to belong to this society, severer than
the Athanasian creed. There were only two or three persons with whom Thoreau, for one, felt that he could afford to walk, his hours were so precious. Was Emerson
less exacting? He was only more polite. In the presence
of cranks and bores, he masked his irritation. Henry
trampled on them; and when, by chance, a bore shadowed him on one of his walks, he took every ditch at a
run, hoping to shake the shadow off. He detested these
mere strenuous pliers of legs, these broachers of mighty
arguments who spoiled one's day and talked the bobolinks under. With his long swinging gait, his eyes on the
ground, his hands clasped behind him, his legs like steel

springs and his arms as powerful as a moose's antlers, thrusting the brush aside; with his wary glance, his earnest energy, as if, on the lookout for squirrels, rabbits and foxes, he was in the thick of a day's battle, Henry was no man to trifle with. He was impatient even with the farmers, who were always standing on their good behaviour, moralizing and philosophizing, instead of giving a brisk report of their crops. He preferred the sportsmen and loafers, or anyone who had seen a painted tortoise, or taken a good look at a flying lark, or who shared his feeling about the encroaching railroad, that seventh abomination. Henry had grown so formidable, in fact, that the village-folk had ceased to call him Henry, especially now that he was earning a living, by lecturing, writing, surveying, by means that anyone could understand. He was Mr. Thoreau, the surveyor, who gave you fair warning to keep your distance.

No use to attempt to join the Sunday walkers unless you were able to meet the test. Were the woods for you full of solicitations, were there forms and colours everywhere, powers on every hand, locked away from ordinary Christians, to which your wit afforded you the key? The churches on the square were ready to welcome the dry souls whom life, as Ellery said, had put away on the shelf like so many rinds of cheese. You had to be up to the mark to keep pace with the Walden associates,—Emerson, twirling his stick, while he drew rhymes from the upper air, Ellery touching off his sudden fuses, dressed in his red flannel shirt, suggesting an indolent bandit, Thoreau with his taut mind and wound-up muscles, ready to crush idle talkers with a merciless phrase. He tied his boots in a hard lover's-knot, while Ellery, half the time, went about with his shoe-strings dangling, or even wore no laces,—just as he wrote his poems, loosely strung, to the scandal of his conscientious friends. He should have been compelled to write in Latin, Henry said and Emerson agreed; then he would have used a dictionary and written firmly and clearly, instead of in the dangling-shoe-string style, the sublimo-slipshod style, as Henry called it. But Ellery would not pay the going-price, he would not stoop to conquer. Henry, as they walked, pulled out his note-book and jotted down his careful observations. Ellery half-heartedly followed suit, scrawled away for a moment, then drew some hasty sketch and stuffed the book away in his pocket again. He had no use for the "definite" and left the "facts" to Henry. Only the "ideal" was good enough for him.

No matter, he was a virtuous walker. He had eyes for every line and every colour, for every fleet of yellow butterflies, ears for every sound, the wood-thrush pitching his notes in the pine-alleys, the oven-bird beating his brass in the heated shades of noon, the partridge's feathery roll-call, the gossiping dialogue of the brown thrashers, a comforting sound, this latter, enough to cure the heartache of a world, on one of those summer days when the sky bends over a walker with a face like Jerusalem Delivered. A fit companion, Ellery, for a dozen poets, or two, at least, Emerson and Henry, or any combination of two or three. What was the programme for the afternoon? A stroll to Conantum, perhaps, or White Pond, or to Round Hill in the Sudbury meadows. Thus the talk flowed.—We'll stop at Duganne's spring and get a drink. —Or suppose we go to Flint's.—Agreed.—That country with its high summits is good for breezy days. And we must not forget the mountain view from the Three Friends' Hill, beyond the pond. Across the pastures, in any case, the broad, healthy new-springing pastures, ornamented with apple-tree pyramids, the pastoral architecture of the cow, and the waving saxifrage and the delicate houstonia, the dark belts of pines stalking over the landscape.—The air is fairly spotted today with the rigmarole of the bobolink, buttery, scattery, wittery, pittery, a few yellow, a few black feathers, a summer-warming song.—Soaring over the tallest pine, the fierce hen-harrier screams and hisses.—And see the peach-trees yonder. Montaigne took pains to be made a citizen of Rome. I should much prefer to have the freedom of a peach-orchard.—Or of an accommodating trout-stream, such as Goodwin loves, the one-eyed Ajax.—What do you think of the farmhouse we are passing? Aren't the clapboards needlessly stiff? Is there not too little ornamentation? In Italy and Switzerland and England, the picturesque seems to spring from the soil, in the shape of barns and buildings, as naturally as the trees and flowers. —Moderate your words, dear Gilpin. Utility lies at the bottom of our village architecture. The structure springs from that. The simple edifice you see, created out of white-pine boards, a mere casing of shingles and clapboards, as it appears to you, appears to its owner, who built it and lives in it, anything but ugly or unpicturesque. It fits him like a shell. Comfort, economy, use, a dry, warm cellar, a sweet, airy milk-room, a barn with its cellars and accommodations, all in the solidest style,—these matters make the study of the farmer.—I say that beauty must have an equal place with utility, if not the first place. Your farmer shirks architecture and landscape-gardening, with his one leg in the barn and his other in the kitchen, and the compost-heap in the midst. And his highest ambition is to have a patent-leather top to his carriage.—Go to, you libel my jolly countryman. He is no such thieving rat as this. O brother Gilpin, hearken ere you die. Those prejudices of yours for Inigo Jones have left you too little sympathy for the industrious yeoman of New England. He stands like a king in the midst of the general penury.—Have you read those old farmers Cato and Varro? "Study to have a great dung-heap. Carefully preserve the dung. Break it up fine." There speaks the New England yeoman. If you would understand him, read this manual of the Roman farmer, how they got their living, what they did from day to day. —But, come, here's the brook. Let me rest a fraction on the bridge.—I am your well-wisher in that. The manners of water are beautiful, playing its sweet games, all circles and dimples and lively gleaming motions.—The brook, the petted darling of the meadows, wild minstrel of an ancient song, poured through the vales forever.—And those eddying pools, where the old experienced trout sleeps on his oars.—Rest a little longer here.—Are not those gulls yonder, gleaming like spots of intense white light far away on the meadow?—And observe that ridic- ulous colt, the colour of sugar-gingerbread, set upon his four long legs and swishing a bald tail, laughing at us men-folks nibbling our crackers and herring.

Thus the talk rambled, while Peter, Ellery's dog, ca- pered through bush and brier, plunging into the brook with his smiling tail. Peter lived as Henry aspired to live. As the Indians had amused the Jesuits by sitting all day naked on the ice, fishing through their holes, as if they were lolling on feather-beds, so Peter would sleep all night on a snow-bank in January. It was enough to make one shiver to think of, on a day like this, by Clematis Brook, when the ants, bees and millers kept open shop, when the woodchucks sat up at the mouths of their houses, when the Maryland yellow-throats and the bull- frogs and robins performed their operas all day long, and the learned advocate, the *Mephitis chinga,* probed the roads for beetles. A day for three friends to expand their fancies. Anon they took their way to the Estabrook country, or embarked on some riparial excursion, a walk along the river-bank, or a paddle in Henry's boat, leav- ing the boat, perhaps, for an inland stroll, at the rear of the blacksmith's house, five miles up the river. Sometimes they went for a voyage in the pinnace as far as the Port of Lilies, along the river which, in its glassy folds, laid its unswept carpet over the fragrant meadows. Anon they set forth on a wintry day, under a lead-coloured sky, to the steady, silent, windless fall of the snow, when all the pines and oak-leaves were moulded in silver. Sometimes, after dark, they dropped in to see Perez Blood, the farmer-astronomer, over towards Carlisle, sitting in his wood-shed, in his astronomical chair, with his skull-cap on his head and his short Northern figure, a Concord Tycho Brahe. They peeped through his telescope and saw Saturn's rings and the shadows of the mountains on the moon. If it was spring or summer, they reappeared in the village streets with flowers and rare insects in their hats and pockets. They might have been Linnæus and his pupils on one of their "herborizations."

Thoreau was in danger of losing his solitary habits. What with lecturing, what with surveying, what with the acclaim that followed his *Walden,* he was becoming almost a man of the world. He had had to spend ninety days surveying to pay for his *Week on the Concord,* but *Walden* was actually selling. It was finding the kind of friends that make a classic. He had had his name posted for public lectures, two or three a year, wherever—in Worcester, Nantucket, Salem, Plymouth—they absolutely required his presence. Not that he wished for "experience": one might as well have advised a bear to leave his hollow tree and run about all winter, scratching at all the hollow trees in the woods. The bear would have been leaner in the spring than if he had stayed at home and sucked his claws. But Henry was willing to go, to make a few dollars, whenever it was convenient to drop his work, provided it was clearly understood that what he said on the platform was nobody's business. It was just another chore, like surveying. Nothing one did for money was ever worth doing, but one had to pay one's way and hold one's peace. As for the surveying, it was like Peale's and Morse's portrait-painting. Peale and Morse had wandered through the country, painting the portraits of the gentry. Henry went about in a similar fashion, to the houses of the farmers and the squires. With his staff and chain, he, too, had to paint his portraits, while his mind was filled with more important matters.

Still, he acquired thereby, and through his writings, a number of new acquaintances who were almost as rewarding as the muskrats. Agassiz, the great professor in Cambridge, was studying the American fishes. Henry was glad to send him four firkins of Concord fish, including one and probably two species that Agassiz had not seen. Agassiz, greatly pleased by this, came out to Concord and examined turtles with him. The lecturing-business also took him to Nantucket, where, as the natives said, you had to strike a whale before the girls would dance with you. This was no great news, to be sure, for Henry. That a young woman had regular features might be a reason for looking at her, but it was no reason for talking to her. Still, it was something to meet the natives; and surveying was a pleasant occupation when one had good friends to set up the staff and carry the chain. Henry was glad when Alcott offered to do so, and it was a question of surveying Hillside, Marston Watson's country-place at Plymouth. Alcott was in his element there, for Marston Watson, having the means, had had an inspiration. On his beautiful slope overlooking the harbour, he wished to lay out a park and garden, and he proposed to build a summer-house, with front gables facing south and east, and a lookout with winding stairs, all of rustic wood. Alcott gathered the timbers, with plenty of knots and sylvan ornaments, and soon constructed the bower, a riot of natural curves, fit for a Pythagoras to talk in; and he and Watson carried Henry's chain. As they trod the warm, sandy Plymouth wood-roads, or lingered on the slope, they talked over the virtues of pears and apples, golden russets, Tolman sweetings, greenings. Pears were too aristocratic, Henry thought. He much preferred the democratic apples that were left to the hired man to gather and barrel, while the land-owners plucked their own pears and had their daughters wrap them in separate papers. Judges and ex-judges,—Squire Hoar, for instance,—were connoisseurs of pears and named them after emperors and kings, queens and dukes and duchesses,—glout-morceaus, Bonne Louise. Henry thought they were less poetic than apples, the apples that children dream of. He meant to wait for his pears until they got American names.

But when one writes a *Walden,* one has to be prepared for consequences. Much as Henry preferred the republican apple, Marston Watson sent him a gift of pear-trees. Somebody else, in Brattleboro, sent him a box of may-flowers. Another friend in Worcester sent him a humming-bird's nest. All in two days. In Worcester, they were developing a Thoreau "cult." There Thomas Wentworth Higginson lived, the literary minister, one of the active Abolitionists. There lived Theophilus Brown, the literary tailor, who sent forth sparkles of wit as he bent over his measuring-tape and scissors; and there, above all, dwelt Harrison G. O. Blake, a terribly conscientious Harvard man, who, as Emerson said, would even return a borrowed umbrella and who was Henry's firmest partisan. Attracted by Henry's writings in *The Dial*,—the essay on Persius first,—he had persuaded him to go to Worcester, to give a sort of annual parlour-lecture, so that his friends could really look at him. He had led Henry into a correspondence, which was conducted on the highest plane; for "Mr. Blake" was so Transcendental that Henry had to walk on stilts to please him. But he was a loyal adherent. The moment the postman arrived with a letter from Concord, he gathered his neighbours together and read the letter aloud at the breakfast-table.

One of Henry's expeditions took him to New Jersey,

where he surveyed the two hundred acres at Eagleswood, Perth Amboy. Marcus Spring was founding a colony there, with the Grimkés and the Welds and other Abolitionists. They wished to propagate, in combination, radical views and old-fashioned culture, and Henry laid out the streets of the village they were planning. Alcott joined him there, and they spent a night with Horace Greeley and went over to Brooklyn to see Walt Whitman, whose *Leaves of Grass* Henry had just been reading. He wished to pay his respects to the great new poet, whom Emerson had recently greeted, although he had small use for the politicians whom Whitman included in his cosmos. He had, for the rest, all manner of reservations in regard to this great America, and he also thought that Walt was a little rank,—although, when it came to that, if you blushed when you read the *Leaves,* at whose thoughts were you blushing, your own or Walt's? He felt that Whitman had written a great primitive poem, as wonderful in its way as the Bhagavad-Gita. It was an alarm or trumpet-note, ringing through the American camp.

Meanwhile, he had found another friend, sufficiently near home to pay him an annual visit, a Quaker and poet, like Whitman, albeit quite unknown in the world of letters. This was Daniel Ricketson, who lived at Brooklawn, his ancestral home at New Bedford. The Quaker ship-owners in the whaling metropolis were shrewd, quick-witted traders. Ricketson had inherited some of their money, but none of their mercantile instincts. He was a naturalist and a man of letters, whose favourite authors were Virgil and Cowper and who had corresponded for many years with Howitt and William Barnes, the Dorset poet. A lover of Gilbert White and William Gilpin, he lectured now and then, especially on "Cowper and His Friends," and he liked the ancient saying, "A spare diet and clear skies are Apollo and the Muses." He was at home with partridges, quails and rabbits, and had tramped thousands of miles through the winter woods; and he looked after his farm, his fruit-trees and garden, avoiding forms and ceremonies, seeking a simple, quiet life. A quick man, quick in heart, quick in all his movements, with a taste for free thinking and social reform, he liked to get hold of some outcast and hold him up by the chin and whisper weighty matters in his ear; and, as for the anti-slavery movement, how could he listen to the woodland songs, or look at the great clouds and the starry heavens, and not be a friend of the poor and the oppressed? In the midst of his rural pursuits, he fought for justice. He hoped to see the quarrels of nations settled by arbitration, the factory-system humanized, the prisons without tenants. He longed to see machinery, now so destructive of life, turned into safe and useful channels. An inveterate journalizer, the author of a *History of New Bedford,* a rural poet with a clear vocation, Ricketson was one of those happy readers who create for other men of letters an atmosphere in which they can breathe and work. "In proportion as we see the merits of others, we add to our own," he said. Thoreau had been touched by the word of greeting that Ricketson sent him after reading *Walden.* The modest and perceptive Ricketson had also built a shanty, like his own; and when Ellery Channing went to New Bedford, to write for one of the papers, Thoreau had a double reason for visiting the town.

These friends had high times in Ricketson's shanty, then and every year thereafter, especially when Alcott joined the trio. They went for walks in the neighbouring woods, and Henry found marine plants he had never seen before and an old Indian woman, living alone in her hut, the last of the Nemaskets. The shanty recalled his Walden days. It was much the same in size and style, bristling with evidences of Ricketson's hobbies, twenty rustic walking-sticks, a dozen pipes, a spyglass, Indian

relics, stuffed birds, old guns and swords, slips of paper
pinned on the walls with verses in praise of country life.
In the surrounding woods, the quails incessantly whistled, and morning and evening one heard the strain of
the bay-wing. There the happy sages sat, like so many
gymnosophists of old, ready to stamp on the ground if
any Alexander thrust himself in at the door. Ellery
smoked his pipe and joked with Alcott, and Ricketson
stood boldly up to Henry. One day, Walton Ricketson,
the sculptor-son of the house, named after Izaak Walton,
made a medallion of Henry, wearing the full black beard
he had recently grown; and, as if to belie his beard,—
on another occasion,—Henry, unable to contain his joy,
jumped out of his chair and began to dance. He pranced
and leaped about, like an Indian in the forest, taking
pains to step on Alcott's toes.

CHAPTER XXIV

CAMBRIDGE IN THE FIFTIES

THE GREAT months in Cambridge were June and October. June was Lowell's month. When the trees were heavy with leaves and the gardens full of blossoms, when the insects chirped in the grass and the white clouds sailed aloft, Lowell, pitching his hay in the meadow at Elmwood, felt the metres of Chaucer, Shakespeare and Keats pounding in his blood. Longfellow loved October. He always uttered the word with a curious pleasure. Every year, when the leaves turned scarlet and yellow, his mind stirred with thoughts and fancies. "Welcome, O brown October!" he wrote in his journal. "Like a monk with a drinking-horn, like a pilgrim in russet!"

At the rear of the Craigie house, he had laid out a more elaborate garden, following a Gothic pattern, with borders of box. He made a little pond under the willows. It was 1854, and he had resigned from his professorship. In his brief novel, *Kavanagh*, the story of a minister in Maine,—who might have been Sylvester Judd, for his aim was to remove all prejudices and bring about a union of all the sects,—he had pictured his own predicament. Kavanagh, the youthful poet, who had been brought up on the lives of the saints, was forced to teach grammar for his living, while his mind overflowed with verses; interrupted and hampered by trivial things, he postponed his great designs from year to year and never found the courage to begin. The tale was feeble enough, for Longfellow's mind was poor and thin without its mantle of verse; but it expressed his feeling at the moment. His college work was like a great hand laid on the strings of his lyre, stopping their vibrations. He was the Pegasus in pound of whom he wrote in one of his poems. Still, he had written *The Golden Legend,* based on a story of the minnesingers, in form suggesting *Faust.* It was an evocation of the Middle Ages, softly melodious and picturesque, redolent of ivy and ancient ruins, with a fervent strain of religious feeling. Some of the scenes were among the best in the Longfellow picture-gallery, especially the scenes of monastic life.

The first result of Longfellow's freedom was the Indian idyll, *Hiawatha.* This was an October poem, floating in an air of Indian summer, a haze of yellow harvests and autumnal quiet and the smoke of camp-fires and far-away lodges. Ever since his boyhood in Maine, Longfellow had felt the poetry of the ancient forest people. He had seen the last of the Algonquins, stragglers in the Maine woods, and he had never forgotten the words of the Choctaw chief who said that his tribe would hear the news of his death "like the sound of the fall of a mighty oak in the stillness of the forest." He had entertained an Ojibway chief who was lecturing in Boston, and one of his students who had returned from the West and told him legends of the lodge and camp-fire had urged him to weave them into a poem. He had ploughed through School-craft's collection of Indian folk-lore, and then he had remembered the *Kalevala,* the Finnish folk-epic that he had read during his summer with Freiligrath. There was much in common between these primitive peoples and their legends. Many of their metaphors were the same, and the repetitions of the *Kalevala* were characteristic of the Indian songs, so like the wind in the pine-trees. The vague myth of a sunset land, a paradise in the West, where the mountains and forests were filled with deer and the lakes swarmed with fishes, the happy hunting-ground of the Indian braves, swept through his mind, when autumn came, with the sighs of the south-wind, Shawondessa. He saw it all in a wondrous light, in the mist of leaves, in the flash of the river. The Indians that emerged in the poem were not the warrior-stoics of flesh and blood. They were not Indians even as Concord saw them, for Longfellow was not Thoreau. He had reshaped the legends to suit himself, omitting all the savagery and malice. He had softened and simplified and humanized them, picturing the father of the lodge, the patriot, the sportsman and the hero. There was a touch of Channing in Hiawatha, the bringer of light, peace and the household arts, and the elements of romance were European. The mild humanitarian glow of the poem savoured of the poet's Cambridge circle. But why not? Of what did the Indians savour in *Atala* and *René*, if not Chateaubriand's circle across the ocean? There was a quiet magic in the story, a golden languor as of afternoon, of corn-fields in the setting sun, purple vapours and the dusk of evening.

It was not for children that Longfellow wrote, although children were his best readers always. *Hiawatha* travelled round the world; Cardinal Newman's brother translated it into Latin, and Freiligrath, the German translator, amply defended Longfellow's use of the metre. He had been accused of plagiarism, as erstwhile by the author of *The Raven,* which had occasioned the lines that he wrote in his journal,—

> In Hexameter sings serenely a Harvard professor.
> In Pentameter him damns censorous Poe.

Everybody read him, and the critical public recognized that in his use of metres Longfellow had shown himself an original artist. Still, the children liked him best, and Cambridge and the Craigie house were full of children. Dr. Worcester had built the house next door, and the Longfellow boys, perched on the fence, swooped down on the lexicographer's pears and apples. Then Dr. Worcester, roused from his studies, issued from his cave of notes and told the little boys what they were made of. Their father knew already. He had composed a jingle on the subject and also asked what little girls were made of. The Longfellow girls were more discreet. Longfellow wrote several poems about them. Brattle Street, in fact, was a garden of girls, quite in the Tennysonian vein, and Longfellow liked to go to balls in Boston, where he could see them, fair and slender, waving, like lilies on their stems, to the music as to a wind. At the Craigie house, they were always reading aloud, every day at the children's hour, often by the cozy fireside, while they looked over pictures from Florence and Dresden. There were many new authors to keep up with, Hawthorne, who had gone to Liverpool, to serve as American consul there, Thackeray, Charlotte Brontë, the Brownings, Ruskin. Longfellow watched the moon, through the open window, rising in the autumnal air. Like a delicious perfume, like far-off music, floated through his mind, as through parting clouds, glimpses and visions of Tyrolean lakes.

But Europe was drifting more and more to Cambridge. Every Cunarder brought some visitor, Adam Gurowski, for one, the terrible count,—the one-eyed Pole who called himself "the homeless,"—Ole Bull from Norway, Frederica Bremer from Sweden, gathering notes on the "homes of the new world," Thackeray, Clough the poet, Luigi Monti, the Italian scholar,—the Sicilian of Longfellow's *Wayside Inn,* who presently married the sister of the poet Parsons,—or Professor Sophocles, the scholar-hermit, bred in a monastery on Mount Athos, a strange Diogenes with a wild, grey beard who looked like Byron's Corsair, who lived like a monk of the Thebaid in his room in Holworthy Hall and whom one encountered on his lonely walks. Felton, the great professor of Greek, Longfellow's closest friend and the friend of Dickens, the huge, hearty old-fashioned scholar who liked to apply the epithet forcible-feeble to those who simulated his own robustness, and who often reminded his hearers that Agamemnon had honoured Ajax with a whole sirloin after his fight with Hector,—for he shared the Homeric enjoyment of eating and drinking,—was lecturing at the Lowell Institute. He had made his own collection of Swiss folk-poems and had visited Jacques Jasmin, the barber-poet, who lived at Agen in Provence and whose *Blind Girl* Longfellow translated; and in Greece he had made friends with farmers and sailors, travelled through the mountains in search of ballads and met all the living Greek writers, whom he brought out presently in a book of selections. He took the modern world-historical view in his great courses of lectures, which later appeared as *Ancient and Modern Greece*. At Harvard, everything was "comparative" now; the studies overlapped one another. With the humorous, copious Felton, all fire and energy and poetic feeling, with Asa Gray, the botanist, with Peirce the mathematician and Jeffries Wyman, with Agassiz in the chair of natural history, the lines and angles of the checker-board had gradually faded out. There was a genial glow in the Cambridge air. Agassiz had brought full summer with him.

The great Swiss professor had settled in Cambridge in 1848. A sort of Johnny Appleseed of science, sowing trees of learning wherever he went, he had lectured to vast crowds from Boston to Charleston, making the great types of the animal kingdom, articulates, radiates, molluscs, as real and vivid as historic human races. Talking with his enchanting verve and drawing his illustrations on the blackboard, so that one saw the insects and fishes bursting from their eggs, he infected everyone with his zeal for nature. Museums rose over-night as the great showman of science passed through the country, and, as his fame grew, every strange rock that was unearthed, every queer creature that anyone caught, in pond or stream or forest, was sent to the professor for an explanation; and when he issued a circular, asking for collections of fresh-water fish, specimens came in from every quarter. He could scarcely handle his correspondence. He was never without his blackboard and his bit of chalk and was always ready to teach at a moment's notice, in camp, on the road, on the shores of lakes. All creation was his lecture-room. He carried snakes in his pockets; every room in his house was a laboratory; garret and cellar were filled with his collections. Everyone quoted his sayings. He had never known a dull hour. He had never been a dollar ahead in the world and never expected to be. He had no time to waste in making money! This made a great impression in New England; and everyone heard how he rejoiced, for science, when a book appeared that demolished a theory which he had been toiling for years to establish. It was known that, to keep his chair at Harvard, he refused the directorship of the Jardin des Plantes, offered him by Napoleon III, and a seat in the French Senate, a rank equal to Cuvier's. Nothing kept the Americans back, he said, except a consideration for the opinion in which they were held in Europe. He hated to see an American man of genius elated by some foreign recognition, taking it as a mark of honour that set him apart from his countrymen. Contemptible provinciality! America could so easily be a centre if it once discarded the foolish notion that Europeans were its proper judges.

Agassiz, with his joyous magnetism, for whom all the species of human beings, emperors, farmers, scientists and poets were so many bipeds and bivalves, save for his impetuous affections, who made science a national cause and charmed money out of the politicians with which to found museums, as if they were asylums for the blind, Agassiz, the Pied Piper of Cambridge, soon became Longfellow's alter ego. He took his class one summer to Nahant, where Longfellow had a cottage, not far from Prescott's. Agassiz caught nature "in the act," while Longfellow rejoiced in the northeast storms, the fringes of the foam about the rocks, the wet sails struggling in the wind, the kale, the seaweed and the waste of waters, the scent of the wild roses about the cottage mingling with the odour of the sea. This was Longfellow's element. He was at home with the ocean, like Ole Bull, the Norwegian violinist, who had come to Cambridge, where he was to find his second wife. Ole Bull had swept through the country, a musical Agassiz with his "storm-organ," the whirling spray of sound in which one heard the thunder of the northern avalanches, the wind in the pines and the sun-flecked hollows of Norway, filled with gnomes and elves. All the young girls had heard his music, like the mist scattered by a fountain, and wrote about him in their diaries. They thought he was like Adam in Paradise. He had shared in the Norwegian national movement, working with Ibsen at the Bergen theatre. There, as in America, a fresh, youthful spirit was in the air. Norway had declared its independence and separated from Denmark, and the Norwegian writers were building a literature of their own, one which they hoped would express the dreams and hidden talents of the people. P. A. Munch was their Bancroft, and Ibsen wished to be the national poet. He was writing odes for the May 17th celebrations, much like the American Fourth of July, and festival poems such as Dr. Holmes was writing for the Berkshire cattle-fairs,—even so, Ibsen, the author of *Ghosts,* who said that culture was "unthinkable apart from national life." He was gathering folk-tales among the fjords, as Hawthorne had gathered them on his excursions.

Ole Bull spent a winter at Elmwood, which he had rented during Lowell's absence; for Lowell, appointed to Longfellow's vacant chair, had gone abroad for a year of study. At the Craigie house, he would talk half the night about Paganini, Malibran and Liszt. He played and chanted his old Norse melodies, like one of Longfellow's gleemen of the Viking days, and spoke of his childhood in the northern forests, the flower-clad valleys, filled with singing birds, the rocky coast, the rushing cataracts, the glittering lakes of Norway, so like the woods and valleys of Maine and New Hampshire. He might have been born in Portland, as Longfellow might have been born in Bergen. Hawthorne was more like Ibsen in the sense of fate that wrapped his folk-tales in a Gothic darkness. Hawthorne, too, had appeared at the Craigie house, during the years before he went abroad, coming and going like a shadow, hiding behind the curtains, where he spent whole evenings undisturbed, a Viking under a veil. Arthur Hugh Clough, the English poet, who spent a winter in Cambridge, also had a touch of the Viking in him, although it was sicklied o'er with the pale cast of thought. He had written his poem, *The Bothie*, largely suggested by *Evangeline*, filled with a feeling for the out-of-doors, high-spirited youth and the wildest nature. His Scotland was another Maine or Norway. He stayed at Shady Hill, as a friend and guest of Charles Eliot Norton, coaching a few young men in Greek and making a revision of Dryden's Plutarch. The calm and repose of Cambridge soothed his mind, torn and bewildered by scruples and speculation, and brought back his earlier days at Oxford.

Then suddenly who should appear but Horatio Greenough, just returned from Florence. The tall, handsome, fiery Boston sculptor, a Viking or a Greek, as one chose to see him, had come home to superintend the erection of one of his monuments at Washington. As a Boston and Cambridge boy, two of whose brothers were also artists, he had copied a marble Phocion in his father's garden, studied anatomy under a Boston doctor, modelled in butter, wax and chalk and spent his happiest hours with Washington Allston, during his years at Harvard. In Rome, he had worked with Thorwaldsen, and Cooper had given him his first commission, for the well-known "Chanting Cherubs," the first marble group that had ever been made by an American sculptor. For twenty-three years he had lived in Florence. He had introduced Emerson to Landor, his vehement friend and fellow-republican there, and he had written to the younger Dana, "America has always acted towards her artists like a hen that has hatched ducklings. She cannot understand why they run to the water, instead of thriving on the dung-hill, which only asks to be scratched in order to feed them. She will learn better, but not yet." But he had not been able to endure the repressions of Italian life since 1848. He had come home in a blaze of vigour, braced by the American air, with little respect for the Tories he found about him. He made the rounds of Boston, Concord and Cambridge before he settled in Newport for the winter.

The lectures he presently gave amplified the exciting ideas which he had been spreading among his friends. They were fragments of a book that he was planning. It was he who surprised the Boston people by praising the clipper-ship as a work of art. He said that the American trotting-wagon and the bald, neutral-toned Yankee farm-house were actually closer to Athens than the Grecian temples that people were building for banks. This seemed odd enough, but there was a method in Greenough's madness, as those who heard his lectures soon discovered. He wished to explain what was the proper basis for a native American art, observing that the true way to follow the Greeks was not to transplant their forms,—a kind of impotent dilettantism,—but to accept their principles and build from the needs of one's own climate and country. This was the strength of the clipper-ship, the type of what our architecture should be. It perfectly fulfilled its natural function. All its details were organic. Would anyone retain a bellying sail, however picturesque it was, however it pleased one's sense of association, when a flat sail went closest to the wind? That was the strength of the farmhouse, too. It seemed to belong to the ground on which it stood, as a caterpillar belongs to the leaf it feeds on. The monuments of the Egyptians and the Greeks were sublime as expressions of their power and feeling, but what did a Greek temple express in State Street? Money and ostentation, nothing else, like a frock-coat on an African king. Did not nature provide a form for every function, and were not all the absurdities of modern usage due to the fact that they were nonorganic? Instead of adopting the outward shape first, for the sake of the eye or of association, without reference to the inner distribution, forcing the functions into a general form, one should begin with the heart and work outwards.

Three generations later, one was to hear much of this "functional" theory, which Greenough preached up and down the country, with a Yankee wit and a foreign culture mixed, as he said, like the matrix and pebbles in the pudding-stone of Roxbury, Massachusetts. It all came down to the doctrine that the one principle of structure was "the principle of adaptation of forms to functions." The obelisk was the simplest type of this. Its function was to signalize a spot that was memorable in history, and how completely it achieved its end! It said but a single word, "Here!"—but everyone heard this word and understood it. Greenough's "Artist's Creed" summed up his faith. There were three things he had seen in man worthy of love and thought, Beauty, Action, Character: "By beauty I mean the promise of function, by action I mean the presence of function, by character I mean the record of function." A stirring combination of New England ethics with an aesthetic point of view that was to grow in meaning.[1]

At Shady Hill, Charles Eliot Norton was also preparing to preach the gospel of art. There, in the gracious house with the wide verandahs, surrounded by its rolling lawns, the beeches and the willows, filled with the clatter of crows, the Cambridge circle met, over a game of whist, for music or for conversazioni, suggesting the "Dante evenings" of the future. There the elder Professor Norton beguiled his leisure with Shakespeare, Pope and Scott; and there, or at the house they had built at Newport, where they passed the summer months and where Greenough suddenly died before he could finish his book, the Nortons entertained their younger friends. Among these were Clough, Rowse the artist, who was making his red-chalk portrait-drawings of literary celebrities, William J. Stillman, the painter and writer, the editor of *The Crayon*, the first American art-journal, and later the friend of the Rossettis, Thomas G. Appleton, Longfellow's brother-in-law, and Francis J. Child, the collector of ballads. Charles Eliot Norton, a young man of low

---

[1] See Louis Sullivan's phrase, "Form follows function, function creates form," and the writings of Lewis Mumford. In the light of these recent discussions, one should read Greenough's lectures, *Æsthetics at Washington, American Architecture, Structure and Organization* and *Criticism in Search of Beauty* in H. T. Tuckerman's *Memorial of Horatio Greenough*.

See also Emerson's comment on Greenough: "His paper on Architecture, published in 1843, announced in advance the leading thoughts of Mr. Ruskin on the *morality* in architecture, notwithstanding the antagonism in their views of the history of art. I have a private letter from him—later, but respecting the same period—in which he roughly sketches his own theory: 'Here is my theory of structure: a scientific arrangement of spaces and forms to functions and to site; an emphasis of features proportioned to their *gradated* importance in function; colour and ornament to be decided and arranged and varied by strictly organic laws, having a distinct reason for each decision; the entire and immediate banishment of all make-shift and make-believe.' "—*English Traits.*

vitality, always a semi-invalid, a born collector of autographs and coins, books, engravings, paintings, with ample means to satisfy his tastes, with an acute sense of his
social duty, devout, fastidious, learned, a careful scholar,
was cautiously feeling his way towards the world of art.
He and Clough had sworn eternal friendship, and, in
fact, Norton's talent for friendship was the most remarkable thing about him. He was a hero-worshipper by
instinct, who only asked that his heroes should be authentic,—good museum-pieces in flesh and blood, classified
and certified,—for he had an extreme distrust of anything new.[2] He was a born confidant. Everyone told Norton everything, for he was the soul of discretion; and one
could be sure that, if he wrote one's memoirs, nothing
would appear that was not in the best of taste. He had
whispered to his mother, at the age of ten, in the midst
of a desperate illness, "I wish I could live, so that I could
edit Father's works." He was to live to edit Carlyle and
Ruskin, who, like Lowell and George William Curtis,
made him their literary executor. Nature had preordained him for this work, as it made other men explorers
and poets. With a conscientious longing to be useful,
Norton felt sure that he had a mission.

As a child, he had been taken to England, where he
had met his father's friends, especially Joanna Baillie
and Mrs. Hemans, the cultivated Low Church circles that
read Andrews Norton's books. Wordsworth had taken
him upon his knee and given him a blessing. He had had
a taste of the India trade, in the counting-house of his
maternal uncles, before settling down to a scholar's life.
He had sailed to India as a supercargo. There he had
found readers of his father, as well as of Everett's

---

[2] It must be added that Lincoln and John Brown were among his
heroes. Their photographs, in later days, stood on his mantelpiece
at Ashfield. Norton, somewhat timid and imitative on his imaginative side, was highly independent in his moral nature.

speeches and Longfellow's poems, and had passed much of his time with the poet Dutt and his Harvard class-mate, Fitzedward Hall, the Oriental scholar.[3] He found good friends in several rajahs, but India struck his New England taste as "showy," and it was not till he reached Venice, travelling round the world, that his aesthetic feeling came to life. Even in Europe, on this first visit, for which he was well equipped with introductions, thanks to George Ticknor, who was one of his uncles, his social and political observations occupied him more than matters of art. Returning home, he drifted out of business, edited a volume of hymns, opened a night-school for the poor of Cambridge, busied himself with model lodging-houses, to meet the new problems of immigration, and published an anonymous book, *Considerations on Some Recent Social Theories*. This was a counterblast to the radical doctrines that interested the Concord thinkers, the theories that had come to a head in 1848, Fourierism, Kossuthism, nationalism, the "offensive declamation" of Mazzini. The British rule in India, Norton thought, was better than any native rule could be. Republicanism as such was not important; and what was the use of trying to change conditions unless the people themselves had "character"? That character was what they did not have was the evident moral of their degradation,—which gave the upper classes their Christian function. Norton was a tender-hearted man who felt that he was personally bound to rescue the world from its folly.

It was on his second visit to Europe, in 1855, that Norton's real career began. His ship-mate, James Jackson Jarves, already known as a writer on art, gave him a letter of introduction to Ruskin, who, although he was nine

[3] Professor of Sanskrit and English in the government college at Benares; later professor of Sanskrit and Hindustani in King's College, London. Hall was the first American scholar to edit a Sanskrit text, the *Vishnu Purana*.

years the elder, soon thought of Norton as his "first real tutor"; for the bright-eyed Cambridge student with the musical voice, who had steeped himself in *Modern Painters*, knew classical literature better than he, showed a surprising knowledge of Italian painting and introduced him to the *Fioretti*. Ruskin, who was still a Calvinist, might have grown up in New England, in spite of his exuberant temperament. His shrewd, sensible, prosperous merchant-father, his grim, repressive mother, who trampled on every innocent pleasure, the atmosphere of piety, thrift and culture in which he had passed his early years, his tours in a travelling-carriage over Europe, the father sympathizing with the son's ambitions, all suggested Boston. Ruskin and Norton became fast friends at once. Ruskin showed Norton his Turners and Rossettis, Norton gave Ruskin the writings of his American friends, Lowell and Dr. Holmes. They travelled together in Switzerland and climbed the mountain meadows of Sallanches. They met again in Italy. Together they stood at the fountain in Siena, under the same arches where Dante had stood, drank of it together and walked together on the hills above, as Ruskin wrote later in his memoirs, where the fireflies among the scented thickets shone fitfully in the still undarkened air, like starlight through the purple leaves.

Thus began the transatlantic friendships that gave Norton much of his later fame. His second great friendship was with Mrs. Gaskell, the Unitarian minister's wife who had described in *Cranford* a village life that also suggested New England. After Mrs. Gaskell, whom he met in Rome and to whom he recited Lowell's poems, while he gave her lessons in the history of Italian painting, he named one of his daughters. In Paris, he met Lamartine, Vigny and Tocqueville, and he was glad to find that Ary Scheffer, like some of his acquaintances in London, thought Longfellow the greatest living poet.

Ruskin, whose passion was the Middle Ages, said that
Longfellow, in *The Golden Legend,* had entered into the
temper of the monk more closely than any historian or
theologian; and Scheffer proved to Norton's satisfaction
that the most poetic imagination was always accompanied by sound sense and practical understanding. Norton
was not one of those dreamers who found in Italy a romantic solace. Recalling his social interests at home, he
scrutinized the Italian charities, the evening schools for
boys, the work of the Misericordia. Finding Keats's grave
in sad disorder, he had the stone firmly set and planted
myrtles and violets around it, with the same New England instinct for tidying-up that he brought to bear on
the impulsive Ruskin,—to "keep him strictly and busily
at his work." Rome was falling to pieces; it was all a helpless mass of weeds and ruins. All the more reason for a
Protestant grave-yard to set it a good example.[4] Curious
about modern Rome, which seemed to him as gaudy as
Calcutta, wanting in simplicity and taste, he talked with
scholarly priests and architects and went to meetings of
academies where cardinals sat on gilded chairs, where
seminarists recited hexameters on the Sacrifice of Isaac
in excellent Latin, and charming young countesses read
their poems on Dante's Beatrice and Petrarch's Laura.
He took notes on the early painters, Giotto, Fra Angelico
and Perugino, whom Ruskin was interpreting for the
modern mind and whom the Pre-Raphaelites were imi-
tating, with a new feeling for colour which, in England,
following the Oxford Movement, represented a recoil
from rationalism and Puritanism. He began his version
of the *Vita Nuova,* the first of the long series of Dante
translations that were to spring from Cambridge. This
was more literal than Rossetti's version, and marked by
the same delicate feeling; for Norton, in truth, was an

---

[4] Keats's grave was tidied again, about 1874, by the daughter of
W. W. Story.

exquisite scholar. He and Rossetti met, as friends of Ruskin, and Rossetti painted a picture for him, "Dante meeting Beatrice." He also began the study of mediæval cathedral-building, the subject of his most important work. The first part of the book he was soon to publish, *Notes of Travel and Study in Italy,* dealt with the cathedral of Orvieto. Later readers were to find this passage as good as Henry Adams on the building of Chartres.

Norton returned to Cambridge, like another Ticknor, with the same sort of apostolic fervour that had filled his uncle's mind. He was the opener of another door, the world of aesthetic studies. For half a century, as a teacher at Harvard, he was to expound the gospel of taste, the doctrines of Ruskin, Dante, Italian painting, the history of architecture, sculpture, Turner, as his father had expounded the Scriptures,—taste as a means of salvation. He who was called "Pope Charles" by his early friends was destined to outlive the days of the New England papacy; but, even in these first few years, before he became professor of the history of art, he was an autocrat in aesthetic matters. Weak in aesthetic feeling, but skilled and learned, as Ticknor, weak in literary feeling, was also skilled and learned, he had the same responsible sense of an intellectual mission. As Ticknor felt, in his heart of hearts, that all the great writers were of the past,— Ticknor, who lived out his days around the corner from Emerson, Hawthorne, Thoreau, scarcely aware of their existence,—so Norton, who made an exception of Ruskin's friends, Turner and the Pre-Raphaelites, felt that the Renaissance had been the end of art. He apologized, in later years, for a Corot that hung in his hall, left him by a friend to take care of. But as Ticknor had sent boxes of his books to enquiring students in Georgia and Maine, and was always ready with counsel for every scholar, so Norton carried boxes of Turners with him, when he gave lectures in the country towns, and left them for the boys and girls to study. He was always lending his gems and precious vases, fragments of sculpture, engravings, drawings, wherever he saw a chance to spread his gospel. Hearing that someone in Portland was interested in Turner, he sent a box of his water-colours there. His tenderness and goodness to the poorer students, his constant wish to be useful and helpful soon became proverbial in Cambridge. He was an archæologist by nature who had learned the alphabet of art after his mental tissues had dried and hardened, and he often seemed like a learned and elegant priest discoursing of the sacred mysteries of which he had scarcely felt the inner fire. But as a teacher, a sage, in days to come, a moralist, an expounder of manners, a master in the art of discrimination, he was the most potent of the Brahmins. No one left more of a stamp on Cambridge than Charles Eliot Norton.

CHAPTER XXV

THE ROMANTIC EXILES

AT LIVERPOOL, in his consul's office, Hawthorne spent four dull years. He had to deal with the beggars and impostors that haunt the official in foreign ports, the brutal skippers, the imbruted sailors for whom the gallant Dana was fighting at home. American claimants called upon him, "lost heirs" of English estates, usually mad or spurious, occasionally some visionary soul,—for instance, Delia Bacon,—on some phantasmal mission. One day Herman Melville came, his old friend in Lenox, wandering in a cloud, drifting to Constantinople. At the Unitarian chapel, William Henry Channing had found a pulpit. There the sunny mist of the Brook Farm doctrines mingled with the smoky fog of England.

Hawthorne plodded through the day's work with his usual mask of impassivity. Most of his troublesome visitors came and went like apparitions of smoke and fog, like figures in some romance that he would have written if he had had the energy to write. The poor, shy, proud Delia Bacon, a Hawthorne figure in real life, was a more insistent problem. As a friend of Elizabeth Peabody and Mrs. Stowe, she had written a few historical tales and novels and conducted classes in history, like Margaret Fuller, first in Connecticut, then in Boston and Cambridge, unfolding an idea that became an obsession. She had become convinced that Shakespeare's plays, actually written by a group of scholars gathered about Sir Walter Raleigh, contained a system of thought, concealed by ciphers, the deepest wisdom of the greatest epoch, a science that the world was waiting for. The question of the authorship of the plays was of the least importance in her mind. Her mission,—she was a missionary's daughter,—was to reveal their esoteric meaning. Carlyle had treated her with the utmost kindness, struck by her personality and her knowledge, and she had obtained, or thought she had, permission to unseal the tomb of Shakespeare, where she believed the final clues were buried. She had haunted the church at Stratford, at midnight, with her lantern, hovering about the grave, then lost her courage with her confidence, lost the last remnants of her reason, and shrunk into the final stage of madness.

Hawthorne might have invented the story. Later, he told it in his book on England. Without accepting Delia Bacon's theory, he had written a preface for her book, *The Philosophy of Shakespeare's Plays Unfolded*. This vast, chaotic treatise was only an introduction to the subject, but the style was impressive, here and there, in the midst of its incoherence, and some of Delia Bacon's intuitions, especially in the passages on *King Lear*, deserved a place in Shakespearean criticism.[1] But Hawthorne could not share Miss Bacon's romantic feeling for England. This tendency to wander back again, to the old home of the Pilgrims, this appetite for English soil, struck him as blind and pathetic. He seemed to be thrice-armoured against the charm that more and more of his countrymen felt, proud to be at odds with it, proud of his New England prejudices, as if he had turned the tables on Mrs. Trollope and wished to see only the too-much beef, the gloom, the slums, the poverty. He was too deeply planted in his own old world across the water to suffer the beguilement of the "claimants," or so it seemed

---

[1] Delia Bacon was the originator of the "Shakespeare-Bacon" movement. For a conclusive refutation of the Baconian theory, see John Fiske, *The Bacon-Shakespeare Folly*, in *A Century of Science*.

at first. For him the Warwickshire elms could not compare with those that had overhung his village street.

Gradually his feeling changed. His old zest for taking notes returned. He spoke of writing an English romance and even found a clue at Smithall's Hall, an ancient house in Lancashire. A few stage-properties were enough to start the machinery of his imagination, a coffer filled with golden hair, a silver snuff-box, a bloody footstep. *Doctor Grimshawe's Secret* began to take shape in his mind, the novel, begun in Rome, never finished, that struck a new note in American fiction. For was not Redclyffe, the American heir, the first of the transatlantic *revenants* that were to fill the novels of Henry James? Irving and Longfellow, many another, had felt the spell of the old world, but Redclyffe's nostalgia was something else than theirs: "The thought thrilled his bosom that this was his home—the home of the wild Western wanderer, who had gone away centuries ago, and encountered strange chances, and almost forgotten his origin, but still kept a clue to bring him back . . . He began to feel the deep yearning which a sensitive American,—his mind full of English thoughts, his imagination of English poetry, his heart of English character and sentiment, —cannot fail to be influenced by,—the yearning of the blood within his veins for that from which it has been estranged, the half fanciful regret that he should ever have been separated from these woods, these fields, these natural features of scenery, to which his nature was moulded, from the men who are still so like himself, from these habits of life and thought which (though he may not have known them for two centuries) he still perceives to have remained in some mysterious way latent in the depths of his character, and soon to be resumed, not as a foreigner would do it, but like habits native to him, and only suspended for a season."

In days to come, this feeling, which Hawthorne had begun to share,—a feeling that unsettled him, indeed,—was to play a part in American culture as marked as that of the "wanderers" of Pushkin's Russia. The most exotic writers, hitherto, had had the unquestioning instinct of homing pigeons, which brought them back from every foreign journey. The great tradition of the Revolution, the feeling of the national destiny, the prevalence of the classical studies that always made the mind its "own place," had rooted them in the Western soil. They had felt that they were building a civilization; and, in fact, it was not until after the Civil War that the great diaspora began and with it the tradition of deracination. Then, as the old causes grew dimmer and dimmer, as the European peasants arrived in thousands, as wealth advanced and tourists multiplied, as the human imagination felt cramped and thwarted in the vast industrial beehive, as classical studies declined and young men forgot the Plutarchian patterns, then this yearning for an older homeland rose in people's minds and men of sensibility flocked to Europe, not to study, as in former days, and carry their spoils back, like travelling Romans, but as if they could reascend the river of time.

The mood that found expression in Hawthorne's Redclyffe was to reappear not only in Henry James but in dozens, even scores of other writers who somehow felt estranged from their native life when the thread had once been broken. The elm-scattered meadows, the hawthorn hedges, the lawns, the castle-towers, the stiles, the heavy-timbered manor-houses, the Norman churches uplifting themselves among the stately trees touched some deepest buried nature in them, as of their English progenitors, a nature that seemed to have lain unchanged under the snows and leaves of ten-score winters and summers, layers of new customs and institutions that melted away in a night. They greeted these English scenes with a sudden flash of recognition. It was like a coming home after an absence of centuries. These intimations of a previous state, almost suggesting Plato, this sense that one had "been there before" was partly due to the reading of English books, partly to the maintenance of English customs in households across the Atlantic. There were thousands of families in New England, as in New York and the South, that had never ceased to be English, for all they had accepted the Revolution. They had fought for English rights against the redcoats. They had defended their country against their country because it was an English trait to do so. Not to be patriotic was not to be English, and they were Americans in a sense because they were English. Meanwhile, Wordsworth and Byron, Thackeray, Dickens, *Punch* and the British reviews had shaped their minds. A thousand times, in fancy, with Dr. Johnson, they had turned at a corner into Fleet Street. A thousand times they had walked down Piccadilly, among the yellow chariots of Vanity Fair. Shelley's larks were still more real to them than all the bobolinks of their native pastures, and they saw Oliver Twist and Little Nell even under the trees of their village lanes.

There had always been good Bostonians, like Edmund Quincy, for whom their first pilgrimage to London was like the Musselman's visit to the tomb of the Prophet. They saw it as the ancient Jews beheld their holy city after the years of bondage in a foreign land. Deep in their minds lurked the feeling that T. G. Appleton ascribed to the Yankee: "Europe is the home of his protoplasm, of the long succession of forces which make him what he is." It was against this feeling that Emerson fought, or rather against its consequences, in everything that he said of the "tape-worm of Europe." Those who had made England what it was had done so by sticking where they were, regardless of their own atavistic instincts, which might have led them back to France or

Denmark. When would Americans cast out the passion for Europe by the passion for America that would give them repose? Old and new countries were all the same to one who looked at the world with the eye of wisdom. Why this superstition for a mushroom Europe, which only had gravity and domestic rest because it lived a self-contained existence? Emerson, who travelled and believed in travel, whenever there was a reason for it, said that one should fill a place at home before one tried to find a place abroad. Who provoked pity, he remarked, like that excellent family just arriving in some foreign city, in its well-appointed travelling-carriage, as far from any honest end as ever? Each nation had asked successively, "What are they here for?" until they were all embarrassed, expecting to be asked the same question at the gates of every town. But this idle and pathetic nostalgia for Europe, which had always existed in the Yankee mind, was a minor strain before the Civil War. Two hundred years had left their stamp on almost every American, and those who had amply shared the life of their country were as self-possessed as any European. The eminent Americans of the forties and fifties confronted England with a serene aplomb. Proud of their nation, proud of themselves, proud of their own good work, objective in their point of view, contemptuous of trifles, they were eager for the welfare of the world and they were convinced that America had a mission.[2] The apologetic note of later years was wholly absent from their tone and manner. They met the Englishman as Greek met Greek, as men who spoke their minds on all occasions, as the Romans of Spain met the Romans of Rome.

The relations between America and England had

[2] "Why do foreign lands regard us with this intensity of interest? Is it not because the whole world looks hopefully toward America as a nation especially raised by God to advance the cause of human liberty and religion?"—Harriet Beecher Stowe, Letter of 1853.

reached a sort of equipoise in the eighteen-fifties. The acrimony of earlier years had largely passed away, the Civil War had not yet revived it; and English and American writers and statesmen found that they had more in common than at any time before or since. A dozen American authors of the moment, Prescott, Longfellow, Motley, Mrs. Stowe, Emerson, Hawthorne and others were greeted in England with the kind of *éclat* that Dickens met in America, or Thackeray or Trollope. Sydney Smith had said, before Prescott's visit, that a "Caspian sea of soap" awaited him. The English admired his pluck and his glorification of the life of action; but even Prescott's triumph was a trifle beside the royal progress of Mrs. Stowe. Hundreds of thousands, like the Queen herself, had been stirred and moved by Uncle Tom and Dred. They had wept over the death of Nina and shared the Queen's annoyance that fate had not chastised Tom Gordon. Mrs. Stowe, like Prescott and Sumner, found her portrait in English castles, and crowds trooped after her carriage as if she had been a prima donna. Much of the cordiality that united the countries was of a purely social kind. Outside the political sphere, Sumner, Dana, Charles Francis Adams found everything in English life congenial; and Sumner cultivated his English connections all the more because his political views had made him an outcast in social Boston. His pockets were always full of letters from duchesses and noblemen, and his diaries in England suggested Ticknor's, almost as copious and entertaining. But behind this social interest lay another, the humanitarian feeling that England and New England shared in common. Channing, Garrison, Whittier, Mrs. Child had spoken the language of Wilberforce and Clarkson, and their unaffected, intelligent goodness had touched thousands of English hearts. Philanthropic England, the England of the great liberal circles, busily building model dwelling-houses, raising the condition of the poor, occupied with popular education,—in a spirit, often pharisaical, that was sometimes saintly,—rejoiced in these American allies, of whom Mrs. Stowe was the largest-hearted. The Anglo-American friendships of this time, Mrs. Stowe's friendship with Lady Byron, with Mrs. Browning and George Eliot, Norton's friendship with Ruskin, Emerson's with Carlyle,—a reformer of another stripe,—were fruits of this moral solidarity. Another fruit was Emerson's *English Traits,* the best of American travel-books and one of the great and permanent works of its kind. Every candid English reader, Thackeray, Browning, Clough, felt that Emerson over-praised England; but everyone felt that the praise was the praise of a master and that Emerson spoke as befitted a sage. In point of composition, *English Traits* was Emerson's masterpiece, the only book, save one, *The Conduct of Life,* that he ever really composed. What made it sovereign, as a book on England, was its realistic grasp of essential facts, its Olympian air of detachment and self-possession. It was the work of an intellect that was always dominant and always open. One felt as if the eye of God had fallen upon England, after having refreshed its impressions of India, Egypt, Greece.[3] If God had a special regard for England, that was his own affair.

The romantic-pusillanimous view of England was the product of a later generation. Italy, meanwhile, was the goal of those who sought, without benefit of Argo, the golden fleece of the past. Paris, for twenty years, the years of the Second Empire,—the Paris of the Empress Eugénie's hats,—was all that London later became as a

---

[3] "England has inoculated all nations with her civilization, intelligence and tastes; and, to resist the tyranny and prepossession of the British element a serious man must aid himself by comparing with it the civilizations of the farthest east and west, the old Greek, the Oriental, and, much more, the ideal standard, if only by means of the very impatience which English forms are sure to awaken in independent minds."—*English Traits.*

goal of American fashion, of those who never trod their native shores without a steamer-ticket in their pocket; and other Americans, on special errands, flitted all over the continent, collecting twigs for their various nests at home. Lowell Mason wrote, in 1852, his *Musical Letters from Abroad,*—reports on the state of music in Germany and England,—before he returned to Massachusetts with an apostolic mission like Ticknor's and Norton's. Jacob Abbott's Rollo and Mr. George were types of a thousand other tourists who roamed over Europe for their improvement, visiting silk-mills and iron-foundries, marble-quarries, mosaic-factories, gathering hints for their future in Fitchburg and Lawrence. They did not neglect the sights, the Dying Gladiator and the Coliseum, but they never lost their practical sense of proportion.[4] They felt that their minds should be furnished but not upholstered. If Rollo had his doubts at times, he always saw that Mr. George's view was reasonable and right.[5]

For those who were tropical by organization, who longed for the myrtle and orange, Italy was another matter. In Rome and Florence, when Hawthorne went there, in 1858, little bands of exiles dwelt already, grouped about the sculptors and the painters, precursors of the colonies to come. These were new types, lovers of the picturesque who, far from seeking another homeland, wished to be strangers and sojourners. For them, the charm of Italy was its strangeness, not the familiarity that one found in England. Fugitives from the land of calculation, from the east wind, the "whip of the sky," as T. G. Appleton called it in one of his poems, the grey-

[4] "The Coliseum may have cost the most labour," said Mr. George, "but the Great Eastern is far above it, in my opinion, in every element of real greatness."—*Rollo in Rome.*

[5] "We are travelling for improvement, not for play. We are making a tour of Scotland for the purpose of learning all we can about Scotland, with a view to obtain more full and correct ideas respecting it than we could obtain by books alone. So we must attend to our duty."—*Rollo in Scotland.*

ness and chilliness of coast and headland, from "cold roast Boston" and expectant Concord, which asked them either to be men of business or to make bread of the stones in their native pastures, they found balm and solace in the weeds and the ruins, the lichens and the ancient walls, the colours and the forms that caressed the eye, the flowing life, the *dolce far niente*.[6]

> Nature abhors what housewives love—the clean,
> And beauty hides when pail and brush come in.

So William Wetmore Story, the sculptor, wrote,—the son of Justice Story, who had settled in Rome,—recalling his native Salem. All his fellow-exiles shared this feeling. Some of them, like Story, in taking flight, had been warned by the example of Washington Allston, whose mind had withered away in Cambridgeport. Depressed at home, humbled before the men who were building towns and railroads, turning villages into factory-centres, they revelled in a world that was tumbling to pieces. They had heard too much about the "improvement" that seemed to signify only money and comfort; they were weary of the "perfectibility" that left their sensuous needs unsatisfied. Emerson had talked too much, they thought, about the "rococo toy of Italy." He did not understand painters and sculptors. He had seen the case in too abstract a light, as one of them told the sage on a visit to Concord. Nature, he said, might be the same on the banks of the Kennebec and the banks of the Tiber, but, however it might be with writers, who had their books to study from, artists, whose books were pictures,

---

[6] "It is this which makes Rome so admirable as a residence for an artist. All things are easy and careless in the out-of-doors life of the common people,—all poses unsought, all groupings accidental, all action unaffected and unconscious. One meets nature at every turn,—not braced up in prim forms, not conscious in manners, not made up into the fashionable or the proper, but impulsive, free and simple."—W. W. Story, *Roba di Roma*.

needed Europe. Concord, for them, was another Patagonia.[7]

In fact, the colonists in Rome and Florence were all painters and sculptors rather than writers, or writers whose principal interest was painting and sculpture. James Jackson Jarves lived in Florence, where he was to remain for a generation. A man of more vigorous mind than Norton or Story, though less accomplished than either, he was producing a series of books on art that had a sort of missionary value. He had settled in Italy about 1850, after a stay in Paris and a long and adventurous youth in the South Sea Islands. The son of Deming Jarves, the glassmaker, the "Father of American Glass," who had founded the glass-works at Sandwich to utilize the fine Cape Cod sand, he had inherited a little fortune, most of which he spent in collecting pictures. He had passed several years at Honolulu and written a standard *History of the Sandwich Islands* and two amateurish novels,—with a few good pages of description, sketches of Polynesian scenes and manners,—before he happened upon his real vocation. A lively, shrewd, unworldly, honest soul, with a rare aesthetic taste, a born collector, familiar with the New England country auction, at which, as a boy, he had spent his pocket-money, buying books, especially histories,—he had a passion for Prescott,—he was engaged in a nine-years' search for his great collection of Tuscan paintings.

These were the days when the Primitives were still regarded as of dubious value, when gold-background pictures of Carlo Crivelli were burned for the sake of the gold one found in the ashes and Walter Savage Landor was called a madman for wasting a handful of silver on such rubbish. At least, if this fabulous hour had passed, largely thanks to Ruskin's eloquent writings, one still found an occasional "Muse of Cortona" used by a peas-

[7] Elihu Vedder, *The Digressions of V.*

ant to stop a hole in an oven, a Titian, painted over by
some bungler, that sold for six dollars, a Correggio, tat-
tered and torn, in the hands of an old-clothes dealer.
The age of wild buying had begun, the forgers were busy,
the couriers were swindling millionaires who proudly
carried back to New York and Boston their false Muril-
los, Claudes and Leonardos. With no fixed standards of
authentication, the art-market was a house of darkness.
Jarves taught himself to see in the dark. He tramped
through villas, palaces and convents, picked up a canvas here and there, cut from its frame, in a pile of earth
and rubble, or tossed aside in a lumber-room, and slowly
formed the collection, so famous later. It was a triumph
of discrimination. It was a task of devotion, like Agassiz's,
for Jarves had no thought of personal gain. He was an
Agassiz of art-museums, one who found, however, that
his country, ready as it was for the gospel of science, was
far from ready for this other gospel. Neither New York
nor Boston would accept his collection, though Norton
tried to find a place for it. The critics laughed at Jarves's
"wiry madonnas" and called him a scamp for all his
pains; and the pictures found their dwelling-place at
Yale,—where a little gallery existed, the first of its kind
in America, founded in 1832,—only through a comedy
of errors. But Jarves was a patient man. Italian art was
the fruit of a working epoch, not unlike his own, an age
of democratic energies; and he thought that the same
faith was preparing his country for a similar efflorescence. He bequeathed collections of textiles and Venetian glass to the New York museum and Wellesley
College. He studied the glass-making at Murano and
tried to introduce the Venetian methods into the works
at Sandwich.

In the books that Jarves wrote in the fifties and sixties,
Art Hints, The Art-Idea, Art Thoughts, Art Studies,—a

highly intelligent history of Italian painting, with illustrations from his own collection,—he preached like one of the missionaries with whom he had spent his youth at Honolulu. He urged the cause of art-teaching, museums, galleries, schools of design. He explained the success of the British efforts to introduce art into manufacture and asked why river-banks and public buildings, parks, shop-windows and railway-cars should not have their beauty and interest. In a strain of religious feeling that be-clouded his style, for his thoughts were often wrapped in ethical phrases, he asked, in fact, more questions in his field and made more intelligent observations than any other writer of his time,—"an epoch," as he described it, "of monstrous plaster figures, daubed with crazy paint, of mammoth cast-iron wash-basins, called fountains, of cast-iron architecture and clumsy gate-ways to public parks, of shoddy portrait-statues and inane ideal ones." His writings were full of astute perceptions. Like Green-ough, he praised the clipper-ship and the old-fashioned farmhouse. They were appealing and true because their style was suited to the realities behind them, the climate, the materials at hand. They were as successful in their way as the Greek temples and the Gothic churches. Why? Because the American merchants and farmers took pride in a work that really met their needs. Had any American patron of painting or sculpture shown the kind of feeling the merchant expressed in Longfellow's *The Building of the Ship?*—

> Build me straight, O worthy Master,
>   Staunch and strong, a goodly vessel
> That shall laugh at all disaster,
>   And with wave and whirlwind wrestle!

Well might the poet say:

> The merchant's word
> Delighted the Master heard,—

for this was the tone of Lorenzo de' Medici, in days when painting had really mattered, too. Jarves, who predicted that architecture would be the first great American art, said that it could have no healthy growth until it represented the people's life and shaped itself in conformity to local causes.[8]

With a somewhat forbidding style, all thumbs, too often, Jarves was an independent critic who did not spare the feelings of his friends, the American painters and sculptors in Rome and Florence. Greenough had gone home to die, but Powers lived in Florence; and, in Rome, Story, Crawford[9] and Harriet Hosmer, a pupil of the English sculptor Gibson, who gave her one of the rooms where Canova had worked, carried on a school of Yankee sculpture that showed what will could do, if little else. Eager workers all, anxious to justify their expatriation, they turned out busts and heroic groups, statues of American statesmen, histories in granite and romances in marble, such as the "Greek Slave" and the "Libyan Sibyl." These story-telling figures possessed every accessory and association that spoke for literature as it spoke for learning and uttered an occasional word for sculpture. Zenobia was a favourite subject, the heroine of William Ware's novel, a true New England woman born too soon, and the drapery of Cleopatra, as Story conceived her, was almost a novel in itself. The school excelled in allegories, representing, for instance, the struggles of genius, a sculptor in despair, while a hand pours oil into his dying lamp. The hand was the hand of the patron, and patrons

[8] One of Jarves's early books contained an excellent sketch of Hokusai, who was all unknown to Ruskin. This was the first suggestion of his later handbook, *A Glimpse at the Art of Japan*. Jarves was one of the first students, with Millet, Whistler and La Farge, who, when Japan was opened in the early fifties, became aware of Japanese art.

[9] Crawford's figure of Beethoven, erected in the Boston Music Hall, in 1856, is said to have been the first statue raised in America to an artist of any kind.

were not wanting, after all. Commissions came from Congress, from Cooper, Sumner, Ticknor, and the fame of Powers's busts had gone abroad. Thorwaldsen had said that his bust of Webster was the best work of the kind in modern times. Powers's vogue was world-wide, and travelling magnates from across the sea, manufacturers, diplomats and scholars, haunted his Florentine studio. No European journey was complete unless one carried home a bust by Powers.

To warm themselves in one another's presence, the artists in Rome met at the Caffè Greco, the dark and dingy haunt in former days of Allston, Cooper and Turner. Little groups of aspiring students went for moonlight rambles in the Coliseum. They strolled through the Forum, singing "Hail Columbia" in chorus. They stopped at the Fountain of Trevi, where Lord Neville had talked with Corinne. They sallied forth with sketchbooks for picnics on the Appian Way. They pored over one another's portfolios and wrote "Campagna bits" in their journals and letters. They gathered for musical soirées, perhaps in Charlotte Cushman's rooms, for the great Boston actress with the "thoughtful" style often spent her winters in Rome. They talked about Guido's "Aurora" and Canova, who seemed to have brought back the repose of the Greeks, and the mystery of Beatrice Cenci. They sat on ruined columns, with their colours beside them, sketching some model with dishevelled hair, a beard that suggested Moses or a well-turned arm that might have belonged to Apollo. Some of them aired their distaste for the Puritan ways that had made their life at home so drab and sober. In others the New England strain seemed only accentuated in the foreign air. They clung to their Calvinistic views and lived in the Rome of the Popes as they had lived in Lynn or Brattleboro. Powers cultivated his Yankee speech, as if it gave him a dramatic pleasure; and he and Joel Hart abounded in mechanical shifts that would have made their fortunes in Lawrence or Lowell. The tone of the little colonies, of all the foreign artists in Rome and Florence, set by Thorwaldsen and the German painters, Overbeck and Cornelius, was rigidly moral and highly religious. One might well have found some Yankee maiden, like Hilda in *The Marble Faun,* living in her tower among the doves and trimming her evening lamp at the Virgin's shrine.

This was the little world that Hawthorne found. Story, his old acquaintance in Salem, had come to spend his life in Rome and Florence. Others came and went, Lowell to visit Story, Norton taking notes on Giotto and Dante, Bryant the poet, George Stillman Hillard, Hawthorne's old friend and Sumner's partner, who published, in *Six Months in Italy,* a glorified and even glorious guide-book that was destined to serve a generation of tourists. Story, who took Hawthorne under his wing, a slight, wiry, nervous little man, witty, swarthily handsome, abounding in every social grace, clever at acting, singing, sketching, writing, passionately ambitious as a sculptor, had passed his earlier years as a lawyer in Boston. He had written his father's life and various legal treatises; he had shared in Margaret Fuller's Conversations and dreamed and talked of art and Rome, with Longfellow, in Lowell's study. Everything in New England annoyed and bored him, even the growing interest in German thought, for Italy had captured his imagination. His closest friends there were the Brownings and Landor, who had taken refuge with the Storys when, like King Lear, at eighty-four, he had been turned adrift by his wife and children. Browning had encountered the grand old poet, as terrible as he was grand, wandering aimlessly in the streets in Florence, under the burning sun, with a few coins in his pocket, and Landor had joined the Storys in Siena, where he continued to write his Latin verses attacking Napoleon III. Browning took lessons in modelling from Story, who remained his intimate friend for forty years. Once, at the Palazzo Barberini, Stor,'s house in Rome, he recited *The Pied Piper* to the Story children; Hans Andersen read *The Ugly Duckling*, and Story, playing on his flute, headed a march of the children about the house. But, as a poet, Story followed Browning like one of the children who had heard the piper.

Hawthorne surveyed the scene of *The Marble Faun* with a certain distrust and suspicion. For strangers, he felt, the Italian air had something sinister in it. The years were empty. Postponing the realities of life, one had no present, and gradually one ceased to have a future.[10] The artists "linger," he wrote, "while their originality dies out of them, or is polished away as a barbarism." This was surely true in Story's case, at least in the matter of his writing. What Story might have achieved under other conditions as the poet that he always wished to be remained an open question. His first Italian poems were certainly better,—if only because he was older,—than those he had written at home, the pale Tennysonian verses, the imitations of German ballads that had given him a little name in Boston. In fact, his *Castle Palo*, his *Orestes* and some of his dramatic monologues, *A Roman Lawyer in Jerusalem*, *A Jewish Rabbi in Rome*, would have been surprising in their power if they had not been virtually written by Browning. Story was the cleverest of chameleons, an actor, a ventriloquist

[10] "The years . . . have a kind of emptiness, when we spend too many of them on a foreign shore. We defer the reality of life, in such cases, until a future moment, when we shall again breathe our native air; but, by and by, there are no future moments; or, if we do return, we find that the native air has lost its invigorating quality,—and that life has shifted its reality to the spot where we have deemed ourselves only temporary residents. Thus, between two countries, we have none at all, or only that little space of either, in which we finally lay down our discontented bones. It is wise, therefore, to come back betimes, or never."—*The Marble Faun*.

in verse, and several of these poems were brilliant sallies. But less and less one found in his work the quiet, truthful, natural note that marked such earlier verses as *The Locust;* and the same thing was true of his writing in prose. His *Roba di Roma,* the fruit of his first impressions, charmingly pictured the surface of Roman life. It was a treasury of the sort of scenes, caught by an eager artist's eye, that appeared on a thousand canvases of the eighteen-fifties, the *panem et circenses* of the streets and the markets. This was the work that Story was to live by, one that he never equalled in later years. His pretty little novel, *Fiammetta,* like some of Henry James's early tales, suggested that Story ended where James began. The *Conversations in a Studio,* filled with sophisticated schoolboy-talk,—on Shakespeare, on capping quotations, on spirit-rapping,—bespoke a mind that never found its focus, a snapper-up of trifles, not unconsidered, but without the justification of a point of view.

Was Hawthorne right in feeling that "it needs the native air" to give a writer's work reality? Rome had provided him with a fairy setting for the last of his own romances,—the last he was ever to finish,—the tale of Hilda, Miriam and Donatello, the dusky Miriam of the shrouded past and the delicate wood-anemone of the Western forest. This dance of Yankee girls and fauns and spectres was like a Pompeiian fresco or something immobilized on a Grecian urn. A bituminous light suffused it, as of an afternoon in the realm of shades. One caught in the shifting groups the magical, mythological grace of Poussin. One heard Mignon's song rising from the depths in the fitful measure of a wind-harp. Hawthorne had drawn enchantment from the Roman air; and yet, for all the spell of *The Marble Faun,* it was hardly comparable with *The Scarlet Letter* or *The House of the Seven Gables.* The orchidaceous existence of most of the exiles seemed to bear him out in his distrust. One could dream forever in these Roman gardens, under the cypress and ilex, while all one's mental muscles atrophied. Norton, with his acute social conscience, his sense of a mission at home, probed under the surface of Italian life. The repressive political system disturbed him, and he had understood, from his own observation, the sorrows of Petrarch, Dante and Alfieri, who had mourned over their country and its degradation. Norton's critical faculties were alert; he had ridiculed the old romantic guide-books and the cold and pretentious work of the German painters who were dominant in modern Rome. He had cared for the realities of Italian life, as Greenough and Margaret Fuller had cared before him. The others did not wish to care. It was to escape from the prose of existence that they had left America. If their writing lost all grip and bottom, was not this the reason and the explanation?

CHAPTER XXVI

THE AUTOCRAT

THE WELL-KNOWN house of Ticknor and Fields was the publishing centre of Boston. William D. Ticknor, the senior partner, a cousin of George Ticknor, had built up a large business with English authors by paying for their books, an act of justice that was not required by any law of copyright. He had attracted Tennyson and Browning, Coventry Patmore and others, in several cases creating a public for them when they were still unknown at home.[1] The younger partner, James T. Fields, a man of letters in his own right, was a big, jovial creature, always dressed in Scotch tweeds, with a full beard, abundant hair, keen, twinkling eyes and a hearty manner. The Old Corner Bookstore in Washington Street, where Fields sat behind his green curtain, laughing and manufacturing reputations, was already an institution. There was always some author in Fields's cozy nook, Longfel-

---

[1] Many English authors of the time bore witness to the American "general gift of quicker and more subtle recognition of genius than the English public,"—as Coventry Patmore described it in talking with Hawthorne. Miss Mitford said to Fields: "It takes ten years to make a literary reputation in England, but America is wiser and bolder, and dares to say at once, 'This is fine.' "—Fields, *Yesterdays with Authors.*

See also Richard Garnett's remarks in his introduction to Lowell's *My Study Windows:* "Americans far surpass us English in the prompt recognition of excellence. Carlyle, De Quincey, Coventry Patmore, James Martineau, found their first considerable audiences across the Atlantic. Americans are quicker to discover the merits of a foreign author, more thorough in naturalizing him, and demand a higher standard of excellence in the translation of his works."

low, Mrs. Stowe or Emerson, sitting on the window-seat in a litter of books and papers. The shop was crowded with visitors, poets, historians, actors and singers,—for concert and lecture-tickets were also sold there,—country lawyers and ministers, on their annual journey to town, and here and there some elderly judge or merchant in search of a calf-bound set of Burke or Gibbon.

James T. Fields was a sort of liaison-officer between the European celebrities and the literati of Beacon Hill and Cambridge. He had a grand idea of the publishing business. As a Portsmouth boy, a shipmaster's son, like Hawthorne and Jones Very, a passionate lover of reading, he had watched the rise of New England letters and made up his mind to forward it. He had served his apprenticeship as a bookseller's clerk and had startled all the other clerks by guessing, whenever a customer entered the shop, the sort of book the customer presently asked for. His hero-worshipper's instinct would have pleased Carlyle. He knew the London publishers and bookmen as well as he knew New York and Boston, and he had visited all his British authors, Leigh Hunt, Miss Mitford, Wordsworth, Barry Cornwall. He had gathered together De Quincey's scattered writings and published the first collected edition of them. In rare-book rooms and auction-rooms, Fields was a familiar figure. He had read all the marginal comments in Wordsworth's little library. He had lovingly handled Lamb's own copies of Marlowe, Drummond and Drayton and the literary magnificoes at Elmwood. There was nothing he did not know about first editions. His house, which overlooked the Back Bay, was a temple of busts and portraits, autographs and souvenirs of authors, drawings by Blake, heads of Pope and Dickens, Thackeray, Wordsworth, Hawthorne. In later years, inspired by these portraits, all of them painted from life, he was to write his *Yesterdays with Authors,* a notable memoir filled with veracious gossip.

He liked a rough tramp in the Adirondacks or a camping-trip to Moosehead Lake, where one slept on the ground for a mattress with a bundle of faggots under one's head. At present, while he wrote his poems and essays,—the papers collected in *Underbrush* and various songs and ballads,—he gave most of his thoughts to business. He had a shrewd eye for the winning author that would have made the fortune of a racing-man.

The chief reader of Ticknor and Fields was Edwin P. Whipple, a self-made man of letters, like Fields himself, who had been a broker's clerk when Fields was a clerk in the bookshop. The two had been inseparable friends since the days when they had met, as fellow-bookworms, in the rooms of the Mercantile Library. Whipple was a short, slight man, always dressed in black, with a square, prim face and a manner all precision and decorum. Beside the exuberant Fields, with his overflowing air of the world, there was something ministerial in his appearance. He was extremely myopic and excessively shy, and yet this bespectacled man had a vigorous mind that often suggested Macaulay, who had praised him highly. His reputation was already brilliant, in England as well as America, and some of this reputation was deserved. As a writer for the *North American Review*, he had formed a method of his own, discriminating, acute and often subtle, with none of the ponderousness of his early models; and he was discussing, in his essays and lectures, such subjects as wit and humour, the ludicrous side of life, genius, intellectual health and disease, character, success and its conditions. His estimates of the early American writers were undoubtedly over-friendly, but his papers on the English dramatists and the Scottish and English critics were the best of their kind in America, by far. He had summed up Francis Jeffrey to perfection, and some of his essays, on Fielding, Thackeray, Dickens, were admirable characterizations and definitions. His only

American rivals were Poe and Lowell. Whipple, at the moment, was highly regarded; his volumes went through eight and ten editions, and he was to live obscurely as one of those writers whom people rediscover with surprise.

This very intelligent, shy and modest Whipple had long been moving about in Boston and Cambridge, watching the unusual men who lived there and noting their conversation and personal traits. He had formed this habit as a boy in Salem, observing Rufus Choate in his pew at church, so strangely different from the stolid merchants, and had later followed and studied in similar fashion Webster, George Ticknor and Charles Sumner, Prescott, Agassiz, Emerson, Alcott and others. He had a way of meeting them on the street at moments that revealed their oddities, stopping to see them when some bit of news had thrown them off their guard, catching two or three of them together when something in the air satisfied his eye for character. As a bank-clerk, in the Transcendental days, he had been struck by Emerson's sound sense, as compared with the delusions of the Boston merchants. The manias that possessed the business men, who bought up waste and worthless lands and recklessly sunk their millions in hopeless railroads, convinced him that Emerson knew the laws of trade better than Amos Lawrence. And so with all these other remarkable minds. He felt he was living at a historic moment, that a group of worthies had appeared who were to be of interest in the future. Scarcely observed by them, he was the chiel among them taking notes. These notes appeared later in his liveliest book, the excellent *Recollections of Eminent Men*.

That the New England mind had crystallized, that there was a renaissance in Boston,—one of those "heats and genial periods" of which Emerson spoke in *English*

Traits, "by which high tides are caused in the human spirit,"—had not escaped the firm of Ticknor and Fields. In fact, they were the practical centre of it. The publishers of Emerson, Hawthorne, Holmes, of Longfellow and Mrs. Stowe were able to feel that they were creating classics; for their authors were becoming national figures, and even international. Their little brown editions were known wherever books were read; and the day had long passed when Andrews Norton, making up a list of American writers, had placed Emerson, Longfellow and Hawthorne as minor figures in the second fifty. In Russia, even in India, even in China, all these names were favourably known, and lecturers in the West, like Whipple and Alcott, found that in St. Louis and Chicago they had an almost sovereign reputation. Seen from a distance, the New England writers appeared like fixed stars in a constellation that grew more brilliant with every decade. In fact, they were widely scattered. Aside from the groups in the capital, they rarely met. The Cambridge authors never went to Concord; the Concord authors seldom went to Boston; Whittier, Mrs. Stowe, Thoreau and others revolved in worlds of their own, and Ticknor's circle scarcely crossed the circles of Holmes and Lowell. Connecticut and Massachusetts were like different nations. Their unity was an abstraction still, largely so to remain, in fact; but Fields, the clever impresario, made a reality of it. He issued souvenir volumes of "Boston Authors," with plates of the Craigie house and Lowell's Elmwood, Webster's house at Marshfield and Ticknor's in Park Street. His "blue and gold" editions stamped his poets with authority. Willis wrote to Fields, in his flowery way, "Your press is the announcing-room of the country's Court of Poetry." From this press the English writers and the New England writers came together, and each drew something from the general glamour. Browning and Longfellow, Emerson, Tennyson, Hawthorne, Holmes, De Quincey, Mrs. Stowe presented a common front as standard authors.

One of Fields's jokes was about the Boston man who read Shakespeare late in life but found him far beyond his expectation. "There are not twenty men in Boston who could have written those plays," he said. More than twenty were engaged at present in work that Boston men were fitted for. Sparks's aspirations for the Athenæum seemed almost to have been fulfilled. There were dozens of more or less productive students in the alcoves that had once been empty; and Prince Jerome Napoleon, visiting Boston, surprised by the freedom of opinion, the absence of Puritanism that he found there, remarked that the New England capital had much more intellectual movement than any other part of the country. Among the recent minor men of letters were several whose names were to be remembered. The librarian of the Athenæum, William Poole, was at work on a well-known compilation. As one of the librarians at Yale, he had started the custom of keeping on slips of paper notes on current periodicals that might be useful in student-debates, and this was developing in Boston into *Poole's Index*. Thomas Bulfinch, the architect's son, a class-mate of Prescott at Harvard and a clerk at the Merchants' Bank, whose rooms, overlooking Scollay Square, were piled high with books, published *The Age of Fable* in 1855. In this same year, another book appeared that was equally useful. "Ask John Bartlett" was the phrase in Cambridge when anyone wished to find a familiar quotation. Bartlett owned the University book-store. A notable angler, a lover of whist, who edited Izaak Walton and later wrote a concordance of Shakespeare, he made his shop a centre for literary gossip and wished to live up to his reputation. He had kept for years the voluminous commonplace-book that finally emerged as Bartlett's *Familiar Quotations.*

The founding of the *Atlantic Monthly,* in 1857, marked this high tide of the Boston mind.[2] In the "new magazine," as it was called from Maine to Minnesota, all the established writers appeared together. Lowell, the editor, assembled for the first number contributions from Emerson, Motley, Holmes, Longfellow, Norton, Whittier and Mrs. Stowe. It seemed, from a distance, like a family party, in spite of the diversity of these minds, and murmurs were heard in other regions against the self-complacency of Boston and the mutual admiration that flourished there. But, as Dr. Holmes remarked of his commensals, if they had not admired one another they would have shown a singular want of taste. It was true that at this moment the New England mind began to reveal signs of degeneration, traits that in later years grieved or vexed those that knew not the Boston Zion, and sometimes did not even wish to know it. The "breaking of the seedling tulip into high-caste colours," as Dr. Holmes described this hour in Boston, was not without unhappy consequences. It destroyed the noble unconsciousness of the past. But the note of *The Atlantic* was not self-conscious, in spite of Lowell's tendency to be so. The magazine was born mature. The regard of the writers for one another sprang from an impersonal respect

[2] The American mind in general reached high tide at about this time. Samuel G. Goodrich ("Peter Parley") presented in *Recollections of a Life-time* the following statistics of American book-manufacture: In 1820, American authors, 30%, British authors, 70%; in 1830, American authors, 40%, British authors, 60%; in 1840, American authors, 55%, British authors, 45%; in 1850, American authors, 70%, British authors, 30%; in 1856, American authors, about 80%, British authors, 20%. In 1800, American school-books were wholly of English origin; by 1820, they had been adjusted to the needs of American readers; in 1856, they were wholly American. Goodrich added, "We produce annually more school-books than the whole continent of Europe."

for their characters and their work; and, if they over-valued one another, they set a better example than most of the other American writers and artists, who were all too prone to self-depreciation. They increased the self-respect of their fellow-craftsmen; they won for American letters and art the respect that American letters and art had always needed.[3] It was observed, moreover, that, sooner or later, almost everything *The Atlantic* published, essay, poem and story, found its way into a book and had at least a measure of permanent interest; and, as time went on, and Ticknor and Fields took over the publication, and Fields became the second editor, and the Civil War came, and Howells followed, the scope of the magazine grew broader and broader. It became a national institution.

Dr. Holmes had named *The Atlantic Monthly*, as Alcott had named *The Dial*; and he was the first contributor. He had had little time for writing prose in his active professional life, but he recalled that many years before he had published two papers entitled *The Autocrat of the Breakfast-Table.* Nothing could be salvaged from these old essays, but the venture had given him a good idea, to carry a note-book with him and jot down his own conversation. A Boswell writing out himself. Two other contributions to the monthly, evoked by the Civil War, were the *Battle Hymn of the Republic* and *The Man Without a Country.* Julia Ward Howe and Edward Everett Hale, a nephew of Edward Everett, were destined to outlive the century and write their memories of a hundred years. Hale, whose father was Nathan Hale, the editor of the *Daily Advertiser,* the oldest of New England daily journals, remembered seeing his

---

[3] "We every day too easily undervalue our own artists. It is sad to say that to a remark of Thackeray they owe some of the consideration they enjoy. 'Never neglect or forget Trumbull,' he said, and poor America accepted the boon of praise, and thought better of her Revolutionary artist."—T. G. Appleton, *A Sheaf of Papers.*

mother rock the cradle in which reposed his sister, the infant Lucretia, who wrote *The Peterkin Papers* in after years, while Webster and Justice Story dictated to her the speeches that were to appear in her husband's paper. To write a book, for one of the Hales, was as natural as to breathe; the father, the mother, the sisters, Lucretia and Susan, were all authors by instinct and almost by habit; and Edward Everett Hale, a minister, whose mind was ingenious and alert, breezy and even salty, had begun to write for the press at seventeen. He was quite outside the literary currents that had flowed through the centre of the Boston mind. His models were the familiar essayists, and his mode was evangelical journalism. But he had a "new idea" once or twice, in *My Double, and How He Undid Me,* and especially in *The Man Without a Country.* New ideas are rare in story-telling, and Hale's Philip Nolan, like Rip Van Winkle, became a folk-figure, a national myth. That the story appeared at a moment when patriotic feeling was at a pitch, when men like Thoreau, whose interests were universal, felt for the first time that they had a country, accounted for its impression on the public mind; but it was a bold and fresh conception. Julia Ward Howe, a banker's daughter from New York, a clever and charming young woman with a passion for learning, had met Dr. Howe, the teacher of the blind, on one of her visits to Boston. He was riding on a black horse, and she had straightway fallen in love with him. Miss Julia Ward's friends in New York thought that her pink stockings should have been blue, for she had herself roped to her chair, in the manner of Alfieri, during her hours of study. In Boston, they understood these matters better. As the universal reformer of the future, ready for every new crop of "causes," almost the only person who knew the New York "four hundred" as well as the Boston "forty," she was a more gracious Margaret Fuller.

Half a century later, Mrs. Howe and Dr. Hale had become folk-figures in actual life. They were almost as mythological as Philip Nolan, so many associations had gathered about them. These were the days when every child in Boston had sat on Dr. Hale's knee, when the patriarch who looked like Homer was chaplain of the Senate at Washington and the romantic old sibyl, travelling with her lecture, her cap and her laces tucked away in her hand-bag, recited the *Battle Hymn* on every occasion. They were the last leaves of the flowering thorn-bush, the Boston, historic, prehistoric, of the eighteen-forties and fifties. Dr. Holmes had fallen long before them, and Holmes had flowered late. He had outlived the life-span of Goldsmith when he appeared in prose in *The Atlantic*. No matter, the pear-trees had reassured him. Some were ripe at twenty, the Jargonelles, and one had to make the most of them when they were young, for their day was soon over. Others came into their perfect condition later. These were the autumn pears that lasted better than the summer fruit. Best of all were the Winter Nelis, hard and uninviting until all the rest of the pears had had their season. Long after the frost and snow had nipped and wrecked the orchards, the Winter Nelis got their glow and perfume. How much worm-eaten fruit, how many windfalls the doctor had seen under the boughs when the sap in his own tree was just beginning to stir!

Thus it was that, at the breakfast-table, the Autocrat resumed his seat one morning and found himself addressing his fellow-boarders, the schoolmistress, the divinity-student, the landlady's daughter, Benjamin Franklin, all the characters he had known so well, in Boston or the "huckleberry districts," during his lecture-tours. The boarding-house was a microcosm of a larger world, for what American did not find himself suggested in one of the characters? The Autocrat had earned his right to speak; he had plucked the flowers of life and come to the berries, and who could say that he was not a teacher fit for a great occasion, he who had fed with the fox in the matter of knowledge and used such Machiavellian astuteness in passing on all that he had learned? What was his mission? It was very simple: the mission of conversation. Was it not very bad to have thoughts and feelings, which ought to come out in talk, *strike in,* as people said of certain diseases? There was the great American evil, morbid introspection, class-distinctions that were unconfessed, scruples of conscience, secrets that ought to be exposed to common sense, forms of speech and phrases, ugly and distorted, the outward and visible signs of the twisted life within. Fruits of the old religion of Calvinism, fruits of isolation and provincial conditions, fruits of unconscious living. Out with them, and talk them over! The boarders knew they could trust a family doctor who read them through and through, who saw their maternal grandfathers in the way they held their tea-cups, and who would never abuse their confidence, a doctor who was used to dealing with secrets and who, without hurting their feelings, could give them the right prescription to set them on the road of mental health.

The boarders listened like a three-years' child. All America had begun to listen, and well the doctor knew it. Did people think that talk was merely a tool with which to chop a path for one's primitive wants? Did they think that absolute truth, in the form of rigidly stated propositions, was all that conversation ought to admit? Did they not see how difficult it was for two persons engaged in talk to make the most of one another's thoughts, when both had so many? (Here the boarders stirred and looked as if they wished for an explanation; for they did not know they had so many thoughts, never having put them into words.) Conversation must have its partial truths, even its exaggerated truths,—the boarders stirred again,—if, as one of the fine arts, it is to serve a greater art, the art of human relations. It must not merely express the "logical mind" that builds a bridge of asses over chasms that wit leaps across.

Thus, in his diplomatic way, the Autocrat attacked all the mental habits of his hearers. What was this "logical mind," the fruit of generations of preachers and lawyers, but the One-Hoss Shay of Calvinism? The doctor had no use for Calvinism, and he knew that, while they laughed at the one-hoss shay in Boston and at Harvard, it was no laughing matter in the country. He was determined to break it up,—if laughter failed, by other means, by quoting half a dozen sciences, by the use of analogies and comparisons, by every method but controversy, since controversy equalized the foolish and the wise and no one knew this better than the fools. For what was the "logical mind" of Calvinism but the parent of all injustice, the *a priori* and the *parti pris,* narrow judgment, rigid condemnation, all those moral plagues, in other words, from which the American mind so patently suffered? Did he mean to weaken moral obligations by drawing up the blinds of this dark chamber and letting in the light? His object was merely to define them; for the light he let into the dark chamber was the light of common sense, a doctor's view of the problem of cause and effect as it really expressed itself in human nature. Was some question of crime involved? The "logical mind" spoke of original sin and anathematized the doctor. The rational mind spoke of the effect and anathematized the cause. As for the fruits of the old religion, many of the minister's patients were fools and cowards, and all too many of them were also liars. (Immense sensation at the table.)

The doctor was prepared for the sensation. The religious weeklies and monthlies, all over the country, began to throw brickbats at him. The Autocrat was imperturbable. One cannot turn over any old falsehood without a terrible squirming and scattering of the unpleasant little population that dwells under it. No one can ever say anything to make his neighbours wiser or better without being abused for doing so; and, if there is one thing that people detest, it is to have their little mistakes made fun of. The Autocrat continued, with calm good humour, always ready to talk as long as a few boarders remained at the table, twirling their knives, perhaps, balancing their spoons on the edge of their tea-cups or tilting on their chairs against the wall. Was he named Holmes for nothing? A holme is a meadow surrounded by brooks; and, as long as two or three brooks, were they only trickles, fed it with their attention, how could a meadow run dry? Now, these little mistakes, this tilting of chairs against walls, this pronouncing the name of one's town as if one did not know that it ought to be "Norridge," this calling an entry a "hall" and a buggy a "kerridge," this saying "Yes?" when somebody told one something,— did they think these vulgarisms were trivial matters? Was it not plain enough that a man with a future had to get rid of all these odious tricks? What hope could he have when he said "How's your health?" when people liked to hear "How do you do?" Did not Sydney Smith say that no public man in England ever got over a false quantity uttered in early life? And might it not be similarly said that the woman who "calc'lates" is lost? Worldly wisdom, merely, not at all the wisdom of the angels; but surely the woman who "calc'lates" is not an angel, and, since she is given to calculating, she might calculate to better purpose. And what was one to say about those rural visitors who do not know how to get out of a room when their visit is really over? They wish to be off, you wish them to be off, but they do not know how to manage it. One would think they had been built in one's parlour and were waiting to be launched. One had to contrive for them a sort of ceremonial inclined plane and back them down, stern foremost, so to speak, into the great ocean of out-of-doors. Then what was one to say of the "terrible smile," the smile of those persons whose mouths, the moment they see us, begin to twitch with an uncertain movement, conveying the idea that they are thinking about themselves and thinking that we are thinking that they are thinking about themselves? What was one to say of the pretty women who do not understand the law of the road in regard to handsome faces? Nature and custom agree, the Autocrat remarked, in granting all males the right of at least two distinct looks at every comely female countenance, one to define the person, one as an appreciating homage. The lady of whom he approved was she who left at home her virtuous-indignation countenance, knowing that the street is a picture-gallery where pretty faces framed in pretty hats are meant to be admired, and everybody has a right to see them.

Trifles, perhaps, but not unkindly mentioned. Was not the art of living made up of trifles? And were these awkward postures and rustic phrases as merely superficial as one might think? Were they not the signs of inner dislocations, the rigidities, false reserves, distortions, torments that render human relations so difficult and make men so unhappy? Expression was the greatest need of this unexpressed New England, which almost seemed to enjoy its cold and taciturn ways, ways that concealed what tragic depths! Emotions that can shape themselves in language open the gate for themselves into the great community of human affections. That was why the Autocrat loved words, expressive words, euphonious and pleasing, just as he loved song. As long as a woman could talk, or had some musical utterance, there was nothing that she could not bear. How many a tragedy had found its outlet in a strenuous bravura or a fierce roulade on one of Jonas Chickering's pianos! Therefore the Autocrat loved to hear the all-pervading tum-tum issuing from the window of the unlovely farmhouse, with the brown stream flowing beside the door, in which Almira or Louella might have been found floating, face downward, had she not been able, in these harmless discords, to throb her wild impulses away.

The boarders listened, all America listened, as the Autocrat unfolded his amusing wisdom, unrolled that inexhaustible scroll which only those possess who have kept their wits alive by constant use. Never had they heard of such a man for breaking up the ice of mental habits, for harrowing people's minds and planting in them flowers that out-shone even "Macaulay-flowers." They listened round the table, reading *The Atlantic,* drawing virtue from it, as hot water draws the strength of tea-leaves; for society, as the Autocrat said, is a strong solution of books. The old gentleman opposite smiled benignly, and Benjamin Franklin gathered some valuable hints. As for the theological remarks, the divinity-student honoured himself by the way in which he received them: he did not swallow them at once, neither did he reject them, but he took them as a pickerel takes the bait. He carried them off to his cranny upstairs to ruminate over them at leisure. The schoolmistress pondered these things in her heart and presently passed them on to her flock. All Young America, sooner or later, heard her say that "those who ask your opinion really want your praise and will be contented with nothing less." Did she not remark, "Sin has many tools, but a lie is the handle which fits them all"? Did she not refer to the cubes and spheres, the little cubes of Truth that are always white and the spheres that have "lie" written on them but that roll so easily and so pleasantly, although they are always rolling into the wrong corner? One had no real excuse for mistaking the cubes, because they always stayed

where they were left; but Timidity and Good-Nature
and Polite-Behaviour insisted that Truth must roll, and
they filed and polished away the snow-white cubes till
one could hardly tell them from the spheres,—a sad mistake, since Truth is always square. No doubt, there were
members of the rising generation who did not hear this
fable in their youth; but they were not born under the
Stars and Stripes.

For schoolmistresses, Dr. Holmes had a tender feeling.
He was well aware of the part they played in a nation
and generation in which the men shirked the tasks of
culture. Who but the schoolmistress, and usually the
New Englander of the species, followed the pioneers
wherever they went, even to the remotest corner of the
Rocky Mountains, and sowed the furrows they ploughed
with the seeds of education which, but for her, would
have remained unsown? Well the doctor knew this heroism, and he knew it imposed on the heroine a biological
handicap. "The great procession of the Unloved" filled
him with compassion, for he was a match-maker on all
occasions. Besides, they belonged, as often as not, to the
Brahmin caste of New England, that mystical brotherhood and sisterhood in which the doctor took a special
pride and which he was the first to designate. He grieved
when people supposed that he meant by the Brahmins
a bloated Boston aristocracy. His innocent and service-
able caste was no such thing. Its members were commonly sensitive, pallid and shy, and their only birthright
was a taste for learning. Bred from races of scholars, descended from gentle souls who had stepped off the "Mayflower" or the "Arbella" with books in their hands, races
that had acquired, by the repetition, generation after
generation, of the same unworldly influences, a distinct
organization and facial type, they took to their books at
school as a pointer or a setter to his field-work. Their
names were constantly rising to prominence in connec-

tion with some learned labour, and the nation owed to their devotion countless unrequited benefits. Indeed, they were a caste to which only a niggard could wish to refuse a decent homage; for, in exchange for all their lofty efforts, what were their worldly claims, their prescriptive titles?—that they wore white linen by inherited instinct, that they were able to pronounce the sacred word "view," a word not to be spelled or, by others, pronounced, the touchstone of New England Brahminism. Dr. Holmes was not to be blamed if other times brought other customs, if, in days to come, the Brahmins ceased to perform their function and, in proportion as they lost their vigour, advanced their worldly claims.

Everyone listened to the Autocrat, except a little group of serious thinkers who called themselves Humanists later. Perhaps they were not in the room when he remarked: "Beware of making your moral staple consist of the negative virtues. It is good to abstain, and teach others to abstain, from all that is sinful and harmful. But making a business of it leads to emaciation of character, unless one feeds largely also on the more nutritious diet of active, sympathetic benevolence." Perhaps this little group considered the doctor frivolous, with his marked distaste for a "soul-subduing decorum." But everyone else was prepared to listen when he wrote a novel, *Elsie Venner;* for he had long believed that every intelligent man had the stuff of a novel in him, and therefore why not he? In fact, he wrote three novels, as he wrote three books about the breakfast-table, proving his theory about continuations, that they were not always justified. Good jockeying, he thought, was important for authors. One should let the public see one's horse only just enough and not too much, hold him up hard when the market was too full of him, always gently feel his mouth, never slack and never jerk the rein. He let his own horse out only when the horse grew too impatient, and sometimes with not too much success. His novels were "medicated novels"; and, as the doctor was always a talker, he strolled about from page to page, airing his views about his characters, dismissing them at times with a turn of the hand as if they were so many cases at a medical meeting. His composition was very untidy. But he always had a new story, even when it was only a ghost of a story, as in the breakfast-table series, and he always had a problem to deal with,—hysteria in a young girl, a young man's misogyny, morbid religious excitement and its effects. There were happy streaks in all his writings, and striking applications of modern science; and his essay on *Mechanism in Thought and Morals,* the "underground workshop of thought,"—the unconscious,—was a brilliant anticipation of Dr. Freud. In fact, although *Elsie Venner,* of all these later books, was the only one that seriously counted, the doctor knew so much about human nature, and had such a tang of his own, that one could read him at his worst with pleasure.

He was always putting two and two together, and *Elsie Venner* stood for a large sum in this species of multiplication. He had taken one of his twos from the old medical books over which he was constantly poring, Schenckius, Andreas Baccius and Cardan, books that amused the imagination. They were full of Æsculapian gossip concerning girls who had fed on poison and who acted out the influence of the poison, gossip about men, bitten by serpents, who became the fathers of daughters whom serpents could not harm, however the daughters might mistreat the serpents. *Christabel* and Keats's *Lamia* were favourites with the doctor; and recent experiments had seemed to suggest that snake-bites might produce an influence over the moral faculties of the victim. But all these mythical and half-mythical data merely served to fertilize the doctor's fancy. He was out for larger game when he imagined the beautiful, cold girl with the glittering eyes who was destined for a tragic end, the gliding, sliding Elsie, with diamonds on her breast, and her asp-like bracelet, and the barred skirts in which she liked to dance, to the rhythm of castanets. She was still and dangerous and watchful, silent in her anger and swift in vengeance, and the village folk believed that she was able to twist herself into all sorts of shapes and tie herself in a knot. In short, she suggested the rattlesnake that Dr. Holmes kept in his cage; and the story was that a snake had bitten her mother, just before Elsie was born. Was it a case of physical cause and effect? How could any honest doctor say so, even if he liked to tease his readers? Besides, there were plenty of Elsies in New England whose mothers had not been bitten by rattlesnakes. Several of them had been hanged as witches; and who but Margaret Fuller had narrowed her lids, just as Elsie did, till her eyes were small and bright as diamonds? The doctor was interested indeed in the subject of prenatal influences, but not in quite so simple a way as this. He wished to test the doctrine of original sin, which was still raging in New England, or, to place it on a larger ground, the doctrine of human responsibility for the aberrations of a disordered will. Was Elsie "shapen in iniquity," as the farmers and the country parsons thought? Not if one saw her life as the doctor saw it and did his best to make his readers see it. Was she a subject for wrath or a subject for pity? The rattlesnake's bite was only a figure of speech for any kind of untoward circumstance,—a couple of drunken grandfathers or abuse in childhood,—that might explain anyone's aberrations of will. If one saw this clearly in Elsie's case, what about all the other unhappy creatures who were born with poison in their system?

This time the doctor cast a bombshell into the circle of his fellow-boarders. Every breakfast-table in the country resounded with *Elsie Venner*. Were you a Unitarian or a Calvinist, or any other variety of Jew or Christian, were you interested in the recent theories about heredity and environment, in medical and therapeutic questions, philosophy, criminology, education? Then *Elsie Venner* had something to say to you, and sometimes it was not a pleasant message. If, as a good Unitarian, you liked to think of the soul as an "unstained white tablet," then Elsie with her wicked little powders was an awkward nut to crack. The question whether Elsie could help herself was even more of a dose for the Orthodox. If you were a Pharisee, you fared still worse; for, if Elsie was not responsible, if she could not be accused of sin,—however one might punish her for crime,—what became of your own pretensions? Were you not obliged to see that your valour and justice, your strength, truth and virtue were merely the result of your happy fortune? What was your aristocracy but a sum that began with a one in tar and a two in tallow, and perhaps a three in whale-oil, however maintained by pluck? Your elevated type of face and figure were due not to you and your father's virtue, beyond a certain measure, but to the money made from the tar and the tallow that bought the air and sunshine, the healthy, happy summers, the good nursing and doctoring, the best cuts of the best beef and mutton, which enabled your father, and his father and his, to grow up in such a kindly fashion and, when they were grown, to afford the costly luxury of beauty and marry the finest specimens of the other sex. This train of reasoning went a long way when the valour and the truth, the strength and the virtue were so obviously poisoned *out* of a race by the food of the bushman in his forest, by the foul air and darkness of the tenement-houses where half one's fellow-Christians were constrained to live. Just how far it went, the doctor might not have cared to think, for the "sunny street that holds the sifted few," the "swell-fronts and south-exposure houses" had a singular charm for him, as for other mortals, and the people who lived inside these houses were not only just as good as other people but the pleasantest for a doctor to take care of. "Why not take the tops of your sparrowgrass? Somebody must have 'em,—why shouldn't you?" Such was the doctor's advice to a young disciple; and, in fact, he never pretended to be a sage, too lofty for these trifles. He knew that a certain amount of glass was mingled with the bricks in the house he lived in, a knowledge that disarmed the caster of stones; and meanwhile he had discharged a thunderbolt that fairly rocked the walls of Philistinism. Who, after reading *Elsie Venner*, could talk about "total depravity"? Who was to condemn? Who to judge? Or pride himself too much on his family portraits? Or think that God had given him his lands and chattels in recognition of his Christian virtue? Dr. Holmes, perhaps unwittingly, had played into the hands of Dr. Darwin. He had played into the hands of Dr. Freud. He had played into the hands of another doctor of whom perhaps he had never heard, Dr. Marx. One never knows how far a doctor's table-talk may carry him.

for him, as for all the world, and the people who lived
within these walls were not only just as good as white
people but in that all but the culture to make care of...
...not like the ignorant poor people and...
...men have come, very shocking, poor such was the that
in "Spider" to I young, (Bridie," and in fact, he never
pretended to be a bigot and only for these. But it always
seemed that a certain amount of pay was mingled with
the back in the house. He lived for it knot felt...
...dreamed the cares of women may meant that the top
encouraged a friendship that felt packed the walls of
Plantation. When after reading this I gazed thoughtfully
about, and despaired. Who was to understand. What is
under the subscription...

...raise Or think that God had given him his hands and
shoulders in recognition for his Christian service. On
Holm... perhaps unwittingly, had placed into the hand
of Dr. ..., He had ..., He had ... into the hands of Dr.
...ford. He had placed into the hands of another doctor
of whom perhaps he and many in him, the More. One
never knows how far a thought's table but may carry him.

CHAPTER XXVII

THE SATURDAY CLUB: LOWELL

PRESCOTT died in 1859. Almost totally blind, at the last, and racked with rheumatism, able to read only a few lines in the artificial twilight of his dark blue curtains, lying flat on the floor, with his noctograph before him, when any other posture was impossible, he had never ceased to work at the vast *History of Philip II,* of which three volumes were completed. "My spirits," he said, "are always as high as my pulse, about fifteen points above normal." He was merry and laughing as usual a day before the end. Longfellow's last remembrance of Prescott was a sunny smile at the corner of the street.

The faithful Ticknor, inconsolable, recalled the happy times at Pepperell, the drives and walks with Prescott in the Fairy Grove or along the Nashua river, the evenings when they had read *The Antiquary,* with two generations of children to share the pleasure. At Lynn, where Prescott had also had a villa, looking over the water towards Nahant, an old cherry-tree stood near the house. Round and round this tree, to protect his eyes in the shade, Prescott had walked every day until he had worn a path in the greensward. The traces of this path remained for years, worn by no foot but his, while Ticknor, touched by all these memories, slowly composed his *Life of Prescott.* This was a rare biography, picturesque and circumstantial. New England had produced no other that could be placed beside it; for Ticknor's affection for his subject had brought out all the skill, the gift for observation and characterization that made his own Journal so entertaining. The unfinished *Philip II* contained some of Prescott's most spirited writing, the Battle of Lepanto, the Siege of Malta. It was a history of Europe in the latter half of the sixteenth century, when the doctrines of the Reformation were dividing the world; and Prescott had had to spread his investigations over the whole continent. On his visit to Europe in 1850, he had spent several weeks in Belgium and Holland, studying the topography of the country, the scenes of Philip's reign, the spot where William the Silent had fallen at Delft. He had had the help of Pasqual de Gayangos, the great professor of Arabic at Madrid, who translated Ticknor into Spanish. Gayangos searched for him the manuscript collection of Sir Thomas Phillips, twelve thousand pages, gathered in boxes and closets in Phillips's house, some of them under his bed; and Prince Corsini also assisted Prescott, collecting documents in Italy. The archives of Simancas, which no historian had even seen, Philip II's own original papers, two hundred and eighty-four dusty bundles, rolled up at random, that lay like bottles of forgotten wine in the lumber-room of a Spanish castle, were sorted and scrutinized for him, along with the archives of Leyden, the Hague and Paris. In all, there were eight thousand sheets to be turned into threads for the Gobelin-loom in Boston, where the tireless Prescott wove his tapestry.

Never again perhaps were historical works to excite so much attention as at present. A generation later, Parkman's great books appeared in little editions of seven hundred copies. Only a handful of readers noticed them. Prescott's *Conquest of Mexico,* a large and expensive work in three volumes, had sold four thousand copies in four months, and *Philip II,*—like Robertson's *Charles V,* which Prescott revised and continued, to fill the gap in Spanish history between Ferdinand and Philip,—was published in England in four simultaneous editions.

These splendidly printed books,—for Prescott and Ticknor took pains to appear in the grand manner,—put Peter Parley out of countenance; and the interest in history grew with the interest in public affairs, which were rapidly shaping for the Civil War. Ticknor had returned from his last European journey, with a great new collection of books for Boston. The rival Astor Library in New York, with Cogswell at its head, had filled the old scholar-courtier with apprehension. Unless something similar were done in Boston, the literary culture of New England would follow trade and capital to the rapidly-growing metropolis. Ticknor had taken the lead for the Boston Public Library, collected lists of necessary books from every interested citizen, established agencies in Florence and Leipzig and bought books in London, Paris and Rome. He had made Boston, once for all, a centre of historical research.

Prescott's example had also had its effect. He had won for Boston the interest of historians everywhere and had opened up facilities for others; and his winning personality and heroic labours made history still more attractive to younger men. Of his own generation, Bancroft, who had withdrawn for a while from public life, carried on his work from volume to volume. He had long since settled in New York, but he had a summer villa at Newport, where he took special pride in his roses. He corresponded with rosarians all over the world. Every evening, at Newport, he read to the ladies of his household the pages he had written during the day, asking for suggestions in regard to style; for the more the flowers grew in his garden, the more he plucked them out of his prose, which soon became monotonous and bare. Everett, who had helped both Prescott and Bancroft, had also retired from politics and withdrawn to his "temple of peace" on Summer Street. His brief term as president of Harvard had not been too agreeable, for the kindly old soul, as

vain as he was kind, had grieved because the undergrad-
uates did not touch their hats to him enough. But the
aging figurehead of the Boston ship, beaten by so many
storms, made of soft pine instead of oak, still Apollonian
in its wrinkled beauty, was ready for another voyage.
Fearing that a civil war was coming, Everett did what
he could to stave it off. Washington's house at Mount
Vernon was dropping to pieces. The columns of the
portico were falling, the offices were in ruins, the floor of
the summer-house was gone, there were pales missing
from the staircase. The magnolias had been whittled
away by tourists and even the tomb was in decay. Everett,
who had tried in vain to save Franklin's early home in
Boston, hoped to unite the North and the South in one
last touch of common sentiment. He composed an oration on Washington, which he delivered in almost every
city in the country, and saved Mount Vernon with the
proceeds. The day had passed for Everett's oratory, but
there were always crowds to applaud a speaker who held
his glass of water aloft and slowly and dexterously spilled
it as he spoke of the cleanliness of Washington's soul.

The wheel of time had turned again. On winter afternoons, in Beacon Street, when George Ticknor passed,
strolling in the sunlight, with his air of conscious importance, one recalled the days of Gilbert Stuart. The renaissance in Boston had scarcely existed for Ticknor. It
scarcely existed for the elder Dana, the author of *The
Idle Man,* who had outlived his little fame and whom
one also saw, on sunny days, warming his bones in the
Common, although the Saturday Club, recently organized by the younger writers,—touched by his charm and
silvery courtesy,—elected him an honorary member. The
old guard looked askance at the reigning talents, which
were too informal to please them. Emerson's high-flown
manner offended them still. They did not like Holmes's
style, his way of referring to "Roxbury and Dorchester

boys." This made the younger people feel akin, but it struck their elders as too familiar. It was almost as bad as Whittier, so plain that he might have been common. Lowell was too clever to be sound. If Burke and Johnson were no longer read, what was more to blame than Lowell's brilliance?[1] Thackeray had scandalized Boston, on his reading-tour, by driving to the lecture-hall with his long legs thrust out of the carriage-window. His friends had had to repress his jollity, as he ploughed through the snow on Beacon Street with *Henry Esmond,* just issued, under his arm. The old Bostonians knew that Englishmen often behaved like this, but they had never expected to see a Boston man cutting undignified capers; and Lowell's puns and Holmes's boarding-house almost savoured of the vulgar.

The temperature, if not the tone, had risen; and no one from other regions ever complained that the Boston tone was low. When Thackeray wrote to Fields, "I always consider Boston my native place," he was referring to the temperature, the warm and genial air of the Yankee Athens in these days of its efflorescence. Agassiz's beaming face at the Saturday Club, and Longfellow, benign, all unconscious of the spell he wove, at the other end of the table, set the pitch of the gatherings. If the club had not existed, Dr. Holmes would have invented it, for such an association, in his opinion,—a club strung like a harp, with a dozen ringing intelligences, each answering to some chord of the macrocosm,—was the crown of a literary centre. What would literature and art have been if Shakespeare had not had his Mermaid Tavern, and Addison and Steele their coffee-house, not to speak of Dr. Johnson, Goldsmith and Gibbon? It was one of the doctor's convictions that a handful of men, at any given moment, carry in their brains the ovarian eggs

[1] Professor Bowen, editor of the *North American Review,* rejected Lowell's earlier essays because they were "too brilliant."

of the future, and that one should talk with them in order to seize in advance these germs of thought, not yet developed, germs that were moulded on new patterns which had to be long and closely studied. For no fresh truth ever got into a book: an egg once hatched was already old. There were jobbers of thought and retailers of thought; but he wished to know the producers of thought. That was why he loved his club so dearly. One could listen to Asa Gray on botany, Peirce on mathematics and Lowell on language, Agassiz on geology and fossils, Motley on history, Norton on cathedrals. If one followed for a dozen years any line of knowledge, every other line would intersect it; and here all the lines intersected, the doctor was happy to find,—in this carnival-shower of questions, replies and comments, axioms bowled over the table like bomb-shells from professional mortars, while wit dropped its explosive trains of many-coloured fire and pelted everyone who exposed himself. Emerson enjoyed the club for much the same reasons. Of the lonely men of Concord, he was the only member, with Judge Hoar, who drew any virtue from the meetings; for Hawthorne, who joined the club after his return from Italy, sat with his eyes fixed upon his plate. Thoreau's feeling in regard to clubs might have been described as detached.[2] But Emerson, who said that he fed on genius and who liked to see feats of every kind, feats of mathematical combination, of memory and the

---

[2] "As for the Parker House, I went there once, when the Club was away, but I found it hard to see through the cigar smoke; and men were deposited about in chairs over the marble floor, as thick as legs of bacon in a smoke-house. It was all smoke, and no salt, Attic or other. The only room in Boston which I visit with alacrity is the gentlemen's waiting-room at the Fitchburg depot, where I wait for the cars, sometimes for two hours, to get out of town. It is a paradise to the Parker House . . . A large and respectable club of us hire it (Town and Country Club), and I am pretty sure to find someone there whose face is set the same way as my own."—Thoreau, *Familiar Letters*.

power of abstraction, who rejoiced in a gymnasium and a swimming-school, where one saw the power of the body, a race-course, a training-ground for horses, a laboratory, a surgeon's demonstration, who never heard of any skill or vigour without fresh resolution,—Emerson sat like a child at the meetings. Every word that was dropped set free his fancy. He talked, but rarely; he preferred to listen.[3] His was Goethe's gift, the "highest to which man can attain," wonder.

Lowell walked in from Cambridge to his office at *The Atlantic*. Once his hat blew into the river, as he was crossing the bridge, with a hatful of rejected manuscripts. He scarcely had to look for his contributions beyond the Boston, Cambridge and Concord circles. The Porterhouse steak at the Porter House, the Parker-house rolls at the Parker House, guinea-fowl and venison on all occasions, and wine, "the grand specific against dull dinners," as Dr. Holmes called it, sped the festive enterprise; and even the abstemious author of *Snow-Bound,* who had never entered a theatre and who cared as little for dinners as the men of Concord, caught the contagion of the magazine and grew more and more the man of letters. Lowell published a series of Agassiz's essays, which spread the popular knowledge of science. A poem that attracted much attention, *On a Bust of Dante,* was the work of a Boston dentist, Thomas W. Parsons. It was a good poem, although notable chiefly as an expression of the *zeitgeist,* the ever-growing interest in Dante studies. Dr. Parsons, at seventeen, had spent a year in

[3] "I sat by the side of Emerson, who always charms me with his delicious voice, his fine sense and wit, and the delicate way he steps about among the words of his vocabulary,—if you have seen a cat picking her footsteps in wet weather, you have seen the picture of Emerson's exquisite intelligence, feeling for its phrase or epithet,— sometimes I think of an anteater, singling out his insects, as I see him looking about and at last seizing his noun or adjective,—the best, the only one which would serve the need of his thought."— *Life and Letters of Oliver Wendell Holmes.*

Italy, where he had formed his life-long love of Dante. He had learned the *Paradiso* by heart in Florence and had translated the *Inferno* years before Norton began his studies.[4] Some of his other poems were good, especially *The Shadow on the Obelisk*. They represented a kind of verse, graceful and correct, that was rapidly multiplying. Often the expression of poetic natures, of cultivated and scholarly minds, usually written with taste but almost if not quite devoid of magic, this verse, which would have seemed miraculous a generation before, was a staple of every journal in later days.[5] In the country towns, as in the Western cities, thousands of eager faces, by the evening lamp, scanned each new issue of *The Atlantic,* thrilled by a new poem of Whittier or Lowell, perplexed by Emerson's cryptic rhymes. "If the red slayer think he slays" was better than a dozen cross-word puzzles. A paper by Thomas Wentworth Higginson, *Letter to a Young Contributor,* fluttered a breast in Amherst that was to sing to better purpose than most of the famous poets of the eighteen-sixties. To Emily Dickinson, "moving to Cambridge" seemed "like moving to Westminster Abbey, as hallowed and as unbelieved, or moving to Ephesus with Paul for a next-door neighbour."

Cambridge still had much of the village look. A mighty elm shaded Harvard Square, and the groups of youths and maidens in summer dresses who danced on the green, on Class Day, in front of Holworthy Hall, brought back the May Day of merry England. Old Royal Morse, the driver of the stage in the days of President

[4] A copy of Parsons's *Inferno,* translated in 1843, was placed under the cornerstone of the monument to Dante in the Piazza Santa Croce.

[5] American poetry has had its own "law of acceleration." Rufus W. Griswold, the anthologist, said that he had read all the American poetry published before 1850. He estimated this at about five hundred volumes. Three generations later, at least as many volumes appeared every year.

Kirkland, still haunted the square to tell his tales of a time when President Kirkland had scarcely been heard of. Agassiz strolled across the Yard, smoking his cigar, oblivious of the university statutes. Agassiz represented all that was new, while old Cambridge was John Holmes's special province. For Dr. Holmes's shy and modest brother, whose occupation was friendship, the period since 1832 was "margin" and sometimes "leavings." A "ripe local man," as he wished to be, he lived in a little house on Appian Way, full of cats and birds. "I sha'n't have better quarters," he said, "till I have a better half." For a bit of foreign travel, he went to Nantasket. He even made three short trips to Europe, where he could find nothing to compare with Cambridge. Every day in Venice he repaired to a spot that reminded him of a corner of the port, where Broadway and Cambridge Street met. Besides an occasional poem, he wrote a series of letters to one of his nephews about Goliath Tittle, the Kennebunk sailor. Goliath was tattooed in circles by a tribe in the South Sea Islands, and then he was captured by another tribe who changed all the circles into squares. John Holmes's only ventures into print were addressed to esoterics in Cambridge lore, those who could answer the following questions: "Where was the old Court House? The old jail? The Market House? Where was the college wood-yard? Where were the old hay-scales? Where was the little brook that ran over gravel toward the Charles and, like the two princes, was stifled in its bed?"

In Cambridge, as in Concord, where the "little women" and the "little men" were about to appear in books, children filled the scene. All the New England writers understood them and wrote about them, sometimes with exquisite feeling.[6] *Uncle Tom's Cabin* was

---

[6] "Pliable as she was to all outward appearance, the child had her own still, interior world, where all her little notions and opinions

composed, under the lamp, on a table surrounded by children conning their lessons, in a hum of earnest voices asking questions. Hawthorne's stories were as full of children as ever the summer woods were filled with birds; and Whittier's shy affections and Holmes's salty humours were addressed as often as not to boys and girls. Lowell, so self-conscious in most of his letters, only showed how deep his feelings were in these domestic relations. Perhaps they were deep only in these relations, like the feelings of Henry James. In later times, when boys and girls were "problems," and most of their fathers and mothers were also problems, more problematic than the children, when the old cultural forms had broken down, and literature was produced by childless rebels,—or largely so produced,—against the abuses of the older culture in the hour of its rigidity and decay, when the nation had lost much of its faith and even so much of its will-to-live that "race-suicide" was a pressing question, one found it difficult to return in fancy to Longfellow's "children's hour," when life flowed so freely between the generations. This ever-present consciousness of children, in minds so unconscious of themselves, spoke for a culture at its highest tide, a community that believed in itself, serenely sure of itself and sure of its future, eager to perpetuate its forms.

Longfellow had bought an orange-tree, with a hundred buds and blossoms. It flourished in his window beside the lemon-tree, which, for the last ten years, had kept the summer blooming through the winter in his

---

stood up crisp and fresh, like flowers that grow in cool, shady places. If anybody too rudely assailed a thought or suggestion she put forth, she drew it back again into this quiet inner chamber and went on. . . . There is no independence and pertinacity like that of these seemingly soft, quiet creatures, whom it is so easy to silence, and so difficult to convince."—Harriet Beecher Stowe, *The Pearl of Orr's Island.*

See also Emerson's remarks on children, in the opening paragraphs of his essay, *Domestic Life.*

white-panelled study. A springtime fragrance of Italy
filled the room. On his table stood Coleridge's ink-stand,
the gift of an English admirer. A Tintoretto hung near
by. One saw an agate cup of Cellini. The folding doors
opened into the spacious library, with its two Corinthian
columns. There was something large, bland and sweet,
something fresh and sunny in the atmosphere of the
house that reflected the soul of the generous poet, he
whom neither fame nor the praise of kings could ever
spoil or alter. A fathomless calm of innocent goodness
brooded in the air that spread with Longfellow's poems
over the world.[7] Nothing disturbed the poet's magnanimous mildness, neither the vanity that he never knew
nor the fools whom he suffered gladly. By no effort of
any man could any malicious phrase be drawn from his
lips. Were you pulling some rhymester to pieces, Longfellow had culled and was ready to quote, in the poor
bard's favour, the only good line he had ever written.
Did you beg him not to waste his time on the cranks who
were always besetting him. "Who would be kind to him
if I were not?" was Longfellow's only possible answer.
As his fame spread like the morning sun over the English-speaking peoples, with its notes of domestic affection
and the love of the sea, of landscape and legend, till
twenty-four English publishing-houses brought out his
work in competition and ten thousand copies of *The
Courtship of Miles Standish* were sold in London in a
single day, as the royalties of his poems rose till they
rivalled those of Byron and even those which, in ancient
Rome, Tiberius lavished on his poetasters,—four hundred thousand sesterces for a dialogue,—the flood of
interruptions became so great that he longed for a snow-

[7] "I had many things to say about the sense I have of the good
you might do this old world by staying with us a little, and giving the peaceful glow of your fancy to our cold, troubled, unpeace-
ful spirit. Strange, that both you and Norton come as such *calm*
influences to me and others."—Ruskin to Longfellow.

storm to block the door. A stranger who came to see Washington's rooms asked him if Shakespeare did not live near by. Some of his visitors thought he was greater than Shakespeare. An Englishman stopped to see him because there were no American ruins to visit. Longfellow smiled when a Frenchman asked him for *révelations intimes* regarding his domestic life, to appear in a Paris newspaper; but he gave a loaf of bread to every beggar, even when the beggars, disappointed, left the loaves upright on his gatepost. Now and then a great man came of whom Longfellow had never heard but who had heard of Longfellow, perhaps in Russia. One day, in 1861, Bakunin arrived at noon. He had escaped from Siberia. Longfellow asked him to stay to lunch. "Yiss, and I will dine with you, too," Bakunin replied, and he stayed till almost midnight. There was another Cambridge tableau.

Walking in his garden, among the birds, to the trilling of the frogs in his pond, like the chorus of a Grecian tragedy, Longfellow revolved in his mind the stories he was telling his children, passing them on to a larger world that was an extension of his household. He told them with a childlike air of trust, as if he knew in advance that the listening earth shared his faith in true love and homeland, his hatred of cruelty and his joy in nature,—the humble sweetness of a courteous heart. He ranged, in the *Tales of a Wayside Inn*,—the old Sudbury tavern, on the post-road to New York, where he assembled, in fancy, in imitation of Chaucer, some of his friends, the poet, Dr. Parsons, the Sicilian, Luigi Monti, the landlord, Mr. Howe,—over New England, Norway, Italy, Spain. Most of these tales were of the pretty kind in which the romantic poets abounded. Longfellow, who liked to say, "To stay at home is best," who had nothing of the adventurous in him and did not like extremes or excess, the extreme of heat, the extreme of cold, treated

the tragic in the tales with the guileless impassivity of a
Florentine monk picturing the miseries of the damned.
He, whose eye had never missed an old stone church or
a winding lane, an unusual tree, a wall, a crumbling
house, in his own American country, by which to endow
the scene with associations, paused at every page of the
story-book of history and read it again aloud with a
smile of his own. But in the New England stories, *Paul
Revere's Ride, The Courtship of Miles Standish,*—"full
of the name and the fame of the Puritan maiden Pris-
cilla,"—another tone appeared in his voice. He spoke
with a spirit or a tender conviction that sprang from
the blood within him. One heard this note in *My Lost
Youth;* one heard it in the sea-poems, the ballad of
The Cumberland, The Warden of the Cinque Ports.
One heard it in *The Saga of King Olaf,* the songs of the
Norsemen. In these runes and rhymes one heard

the ocean's dirges,
When the old harper heaves and rocks,
His hoary locks
Flowing and flashing in the surges!

Longfellow's soul was not an ocean. It was a lake,
clear, calm and cool. The great storms of the sea never
reached it. And yet this lake had its depths. Buried cities
lay under its surface. One saw the towers and domes
through the quiet water; one even seemed to catch the
sound of church-bells ringing like the bells of the city
of Is. Transparent as this mind was, there were profundi-
ties of moral feeling beneath the forms through which
it found expression, the fruits of an old tradition of
Puritan culture, and, behind this culture, all that was
noble in the Northern races. If Longfellow's poetic feeling had had the depth of his moral feeling, he would
have been one of the major poets, instead of the "chief
minor poet of the English language,"—a phrase of

Arnold Bennett's that strikes one as happy, if "minor"
is understood as "popular," popular in the high sense,
not the machine-made popular of later times. Longfellow's flaccidity debarred him from the front rank; but
his work possessed a quality, a unity of feeling and tone,
that gave him a place apart among popular poets. Of all
the sons of the New England morning, save only the
lonely men of Concord, he was the largest in his golden
sweetness.

In Lowell, too, there was something large, or, shall
one rather say, robust; for the noble unconscious New
England of old had begun its decline in Lowell. The
"clever" note that had appeared in his earlier verse and
prose, along with Holmes's cleverness, was the first streak
of decay in the "high-caste tulip"; and Lowell, unlike
Holmes, was self-consciously clever. Something uneasy
and insecure lurked in the depths of his soul. The serene aplomb of Longfellow, Prescott and Holmes, well-
seasoned men of the world, the equipoise of Emerson
and Hawthorne, citizens of the over-world, was a state
of mind that Lowell never knew. His judgment seemed
to have no bottom. He never struck a balance between
his radicalism and his Tory instincts.[8] His schoolmaster-
ish pleasure in snubbing others, one of the unlovelier
traits of the Cambridge mind,[9]—so marked that Ruskin protested against his "all-knowing attitude," [10] was
matched by his capacity for feeling snubbed by those

[8] "I would not give up a thing that had roots to it," Lowell wrote
on one occasion, "though it might suck up its food from graveyards."

[9] "What a delightful, generous and human sound Dr. Holmes's
letters have, especially in contrast to the self-conscious Lowell. It
makes one understand father's enthusiasm for the Doctor, who,
he used to say, was worth all the men in the club put together;
and how indignant he used to be with Lowell's manner of snubbing him, and admiring of the perfect way the Doctor took it."
—*Journal of Alice James.*

[10] "Lowell speaks of Dante as if Dante were a forward schoolboy,
and Lowell his master."—Ruskin to Norton.

whose superiority he recognized. Emerson, Longfellow, Hawthorne never felt, as reflecting on themselves or their country, the "certain condescension in foreigners" that troubled Lowell all his life. A sense that he was patronized lay behind the animus that made him a "defiant American," [11] when he was minister to England. The English knew why he was defiant, and the Romans of Rome who had known the Romans of Spain knew that Lowell was not one of them. He was uncertain of his own values. Something in him doubted the ground he walked on, and this accounted for the painful way,— painful because it was so self-conscious,—in which, in later years, he "wore a top-hat and looked askance at the Common." [12] Lowell must have blushed when his eye fell on the sentence, in his essay on condescending foreigners, "I am a man of the New World and do not know precisely the present fashion of Mayfair,"—in the days when he had abandoned the "round hat and sack-coat business" and wished Howells to "feel all the honour" involved in the admiration of "some titles" who had enjoyed his books.[13]

This draws the curtain of another age, the age that followed the Civil War. "One thing seems clear to me," Lowell wrote, when the new age was under way, "and that is that the Americans I remember fifty years ago had a consciousness of standing firmer on their own feet and in their own shoes than those of the newer generation. We are vulgar now precisely because we are afraid of being so." [14] Lowell, who was referring to Henry James, included himself in the "we" with a measure of reason. The high-caste tulip was in full decay, in these days of the "furtive apology," [15] when people forgave

[11] Leslie Stephen.
[12] John Jay Chapman.
[13] Howells, *Literary Friends and Acquaintance*.
[14] Letter of Lowell, 1879.
[15] Robert Grant, in reference to Henry James.

the self-conscious because it was conscious, forgetting
that the noble is only noble when it is unconscious. All
that was grand in the older America, the simple elevation, the magnanimous faith, which Lowell had praised
in his essay on Quincy, had withdrawn from the foreground of the national mind, and many of the Yankees
ceased to be proud of their country. There were other
elements in the situation that became significant in later
times, when urban life spread, with its special demands,
and the old American social forms, adequate for a
patriarchal world, could not meet the new requirements.
The "problem" of Henry James was more complex than
any similar problem that Lowell encountered; but Lowell, whose roots had never been deeply planted, as the
roots of the men of Concord were, whose youth had
been fundamentally literary, foreshadowed the beginning of the end of the old New England culture. The
weakness of his position was reflected in his verse and
prose, the rhetorical factitiousness of most of his poems,
the exalted commonplace, so essentially empty, of his
political writings. To later ears, the sentiment in these
rang hollow.

But this was only an aspect of Lowell. Lacking the
largeness of the whole-souled men, he had his own ingenuousness and warmth. He had a dozen literary virtues and practised them in all sincerity. It was a pity that
he went to England. He was not sufficiently mature, and
in this respect his case resembled Motley's. The ambassa-
dorial habit, to which American writers are prone, has
spoiled many a good man of letters who was not well-
seasoned enough to survive the test. Emerson or Holmes,
as minister to England, would have remained the men
they were before. The adventure relaxed the fibres of
Motley and Lowell, who had an exaggerated sense of the
value of honours and the "flattering conditions of life
abroad," as Lowell described them to Howells. Neither

of them wrote as well after the experience as before it. Motley might almost have been another Gibbon, he could certainly have been another Prescott, if, instead of spending years floating about in drawing-rooms,—"suitable for women and people of rank," in Goethe's useful phrase,—breaking his heart because he lost his post, he had buried himself in his own mind; and Lowell would have been a sounder man if he had never left his cherished Cambridge. His Cambridge sometimes irritated others, and his capacity, in Paris, for making the Rue de Rivoli a mere continuation of Brattle Street occasionally amused his friends at Lowell's expense. But his Cantabrigianism was his stoutest virtue. His way with his calves and pigs, and his melons and pears, his making hay when battles were on, even the Battle of Gettysburg, his honest bookishness and his wholesome pleasure in all who loved books like himself,—this bespoke the worthy Lowell who had something transparently simple in him, the boyish frankness his friends enjoyed so much.[16] One saw the "green, live Yankee" under the cosmopolitan surface. This was the racy Lowell who had written *The Biglow Papers;* and Lowell's bookishness was a Cambridge trait. If one smiled away the shell, or pierced the armour with a shaft of wit, if one held the key that unlocked the door, one liked and rejoiced in the man one found inside.

This was the Lowell whom everyone liked and respected, the compact little man in the velvet jacket who loved his pipe and his fire of logs and turned round *rounder* than anyone else, as Howells said in later years, when he turned to take a book off the shelf. This was the Lowell who sat in his study, winter and summer, for

---

[16] "My temperament is so youthful that whenever I am addressed (I mean by mere acquaintances) as if my opinion were worth anything, I can hardly help laughing. . . . A boy of twelve behind a bearded vizor."—*Letters of J. R. Lowell.*

years on end, feeding like a silkworm on his books, only stirring abroad for his daily walk. Lowell was a book-man, pure and simple, born and bred in an alcove; and he basked and ripened in the sun of books until he grew as mellow as a meerschaum. He hardly professed to be a critic, except in textual matters, in which he was both learned and conscientious. He would spend a week, at twelve hours a day,—a fortnight, if need were,—writing a six-page notice of a dictionary. He would run through the whole of Ovid and Lucan to find a word for one of his poems. From dawn to dusk in summer, oftener in winter, in the "tumultuous privacy" of a snow-storm,— for he drew all the virtue from Emerson's line,—he read his Boccaccio, and his Hakluyt and Purchas, his old French metrical romances or all he could find on the Yankee dialect. Ever since 1855, when he had lectured on the English poets, at the Lowell Institute in Boston, he had been regarded as a man of letters who had no equal in the United States for literary knowledge and grace of style; and all this, combined with his animal spirits, made him a capital teacher. Ticknor and Long-fellow had explored for Cambridge the foreground of the history of letters. Lowell's task was one of interpreta-tion; and, if his own mind was not quite in the grand style, he still communicated a feeling for it.[17] He loved his books and he liked his students. He asked them to read with him privately in his study.

Such was the notable Cambridge bookman, the liter-ary recluse and the teacher of letters. When you dropped in and found Lowell reading a play of Calderon or a

[17] "Thirty odd years ago I brought home with me from Nurem-berg photographs of Peter Vischer's statuettes of the twelve apostles. These I used to show to my pupils and ask them for a guess at their size. The invariable answer was 'larger than life.' They were really about eighteen inches high, and this grandiose effect was wrought by simplicity of treatment, dignity of pose, a large unfretted sweep of drapery."—*Latest Literary Essays.*

canto of Dante, you knew you were in the presence of
something real. It was not the reality of a critic and made
small pretence of being so. The critic's seat is not an
easy-chair. Its rushes are iron spikes; and he who writes
about books in relation to life, or life in relation to
books, distrusts that "precious feeling of seclusion in having a double wall of centuries" [18] between himself and
the world in which Lowell revelled. The rounded curves
of a velvet coat are not for him whose proper atmosphere, as Emerson said of the scholar, is "poverty and
reproach and danger." Lowell, as a critic, was not important, in spite of the golden opinions he won from those
who had a right to give them,[19] in spite of all his authority in other circles, wherever the English tongue was
spoken.[20] Those who compared him with Sainte-Beuve
forgot Sainte-Beuve's psychology and his feeling for life,
—not to speak of his scope and massiveness,—the life
that in Arnold, Taine and Renan, even in Walter Pater,
served as a touchstone in the world of books. Lowell, who
had no philosophy, whose general ideas were so few that
only two of his essays might be said to contain them,—
the essays on Rousseau and Swinburne,—had no psychology either, and wished to have none; or, rather, he
had enough when the subject pleased him, when it con-
formed with the local proprieties, but none when it
shocked the proprieties. He said it was "fortunate" that
we know so little about the lives of Shakespeare and
his friends, "literary bohemians, living from hand to
mouth," but he could hardly know too much about the

[18] *Library of Old Authors.*
[19] "I think he is altogether the best critic we have; something of
what Ste. Beuve is in French."—*More Letters of Edward FitzGerald.*
[20] "My father, who would never accept the authority of an encyclopædia when his children got him in a corner on some debated
question of fact, held James Russell Lowell as the supreme judge
of letters, from whom not even he could appeal. (It is true, he
had never heard of Sainte-Beuve, and regarded Matthew Arnold
as a modern fad.)"—Arnold Bennett, *Your United States.*

virtuous Gray and the innocent Walton. It pleased him
to contemplate the latter; it shocked him to contemplate
the former, the evil in whose lives his conventional mind,
all too conscious of the fig-leaf, greatly exaggerated;[21]
and sometimes he was disingenuous in his suggestion
that these prejudices had an objective basis.[22] All this
was to breed a reaction in later generations, when the
cache-sexe that emphasized the sex was rudely torn away,
and the spotlight fell on the sex that had fallen on the
fig-leaf. Sometimes, in Lowell, a whim of taste triumphed
over the *convenances,* as in a casual remark on Fielding;[23] but psychology and the objective were the last of
his cares. Life had to be as Brattle Street desired, though
the heaven of intellect fell. It had to be as nobly good as
Longfellow really was, and as others wished to think it.

For the rest, Lowell's sympathies were all but exclusively literary; and, in his rare digressions into other
fields, painting, for example, or architecture, he showed
an ineptitude that was almost surprising. He said that
Paul Potter's "Bull" could no more be compared with
Rosa Bonheur's "Horse Fair" "than a stuffed and varnished dolphin with a living one," a judgment that sug-

[21] "Is it not after the discreditable particulars which excite a
correspondingly discreditable curiosity that we are eager, and these
that we read with greatest zest? So it would seem if we judged
by the fact that biography, and especially that of men of letters,
tends more and more towards these indecent exposures . . . There
are certain memoirs after reading which one blushes as if he had
not only been peeping through a key-hole, but had been caught in
the act."—Lecture on Chapman.

[22] "The so-called realist raises doubts in my mind when he assures
me that he, and he alone, gives me the facts of life . . . But are
they the facts? I had much rather believe them to be the accidental
and transitory phenomena of our existence here."—*The Old English
Dramatists.*

[23] "He painted vice when it came in his way (and it was more obvious in his time) as a figure in the social landscape, and in doing so
he was perhaps a better moralist than those who ignore it altogether,
or only when it lives in a genteel quarter of the town."—*Literary
and Political Addresses.*

gests Mark Twain; and in Rome he had "doubts about domes," which seemed to him "the goitre of architecture." [24] Only a Boston or a Cambridge man could ever have "doubts about domes,"—despite the shades of Bulfinch and the State House. Lowell's words on Michael Angelo,—one part truth, ten parts misapprehension, which he retracted in the sequel, indicated his want of intuition, the vacillating nature of his mind, and, more than all, his fear of the great and the vital.[25] With the great and the vital he felt unable to cope, except when he was aware of the stream of tradition that backed him up in his authority. Hence the insinuation of a grudge in the tone with which he spoke of the great and the vital, the unconsecrated great, the newly vital. He felt that the great must be "exaggerated"; the original was original by "conscious intention." Of the stream of tradition in the plastic arts, Lowell was unaware, if only because he lived in Cambridge, the Cambridge of the pre-Nortonian era. Besides, a certain levity of judgment in regard to the plastic arts was quite in the form of his age, in London as in Cambridge. Lowell's free-and-easy way with domes and Michael Angelo was all of a piece with that of other writers who spoke for the centre of the world where literature was concerned. Carlyle was a case in point. But Lowell's tone in literary matters, where he could not feel the stream of tradition behind him, was equally presumptuous and inconsequential. The list of his ineptitudes, in relation to all that was vital, all that was original and strong in the world of his day, where

[24] *Fireside Travels.*

[25] "Shall I confess it? Michael Angelo seems to me, in his angry reaction against sentimental beauty, to have mistaken bulk and brawn for the antithesis of feebleness. He is the apostle of the exaggerated, the Victor Hugo of painting and sculpture. I have a feeling that rivalry was a more powerful motive with him than love of art, that he had the conscious intention to be original, which seldom leads to anything better than the exaggerated."— *Fireside Travels.*

he had to think for himself, was more than surprising. His instinctive response to Whitman,[26] Poe[27] and Swinburne,[28] their personalities and their work alike, never corrected in regard to Whitman,[29] scarcely in regard to Poe and Swinburne,—since the essay on Swinburne was non-committal and Lowell could never speak of Poe without qualifications and disclaimers, as if he were eager to forestall any misapprehension of his admiration, —were in keeping with his verdict on Thoreau, that "his whole life was a search for the doctor," which was not merely false but singularly stupid. What, moreover, could one say of his final remark on Emerson's poems,[30] in which the impression left in one's mind obliterated the truth that it contained? A critic who regards the truth may well retract and qualify in order to present his theme in all its ramifications; but a substantial critic never leaves the reader in doubt about his final judgment. What was Lowell's real opinion of Poe, Swinburne, Emerson, Thoreau?—since we know his opinion of Whitman. Fine pages do not make a verdict, and Lowell wrote many fine pages about Thoreau and Emerson. But the *I-am-afraids* and the *Shall-I-confesses*, the doubts, the hesitations and the doublings, the notes of patronage and condescension, the reluctances, the conventional phrases, the foolish condemnations, the unworthy suspicions that marked Lowell's critical essays concerning living men proved that his judgment had no sure footing. He was

[26] "No, no, the kind of things you describe won't do. When a man aims at originality, he acknowledges himself consciously un-original." —*Letters.*

[27] "He probably cannot conceive of anybody's writing for anything but a newspaper reputation, or for posthumous fame."—*Letters.*

[28] "I am too old to have a painted hetaira palmed off on me for a Muse."—*Letters.*

[29] Apropos of *Leaves of Grass:* "A book I never looked into farther than to satisfy myself that it was a solemn humbug."—*New Letters.*

[30] "As for Emerson's verse (though he has written some as exquisite as any in the language), I suppose we must give it up." —*Letters.*

the father of a school of American essay-writers that blossomed in the age that followed him. These lesser Lowells exercised a style that shambled and wobbled self-consciously in a welter of qualifications. One might call this style the Indian-giver style, for it took back everything it granted.

Boston was to produce, as time went on, many minds of this sort. What these minds could never see was that their knowing humility, their treating great men as refractory children, disqualified not others but themselves. The pride of Boston gave birth to the pathos of Boston. But in Lowell himself one saw that much was real, much, if one looked for it in the right direction. As an editor, he played a historic role. He brought to the work his learning and his taste; and his understanding of the national feeling, in the years before the Civil War, gave him a double authority. It was true that, if *The Atlantic* was full of cream, he had the top of the bottle; true, that when manuscripts came to him which could not be weighed in the scales he knew, he had a way of missing them. He thought Rossetti was "too foggy" to be printed in his magazine. His merit was that he did not doubt the value of the men he understood and found about him; and he was a bookman beyond compare in literary America. How does a bookman differ from a critic? He differs in that he assumes as given the whole sphere of values. The bookman does not judge, nor is he asked to judge. He appreciates, he enjoys, he communicates pleasure. In the world of the bookman, taste is the main affair, enthusiasm, gusto, relish; and it was in these that Lowell excelled. When he felt behind him the stream of tradition, when he was not obliged to judge for himself, when he could follow his whims and prejudices, his preferences, his instinctive admirations, when he could let out sail, without any danger of reefs and shoals, then one saw the master. Who asks for judgments of Dante and

Shakespeare, of Chaucer, Spenser, Dryden, Gray and Walton? Humanity judged these authors long ago and found them worthy of enduring fame. What one is asked to do, if one writes about them, is to evoke new aspects for appreciation; and this was Lowell's gift,—here lay his glory.

"In my weaker moments," he said, "I revert with a sigh, half deprecation, half relief, to the old notion of literature as holiday, as

'The world's sweet inn from pain and wearisome turmoil.' " [31]

Lowell's weaker moments were his stronger moments. When, abandoning the sphere of the critic, he yielded to the secondary role for which his talent equipped him, the cold, self-conscious Lowell of the world became the winning Lowell of the study. He "deprecated" it, but it "relieved" him; for his efforts as a critic were conscious efforts, while all the force of the unconscious Lowell lay behind his bookishness. His mannerisms vanished at once, all that was factitious, arch and coy in the essays in which he stood on his good behaviour; and miracles, in his zest for letters, happened. The indecisive Lowell, the conventional Lowell, the condescending Lowell, the defiant Lowell,—all these Lowells were absorbed in the passionate lover of reading; for in love one feels the world well lost, even when the love is the love of books. What joy, what shy delights this man revealed when he wrote of the authors he loved, and even, let us add, what judgment! He who could never judge when he had to judge judged like the best when no one was looking, and men are not born every day who can write such essays as Lowell's on Walton and Dryden.

When one took Lowell as one found him, yielded to his tastes and preferences, then one began to share his pleasures. He revelled in Spenser's charms and in Chau-

[31] *Latest Literary Essays.*

cer's beauties as he had revelled in puns and Yankeeisms. His muscles grew springy and his lungs dilated in this atmosphere of books, as in his winter walks through the streets of Cambridge. Even his puns had a respectable meaning because his beloved Elizabethans used them. Was not Queen Elizabeth an ardent punster?—and was not Lowell's love of puns, even more extravagant than Browning's and quite in the tone of his time, a symbol of his delight in reaching back, behind his Puritan heritage, to the warm and sunny world of Shakespeare and Spenser? One would hardly know this glowing Lowell, who seemed to lose all his reserves in the joy of books. Warmed with Villon and Marlowe, he admitted that Poe was a man of genius, and he was all for Emerson the man, even if he had doubts about the poet. He said the happiest things about Thoreau,—"as if all out-of-doors had kept a diary and become its own Montaigne,"— and no doubt, he would have liked Whitman also if he had cared for Blake. In his felicitous insights and luckier phrases,[32] as in the tone and texture of his style, Lowell deserved his fame and was long to deserve it.

[32] On Dryden: "We always feel his epoch in him, and that he was the lock which let our language down from its point of highest poetry to its level of easiest and most gently flowing prose."
On Carlyle: "He goes about with his Diogenes dark-lantern, professing to seek a man, but inwardly resolved to find a monkey."

CHAPTER XXVIII

CONCLUSION

THE CIVIL WAR brought to a head, however inconclusively, a phase of American culture that later times described as the New England "renaissance." This movement of mind continued in the generation that followed, and many of the writers who embodied it long outlived the war. Some of them produced their best work, or work, at least, equal to their best, during this later period. But all had given their measure before the war, and several had disappeared before it. That they stood for some collective impulse, exceptional in the history of the national mind, no one questioned then or questioned later.

This movement of mind in New England followed the typical pattern of the "culture-cycle," as Spengler convincingly described it. Setting aside the question of scale, one finds in it the same succession of phases that one finds in the great culture-cycles,—for Spengler, in this, at least, made a case that is so suggestive as to seem conclusive. Here we have a homogeneous people, living close to the soil, intensely religious, unconscious, unexpressed in art and letters, with a strong sense of home and fatherland. One of its towns becomes a "culture-city," for Boston, with Cambridge and Concord considered as suburbs, answers to this name, which Spengler accords to Florence, Bruges and Weimar, as no other town has ever answered in either of the Americas. There is a springtime feeling in the air, a joyous sense of awakening, a free creativeness, an unconscious pride, expressed in the found-

539

ing of institutions, intellectual, humanitarian, artistic, and—at first a little timid, cold and shy—the mind begins to shape into myths and stories the dreams of the pre-urban countryside. There is a moment of equipoise, a widespread flowering of the imagination in which the thoughts and feelings of the people, with all their faiths and hopes, find expression. The culture-city dominates the country, but only as its accepted vent and mouthpiece. Then gradually the mind, detached from the soil, grows more and more self-conscious. Contradictions arise within it, and worldlier arts supplant the large, free, ingenuous forms through which the poetic mind has taken shape. What formerly grew from the soil begins to be planned, and the Hawthornes yield to the Henry Jameses. Over-intelligent, fragile, cautious and doubtful, the soul of the culture-city loses the self-confidence and joy that have marked its early development,—it is filled with a presentiment of the end; and the culture-city itself surrenders to the world-city,—Boston surrenders to New York,—which stands for cosmopolitan deracination. What has once been vital becomes provincial; and the sense that one belongs to a dying race dominates and poisons the creative mind.

Not to press a formula too far, is not this the story of New England, as the New England mind has confessed it, from the days of Channing and Webster to those of Barrett Wendell and Henry Adams? In religion, the springtime faith of Channing, with its feeling of a world to create and redeem, yielded to the conception of religion as hygiene in the valetudinarian Mrs. Eddy. In politics, the robust and confident Webster gave place to the querulous Henry Cabot Lodge. The scholars and historians lost themselves among their documents; and the cheerful, unconscious, generous note of the essayists and poets of the eighteen-fifties made way for the analytical and the precious. No doubt, the New England mind exaggerated its own decline and decay. But that it had passed through a cycle, and some such cycle as Spengler pictured,—this grew more and more apparent.

"Men are free," said D. H. Lawrence, "when they are in a living homeland, not when they are straying and breaking away. Men are free when they are obeying some deep, inward voice of religious belief. Obeying from within. Men are free when they belong to a living, organic, believing community, active in fulfilling some unfulfilled, perhaps unrealized purpose." This was the case with the New England authors, in the epoch of the building of the nation. Perhaps it was never more truly the case with any group of authors, all question of intensity aside. They were as completely of their people as any authors of the oldest nations; and they saw, if not themselves,—for they were not self-conscious,—at least their profession as having a Promethean role to play. They were teachers, educators and bringers of light, with a deep and affectionate feeling of obligation towards the young republic their fathers had brought into being. That New England was appointed to guide the nation, to civilize it and humanize it, none of them ever doubted, a motive that was evident in all their writings, from Emerson's early addresses to the table-talk of Holmes, from Longfellow's *Hiawatha*, in which an Indian myth conveys the poet's notion of his role, to the prophecies of *Uncle Tom's Cabin*. Sometimes they suggested Miss Ophelia reforming Dinah's kitchen; but there was so little of the condescending, so much of the humble and fraternal, in their state of mind and point of view, and they threw so many ideas into circulation and wrote so sincerely and so well that they came to be accepted as fathers and sages.

What was the cause of this transfiguration? The breadth of their conscious horizon, the healthy objectivity of their minds, their absorption in large preoccupations, historical, political, religious, together with a literary feeling, a blend of the traditional and the local, that gave the local wider currency while it brought the traditional home to men's business and bosoms. They filled the New England scene with associations and set it, as it were, in three dimensions, creating the visible foreground it had never possessed. They helped to make their countrypeople conscious of the great world-movements of thought and feeling in which they played parts side by side with the intellectual leaders of the older countries. In their scholarship, their social thought, their moral passion, their artistic feeling, they spoke for the universal republic of letters, giving their own province a form and body in the consciousness of the world. Moreover, there was something in their temper that made them seem friends of the human spirit. They stood for good faith and fair play and all that was generous and hopeful in the life of their time. The hold they gained and kept over the nation possessed an extra-literary sanction, as if they were voices of the national ethos. If they found themselves "done up in spices, like so many Pharaohs," as Dr. Holmes remarked in later years, it was because they were looked upon as classics,—

> In whom is plainest taught, and easiest learnt,
> What makes a nation happy, and keeps it so.

This process of canonization went hand in hand with the spread of New England culture over the country. As the New England strain died out in the West, with the second and third generations of the pioneers and the growth of a native point of view, the reputations of the New England authors had to face another test. They encountered an increasing neglect and indifference, and even a widespread hostility. This was partly due to the reaction against the romantic authors in every country; but it was inevitable that the West should have turned against New England. In order to establish its independence, it was obliged to do so, as the East had turned against the mother-country. Of the popular writers, Longfellow, Whittier, Holmes, something seemed destined to survive in the general mind of the nation, when the life of all the regions, taken together, formed a final synthesis; but much of their work was ephemeral, and most of it was so bound up with regional modes of feeling and local traditions that it could only endure in the regional mind. For the rest, there are two kinds of classics, the popular and the esoteric, those that yield their meaning at the first encounter and those that one has to discover by effort and insight, the classics of the intellectual surface and the classics of the spiritual depths. The popular New England authors, whom every child could understand, remained as classics indeed, but mainly for children; while the handful of esoteric authors,—Hawthorne, with his cloudy symbols, whom one could only see through a glass, darkly, Thoreau, who "listened behind him for his wit," and Emerson, who, in life, never gave a direct answer and said that one should speak in parables,—came more and more into their own. Ironically enough, it was Boston and Cambridge that grew to seem provincial, while the local and even parochial Concord mind, which had always been universal, proved to be also national. Whatever doubts the country at large felt regarding the other New England authors, Hawthorne, Thoreau and Emerson were clearly of the main stream, with Emily Dickinson, Whitman, Poe and Melville.

*
* *

Thoreau died in 1862. He had caught cold from over-exposure while counting the rings of some trees on a snowy day and had fought for a year and a half with tuberculosis. He had outlived his juvenile-braggart phase and had grown more and more to seem the sage, whose life and opinions might have appeared in the pages of Diogenes Laertius. In an effort to regain his health, he had journeyed to Minnesota and had made friends with some of the Indians there. Then, knowing that nothing could save him, he had settled down among his papers, with an Indian's indifference to the future, completing some of his lists of birds and flowers and finishing *The Maine Woods.* No more walks to Bateman's Pond, to Becky Stow's swamp or Nine-Acre Corner. But he said he enjoyed existence as well as ever. His thoughts had entertained him all his life, never so much as at present. Fields, the second editor of *The Atlantic,* had asked him for some of his essays, and he spent his last months revising these.

His friends could hardly imagine Concord without him. Solitude peered out from the dells and wood-roads, and the bobolinks seemed to sing a minor strain. One had thought of Henry Thoreau as a part of nature, destined to be transformed perhaps at last into a mossy rock or a leaf-strewn spring. At least, he was like the hourglass apple-shrub of which he had written in his journal. By the end of October, when the leaves had fallen, one saw the wild yellow fruit growing, which the cows could not reach over the thorny hedge. It was so with the rude, neglected genius of the Concord woods and meadows. He had suffered many a check at first, browsed upon by fate, springing up in a rocky pasture, the nursery of other creatures there, and had grown up scraggy and thorny, not like the sleek orchard-trees whose forces had all been husbanded. When, at first, within this rind and hedge, the man shot up, one saw the thorny scrub of his youth about him; but, as he grew, the thorns disappeared, and he bore golden crops of Porters and Baldwins, apples whose fame was destined to spread through all orchards for generations, when the thrifty orchard-trees that had been his rivals had long since ceased to bear their en-grafted fruit. It was true that Thoreau's fame was slow in growing. Emerson and Ellery Channing brought out his posthumous books,—he had published only two dur-ing his lifetime; and Emerson collected his poems and letters. But only his friends could imagine why anyone should wish to see his journal. Emerson was convinced that, if it was published, it would soon produce in New England a "plentiful crop of naturalists." This proved to be true a generation later. When volumes of selections from the journal appeared, a school of lesser Thoreaus sprang up at once;[1] and

> The happy man who was content
> With his own town, his continent,

became a teacher of wisdom, even in Asia.

Two years after Thoreau, Hawthorne faded out of the Concord picture. He had come home from Italy and Eng-land just before the outbreak of the war and had taken up his life again at Wayside, the house he had bought from Alcott, where a man was said to have lived who be-lieved he was never to die. Hawthorne built a tower over the house, a reminiscence of the Italian villa in which he had stayed in Florence. There he had his study, reached by a trap-door, with a standing desk fastened to the wall. With England still fresh in his mind, he composed from his note-books the beautifully rounded chapters of *Our Old Home,* a book that was somewhat unhappily named; but a sudden change seemed to have come upon him with his return to America, a blight as of winter, a deadly estrangement even from his own imagination. Had he

[1] Thoreau's manuscript journal consisted of thirty-nine blank-books of all shapes and sizes, packed in a strong wooden box built by himself. It was bequeathed by Sophia Thoreau to H. G. O. Blake, who brought out four volumes of selections, 1881–1892. The complete journal was edited by Bradford Torrey and published in fourteen volumes, 1906.

been too old to be transplanted, so that he could never take root again? He made a few half-hearted efforts to gather up the threads of his former life. He appeared at the Saturday Club for a few of the dinners; but even Alcott and Emerson seldom saw him. Once, at Emerson's house, he picked up some photographs of Concord, the common, the court-house and the Mill-dam, which he passed in his walks every day, and asked what the pictures represented. The sight of a friend or a stranger approaching his house drove him up the hill into the woods. Along the top of the ridge, among the pines, between the huckleberry and sweetfern bushes, he walked to and fro, brooding over the novel he could not finish. He fancied that the grass and the little shrubs shrank away as he passed them because there was something in his broodings that was alien to nature. Seventy-five years later, one could still trace the path that Hawthorne's footsteps wore on the tree-covered ridge.

He had wasted away and the glow in his eyes had vanished; and, hard as he tried to write, pulling down the blinds and locking his door, he could not bring his mind into focus. The novel became two novels, and the two became four. He could not fix upon a single setting: Salem, Concord, England, Wayside and Smithall's Hall drifted in confusion through his mind, their outlines melting into one another. Even his theme eluded him. Was it the unpardonable sin, the "ancestral footstep," the man who believed he was never to die? He made four beginnings, constantly changing his perspective, until he could scarcely bear to touch his blurred and meaningless manuscripts. A few of the scenes took form, with all his old perfection, with the sculptural repose of his earlier writing and a touch of the Gothic imagination that seemed to connect America with the Middle Ages. But life shook before his eyes, like the picture on the surface of a pond when a stone has disturbed its tranquil mirror. His mind

had grown like Melville's in *Pierre,* groping in a fog for
the firm conceptions that turned to vapour as he tried to
grasp them. Then, one day in 1864, the news reached
Concord from Plymouth, New Hampshire, that he had
died in his sleep at the village inn. For years, he had been
in the habit, while idly scribbling, of writing the number
64, which had, he felt, some fatal meaning for him. He
had not disappeared, like Septimius Felton, crushed by
the failure of his dream, but he had wandered away with
as little purpose, knowing perhaps that he would not return.

The Alcotts had settled in Orchard House, next door
to Hawthorne's. Alcott had rebuilt it, leaving the old
beams and rafters, making arched alcoves of the ovens
and ash-holes; and, over the chimney-piece in Alcott's
study, Ellery Channing's lines were inscribed,—

> The hills were reared, the valleys scooped in vain,
> If Learning's altars vanish from the plain.

Alcott had been made superintendent of the public
schools in Concord. His vindication had come late, and
one could only think what he might have accomplished
if he had had this chance when he was younger. Louisa
had begun to write the stories that were to carry his
name around the world. Meanwhile, now that Thoreau
was gone, Emerson was the master of the Concord revels.
He liked to pile the children into the haycart, which they
had bedecked with flowers and mosses, and carry them
off for a swim and a picnic at Walden.

Emerson was travelling, on his lecture-tours, further
and further westward. He was still an impossible puzzle
in the popular mind, even a national joke, a byword of
the country paragraphers. No matter, there were always
a few of his hearers for whom all mythology spoke in his
voice, the Indian gods and the gods of the North, who
felt that the beautiful and the good must also be the true,

if only because Emerson had said so. He seemed to have made his own all the victories of genius, which he invited one to share, he who had never doubted the riches of nature, the gifts of the future, the wealth of the mind. Whatever one's occupation was, mechanics, law, the ministry, he broke the spell of one's routine, relating one's craft and task to the laws of the world: one felt how one's life was intertwined with the whole chain of being. He spoke for magnanimity and the power of thought. In *The Conduct of Life* he had met the objections of those who found his optimism too facile. He had fully recognized the existence of evil, the brutal and barbarous elements in the core of the world, the habits of snake and spider in human beings, the snap of the tiger, the crackle of the bones of his prey in the coils of the anaconda. Even as men rose in culture, fate continued to follow them, as Vishnu followed Maya through all her ascending changes. While their checks and limitations became finer and finer, the ring of necessity still remained perched at the top. But fate had its lord, limitation its limits. It was different seen from above and seen from below. For, if fate was immense, so was power. Man was a stupendous antagonism, and as long as he thought he was free. It was true, there was nothing more disgusting than the crowing about liberty by slaves, as most men were, and the flippant mistaking for freedom of some statute right to vote by those who had never dared to think or act; yet men had the power to look not at fate but the other way. The practical view was the other. Well had the oracle said, "Look not on Nature, for her name is fatal!" as Hafiz described the phrase on the gate of heaven, "Woe unto him who suffers himself to be betrayed by Fate!" Instead of cringing to facts, one could use and command them. Every jet of chaos that threatened extermination, one could convert by intellect into wholesome force. The water drowned ship and sailor.

But, if one learned to swim and trimmed one's bark, one clove the water with it, and the waves were obliged to carry it, like their own foam, a plume and a power.

Thus Emerson spoke to the active forces waiting in his hearers, eager for the word that would set them free. For himself, he found that the more he spent the more he had to spend, the more he communicated the results of his thinking the more new thoughts he had. His zest and curiosity grew with the years; and, for all the discomforts of his lecture-tours, he liked to get away from the Eastern sea-board, where the American current was so superficial. He learned the resources of the country, going to school to the prairies. He had no fear of the future, he did not distrust the rough, wild, incalculable road America would have to travel to find itself. As between the civil and the forcible, he had always leaned, in his sympathies, to the latter. The Hoosiers and the Badgers of the West, the hard heads of Oregon and Utah, the rough-riders and legislators in shirt-sleeves, let them drive as they might. Better than to quote English standards and miss the sovereignty of power. Out of pirates and berserkers the English race had sprung, and no strong nation could ever develop without its own strong, wild will; and the power of the buffalo-hunters, bullying the peaceable and the loyal, would bring its own antidote at last. For liberty in all its wildness bred iron conscience; the instinct of the people was right in the end, and natures with great impulses had great resources and could be trusted to return from far.

There, in the West, he thought, lay nature sleeping, too much by half for man in the picture, with its rank vegetation of swamps and forests, steeped in dews and rains. In this great sloven continent, in its high Alleghany pastures, in the sea-wide, sea-skirted prairie, the great mother still slept and murmured. Man had as yet made little impression upon it. But there, where stars and woods and hills abounded, with all things still untried, could one not foresee a social state more excellent than history had recorded, one that turned its back on musket-worship and lived by the law of love and justice? Let men but know that every day is doomsday, and let them look within, in the populous, all-loving solitude which they left for the tattle of towns; for there *he* lurked and hid, he who was reality, joy and power. So Emerson felt, in the streets of New York, or at Concord, as he strolled through grove and glen. Others, as they saw him, tall and slender, leaving the village behind him, might have said to themselves, with the Swedish poet, "The last skald walks over the meadows."

INDEX

INDEX

DUTTON EVERYMAN PAPERBACKS